Samuel Rawson Gardiner

A History of England under the Duke of Buckingham and Charles I

1624-1628 Vol I.

Samuel Rawson Gardiner

A History of England under the Duke of Buckingham and Charles I
1624-1628 Vol I.

ISBN/EAN: 9783743398184

Manufactured in Europe, USA, Canada, Australia, Japa

Cover: Foto ©ninafisch / pixelio.de

Manufactured and distributed by brebook publishing software (www.brebook.com)

Samuel Rawson Gardiner

A History of England under the Duke of Buckingham and Charles I

A

HISTORY OF ENGLAND

UNDER THE

DUKE OF BUCKINGHAM AND CHARLES I.

1624–1628

BY

SAMUEL RAWSON GARDINER

LATE STUDENT OF CHRIST CHURCH
CORRESPONDING MEMBER OF THE MASSACHUSETTS HISTORICAL SOCIETY
AUTHOR OF 'A HISTORY OF ENGLAND FROM THE ACCESSION OF JAMES I. TO THE DISGRACE
OF CHIEF JUSTICE COKE' 'PRINCE CHARLES AND THE SPANISH MARRIAGE'
AND 'THE THIRTY YEARS' WAR' IN THE EPOCHS OF HISTORY SERIES

IN TWO VOLUMES

VOL. I.

LONDON

LONGMANS, GREEN, AND CO.

1875

PREFACE.

THE present volumes are intended to form, together with the 'History of England from the accession of James I. to the disgrace of Chief Justice Coke,' and 'Prince Charles and the Spanish Marriage,' a connected history which now extends from the death of Elizabeth in 1603 to the assassination of Buckingham in 1628. I believe that much is gained for the understanding of the events of which I am now treating by telling the story of the last year of James's reign in close connection with the first years of his son. To make the division at the accession of Charles is to separate effect from cause, and to account for the reaping of the whirlwind without taking into consideration the sowing of the wind. The five years, too, which followed the return of Charles from Madrid stand apart from those before and after them as a war period; for if peace with France and Spain was not at once concluded when Rochelle was taken, hostilities practically came to an end when Lindsey's fleet returned from the French coast without accomplishing anything. These years of war bear specially the impress of Buckingham's activity. Writers not unfrequently speak of Buckingham's ascendency as commencing at a much earlier period. But this is altogether a mistake, if, at least, these writers mean anything like the ascendency which he possessed after his return from Madrid. Influence he had long had with James in everything, and in matters of personal favour he had more than ordinary influence; but up to the end of 1623 James decided his own political course. From that date to his death Buckingham was the ruler of England.

When I first undertook to investigate the history of this momentous period, I felt a certain hesitation. Libraries positively bristled with the names of great writers who had given their thoughts to the world on the subject of these years. But I was not long in discovering that there was still room for further investigation. We have had historians in plenty, but they have been Whig historians or Tory historians. The one class has thought it unnecessary to take trouble to understand how matters looked in the eyes of the King and his friends; the other class has thought it unnecessary to take trouble to understand how matters looked in the eyes of the leaders of the House of Commons. I am not so vain as to suppose that I have always succeeded in doing justice to both parties, but I have, at least, done my best not to misrepresent either.

Another material objection to the works of recent authorities is the brevity with which they pass over the foreign relations of the kingdom. It was not so once. Carte, for instance, takes pains to tell as much as he can on this subject; but the very fact that attention has been more exclusively drawn to Parliamentary history, and that great discoveries have been made in this branch of the subject, has led to the neglecting of investigation into those diplomatic and military relations with other countries which need to be taken into consideration if we are to understand whether the Commons were right or wrong in refusing a subsidy or in impeaching a minister. Fortunately, new sources of information are now opening up to those who turn their attention in this direction. The French despatches of the period have long been in more than one copy in the Museum library, though they have never been submitted to a thorough and searching investigation. The Dutch despatches of Caron and Joachimi are also in copy in the same repository. The greater part of the Venetian despatches have been, through the kindness of Mr. Rawdon Brown, sent over either in copy or in translation to the Public Record Office. A visit to Brussels has enabled me to elucidate some obscure points of Spanish policy, though it is not to be expected that in war time much interesting matter would be left on record. Having failed to meet with any important despatches relating to the last year of James during my visit to Simancas, I have not thought it necessary to make any fresh attempt, as there seems no likelihood that any good result would be secured, as there was no Spanish ambassador in England during the first four years of Charles's reign. In addition to the despatches of the ambassadors of other nations, the foreign series of State papers in the Record Office has been most useful. I trust that I have thus succeeded in disentangling the course of negotiations with France, a knowledge of which is as important to a proper understanding of English history in these years as a knowledge of the course of affairs in Germany is to a proper understanding of English history in the earlier period.

The negotiations with France fall under two distinct heads—those preceding Charles's marriage, and those which come after his accession. The first period has been treated of by M. Guizot in his 'Projet de Mariage Royal,' and by Mr. Bruce in an unprinted fragment of history which will one day, I trust, be made public. But, though both these narratives contain much that is valuable and interesting, neither of them is founded on any comprehensive view of the entire evidence. M. Guizot had before him some of the despatches of the French ministers, which he interpreted with the help of such fragmentary materials as were already in print on the English side, not being aware apparently, or at all events not making use, of some of the most interesting parts of the correspondence even of the French ambassadors. Mr. Bruce, on the other hand, based his narrative entirely upon the English despatches which he found amongst the State papers, supplemented by remarks drawn from his extensive knowledge of the period, without any reference to the correspondence of Tillières and Effiat which was to be found in the Museum library. It seems obvious that a story founded upon all the letters written on both sides will have more chance of giving a correct account of these transactions than that which is avowedly based upon the unchecked assertions of a single party to the negotiations.

The later negotiations have remained almost wholly

unknown. The romantic idea that the war of 1627 was brought about simply and solely by the persistence of Buckingham in forcing his presence upon the French Queen has seemed so satisfactory that many writers have not only neglected to enquire whether anything more than this is to be discovered, but they have even allowed to drop out of sight facts such as those of the contraband trade of Calais, which were perfectly well known to Carte. Mr. Forster was the first to turn enquiry somewhat in this direction by his investigation into the cases of Pennington's fleet and of the 'St. Peter' of Havre de Grace; and though a further examination of the sources of information has led me to the discovery of unexpected disclosures in the former affair, and to ascribe less importance to the latter than Mr. Forster has done, it must not be forgotten that Mr. Forster led the way in the enquiry into the subject. Nor is it only the history of England which is affected by the narrative. As far as I am aware, French writers know nothing of the abortive peace agreed upon between the French Government and the Huguenot deputies on July 15, 1625; and they are content to tell the story of the peace patched up with Spain in 1626, without a suspicion that the conduct of the English Court had a great deal to do with inducing Richelieu to give his consent to it.

If the harvest to be gathered from a diligent use of materials proved sufficient inducement to me to embark upon the present undertaking, I was certainly not prepared for the wealth of new material relating to those very Parliamentary contests, the documents relating to which seemed to have been so completely ransacked by my predecessors. The Parliaments of 1624 and 1626, indeed, stand mainly on their old basis as far as the House of Commons is concerned, though even here I have met with some materials not hitherto used, and 'Nicholas's Notes for 1624' throw some additional light upon discussions which are given very fully in the two reports in the journals. But for the House of Commons in 1625 we have, in addition to Eliot's 'Negotium Posterorum,' which we owe to Mr. Forster, the Fawsley MS., which I was lately allowed by the kindness of Sir Rainald Knightley to edit for the Camden Society. It is, however, the history of the great session of 1628 which gains most from the new light shed upon it. The debates heretofore were in a state of chaos, two or three speeches, often placed out of order, having frequently to do duty for a whole day's discussion. The first light I was able to throw upon the matter arose from a study of 'Nicholas's Notes,' written in that peculiar semi-shorthand of his which seems to have repelled previous investigators. But the knowledge derived from Nicholas was far surpassed by that which was gained from the admirable report, Harl. MSS. 4771, which, strangely enough, lurked unknown in that well-ransacked collection till I was fortunate enough to light upon it. The history of the struggle which led to the Petition of Right is thus at last made clear, and the part taken by the various leaders becomes more intelligible. Wentworth's character especially receives fresh elucidation, and we come to understand, when the evidence is sifted, how he came to take service under the King without being an apostate. It is a new fact, too, that the Petition of Right was preceded by a bill for the liberty of the subject, for which the petition was finally substituted in consequence of the King's refusal to accept any serious limitation of his powers.

If the debates in the Commons have not hitherto been fully known, the debates in the Upper House have been shrouded in utter darkness. The kindness of Colonel Carew in lending the 'Elsynge Notes' has at last dissipated the darkness for every session dealt with in the present volumes, excepting that of 1625, which was probably the least interesting of the four as far as the Lords were concerned. The details of the way in which the Peers dealt with Buckingham's impeachment are of considerable interest. But the most striking revelation is that of their mode of dealing with the questions arising out of the Petition of Right. Writers have hitherto been content to guess what passed in the House of Lords, and have frequently guessed wrong. Especially is this the case with respect to Bishop Williams, who turns out to have had nothing to do with the additional clause reserving sovereignty to the Crown, which is usually attributed to him, and to have been totally innocent of those intrigues against the petition which have called forth such denunciations of his conduct.

My thanks are especially due to Mr. Forster for the kindness with which he allowed me the use of his copy of Eliot's 'Negotium Posterorum,' and to Lord St. Germans for having, at Mr. Forster's request, lent to me a volume of notes in Eliot's hand, which I have quoted as 'Eliot Notes.' I am under the greater obligations to Mr. Forster, as he was quite aware that my view of many matters differed from his considerably, and was not likely to sympathise with much that I have thought fit to say. It is needless to say how much knowledge I have gained from the speeches and other documents published in his 'Life of Sir John Eliot.'

In conclusion, I would say that I have intentionally abstained from noticing some matters, such as Cosin's 'Book of Devotions,' and Williams's decision on the position of the communion-table at Grantham, which, though they fall chronologically within the limits of these volumes, are better treated of in connection with the debates of the following session. On the other hand, there are some matters which fall chronologically within the next period, which, if the popular account is to be believed, may be quoted against the opinion which I have formed of Charles's conduct in the session of 1628. I may therefore say that, as far as I have yet seen, I can find no ground for supposing that Charles, in the time which elapsed between the two sessions, broke the Petition of Right in the sense in which he understood it, and that it is not true that in the printed copy of the petition he substituted the first for the second answer. What he did was to print both answers together with his speech at the close of the session, as may be seen in the copy of the edition of the statutes of 1628 which is still preserved in the Museum library.

CONTENTS

OF

THE FIRST VOLUME.

CHAPTER I.

THE LAST PARLIAMENT OF JAMES I. AND THE DISSOLUTION OF THE SPANISH TREATIES.

		PAGE
1623	The return from Madrid	1
	Warlike designs of Charles and Buckingham	2
1624	Parliament summoned	4
	A French marriage talked of	4
	Spanish offers	5
	The Commissioners for Spanish affairs consulted	6
	They ask for further information	7
	Opposition to Buckingham in the Commission	8
	Della Rota's negotiation	10
	The question of breaking the Spanish treaties referred to Parliament	10
	The elections	11
	Parliament opened	12
	The King's speech	13
	Buckingham's narrative	15
	Sir John Eliot	16
	His speech on Parliamentary privilege	17
	The Spanish ambassadors complain of Buckingham	19
	The Lords condemn the treaties	20
	Rudyerd's declaration of policy	20
	Feeling of the Commons about Spain and Germany	22
	Petition of the Commons answered by the King	23
	Buckingham expostulates with the King	24

		PAGE
1624	Difference between the King and the Commons about the mode of carrying on the war	25
	The Prince explains away the King's answer	26
	Address of the Houses and reply by the King	27
	Dissatisfaction of the Commons and Buckingham's remonstrance	28
	The Prince declares his father to be ready to go to war	29
	Debate on supply	30
	Subsidies voted for four objects	32
	The King declares himself ready to dissolve the treaties	32
	Public rejoicings	35
	Lafuente robbed of his despatches	36
	James informs the Spanish ambassadors that negotiations are at an end	37
	Spanish intrigues against Buckingham	39
	Recall of the despatch announcing the dissolution of the treaties	41
	The Spanish intrigues detected by Williams	42
	The Spanish treaties dissolved	45

CHAPTER II.

BUCKINGHAM'S ASCENDENCY.

1624	Kensington's mission to Paris	48
	Writes hopefully of the French alliance	50
	Doubts of Sir Edward Herbert	51
	French policy with respect to Germany	52
	French designs upon the Valtelline	53
	Mansfeld's visit to France	55
	Charles pledges himself not to favour the Recusants	56
	Mansfeld arrives in England	56
	James's conditional engagement with him	57
	Nomination of a Council of War	58
	James promises to make no engagement for the Catholics in the marriage treaty	59
	Inojosa complains of Buckingham	60
	James refuses to listen to him	61
	Middlesex supports the Spanish ambassador	62
	Impeachment of Middlesex	64
	His sentence	65
	Bristol's return and confinement	66
	The Monopoly Act	67
	Parliament prorogued	69
	Proceedings against Bristol	70

THE FIRST VOLUME. XV

		PAGE
1624	He refuses to agree to a compromise	71
	Siege and capture of Ormuz	72
	Buckingham's claims against the East India Company	73
	Further demands of James	75
	Money extorted from the Company	76
	The massacre of Amboyna	77
	Treaty with the Dutch for sending regiments to the Netherlands	79
	Coloma's protests	80
	Inojosa leaves England	81
	The Dunkirk ships in the Downs	81
	The programme of the Commons carried out	82
	Embassies to Denmark and Sweden	83
	Wake's mission to Venice and Savoy	84
	Carlisle sent to Paris to negotiate a marriage treaty	85

CHAPTER III.

THE FRENCH MARRIAGE TREATY.

1624	Carlisle and Herbert on the French alliance	86
	The French demand terms for the English Catholics	88
	La Vieuville's diplomacy	89
	French preparations for war	90
	Effiat in England	91
	La Vieuville's disgrace	92
	Richelieu demands an article for the English Catholics	93
	James and Charles refuse to assent	95
	Buckingham's intervention	96
	Richelieu draws up an article	97
	Difference of opinion between Carlisle and Kensington	98
	Lewis promises to support Mansfeld	99
	Buckingham gained over by Effiat	100
	James persuaded to put the article in the form of a letter	101
	Favour shown to the Catholics	102
	Further prorogation of Parliament	103
	Refusal of the Council of War to supply Mansfeld	104
	Richelieu's views about the Valtelline and the Palatinate	105
	Negotiations between England and France about the support of Mansfeld	106
	The French refuse to commit themselves in writing	107
	Buckingham urges concession to France	108
	Charles supports Buckingham	109
	James agrees to sign a secret engagement to favour the English Catholics	109

VOL. I. a

		PAGE
1624	Signature of the marriage treaty	111
	Difficulty of finding money for Mansfeld	112
	The chances against him	113
	Frankenthal demanded from the Infanta	115
	Verbal promise of Lewis XIII, that Mansfeld shall be allowed to land in France	115
	The French wish to employ Mansfeld for the relief of Breda	117
	Objections of James	118
	The marriage treaty sworn to at Cambridge	119
	The Recusancy laws suspended	120
	Value of Richelieu's success	121

CHAPTER IV.

THE LAST DAYS OF JAMES I.

1624	Proposal that Mansfeld shall pass through Flanders	122
	Misunderstanding between Buckingham and the French	123
	Wretched condition of Mansfeld's troops at Dover	124
1625	The French propose to send them to the Netherlands	127
	Buckingham's dissatisfaction	128
	Mansfeld forbidden to land in France	129
	He is allowed to go to the Netherlands, but forbidden to relieve Breda	130
	Arrives at Flushing	131
	Mortality amongst the troops	132
	James repeats his refusal to allow their employment at Breda	133
	The army wastes away	134
1624	Christian IV. and the North German Bishoprics	135
	Anstruther's negotiation in Germany and Denmark	137
	Character and plans of Gustavus Adolphus	138
	Negotiations between Brandenburg and Sweden	141
1625	Conditions on which Gustavus will undertake war in Germany	144
	James shrinks from the expense	143
	Conditions laid down by Christian IV.	144
	Difference between the plans of Gustavus and those of James	145
	Gustavus relinquishes the German war	146
1624	Proposed attack by an English fleet upon Genoa	147
	Plan for sending a fleet against Spain	148
	The French Huguenots rise against Lewis	150
1625	Aid promised to Lewis by England and the Netherlands	151
	Final arrangements for the marriage	152

THE FIRST VOLUME. xvii

		PAGE
1625	Strong position of Buckingham at Court	154
	Advice of Williams to him	158
	Illness of the King	159
	Lady Buckingham offers him remedies	160
	His last hours	161
	Death of James I.	162

CHAPTER V.

MILITARY AND DIPLOMATIC PROJECTS OF THE NEW REIGN.

1625	Character of Charles I.	165
	He assumes the government	167
	His anxiety to meet Parliament	169
	Good order kept at Court	170
	Mansfeld allowed to assist the Dutch	172
	Equipment of the fleet	173
	Plan of a campaign in Flanders	174
	The King's marriage celebrated by proxy	175
	Carlisle warns the King not to expect much from France	176
	Buckingham prepares to go to France	177
	Agreement to lend English vessels to France	178
	Change in the treatment of the English Catholics	179
	Buckingham in Paris	180
	His main demands refused	181
	He makes love to the Queen	182
	Henrietta Maria in England	183
	First domestic difficulties	184
	Morton's mission to the Netherlands	185
	Surrender of Breda—Wretched state of Mansfeld's army	186
	Large sums of money needed	187

CHAPTER VI.

THE FIRST PARLIAMENT OF CHARLES I. AT WESTMINSTER.

1625	Opening of Parliament	189
	The King's speech	190
	Feeling against the Catholics	191
	Proposal for an adjournment rejected	192
	Petition on the Recusancy laws moved by Seymour	194
	Eliot's speech on religion	195
	Recusancy petition sent up to the Lords	197
	Motion of Seymour for a small supply	198

		PAGE
1625	Vote of two subsidies	200
	Charles reluctantly accepts the vote	202
	Wentworth's election	203
	Contrast between Eliot and Wentworth	204
1624	Montague's New Gag for an Old Goose	206
	Abbot's interference	208
1625	*Appello Cæsarem*	209
	English Calvinism	210
	Reaction against Calvinism	212
	Report of the Commons' Committee on Montague's books	216
	The Commons declare against Montague	218
	Laud's O. and P. list	220
	Tonnage and Poundage Bill	221
	Charles determines to ask for more money	223
	Eliot's interview with Buckingham	224
	Further supply asked for	228
	The demand not accepted by the Commons	230
	The Houses adjourned to Oxford	231
	Opposition of Williams	232

CHAPTER VII.

THE LOAN OF ENGLISH SHIPS TO THE KING OF FRANCE.

1625	Charles's domestic troubles	233
	His treatment of the English Catholics	234
	Concessions to the French ambassadors	235
	The ships under Pennington lent to the King of France	234
	Charles's double dealing	237
	Pennington at Dieppe	238
	His return to England	239
	Negotiations between Lewis XIII. and the Huguenots	240
	Pennington's orders	241
	Mission of Edward Nicholas	243
	Resistance of the crews	244
	Secret instructions to Nicholas and Pennington	245
	Pennington returns to Dieppe	247
	Nicholas prepares a mutiny	248
	Mutiny in Pennington's ship	250
	Peace agreed upon in France	251
	The ships surrendered to the French	254
	Condition of the English Catholics	255
	The Houses reassemble at Oxford	256

CHAPTER VIII.

THE FIRST PARLIAMENT OF CHARLES I. AT OXFORD.

		PAGE
1625	The Commons complain of favours shown to the Catholics	257
	Buckingham resolves to throw over the Catholics	258
	Montague's case again	259
	Question of the responsibility of the King's ministers	260
	Report of the bishops on Montague's books	261
	Who was to decide on Church questions?	263
	The King in Christchurch Hall	264
	Financial statement by Conway and Sir J. Coke	266
	Debate on the King's demands	268
	Seymour attacks the foreign policy of the Crown	269
	May's reply	270
	Phelips asks for a change of counsellors	271
	Governmental responsibility demanded	273
	Heath's defence of the Government, and Alford's reply	274
	Terms offered to Buckingham	275
	Attempted compromise	276
	Rich's five propositions	277
	Buckingham urged to accept the compromise	279
	Buckingham resolves not to give way	280
	Declares that the engagement with France about the Catholics had never been taken seriously	281
	Defends his policy before the two Houses	282
	Unsatisfactory nature of his defence	283
	Charles demands an immediate grant of supply	287
	Phelips puts the question of confidence	288
	Mansell appealed to	289
	Wentworth's view of the case	290
	Mansell's testimony unfavourable to Buckingham	292
	Buckingham attacked by name	293
	A dissolution resolved on	294
	Heath's reply to Mansell	295
	Protestation of the Commons	296
	Dissolution of Parliament	297
	Leadership of Phelips characterised	298
	Attitude of the King	299
	Conflict between the Crown and the House of Commons begun	300

CHAPTER IX.

THE EXPEDITION TO CADIZ.

		PAGE
1625	Buckingham's intentions	302
	Breach of the engagements between Lewis XIII. and the Huguenots	303
	Determination of Charles to send out the fleet	304
	The Queen at Lichfield	305
	The treaty of Southampton	307
	Open breach with Spain	308
	Buckingham to go to the Hague	309
	The Essex trained bands at Harwich	310
	Death of Sir A. Morton—Sir J. Coke Secretary	311
	Sir E. Cecil appointed to command the expedition against Spain	312
	He reports on the deficiencies of the troops	313
	Cecil created Viscount Wimbledon	314
	The fleet driven back by a storm	315
	It puts to sea	316
	Arrives at Cadiz	317
	Attack on Fort Puntal	319
	Surrender of the fort	320
	Wimbledon's march to the bridge	321
	Failure of the expedition	222
	The look-out for the Plate fleet	323
	Return of the fleet to England	324
	No serious investigation into the causes of failure	326

CHAPTER X.

GROWING ESTRANGEMENTS BETWEEN THE COURTS OF ENGLAND AND FRANCE.

1625	Blainville's proposals	327
	Buckingham's intention to visit France	328
	Objections of Lewis	329
	Blainville's interview with Charles and Buckingham	331
	Views of the French Government	332
	The Peers of the Opposition	332
	Dismissal of Williams	334
	Coventry Lord Keeper	336
	The Opposition leaders of the Commons made sheriffs	337
	The Dunkirk privateers	338

THE FIRST VOLUME. xxi

		PAGE
1625	Buckingham visits the Hague and proposes to attack Dunkirk	339
	The Congress of the Hague	340
	Treaty of the Hague	341
	Prospect of war with France	342
	Difficulties about the Queen's household	343
	Difficulties about the law of prize	344
	Sequestration of the money on board the French prizes	345
	Orders given for the sale of prize goods	346
	Blainville protests	347
	Reprisals in France followed by an order for the restitution of the 'St. Peter'	348
1626	Mission of Holland and Carleton	349
	Charles determines to relieve Rochelle	350
	The prize goods sold	351
	The 'St. Peter' rearrested	352
	Interference of Charles in French politics	353
	The Queen refuses to be crowned	354
	Charles's coronation	355
	An agreement come to between Lewis and the Huguenots	357
	The Huguenots look to Charles for support	358
	Richelieu proposes to join England against Spain	359
	Charles rejects his overtures	360
	Fresh dispute between Charles and the Queen	363
	Blainville ordered to absent himself from Court	365

MAP OF CADIZ HARBOUR . . . . . . *To face Title Page.*

Errata.

Page 28, line 5, *for* 'hoped to call them together again in the autumn' *read* 'intended to call them together 'at Michaelmas, or within a few days after.''

,, 69 ,, 14, *after* 'prorogued' *read* 'to November 2.'

,, 103 ,, 3, ,, 'November' insert foot-note: 'On March 14 (p. 28) James had promised to summon Parliament at Michaelmas or shortly after. On March 23 (p. 33) he had declared that the business of considering the course of the war should be taken in hand at the next session, and the actual prorogation had fixed the meaning of "few days after Michaelmas" to November 2.'

,, 114 note 1, line 2 from bottom, *for* 'attached' read 'attacked.'

,, 137 ,, 1, last line, *for* 'Niedersachsische' *read* 'Niedersächsische.'

,, 143, line 2 from bottom, *for* 'coasts' *read* 'courts.'

,, 206 ,, 6 ,, *after* 'know,' *read* 'not.'

,, 205 ,, 8 ,,. and side note, *for* 'Stamford' *read* 'Stanford.'

,, 220 ,, 8 ,, *for* 'he' *read* 'Buckingham.'

,, 231 second side note, *for* 'House' *read* 'Houses.'

,, 244 second side note, *for* 'enemy' *read* 'crews.'

,, 246 note 3, line 2 from bottom, *for* 'the 18th' *read* 'July 18.'

,, 316 line 5 from bottom, *for* 'Cecil' *read* 'Wimbledon.'

,, 336 ,, 16, *for* 'Shelton' *read* 'Shilton.'

ENGLAND

UNDER THE

DUKE OF BUCKINGHAM AND CHARLES I.

CHAPTER I.

THE LAST PARLIAMENT OF JAMES I. AND THE DISSOLUTION OF THE SPANISH TREATIES.

THE young man's dream which had lighted Charles and Buckingham on their way to Madrid, was pleasant enough while it lasted. All difficulties, personal and political, were to vanish away before the magic of their presence. The King of Spain would, for the sake of his future son-in-law, compel the Emperor to surrender the Palatinate, and the strife which had desolated Germany for five years would be composed as easily as a lovers' quarrel. The King's sister, brought up in the most bigoted attachment to the faith of her childhood, would give her heart as well as her hand to the heretic prince whose person she loathed, and whose religion she detested. Of the two, Buckingham, not being himself in love, was the first to discover the mistake which had been committed. Quick to take offence at the slightest discourtesy offered to him, he was not long in perceiving that the Spaniards meant to make the most of their opportunity, and to deliver over the

CHAP. I.

1623.
The journey to Madrid.

CHAP. I.
1623.

Infanta, if they delivered her over at all, only upon conditions which would be insupportable to the English people. Whilst Charles was hanging about Philip's court, and promising anything short of his own apostasy, Buckingham was quarrelling with the Spanish ministers, and urging the Prince to return to England as soon as possible.

Warlike designs of Charles and Buckingham.

When at last Charles had convinced himself that his concessions had been made in vain, and that, whatever he might do, he would not be allowed to carry the Infanta with him to England, his faith in Buckingham was more strongly confirmed than ever. Buckingham's life was so completely bound up with his life, and Buckingham's objects were for the most part so fully served by promoting his young master's wishes, that differences of opinion were seldom likely to arise between them. And now that a difference had arisen, Charles had proved to be in the wrong, whilst Buckingham had proved to be in the right, and that too on a point on which Charles might well think that his friend had been more jealous for his honour than he had been himself.

Both Charles and Buckingham came back with the full persuasion that they had been duped by the Spaniards, and with a full determination to take their revenge. To the heated imagination of the youthful politicians, the re-conquest of the Palatinate seemed so very easy. And yet it was far from being easy. Not only was the position of Spain and the Imperialists exceedingly strong, but there were elements of disunion at work amongst the opponents of the house of Austria which would go far to make the task of organising a successful resistance impossible.

James determined to

The first difficulty, however, which Buckingham needed to confront, was greater in appearance than in reality. It might seem easier to drag Theseus from his bed of pain than to move James to a declaration of war. A lover of peace by temperament and by force of reason, he knew too well what faults had been committed on both sides to be eager to join in the doubtful fray. Great, too, as was the influence exercised over him by his favourite and his son, it is hardly likely that this alone would have sufficed to overcome his reluctance to embark on so arduous an undertaking. In 1620, in spite of his unwillingness to displease those with whom he was in continual intercourse, Charles and Buckingham, backed by the almost unanimous voice of his Council and his Court, had in vain urged him to take part in the strife. But at the close of 1623 he was no longer in a position to offer resistance. His plan for settling the affairs of Germany with the help of Spain had broken down completely. Even James was driven to acknowledge that that path was no longer open to him, and that if the Palatinate was to be recovered at all, it must be recovered by force of arms. The only question for him to decide, therefore, was whether he was willing to abandon all hope of its recovery or not. And this he was decidedly not prepared to do. The abandonment of his daughter and her children from considerations of state policy, was so grievous to him, that, though Buckingham would doubtless have much moral and physical inertness to combat, he could always make use of the King's real desire to recover the Palatinate as a lever to move him in the direction of decisive action.

In January 1624, James to a great extent yielded himself into the hands of Buckingham. The marriage ceremony at Madrid had been postponed under circumstances which made it almost a matter of certainty that it would never be heard of again. Bristol, the

CHAP. I.
1624.
Jan.

chief supporter of the alliance, was recalled from his embassy in Spain, and the Earl of Oxford, who had been confined in the Tower for nearly two years on account of a violent attack upon Gondomar's influence, was set at liberty. Writs were issued for a new Parliament. Once more, as in 1620, ambassadors were ordered to make ready to start in every direction. This time they were to be the messengers, not of peace, but of war. Sir Isaac Wake was to stir up the Duke of Savoy and the Republic of Venice. Sir Robert Anstruther was to wait upon the Princes of Northern Germany and the King of Denmark. Sir James Spens would do the like office with the King of Sweden. The States General were invited to send commissioners to negotiate a close alliance, and the invitation was made more attractive by a letter in which Conway was allowed impudently to represent the plot which had been hatched between Buckingham and Gondomar for the partition of the territory of the Republic as a mere unauthorised suggestion of Spanish iniquity.[1]

Hopes of a French alliance.

Yet these steps, important as they were, formed only part of the great plan which Buckingham had conceived. Ever since the war had broken out in Germany, France had given a passive, but not the less a real, assistance to the Emperor. Now, however, hints had reached Buckingham that all this might yet be changed. While he was still at Madrid, an English friar named Grey had formed the wild project of converting the Prince; and, when he found that he had no chance of success, had talked with Buckingham of his influence with Mary de Medici, and of the probability that she might be induced to offer her youngest daughter, the Princess Henrietta Maria, as a substitute

[1] Conway to the Prince of Orange, Conway to Carleton, Jan. $\frac{9}{19}$, (S. P., Holland). Compare *Prince Charles and the Spanish Marriage*, i. 334.

for the Infanta. How far Buckingham gave heed to the friar's prattle it is hard to say. At all events Grey made his way to Paris, saw the Queen Mother, and was sent on by her to London, after the Prince's return, to explain to Buckingham her readiness to assist in forwarding the suggested marriage. It is true that when the affair came to the ears of Tillières, the French ambassador in London, both Mary and Buckingham thought it expedient to disavow all knowledge of the intrigue.[1] But the seed was already sown. James agreed to take up the project as soon as the treaty with Spain was definitively disposed of. In the meanwhile it was arranged that Lord Kensington should be sent over to Paris to feel the ground, and to lay the foundations of a complete friendship between the two courts.

CHAP. I.

1624. Jan.

James had thus given his consent to the opening of a negotiation which would leave little room for any further understanding with Spain. But his resolution was not so fixed as to be entirely beyond the influence of a specious offer from the other side. On January 13, the Spanish ambassadors, Inojosa and Coloma, assured him of their master's anxiety to do everything in his power to regain his friendship. Before the end of August, they asserted, all that part of the Palatinate which was occupied by Spanish troops should be placed in his hands. Negotiations should be opened, at a time to be fixed by himself, for the settlement of all other points at issue. Some middle course was indicated as likely to obviate the difficulty about the education of Frederick's sons; and Philip, though he still refused to promise, as he had once promised in a moment of forgetfulness, to draw his sword against

Jan. 13. Offer of the Spanish ambassadors.

[1] Tillières to Puisieux $\frac{\text{Dec. 30,}}{\text{Jan. 9,}}$ Jan. $\frac{8}{18}, \frac{17}{27}$; *Harl. MSS.* 4593; fol. 7, 16, 25, b.

CHAP. I.

1624.
Jan. 13.
The Commissioners for Spanish affairs to be consulted.

the Emperor, was ready to engage to do anything else in his power to bring about a favourable result.[1]

Much to Buckingham's disgust, James thought the offer worth listening to. But James had not made up his mind either way, and he agreed to consult the Commissioners for Spanish Affairs before taking a final decision. The body thus appealed to consisted of twelve of the leading Privy Councillors, and may perhaps be regarded as the germ of our modern cabinets. It had been called into existence in 1617, to discuss the marriage treaty with Spain, as soon as it was openly taken in hand. Its numbers had been constantly filled up as vacancies occurred. As it had recently, by a majority of seven to five, approved of the issue of writs for a new Parliament, Buckingham had good reason to expect its support in his present difficulties.[2]

Jan. 14.
Questions proposed to them.

When the Commissioners met, two questions were laid before them. In the first place :—Had the King of Spain seriously intended to give his sister to the Prince? In the second place :—Did his conduct about the Palatinate deserve a declaration of war?[3] When the votes were taken, three only, those of Buckingham himself, of Carlisle, who hated Spain as much as his

---

[1] Compare *Valaresso's Despatches*, Jan. $\frac{16}{26}$, $\frac{\text{Jan. } 23}{\text{Feb. } 2}$, with Siri, *Memorie Recondite*, v. 568; and Chamberlain to Carleton, Jan. 17; *Court and Times*, ii. 446.

[2] *Salvetti's Newsletter*, $\frac{\text{Dec. } 26}{\text{Jan. } 5}$.

[3] The two questions are abbreviated from the form given by Hacket (i. 167.) He says they were put immediately after the King's arrival at Whitehall, *i.e.* after Dec. 24. As I find no trace of such consultations elsewhere, I suspect he confused them with a discussion whether writs should be issued for a Parliament. After the King left Whitehall, *i.e.* on Jan. 13, we do hear of consultations in Chamberlain's letter of Jan. 31, for instance, *S. P. Dom.*, clviii. 72. There is a curious draft of a letter (*S. P. Spain*), perhaps drawn up by Buckingham, as what he wished the King to say, and not accepted by James.

placable disposition would allow him to hate anything, and of Conway, who would doubtless have voted the other way if his patron had desired him to do so, but who was only in this case following his own instincts in opposing Spain, were given in favour of war. The other nine members of the Commission stated that they had not sufficient information before them, and asked permission to make a thorough examination of all the despatches bearing upon the subject.[1]

CHAP. 1.

1624. Jan 14. They ask for information.

Buckingham was very angry. He sprung from his seat, pouring out the most unmeasured abuse of the Commissioners as he strode out of the room, 'as a hen that hath lost her brood and clucks up and down when she hath none to follow her.'[2] Taking the Prince with him, he hurried down to Newmarket to complain to the King. "What," he said to Chichester, who was passing near him as he left Whitehall, "are you turned too?"[3] It was Buckingham's greatest misfortune in life that he never could understand that it was possible for men to differ from him without some sinister motive. Divergence of opinion was ever with him a thing not to be met with argument, but to be overcome by violence.

Buckingham's anger.

Buckingham met with better success at Royston. From whatever motive, James had no desire to see the whole secret of the past negotiation unfolded before the Commissioners. He wrote to inform them that their request could not be granted, but that they must nevertheless tell him what they thought of the Spanish offer. On the 20th Charles, leaving Buckingham to keep guard over his father, returned to London. He assured the Commissioners that he would never think

Jan. 20. The King supports him.

[1] Tillières to Puisieux, Jan 17/27: *Harl. MSS.*, 4593; fol. 26, b.
[2] *Hacket*, i. 169.
[3] Chichester to Buckingham, Jan. 25. *Cabala*, 197.

CHAP. I.
1624.
Jan. 20.

again of a marriage with the Infanta. All through the remainder of the week the discussion continued with unabated vigour. The Commissioners were unanimous in wishing to see the marriage treaty at an end, but many of them still shrank from giving an opinion in favour of war upon so little information as that which had been vouchsafed to them.[1]

Nature of the opposition.

Of the nine who had originally voted against Buckingham, five, Calvert, Weston, Arundel, Williams, and Middlesex, had already declared against the summoning of a Parliament, and were all for various reasons the advocates of peace. Pembroke and Chichester, Hamilton and Lennox, had always been counted as the opponents of the Spanish alliance. In Pembroke's case, especially, the hesitation to support Buckingham was so unexpected that it was accounted for at the time as proceeding from jealousy of the favourite's exclusive influence with the Prince. There may have been some truth in this, but motives of public policy may have had still more to do with his behaviour. Himself a man without ambition, the richest peer in England, and universally regarded as the model of a chivalrous English gentleman, he had watched Buckingham's career with deep distrust. Only a few months before, he had been required, as a Privy Councillor, to swear to the observance of the Spanish treaty, and to take part in the negotiations which followed for a peaceful settlement of the Continental dispute. And now he was expected, without being told the reason why, to swing round with his eyes shut in the other direction. Was he without enquiry to give his vote for a war which might possibly be justifiable, but which,

[1] Tillières to Puisieux, $\frac{\text{Jan. 31}}{\text{Feb. 10}}$; *Harl. MSS.* 4593, fol. 35. *Valaresso's Despatch*, $\frac{\text{Jan. 30}}{\text{Feb. 9}}$. Hacket's list of the Commissioners is incorrect.

to all appearance, was being urged on by Buckingham's temper rather than by his reason? No wonder that he was heard to say that 'if the Spaniards performed the conditions agreed on, he saw not how the King, in honour, could fall from the conclusion, nor himself in conscience; being sworn to see all observed in his power.' To the Venetian ambassador, who exhorted him to make up his differences with Buckingham for the sake of the common cause of all European states, he replied that internal enemies must be dealt with before external ones. The cause which they had both at heart would be better served without Buckingham than with him.[1]

Pembroke, however, was not a man to persist long in opposition. His character was wanting in that robustness which is needed for such a task. Again and again, in the course of his career, we find him clashing with Buckingham. This time, at least, it seemed that they would be open enemies. But a few words from King or Prince were always enough to soothe his easy temper, and Pembroke would be again on the old footing, giving the support of his respected name to a policy which he distrusted.

So it was now. In a few days, he and the rest of the Commissioners had agreed in a temporising answer to the effect that they did not see that the King ought to be contented with the Spanish answer about the Palatinate, or to amuse himself any longer about the marriage. The original question concerning the propriety of going to war was left unanswered.[2] It was not long before the Prince used his authority to reconcile Pembroke and Buckingham; and before the session opened

[1] Chamberlain to Carleton, Jan. 31; *S. P. Dom.*, clviii. 72; *Valaresso's Despatch*, Jan. 30/Feb. 9, Feb. 6/16.
[2] Tillières to Puisieux, Jan. 31/Feb. 10; *Harl. MSS.* 4593, fol. 35.

CHAP. I.

1624. Jan.
Negotiation of Della Rota.

the malcontent Earl had changed into an unwavering supporter of the Government.

Charles, too, had, on the whole, good reason to be satisfied with his father's conduct. There were from time to time, indeed, fits of hesitation and reluctance; and rumours reached the ears of those interested in such tidings, that James had declared himself to be tired of Buckingham.[1] But such rumours, if there was any truth in them at all, did not reveal the whole truth. The moment that James gave a serious thought to the matter, he knew that if he was to recover the Palatinate, Buckingham's way was the only way open to him, and that the Spanish proposals had but to be fully stated to be rejected. Just at this time the same proposals which had been made by Spain in the preceding autumn were brought before him from another quarter. A Capuchin friar, travelling under the assumed name of Francesco della Rota, appeared in England, with offers from the new Elector of Bavaria. The Elector, just like the Emperor, was ready to yield much for the sake of peace. The only difference in their terms was, that whilst Ferdinand required that Frederick's son and heir should be educated at Vienna, Maximilian required that he should be educated at Munich. Of course there was much said about offering all possible safeguards for the boy's religion. But what was the value of such safeguards to a youth brought at the most impressionable age within the circle of the ideas of the Catholic priesthood?

The breach with Spain referred to Parliament.

To this plan, at least, James gave a distinct refusal. But it was easier for him to see what was not to be done than to decide, for himself and others, what he wished to do. As the Commissioners would not settle

Valaresso's Despatch, $\frac{\text{Jan. 30}}{\text{Feb. 9}}$. [2] Rusdorf, *Mémoires*, i. 156-239.

his difficulties for him, the whole question was referred to the coming Parliament.

By the time the consultations of the Commissioners were brought to a close the elections were almost completed. In ordinary times the House of Commons was brought into existence under very composite influences. In the counties the choice of the great landowners weighed heavily upon the freeholders. In the smaller boroughs the owner of some neighbouring manor, to whom the citizens were bound by the obligations of ancestral courtesy, or immediate interest, could often dispose of the seat at his pleasure. The Government, too, was not without its influence. The boroughs of Lancashire and the sea-coast towns of Kent, for instance, were in the habit of returning nominees of the Chancellor of the Duchy, or of the Lord Warden of the Cinque Ports. In this way the House came to represent not merely the mass of electors, but also the effective strength of the nation. The men who took part in its debates were men who were accustomed as magistrates, or in other ways, to take their share in the business of government. They were in the habit of acting under responsibility; in the habit, too, of thinking of their actions as subservient to the national good. Their election was very far from being a mere form. Again and again, in spite of the lack of reporters, when measures are proposed in the course of this and the following years, the leaders of the assembly make use of the argument, " What will our constituents say? " as the best rejoinder possible. For some years, as political excitement had increased, there had been a tendency in the electors to shake off the control to which they had hitherto to some extent submitted, and to require independence as the one thing needful. And now, in many places candidates supported by Buckingham, or

CHAP.
I.

1624.
Jan.
The elections.

12   THE LAST PARLIAMENT OF JAMES I.

CHAP. I.

1624. Jan. Coke and Sandys.

Feb. 16. Death of Lennox.

Feb. 19. Opening of Parliament.

even by the Prince, were left unchosen, and the name of courtier was the surest passport to rejection.[1] In two cases James was desirous of overruling indirectly the choice of the constituencies. He had a lively recollection of Coke's attitude in the last Parliament, and he seriously designed to get rid of the old lawyer by sending him to Ireland, as member of a commission appointed to investigate the state of that country. He destined for the same employment Sir Edwin Sandys, whose opposition to the Court was of earlier date than Coke's. Such a step, however, was too palpably unwise to be insisted on, and both Coke and Sandys were allowed to take their seats.[2]

Parliament had been summoned for February 12, but was put off till the 16th, because, as men amused themselves by saying, the King had not yet made up his mind what to reply to the Spanish ambassadors.[3] On the 16th it was again postponed, on account of the death of James's old friend and kinsman, the Duke of Lennox.[4]

The speech with which James opened his last Parliament was couched in a tone of unusual hesitation. The old self-confidence with which, in his happier days, he had sought to school his hearers into submission, had entirely left him. Convinced at last that peace could no longer be maintained unless the object for which he had striven so long was abandoned as unattainable, and yet shrinking with his whole soul from opening the floodgates of war, he was equally

---

[1] *Valaresso's Despatch*, Feb. $\frac{6}{14}$.

[2] These are the only Parliament names in the commission (*Rymer*, xvii. 531), or in Chamberlain's contemporary letters.

[3] *Salvetti's Newsletter*, Feb. $\frac{13}{23}$.

[4] Hacket is quite mistaken in supposing (i. 174) that there is an error in the date of the curious letter in which Williams advised Buckingham to accept the office of Lord Steward. It was written after Hamilton's death in 1625, and will be noticed in its proper place.

unwilling to turn his back upon his old policy, or to enter heartily upon a new one. Casting himself upon the compassion of his hearers, he pleaded before them the anxiety with which he had striven to deserve his people's love ; and told the Houses how, as a pledge of his confidence in them, he was come to ask their advice in the greatest matter that ever could concern any king. He had hoped to settle peace abroad and at home. But he now knew what the pretensions of Spain really were. The whole story should be told them by his Secretaries, who would be assisted by the Prince and Buckingham. "When you have heard it all," he added, "I shall entreat your good and sound advice, for the glory of God, the peace of the kingdom, and weal of my children. Never king gave more trust to his subjects than to desire their advice in matters of this weight; for I assure you ye may freely advise me, seeing of my princely fidelity you are invited thereto."

Feb. 19. The King's Speech.

Having thus removed the prohibition which had brought about the dissolution of the last Parliament, James turned to a subject on which his hearers were peculiarly sensitive. "I pray you," he said, "judge me charitably as you will have me judge you ; for I never made public nor private treaties, but I always made a direct reservation for the weal public and cause of religion, for the glory of God and the good of my subjects. I only thought good sometimes to wink and connive at the execution of some penal statutes, and not to go on so rigorously as at other times ; but to dispense with any, to forbid or alter any that concern religion, I neither promised nor yielded. I never did think it with my heart, nor speak it with my mouth. It is true a skilful horseman doth not always use the spur, but must sometimes use the bridle, and sometimes

Explains what he has done about the Catholics.

CHAP. I.
1624.
Feb. 19.

the spur. So a king that governs evenly is not bound to carry a rigorous hand over his subjects upon all occasions, but may sometimes slacken the bridle, yet so as his hands be not off the reins."

How far was this statement true?

Such words were very far from being a full and fair representation of the past negotiations. But they were at least in accordance with what James had wished to do, and were not very far from that which, by some stretch of imagination, he may have fancied himself to have done. They give an accurate account of his first offers to Spain in 1620; and when, in 1623, he went much farther, he had at least reserved to himself, by a protest, the right of cancelling his obligations, if reason of state should so require.[1] It is hardly likely, however, that the Commons, if they had known the whole story, would have told it in the same way.

Arrangements for Buckingham's appearance.

After a few more words, James retired from the scene. He had thrown down the reins of government, and there was one standing by who was eager to take them from his failing hands. James, it is true, had told the Houses that the information for which they were looking would be communicated to them by his Secretaries, with the assistance of Buckingham and the Prince. But so subordinate a part would hardly have suited Buckingham. Before the appointed day arrived it was understood that the communication would be made by the Duke, and that the Secretaries, and even the Prince himself, would be content to give him what assistance he might need. The Houses were to assemble, not as usual in the Painted Chamber, but in the great hall of the palace, where they were accustomed to wait upon the King. If Buckingham had said, " I am the

[1] Conway to Buckingham, July 23, 1623. *Hardwicke St. P.*, i. 430. Compare *Prince Charles and the Spanish Marriage*, ii. 363.

King," he could not have expressed himself more plainly.

King, Prince, and State were all merged in that imposing personality. We can well imagine how he looked as he stood there, with head erect and flashing eye, to disclose those secrets of which so much was suspected, and so little was really known. The tale which he told is easy to criticise, and it has been judged again and again with unmeasured reprobation. But, after all, as far as it is possible to test it, its fault lay rather in its omissions than in its assertions. Over much of which the historian is bound to take account— over the folly of the journey itself—over Charles's reticence, as long as reticence was possible, with respect to his personal religion—over his solemn promises to make impracticable concessions, Buckingham threw the discreet veil of total silence. But the evidence which he produced to show that the Spanish ministers had never seriously intended giving effect to their master's rash promise to aid with his arms in the recovery of the Palatinate was entirely conclusive; and the narrative, taking it all in all, bears the aspect not so much of a deliberate falsehood, as of the outpouring of a heart upon which fancy and passion had impressed their glowing pictures. When Buckingham ended by asking whether the Spanish diplomacy should still be listened to, or whether, these treaties being 'set aside, his Majesty were best to trust to his own strength, and to stand upon his own feet,' he was sure to carry his hearers with him, and to sit down the most popular man in England.[1]

One effect at least of the Spanish treaties was indelibly imprinted on the English mind. Bringing into prominent relief the connection between the English

[1] *Lords' Journals*, iii. 220.

CHAP. I.
1624.

Feb. 27.
Sir John Eliot.

Catholics and the great Spanish monarchy, they had served to whet the spirit of intolerance. Almost the first work to which the Commons addressed themselves was a bill for increasing the penalties on recusancy.[1]

On the 27th Weston, the Chancellor of the Exchequer, was to deliver the formal report of Buckingham's narrative to the Lower House. Before he had time to rise, he was interrupted by Sir John Eliot, a member whose parliamentary experience had been confined to the few weeks of the abortive session of 1614. When he sat down at the end of his maiden speech, he must have made himself a name as the foremost political orator of the time. Early in life he had accompanied Buckingham, then an unknown youth, on a Continental tour, and had received from him, when he rose to be Lord High Admiral of England, the appointment of Vice-Admiral of Devon. During his patron's absence in Spain, he had been imprisoned on an unjust charge springing out of his unwearied performance of the duties of his office, and his liberation, which was almost coincident with the Duke's return, was doubtless owing to his powerful interposition. But, warm and affectionate as Eliot's nature was, he was not the man to allow any tie to an individual to fetter him in the performance of a public duty; and though there was, for some time to come, no actual estrangement between him and Buckingham, it is probable that the retirement of the King to give place to the minister left a disagreeable impression on his mind. He was to the bottom of his heart an idealist. To him the Parliament was scarcely a collection of fallible men, just as the King was hardly a being who could by any possibility go deliberately astray. If he who wore

[1] *Commons' Journals*, i. 718.

the crown had wandered from the right path, he had but to listen to those who formed, in more than a rhetorical sense, the collective wisdom of the nation. Whoever stepped between King and people, whoever tendered other counsel than the House of Commons had to offer, was a divider and a traitor.

CHAP. I.
1624. Feb. 27.

The time had not yet come when Eliot was to breathe his own lofty and resolute spirit into the consultations of those around him. But from the beginning, great as his intellectual powers were, it was not by mere force of intellect that he won his way to distinction. It was the moral nature of the man, his utter self-forgetfulness, which made him what he was, which taught him to risk his whole life and fortunes for the chance of flinging his protest into the air against securely placed iniquity in high places, and which made him as gentle and placable as the saintly men of old in the presence of opposition the motives of which he believed to be pure.

His moral weight.

This time Eliot rose to beg the House not to forget, in the midst of their fresher interests, to vindicate that freedom of speech which had been refused them at the close of the last Parliament. The privileges of the Commons, he argued, could not be derogatory to the King's honour. "The business," he said, "is the King's. The kingdom hath its representative in the King. In him our resolutions rest. We are only called hither upon either the general affairs of the kingdom, or the special propositions of his Majesty, and thereon to deliberate and consult, not to conclude." The Parliament, he went on to say, was the body; the King the spirit by which it was moved. "He is, in the metaphor, the breath of our nostrils, and the bond by which we are tied one to another. Then can it not be we

His speech on liberty of speech.

VOL. I. C

CHAP. I.
1624.
Feb. 27.
Comparison between Bacon and Eliot.

should attempt against, or in anything neglect, the honour of him who is so much our own."[1]

Such language might have been Bacon's language. But the spirit in which the words were uttered was not the spirit of Bacon. To both Eliot and Bacon the Crown and the Parliament were not contracting parties, each of which was to follow its separate interest, but members of one common body, each fulfilling its functions for the benefit of the whole. But whilst Bacon specially idealised the Crown, Eliot specially idealised the Parliament. When the separation threatened to come at last, Bacon clung the more closely to the active ruling power, whilst Eliot trusted with unshaken confidence to the body in which popular instincts were refined under the influence of word and thought. Viewing from afar the follies and errors of the court, he learned to believe, as no other man believed before or after him, in the representatives of the nation. For him history and philosophy concurred in bearing witness to the greatness of Parliaments, the living mirror of the perpetual wisdom of a mighty nation.

Eliot on liberty of speech.

For the sake of the King, Eliot now argued, the counsel of Parliament should be offered freely and without restriction. "More for his sake than for ours," he said, "it behoved that such liberty be allowed." Freedom of speech was the indispensable condition of trustworthy advice.[2]

The question referred to a Committee.

The question thus raised could hardly be passed over in silence. But the leaders of the House were too anxious to get to the important work before them to give it much encouragement. The whole subject was referred to a Committee, and was never heard of again.[3]

---

[1] Forster, *Sir J. Eliot*, i. 70, 71.   [2] Forster, *Sir J. Eliot*, i. 135.
[3] Mr. Forster thinks (*Sir J. Eliot*, i. 143) that the speeches of Alford

Weston was at last able to proceed with his report. If there had ever been any hesitation in accepting Buckingham's narrative, there was none now. Inojosa and Coloma had done their best to convert him into a national hero. Hurrying to James, they assured him that if one of their master's servants had spoken of the King of England as Buckingham had spoken of the King of Spain, he would have paid the penalty with the loss of his head. James's only thought in the presence of the fiery Spaniards was to shift the burthen of a reply to other shoulders. He had not been present at Whitehall, he said, when Buckingham's narrative was delivered, and he must therefore leave it to those who heard it to justify or to condemn him. In the House of Lords, Pembroke, who had now thrown himself unreservedly on Buckingham's side, led the way in exculpating him, and a motion in his favour was unanimously carried. In the Commons the excitement was far greater. "In the way that Buckingham holds," said Phelips, "I pray that he shall keep his head on his shoulders to see thousands of Spaniards' heads either from their shoulders or in the seas." "And shall he lose his head?" cried Coke. "Never any man deserved better of his King and country." A vote as unanimous as that of the Lords, cleared Buckingham from blame in the words that he had used.[1]

CHAP. I.

1624. Feb. 27. Complaint of the Spanish Ambassadors against Buckingham.

and Phelips leave little doubt that they had received private communications from Buckingham. It is quite possible that some understanding had been arrived at, probably through Pembroke; but there is no proof of this, and there is no necessity to resort to this explanation. According to Nicholas's notes (*S. P. Dom.*, clix), of which Mr. Forster has made no use, Phelips said that 'since this motion is on foot, he thinks it should not rest unresolved,' which looks as if he at least expected something to come of the Committee.

[1] Coloma to the King, $\frac{\text{Feb. 28}}{\text{Mar. 9}}$; *Harl. MSS.* 1583, fol. 329; *Valaresso's Despatch*, March $\frac{5}{15}$; *Elsing's Notes*; *Lords' Journals*, iii. i. 233; *Commons' Journals*, i. 721.

*1624.
Feb. 27.
The treaties condemned by the Lords, Feb. 28.*

In the afternoon the Lords took the Spanish treaties into consideration. Not a voice was raised in their favour. After two days' debate, the Bishops having specially distinguished themselves by their warlike zeal, it was resolved that, unless the Commons should show cause to the contrary, the King should be asked to break off all negotiation with Spain, both for the marriage and for the restoration of the Palatinate.[1]

*March 1.
Rudyerd's declaration of policy.*

The Commons were hardly likely to show cause to the contrary. The great debate was opened on the 1st of March in the Lower House by Sir Benjamin Rudyerd, whose official position as Surveyor of the Court of Wards, together with his close connection with Pembroke, made him a fit exponent of the coalition which had sprung up between Buckingham and the popular lords.[2] At the same time, his own tried devotion to the anti-Spanish policy was likely to secure for him the respectful attention of his hearers.

Rudyerd, even at his best, was apt rather to skim over the surface of an argument than to penetrate to its depths, and those who look coolly back at the events of that momentous year may be inclined to ask whether it necessarily followed, because the Palatinate was not to be regained by negotiation, that an attempt should be made to regain it by war. That such doubts were felt by a few who sat there, by Weston and Wentworth for instance, is all but certain. But Weston had surrendered himself body and soul to Buckingham, and Wentworth, haughty and defiant as he was, was too much of a practical statesman to resist the majority of a popular assembly by argument. Those who on this

[1] *Elsing's Notes.*
[2] There is no direct evidence of this; but the fact that he opened the three debates of March 1, 11, and 19, and that the greater part of his advice was adopted by the King, leaves no reasonable doubt that he spoke with authority.

occasion shared his opinions could probably be counted on the fingers. The objection did not come within the domain of practical politics, and Rudyerd, of all men, was the least likely to conceive its very existence. For him it needed no argument to prove that a breach of the negotiations was tantamount to a declaration of war, and he advised the House to 'petition, that his Majesty would enter into a confederacy with his friends abroad, and endeavour to re-collect and re-unite that scattered and broken party of the religion in Germany; that he would strengthen his forts within this kingdom; that he would send out a competent number of ships to discover and resist such danger as may happen; that he would really and roundly assist the Low Countries; and whensoever he intends to make war for the Palatinate, that he would make it near hand by way of diversion to save charges, whither every younger brother that had but 20*l*. in his purse may go stocked for a profession and course of life; and where the Low Countries, no doubt, will be willing and ready to assist us for their own interest, which is the motive of all States.'[1]

So much was said, at the commencement of the next reign, about an alleged breach of the understanding come to in this session between the House of Commons and the Crown, that it is worth while to pause for a moment to ask what was the nature of the demand made by Rudyerd, undoubtedly with the assent, if not at the instigation, of Buckingham and the Prince.[2] Nothing can be plainer than that the idea of a Continental war was placed in the background, if not negatived altogether. Diplomatic intervention there

[1] Rudyerd's speech, *S. P. Dom.*, clx. 8.
[2] In the next year he stated that he had not received instructions from either. Probably his intercourse was with Pembroke.

was to be in Germany, accompanied, perhaps, with some aid in money from the English exchequer, in order to raise an opposition to the Spanish and Imperialist armies. But English military operations were to be confined to the Low Countries, and whatever more was done was to take the form of a diversion, that is to say, the form of an attack by sea upon the Spanish fleets and the Spanish Indies. A new generation of Drakes and Raleighs was to be called into existence, to continue the work, half patriotic, half piratical, which filled so large a space in the minds of Englishmen of that day.

But if any doubt of Rudyerd's meaning were possible, there could be no doubt of the feeling of the House. Of Germany and of German politics the Commons knew very little, had no chance of knowing anything accurately. But they did know that Spain had been specially prominent in the first attack upon the Palatinate, and they knew that Spain had been meddling in their own domestic affairs to an extent which had roused the disgust of all Protestant Englishmen. That they greatly overrated the strength of Spain in Germany, and as greatly underrated the strength of the Emperor and the Elector of Bavaria, is evident to all who know anything about the condition of Germany at the time; and they were thus easily led to imagine that a blow struck at Spain would have far more important results upon the Rhine than was at all likely to be the case. Though it would be unfair to say that they disregarded the miserable condition of the Palatinate, it is certain that Germany held but a secondary place in their thoughts. It was against the intrigues of Gondomar rather than against the arms of Spinola and Tilly that their indignation was specially directed. Spain, and Spain almost alone, was ever present to their vision. War with Spain was regarded as a good thing in itself, needing no further justification. In the debate which followed Rudyerd's speech, whilst the hint which he had thrown out about the formation of a Protestant confederacy in Germany fell flat upon the House, his proposal to attack Spain was received with rapturous applause. "He that shall go out of the way that Sir Benjamin Rudyerd hath set down," said Phelips, "shall work in a maze, and must return thither again." "War only," cried Eliot, "will secure and repair us." The fleet, he added, might be fitted out by the help of "those penalties the Papists have already incurred," a proposal which, if it had been translated into figures, would have organised a tyranny too monstrous to be contemplated with equanimity.[1]

{CHAP. I. 1624. March 1. Popularity of a war with Spain.}

The feeling which thus prevailed found its expression in the petition which the Commons drew up for presentation to the King. The Lords had been content to assign as their reason for recommending that the negotiations should be broken off, the impossibility of placing further confidence in the Spanish Government. The Commons went over the whole history of the past dangers of Protestantism in England and in Europe, and found special fault with the late alliance with Spain as leading to an increase in the number of the English Catholics.[2]

{The petition of the Commons.}

The petition prepared in this spirit was adopted by the Upper House, and was ready for presentation on the 3rd. But the King had a bad cold, and refused to receive it. The petition, in fact, sounded very like a covert attack upon himself, and the attempt to convert the proposed war into a religious crusade against Spain must have been most distasteful to him. Buckingham

{March 3. The King objects to it.}

[1] *Commons' Journals,* i. 674, 722; *Nicholas's Notes.*
[2] *Lords' Journals,* iii. 246.

CHAP. I.
1624.
March 3.
Buckingham expostulates.

had no such scruples. "In obedience to your commands," he wrote, with that insolence which long familiarity had taught him, "I will tell the House of Parliament that you, having been upon the fields this afternoon, have taken such a fierce rheum and cough as, not knowing how you will be this night, you are not yet able to appoint them a day of hearing: but I will forbear to tell them that, notwithstanding your cold, you were able to speak with the King of Spain's instruments, though not with your own subjects."[1]

And suggests the answer to be given.

This strange letter was, in all probability, accompanied by a paper in which Buckingham had jotted down the heads of the answer which he wished James to make to the Houses.[2] The King, he suggested, should say that he was grateful for the answer given him, and that he did not expect any rebukes from them till he had made up his mind whether he would accept their advice or not. If he became engaged in a war in consequence of his taking that advice, he would not make peace without first consulting them; and finally he would allow them to choose a Committee 'to see the issuing out of the money they give for the recovery of the Palatinate.'

Even this last suggestion, James condescended to

[1] Buckingham's letter (*Hardwicke St. P.*, i. 467) is undated, but the reference to the cold authorises me to place it here. On the 6th of March Tillières writes that the King had received the petition, "ayant retardé deux jours à les voir, s'excusant sur un rheum." (*Harl. MSS.* 4593, fol. 128 b.): and Salvetti, in his *Newsletter* of the 5th, refers to the same circumstance.

[2] It is printed (*Hardwicke St. P.*) as a postscript to a letter with which it has no connection, except that it has been placed next to it by the collector or binder of the volume in which it was found (*Harl. MSS.* 6987). The suggestion of a plan for paying subsidies elsewhere than into the exchequer, must have been made before the King's speech of the 5th, in which that suggestion was adopted. If, therefore, it did not actually accompany Buckingham's letter, it must have been sent about the same time.

accept. Four proposals of Rudyerd's, that the fortifications should be repaired, a fleet fitted out, Ireland reinforced, and the Dutch Republic succoured, he adopted as his own, if indeed they had not been originally made with his approbation. But a comparison between the debate in the Lower House and this reply of James's reveals a radical difference between their respective plans for the future. Whilst the Commons wished to do as much as possible against Spain, and as little as possible in Germany, James wanted to do as much as possible for the Palatinate, and as little as possible against Spain. "As Moses," he said, "saw the land of promise from a high mountain, so would it be a great comfort to me that God would but so prolong my days as, if I might not see the restitution, yet at least to be assured that it would be." He would not own 'one furrow of land in England, Scotland, or Ireland without restitution of the Palatinate.' In this mind he would live and die. But he could not declare war till he knew what means he should have to support it. He was himself miserably in debt. He would allow the money voted for the war, to be placed in the hands of treasurers appointed by the House. But he hoped that over and above this they would give him something for himself. In one thing only did he speak of the war differently from the plan expounded by Rudyerd. Rudyerd had suggested the promotion of union amongst the German Princes. James went a step further, and proposed to send them actual aid.[1]

<small>CHAP. I.
1624.
March 5.
The King's answer.</small>

<small>Different views of the King and the Commons.</small>

The demand for money for payment of the King's debts, and the demand for money for a war in Germany, found no response in the House of Commons. In vain Weston unrolled the whole list of the past expenses of the Crown. Rudyerd, in moving for a

<small>March 11. Debate in the Commons.</small>

[1] *Lords' Journals,* iii. 253.

CHAP. I.
1624.
March 11.

conference with the Lords, proposed to ask their advice on the defence of Ireland, the repair of the forts, the setting out of a fleet, and the aid to be given to the Dutch—the four points, as men soon began to call them—but said nothing either of the King's debts or of the German Princes, an omission which can hardly have been accidental. In the debate which followed, no one rose to recommend a war in Germany.[1] England, said Coke, never prospered so well as when she was at war with Spain. If Ireland were secured, the navy furnished, the Low Countries assisted, they need not 'care for Pope, Turk, Spain, nor all the devils in hell.' A resolution was finally passed that, as soon as his Majesty declared the negotiations at an end, he should be assisted in a parliamentary way.

The Prince's explanations to the Lords.

The Commons seem to have taken for granted that James's demand for payment of his own debts would not be pressed. In the Lords the matter was taken more seriously, and doubts were expressed whether it would be possible to raise subsidies enough for this purpose and for the war as well. The Prince of Wales, now a constant attendant upon the debates, was in his place when these words were spoken. He had long lost all patience with his father's doubts and hesitations, and he was too ardent in the cause which he had adopted to reflect that by bringing royalty into contempt he was menacing an authority of which he would one day be himself the appointed guardian. Without waiting to consult any one, he boldly explained away his father's words. The King, he said, merely meant to let it be known that he was in want of money. But

[1] There are two reports of this session in the Journals. According to the second, Wentworth of Oxford spoke of Germany (i. 732). But the first report (i. 692) substitutes 'The Low Countries,' and is evidently right in doing so.

he did not mean to ask for help himself till after the safety of the kingdom had been provided for.¹ The effect of this marvellous commentary was immediate, all the more because the Prince sought out the leaders of the Commons, and told the same tale to them.² An address, embodying the ideas expressed in debate, was at once agreed to; and on the 14th it was presented to the King at Whitehall by the Archbishop of Canterbury, in the name of the two Houses.

CHAP.
I.
1624.
March 11.

March 14.
Assistance promised.

Even if James had not taken offence at his son's unexpected interference, he may well have hesitated when called upon to sanction a plan of operations so different from his own. At all events his reply was not that which the Houses had expected to receive. He took especial offence at a phrase in the address condemning the insincerity of the Spaniards. He had not yet, he said, delivered his opinion on Buckingham's relation. He had come to no conclusion on the sincerity or insincerity of those with whom he had to deal. When Jupiter spoke, he was accustomed 'to join his thunder with it; and a king should not speak except to maintain it by action.' Then, having got rid of his ill-humour, his speech took a more practical turn. Thanking the Houses for their promise to grant him money, he pressed for more definite information on the amount they were prepared to give. " I must not only deal," he said, " with my own people, but with my neighbours and allies, to assist me in so great a business as the recovery of the Palatinate." In other words, whilst the Houses were proposing to fight Spain at sea or in the flats of Brabant, James was proposing a great Continental alliance for a war in Germany. For this purpose, he said, he should need five subsidies and ten fifteenths, adding, in spite of his son's declara-

The King's reply.

¹ *Elsing's Notes.*   ² *Valaresso's Despatch,* March $\frac{19}{29}$.

CHAP. I.
1624.
March 14.

tion, that he hoped they would give him another subsidy and two more fifteenths for himself. He had almost made up his mind to break off relations with Spain. He trusted they would pass as many good bills as possible, and he hoped to call them together again in the autumn.[1]

Dissatisfaction of the Commons.

This hesitating utterance—in all probability it was nothing more—was understood by the Commons to imply that there would be no war after all. They left the presence without the usual cry of "God save the King!" The Prince showed his annoyance at his father's disavowal of his words by remaining in sullen silence for the remainder of the day, whilst the friends of Spain went joyously about with smiling faces.[2]

Buckingham's letter to the King.

Buckingham, unlike the Prince, was not likely to take refuge in silence. It was probably a day or two before this that he had written to James another of those strange and insolent letters in which the position of master and servant was completely inverted. "I beseech you," he wrote, "send me your plain and resolute answer whether, if your people so resolve to give you a royal assistance, as to the number of six subsidies and fifteens, with a promise after, in case of necessity, to assist you with their lives and fortunes; whether then you will not accept it and their counsel to break the match with the other treaties, and whether or no, to bring them to this, I may not assure some of them underhand, because it is feared that when your turns are served you will not call them together again to reform abuses, grievances, and the making of laws for the good government of the country: that you will be so far from that, that you will rather weary them with it, desiring nothing more than their loves and happiness, in which your own is included. Sir, I beseech you think seri-

[1] *Lords' Journals.* lii. 265.
[2] D. Carleton to Carleton, Sir R. Cotton to T. Cotton, March 17 *S. P. Dom.* clx. 19, 20; *Contarini's Despatch,* March $\frac{19}{29}$.

ously of this, and resolve once constantly to run one way. For so long as you waver between the Spaniards and your subjects to make your advantage of both, you are sure to do it with neither.'[1]

Full of these thoughts, Buckingham now sought an interview with the King. Throwing himself upon his knees he besought him to give satisfaction to his subjects. But if Buckingham was anxious to gain from the unwilling King a declaration of war, his idea of what that war should be approached far more nearly to the views of James than to the views of the House of Commons. If the Commons were for a war at sea, and James was for a war on land, Buckingham was for a war both by land and sea. He now dwelt upon the favourable prospect of obtaining French co-operation. The Spanish marriage treaty, he said, had been 'prejudicial to the present government here, in pressing the abrogation of many good laws, and being contrary to the conscience of the people.' The same conditions, replied James, would be demanded in any other Roman Catholic marriage. Against this conclusion Buckingham argued, and suggested that the Houses should send him a petition, asking him not to consent to the Spanish conditions with any other Popish Prince.

Under these persuasions James gave way once more, and consented to allow Buckingham and his son to explain away his answer. The next day, accordingly, Charles was able to assure the Houses that his father had no further doubts about the justice of the war, and that he would apply to that object the whole sum of six subsidies and twelve fifteenths, if they chose to grant it to him. Buckingham then proceeded

---

[1] *Hardwicke St. P.* i. 466. The letter is undated, but must have been written before the 20th, when a smaller sum than six subsidies was offered by the Commons; and I think before the 14th, when the King seems to have accepted the proposal of six subsidies from Buckingham.

to unfold the history of his conversation of the previous night, and for the first time revealed the secret of the French marriage. It was possibly upon perceiving some signs of dissatisfaction around him that Charles added in a low voice, "My father has a long sword. If it is once drawn, it will hardly be put up again."[1]

Whether dissatisfaction was expressed or not, there can be no doubt that it was felt. "I confess," wrote a member of the House, about a fortnight later, "that my heart beats still as you know it hath done ever, and goeth not with this match neither, and I find so many of the same pulse here, that I am sorry my noblest Lord[2] is employed in the business."[3]

Nevertheless the hint thrown out called forth no open expression of disapprobation. In the long debate which followed on the grant of supply, only one member alluded to it, by proposing that the King should be asked to break off all other treaties, as well as the Spanish, that might be prejudicial to religion. On the prospect opened to them of a Continental war they were more outspoken. Sir Francis Seymour touched the question to the quick. He had heard 'wars spoken on,' he said, 'and an army; but would be glad to hear where. The Palatinate was the place intended by his Majesty. This we never thought of, nor is it fit for the consideration of the House in regard of the infinite charge.' Not a word was uttered in opposition to the view thus taken by Seymour. The House was looking in another direction than the Palatinate. "Are we poor," cried Eliot, "Spain is rich.

---

[1] *Lords' Journals*, iii. 266. *Valaresso's Despatch*, March $\frac{19}{29}$. Account of a conversation between the King and Buckingham; *S. P. Dom.*, clx. 80.

[2] Carlisle, who was to go as ambassador to negotiate it.

[3] Nethersole to Carleton, March 31; *S. P. Dom.*, clxi. 61.

There are our Indies. Break with them; we shall break our necessities together."[1]

In fact, the Commons were in a very difficult position. The task before them was no longer to oppose their own resolution to the inertness of the King. They were called upon to decide between two opposite schemes of political and military action. Instead of looking forward to a war limited in extent and lucrative, as they fondly hoped, in its results, they were called upon to provide for a vast Continental alliance, cemented by a marriage which, taken at its best, would go far to encourage the hopes of that Church which they most detested, and relying for its support upon an expenditure of English blood and treasure so great that they could hardly contemplate the prospect with equanimity. For, as Coke explained to them, six subsidies and twelve fifteenths would bring them in 780,000*l.*, and the six subsidies which might be expected from the clergy would raise the grant to 900,000*l.*, an amount which, however small it may sound in the reign of Victoria, was utterly unprecedented in the reign of James. Even the officials in the House did not venture to support the demand in full. Rudyerd, who had again opened the debate, had contented himself with asking that the subsidies should be in principle voted; part of them being held back to be levied at some future time. Later in the debate, however, Edmondes, Privy Councillor as he was, professed himself to be staggered by the greatness of the demand, and recommended three subsidies as sufficient. Weston too, the Chancellor of the Exchequer, acknowledged that the sound of six subsidies was 'very fearful;' whilst Vane and Conway only ventured to urge the consideration of

CHAP. I.

1624. March 19. Difficult position of the Commons.

[1] *Commons' Journals,* i. 740. *Nicholas's Notes.*

CHAP. I.
1624.
March 20.

Rudyerd's original proposal, according to which the full levy would be contingent on the renewed approbation of the House. In the end three subsidies and three fifteenths, or about 300,000*l.*, were voted. The money was to be paid to treasurers appointed by Parliament within one year after James had declared the negotiations with Spain to be at an end.[1]

Objects of the grant.

The address from both Houses with which this resolution was accompanied plainly declared the objects for which it was intended. They were stated to be 'the support of the war which is likely to ensue, and more particularly for those four points proposed by your Majesty; namely, the defence of this realm, the securing of Ireland, the assistance of your neighbours the States of the United Provinces and others of your Majesty's friends and allies, and the setting forth of your Royal Navy.'[2]

March 22. Its wording altered.

Before this address was presented it was privately shown to James. To one passage, in which it was said that the war was to be waged 'for the conservation of the true religion of Almighty God,' he took objection, as making it difficult for him to find allies beyond the limits of Protestantism. The objection was admitted as valid, and the phrase was cancelled.

March 23. James declares the treaties dissolved.

The address itself, unlike the last one, was graciously received. The King said that he was willing to take the advice of Parliament 'in the annulling and breaking of those two treaties, both of the match and

[1] The comparison sometimes made between the incidence of a subsidy and that of our present income-tax, is altogether misleading. As far as land was concerned, a subsidy was a tax upon rental, which would often be little more than nominal, the chief profit being made by the fines levied as the leases fell in, which would not be touched by the subsidy. The gradual decrease of subsidies in value was generally attributed at the time to the collusion of the collectors. Is it possible that there was also a practice of increasing the fines at the expense of rental?

[2] *Lords' Journals*, iii. 275.

of the Palatinate.' In all his negotiations he had only aimed at the recovery of the Palatinate. "I am old," he added, "but my only son is young, and I will promise, for myself and him both, that no means shall be unused for the recovery of it; and this I dare say, as old as I am, if it might do good to the business, I would go in my own person, and think my travail and labour well bestowed, though I should end my days there." Not a penny of the money now offered, he declared, should be spent but upon this work, and that too by their own treasurers. In the address, the subsidies had been spoken of as a 'first fruits,' and there had been a further assurance of more to come when he was actually engaged in war. He took the Houses at their word, " In the next session," he said, " you will consider how this hath been husbanded, and according to that, think what is next to be done; and it will spur you the more to enable me for the rest whereof I spake to you before." For advice about the conduct of the future war, however, he must be dependent not upon Parliament, but upon military men who would form a Council of War. His plans 'must not be ordered by a multitude,' for so his 'designs might be discovered beforehand.' Without the consent of their Commissioners he would not touch a penny of their money. "But whether," he said, "I shall send twenty thousand or ten thousand, whether by sea or land, East or West, by diversion or otherwise, by invasion upon the Bavarian or the Emperor, you must leave that to the King."

What, then, was the meaning of the engagement thus taken? On the one hand Parliament, with the exception of the vague clause about assisting 'other your Majesty's friends and allies,' distinctly intimated that the money was to be employed solely on the four points originally proposed. Even if that clause were to receive the widest possible interpretation, it could never be seriously contended that out of 300,000*l.* there would be enough left, when the expenditure authorised in the address had been met, to provide for any extensive military outlay. James, in talking of sending twenty thousand men or ten thousand men, was clearly not referring to anything connected with the present vote, but to the use to be made of the further subsidies which he expected in the autumn. He had already promised to call Parliament together for purposes of domestic legislation. He now promised to give an account at the same time of the expenditure already agreed on, and to ask the sanction of the Houses to the further prosecution of the war. He would thus have time to ascertain the feeling of the various European courts in which he hoped to find allies. But he honestly told Parliament that when he proceeded to make war in earnest, he should be guided by military, not by political, far less by religious considerations. What he wanted, in short, was to get back the Palatinate, not to punish Spain for its past conduct, or to join in a Protestant crusade.

Evidently, therefore, neither party was in any way bound to anything beyond the expenditure of the 300,000*l.* already agreed to be voted. When the next session began it would be open to the King to say, if he thought fit, that he had found the enterprise more arduous than he had expected; and it would be equally open to the Commons to say that they declined to support any particular policy which the Crown had resolved to adopt. The blind confidence which Charles afterwards demanded, was neither offered nor assumed on either side, even in the event of the autumn session taking place. Still less could it be fairly expected, if the meeting of the Houses were delayed, that the Commons should sanction without enquiry any further expenditure on which the Crown might have entered upon its own responsibility.

CHAP. I.
1624.
March 23.

For the present, however, there was little thought of future complications. On the afternoon after the King's declaration, the streets were filled with happy faces. As soon as darkness fell, bonfires were blazing on every side. At last the long weary burden of years had been thrown off. Whatever else might happen, it would not be a Spanish Princess who would be nearest and dearest to the future King of England, and mother to the future Prince of Wales. Neither Gondomar nor his master would again find an excuse for meddling with the administration of English law, or for thrusting aside statutes which, whatever we may now think of them, were at that time regarded as the bulwark of our religion and our liberty.

Public rejoicings.

Whilst the bonfires were blazing in the streets, some of the servants of the Spanish embassy in the Strand were foolish enough to crowd to the window to see what was going on. As might have been expected, they were received with jeers by the crowd below, and stones and firebrands were flung towards them. The next day, on Buckingham's motion, the Lords resolved that an attempt should be made to discover the offenders. In the Commons other feelings prevailed. Two members of the House reported that they had been in the Strand on the evening in question and had not witnessed anything improper. On this negative evidence the Commons thought themselves justified in treating the whole story as a pure invention.[1]

The Spaniards insulted.

March 24.

March 25.

If Buckingham had still some regard for decorum, Charles shared the popular feeling to the full. Whilst

The Prince rejects a present

[1] *Lords' Journals*, iii. 280; *Commons' Journals*, i. 750.

CHAP. I.
1624.
March 18.
from the Countess Olivares.

James's decision was still hanging in the balance, three cartloads of fruits and sweetmeats were driven up to the gate of St. James's Palace, at that time the residence of the Prince of Wales. They were a present from the Countess of Olivares, prepared in happier days. Charles would not even vouchsafe to look at them. Turning to Cottington, he bade him divide the good things as he pleased amongst his attendants.[1]

March 17.
Lafuente robbed of his despatches.

A King's son, it would appear, could be lamentably deficient in the elements of good breeding. The day before this scene there had been a deed done in France by which still greater obloquy was brought upon the English name. The Spanish Government, in the hope of obtaining better terms from James, had despatched Gondomar's confessor, Lafuente, to England, trusting that his discreet character and his accurate knowledge of the Court might procure him a hearing where the impatient Inojosa and the blunt soldierlike Coloma had failed.

As he was travelling near Amiens, Lafuente's coach was surrounded by a number of men armed with pistols and disguised with false beards. His baggage was searched with the utmost minuteness, and even the leaves of his breviary were eagerly turned over. His assailants were evidently no common robbers, for, though they carried off every scrap of paper in his possession, they left his money and all his valuable property untouched. The affair was never subjected to any serious investigation, but Lafuente believed that the culprits were Frenchmen employed by the Marquis of Hamilton, whose intimacy with Buckingham made it unlikely that the outrage had been committed without the knowledge of the Lord Admiral.[2]

[1] Chamberlain to Carleton, March 20, *S. P. Dom.*, clxi. 4; *Salvetti's Newsletter*, March 26/April 5.
[2] Francisco de Jesus, 97.

If, as was supposed in England, Lafuente had brought instructions to make fresh proposals about the Palatinate, the loss of his papers must have been very serious to him. On the 29th he was admitted to the King's presence together with the two ambassadors, but he had no credentials to present, and a letter from the King of Spain which he had with him when he left Madrid was equally missing. He was therefore compelled to stand by in silence whilst James was informing the ambassadors that all negotiations with Spain were at an end. According to the jest of the day he had only come to give extreme unction to the dying treaties.[1]

CHAP. I.
1624.
March 29.
The treaties with Spain denounced.

At last James seemed to have made up his mind. As soon as the Spaniards left the room, their places were taken by the Dutch Commissioners, who had come over to discuss the terms on which English military assistance should be given to the States General. Their reception was eminently favourable. The King assured them of his strong desire to maintain the independence of their country, and to regain the lost Palatinate.[2]

Reception of the Dutch Commissioners.

The Commons had now leisure to turn their attention to the subject to which, next to the war with Spain, they attached the greatest importance. The treaties which had just been set aside had done much to repress the growth of a tolerant spirit in England. The men[1] who, like Bacon and Bristol, rose to power in the earlier years of James's reign, were capable of embracing something of the idea of toleration. The men who were looked up to in the Parliament of 1621 and 1624, Pym, Eliot, and Phelips, closed their hearts against the very thought. The reason of this difference it is not difficult to discover. The Roman Catholic creed was

Bitter feeling against the Catholics.

[1] *Valaresso's Despatch*, April 2/12.
[2] *Ibid.*

no longer a mere religious error, endangering, according to the common belief, the souls of men, but accompanied by no very evident political danger. It was now once more aggressive both on the Continent and in England. Every step which had been gained by its champions in Germany, every blow which had been struck upon the Danube or the Rhine, had found an echo in English hearts, more especially as the detested creed had gained vantage ground in the concessions which Spain had wrung from the impolitic compliance of an English sovereign.

And so the mischief which had been quietly growing, had produced another mischief in return. Because James had allowed the reins of government to hang loosely in his hands, and had not repelled with scorn the pretensions of an alien ruler to interfere with the domestic affairs of England, therefore the best and wisest spirits of the age were crying out not merely for the exclusion from England of Spanish influence, but for the administration of the English law, as far as their Roman Catholic fellow-subjects were concerned, in a harsh and intolerant spirit.

On the 3rd of April a petition was sent up to the Lords asking for the full execution of the penal laws against the Recusants, and a request was added to it 'that upon no occasion of marriage or treaty, or other request on that behalf from any foreign Prince or State whatsoever,' his Majesty 'would take away or slacken the execution of his laws against the Popish Recusants.'[1]

To the last clause James had no objection to make. He had learned something from past experience, and he had resolved not to complicate the French treaty with any of those stipulations for the English Catholics

[1] *Lords' Journals*, i. 289.

which had hampered him so terribly in his negotiations with Spain. But the demand for the full execution of the penal laws annoyed him. If he had no well-defined theory on the subject of toleration, and if his practice on this as in many other matters was very much influenced by the special circumstances of the moment, he shrank from avowing an intention to deal harshly with the Recusants at a time when he was persuaded that the Palatinate could only be recovered with the assistance of France and other Roman Catholic countries.

As often happened with James, his vexation threw him violently into a course opposite to that which he had previously taken. He ordered the courier who had already started for Madrid with a despatch announcing the breach of the negotiations, to be overtaken and brought back. He must now, he said, consult more fully with his son. "Ye know," he wrote to Conway in a letter conveying these directions, "my firm resolution not to make this a war of religion."[1]

All this may easily be accounted for by the dislike which James reasonably entertained for the intolerant policy which the Commons were urging him to adopt. But it may be acknowledged that other causes may have contributed to ruffle his temper. The Spanish ambassadors, ignorant, like the rest of the world, of the deep hold which the loss of the Palatinate had taken upon James's mind, saw, in the repulse which they had met, nothing more than the result of the overbearing self-will of Buckingham. It was not hard for them to construct out of rumour, partly true and partly false, the idea that the King was held in moral, if not in actual physical durance, by the arts of his

[1] The King to Conway, April 3. Printed without a date in *Rushworth*, i. 140.

favourite and his son, and they imagined that if they could only succeed for an instant in getting the ear of James, the whole monstrous edifice which Buckingham had constructed would topple down of itself.

Their first difficulty arose from their knowledge that they were never allowed to see James in private. When they were admitted to an audience Buckingham was always present, ready to remove any impression they might chance to make, the moment they had left the room. This hindrance to freedom of speech they determined to 'break through at the earliest opportunity.' On March 29, the day on which they were summoned to hear from the King's lips the announcement that negotiations were at an end, whilst Coloma engaged the Prince and Buckingham in conversation, Inojosa offered James a paper which he requested him to put in his pocket till he found himself alone. The paper, when opened, proved to contain a request that the King would give a private audience to Carondelet, the Archdeacon of Cambrai, who was acting as Coloma's secretary. The audience was granted, and Carondelet made use of it to tell the King that he was little better than a prisoner in Buckingham's hands, and was being used as a tool for the satisfaction of the private animosities of his favourite. On the morning of April 3 Carondelet returned, bringing Lafuente with him.[1] This time a written charge against Buckingham was placed in James's possession, accusing him of having formed a plot to transfer the government out of his master's hands to those of the Prince, whilst James was to be graciously allowed to pass the rest of his life in the full enjoyment of the sports of the field. The soldiers who would be levied as soon as war was

[1] *Valaresso's Despatch*, April $\frac{9}{19}$.

declared would be used to bring the King to submission. Already Buckingham had been speaking disrespectfully of his sovereign, and had been doing his best to make him unpopular with the nation. If the King would but cast off his favourite, Spain would undertake to procure the restitution of the Palatinate in three months.

The alleged intention to dethrone the King had doubtless no foundation in fact. But it is likely enough that Buckingham had spoken of the King in his conversation at least as disrespectfully as he had written to him in his letters. At all events, there was enough of general truth in the charge to make James excessively uncomfortable. He must have known that even if it was not true that he was being dragged against his will by Buckingham into a course of action which he disliked, he had at least entered upon a path which, but for Buckingham, he would never have chosen. He now expressed, in bitter words, the usual dissatisfaction of a man who finds out that he is being led by others. His son, he said, before his visit ' to Spain, was as well affected towards that nation as heart could desire, and as well disposed as any son in Europe, but now he was strangely carried away with rash and youthful counsels, and followed the humour of Buckingham, who had he knew not how many devils within him since that journey.'

That afternoon the despatch for Spain was recalled, as has been already told.[1] The fate of the negotiations was once more exposed to doubt. But the story told by Carondelet was so monstrous that James hesitated to accept it. If the Spaniards, he replied, expected him

[1] P. 39.

CHAP. I.

1624. April 3. Carondelet betrayed to Williams.

to take any steps against the Duke, they must first prove their allegations.[1] Carondelet fancied that the secret of his interview with the King was in safe keeping. But in spite of his clerical character his morals were loose.[2] His mistress was in the pay of Williams, who, provided that he could get important information, cared little what means he employed to obtain it. To Williams the discovery afforded a splendid opportunity to strengthen his interests at court. It was true that Buckingham had assured him that his conduct in opposing the war with Spain would be passed over. But since he had given offence no opportunity had been afforded him of exhibiting his devotion.

April 5. Williams informs the Prince.

Williams went first to the Prince. "In my studies of divinity," he said, after explaining how he had come by his knowledge, "I have gleaned up this maxim, It is lawful to make use of the sin of another. Though the devil make her a sinner, I may make good use of her sin." "Yea," answered Charles with a smile, "do you deal in such ware?" "In good faith," said Williams, "I never saw her face."

---

[1] There are two abstracts of the account of these transactions, given afterwards by Carondelet to Williams (*Cabala*, 275, and *Hacket*, i. 195). If, as I suspect, they are both taken at different times from the same conversation, though the notes given by Hacket are treated by him as an abstract of the paper given by Inojosa to James, Hacket's story, as usual, is in miserable confusion. He fancied that he knew better what happened than appears on the face of the documents he printed, and transferred to the beginning of April events which took place long afterwards when the King was at Windsor, which will be given in their proper place.

[2] The Spanish embassy stood in no good repute since Inojosa's arrival. Tillières is not a very satisfactory authority against it. But even his outrageous statement about Inojosa that 'n'étant pas content de debaucher les filles et femmes Catholiques, il a fait servir des prêtres et confesseurs de maquereaux,' throws some light on the probability of the truth of the story about Carondelet. Tillières to Ville-aux-Clercs, Feb. $\frac{7}{17}$, *Harl. MSS.* 4593, fol. 46, b.

After some consideration, it was resolved that Buckingham should go to Theobalds to feel his ground with the King,¹ whilst Williams remained in London to probe Carondelet's secret to the bottom. He ordered the immediate arrest of a priest whom he knew to be specially intimate with Coloma's secretary. As he expected, Carondelet was not long in asking leave to plead for his friend's life. Late at night, to escape observation, he came to the Deanery at Westminster. At first he found Williams obdurate. How could mercy be shown whilst Parliament, with its watchful eye, was still in session? Carondelet caught at the word Parliament. He knew that Williams had opposed Buckingham at the beginning of the year. He did not know how ready he was to desist from a fruitless opposition. "Let not," he said, "the dread of this Parliament trouble you. I can tell you, if you have not heard it, that it is upon expiration." Then, fancying from Williams's answers that he had found a confederate, he unfolded the whole tale of his secret audiences.²

As soon as Carondelet was gone, Williams sat down and wrote off for Buckingham an account of all that

CHAP. I.

1624. April 7. Gains further information from Carondelet.

Buckingham informed.

¹ Hacket gives a wrong date and sends Buckingham to Windsor instead of Theobalds. From the *Lords' Journals* we know that Buckingham was in his place in the morning of the 5th, and was absent on the 6th and 7th. Conway, in a letter written to Aston on the 7th (*S. P. Spain*), speaks of him as being then at Theobalds.

² *Hacket,* i. 198. Mr. Tierney, in his edition of *Dodd,* argues that the story of the priest arrested is untrue, because an account (*Cabala,* 275), sent off at once to Buckingham by Williams, contains a heading—" The end, as was conceived, of Don Francisco's desiring this conference." I do not see that this necessarily follows. Williams may very well have omitted the story of the priest, which was only needed to show why Carondelet came to his house. What had to be accounted for was, how Carondelet came to confer with Williams on such secret matters; what was his end in " desiring this conference," whether he were already in the Deanery or not. Hacket is most confused in dates, and often mixes up different stories. But I do not think him, or Williams, likely to invent such a story as this.

CHAP. I.
1624.
April 6.

had passed.[1] A few evenings later Carondelet returned with further information, and Williams was able to take credit to himself for having fathomed so deep a mystery. Yet before Buckingham had time to receive the information, he had recovered his mastery over the mind of James. On April 6, the day before Carondelet's first interview with Williams, the delayed despatch announcing the final breach of the negotiations with Spain was at last sent off—a step which would hardly have been taken if the impression made by Carondelet and Lafuente on the King had not been already removed.[2]

[1] *Cabala*, 275.
[2] Williams did not write his notes till two o'clock on the morning of the 8th, and that morning Buckingham was in his place again in the House of Lords.

The following account by Williams of a further conference between himself and Carondelet, is given in Birch's transcripts. *Add. MSS.*, 4164, fol. 280, as taken from *Harl. MSS.*, 7000, where I have not been able to find it. Dr. Birch's name is, however, a sufficient guarantee that the reference only is incorrect.

"He was very inquisitive if I had already or intended to impart what he had told me in secret the night before to any man; to the which he did add a desire of secrecy, because (1) the King had charged him and the friar to be very secret; (2) the ambassadors did not know that he had imparted these things unto me; (3) the paper was secret instructions which they gave the friar to urge and press the same points which himself had done, unto the King.

"2. He confessed that the greatest part of the friar's instructions was to do all the worst offices he could against the Duke, and to lay the breach of the marriage and disturbance of the peace upon him.

"3. He excused his bringing the copy of that paper unto me, because the Marquis (*i.e.* Inojosa) had got it in his custody; but said he would procure it with all speed. I desired him to do it, the rather because, besides my approbation of the form and manner of writing, I might be by it instructed how to apply myself to do his Majesty service therein, as I found by that conference his Majesty's bent and inclination.

"4. He having understood that there was, though [? not] a close, yet an indissoluble friendship between the Duke and myself, desired me to show some way how the Duke might be won unto them, and to continue the peace. I answered I would pursue any fair course that should be proposed that way; but for myself, that I never meddled with matters of

This despatch, written and rewritten several times, announced that the proposition made in January by the Spanish ambassadors could not be accepted. James would never consent to his grandson's education at the Emperor's court, nor would he be satisfied with anything less than a direct engagement that Spain would assist his son-in-law by force of arms if diplomacy should fail. The two Houses of Parliament, he added, 'have given us their faithful advice to dissolve both the treaties, as well of the marriage as of the Palatinate. To which we have given our consent, having not found any example that any king hath refused the counsel of the whole kingdom composed of faithful and loving subjects.' So far the letter was all that Buckingham could have desired. But a passage followed in which James again pressed Philip to aid him, or at least not to oppose him, in his efforts to obtain the restitution of the Palatinate. And though he allowed the Prince to cancel this last clause,[1] he did not countermand the sending of a letter of Conway's which was to go in the same

CHAP.
1.

1624.
April 6.
Breach of the negotiation with Spain announced by James.

state of this nature, but was only employed before this journey of the Prince's in matters of mine owne court and in the pulpit.
" 5. He desired to know if they might rely upon the King, whom only they found peaceably addicted, otherwise they would cease all mediation and prepare for war. I answered that he was a King that never broke his word, and he knew best what he had said unto them.
" 6. He commended much the courage and resolution of the Lord Treasurer, which I told him we all did, as a probable sign of his innocence.
" 7. He said the Marquis had despatched three correos, and expected of large propositions from Spain to be made unto his Majesty concerning the present restitution of the Palatinate, and that if these failed they were at an end of all treaty, and the ambassadors would forthwith return home."
" Indorsed:—Bishop of Lincoln's Relation of Speeches passed between his Lordship and Don Francisco.—11 *April*, 1623." [Sic].
[1] In the draft the passage is scored out, and a note in Charles's hand is appended to it—" These two last are thought best to be left out." The King to Aston, April 5. *S. P. Spain.*

packet, in which the ambassador at Madrid was directed to assure Philip that, though James had promised to listen to the advice of his Parliament, he had never promised to follow it.[1]

Such a reservation could have but little result. The one fact of importance was that the Spanish intrigue had failed, and the treaties were at last abandoned. In all that had passed the weakness and hesitation of James had been most manifest. He had been half driven, half persuaded, to place himself in hostility to Spain. It had not been without many backward glances that he had taken the required step, glances which the Spaniards interpreted as meaning much more than they really did. For it was surely not merely owing to the personal ascendancy of Buckingham that James at last shook off the influence of the Spanish ambassadors. Here, at least, Buckingham had the advantage of a good cause. If he dazzled James by his vigour and audacity, he was also able to convince his intellect. After all that had passed it was impossible even for James to maintain seriously that it would be wise to look again to Spain for the recovery of the Palatinate.

Buckingham's sanguine and incisive temper had carried him safely thus far. Would it serve him equally well when he came to proceed to positive action? It is far easier to put an end to negotiations than to conduct a war. And he would now no longer have the full assurance of the support of the House of Commons. If he had been on the side of Parliament against the King in wishing to make the breach with Spain complete, he was on the side of the King against Parliament in wishing to make a close alliance with France the

[1] Conway to Aston, April 3. Date corrected to April 8. *S. P. Spain.*

main feature of his foreign policy. That he was in the right in shrinking from going to war without French aid cannot reasonably be doubted. But it remained to be seen at what price that aid was to be purchased.

CHAP. II.
1624.
April 6.

CHAPTER II.

BUCKINGHAM'S ASCENDANCY.

CHAP. II.
1624.
Feb. 15.
Kensington in Paris.

HENRY RICH, Viscount Kensington, had arrived in Paris on February 15, charged with a confidential mission. Without making any absolute overtures, he was to sound the disposition of the French court towards a marriage between Charles and the Princess Henrietta Maria, the youngest sister of Lewis XIII. Unlike his elder brother the Earl of Warwick, the speculator in buccaneering adventures in the reign of James I. and the pious Lord Admiral of the Commonwealth, Kensington had been fitted by nature for those successes in the drawing-room which were denied him in the senate and the field. Without force of character or intellectual ability, he had early taken his place in that train of flatterers whose ready services were so pleasing to Buckingham, and were of so little value in the hour of trial; and to the satisfaction which he thus gave to his patron he owed his high position at court, his peerage, and at last his selection as the messenger of love to the French Princess.

La Vieuville's Ministry.

Kensington's journey was extremely well timed. Lewis had at last taken alarm at the position which Spain and the allies of Spain occupied on his frontiers. The golden flag of Philip waved from the Netherlands in the North over an almost uninterrupted series of fortifications, through the Palatinate, Franche Comté, the Milanese Duchy, Naples, Sicily, and Sardinia, to the spot where the Pyrenees lower their crests as they sink towards the waters of the Atlantic. And behind this martial barrier was now arising once more the shadowy form of the old Empire which had been quickened into life by the success of Spinola and Tilly. Lewis had felt that it was no longer a time to be guided solely by his religious instincts. Devoted Catholic as he was, he was a still more devoted Frenchman, or rather, it would perhaps be more correct to say, he was still more devoted to the maintenance of his own authority, in which, for him, the interests of France were comprehended. Yet though Lewis was by no means a cypher in French politics, he was too sluggish and unfamiliar with business to trouble himself with the actual direction of affairs. A minister he must have who would be content to carry out his ideas, except so far as he might be able to mould his master's plans in accordance with his own. He now announced the change which had come over him by dismissing his former ministers who were on friendly terms with Spain and the Emperor, and by calling to his counsels the Marquis of La Vieuville who was pledged to a contrary course.

With the higher political questions which were likely to arise out of this change, Kensington had neither the authority nor the desire to meddle. Easy and graceful in his manners, he had little difficulty in winning his way amongst the ladies and gay gentlemen of the Queen Mother's court. Mary de Medici, at this time under the guidance of the sagacious Richelieu, at once treated the handsome Englishman as a friend. She gladly caught at the idea of making her daughter Princess of Wales, especially as she hoped by this means to obtain a cessation of the persecution of the English Catholics, and thus to do more for her Church

CHAP. II.
1624.
Feb.

than Philip of Spain and his sister had succeeded in accomplishing. This feeling was shared by her son, and Kensington was able to send home the most glowing description of his reception at Paris. Though he was told that no serious negotiations could be opened till his master had openly broken with Spain, nothing was left undone to give him confidence in the eventual success of his mission. With the Queen Mother he was soon at home, chattering gaily in broken French, and whispering airy compliments in the ears of the ladies around her. The day after his arrival he was able to report that he had seen the Princess, a quick, bright-eyed girl in her fifteenth year. "My Lord," he wrote to Buckingham, "she is a lovely sweet young creature. Her growth is not great yet, but her shape is perfect." She had seldom, he had been informed, 'put on a more cheerful countenance than that night.' "There were some," he added, "that told me I might guess the cause of it."

The Princess Henrietta Maria.

Kensington's ideas about the alliance.

Of soft glances and merry speeches Kensington was an apt reporter. It was not long before he had to turn his attention to more serious work. Ill-advised as any marriage with a Roman Catholic would have been in the existing state of English public feeling, both James and Buckingham wished this marriage to be at least the seal of an effectual military alliance, and they expected to proceed simultaneously with the two negotiations. Kensington soon made himself the mouthpiece of the French court in advising the contrary course. "For I doubt," he wrote, "whether it may not be thought a little dishonourable for this king to give his sister conditionally that, if he will make war upon the King of Spain his brother, we will make the alliance with him. . . . But if we fall speedily upon a treaty and conclusion of a marriage, the which will find, I am persuaded, no long delays here, neither will they strain us to any unreasonableness in conditions for our Catholics, as far as I can find ; then will it be a fit time to conclude a league, the which they will then for certain do when all doubts and fears of falling off are by this conjunction taken away." [1]

CHAP. II.
1624.
Feb.

It was truly a golden prospect. But even to Charles it did not seem quite satisfactory after his experience in Spain. The Prince wished the general league of friendship to precede the negotiation of the marriage treaty.[2] Kensington characteristically replied by assuring Charles that all would come right in the end, by praising the Princess, who was 'for beauty and goodness an angel,' and by recounting how she, having borrowed a miniature of the Prince which hung about his neck, 'opened it with such haste as showed a true picture of her passion, blushing in the instant of her own guiltiness.'[3]

March 3.
Dissent of Charles.

All this was very delightful to a lover, but it would not go far to help on the political alliance between the two kingdoms. Sir Edward Herbert, who had been for some years the English ambassador in France, and who knew the country too well to be deceived by the gossip of the Queen Mother or the blushes of a girl of fourteen, formed an opinion very different from that of Kensington. The object of the French he thought was to make themselves arbiters between England and the house of Austria ; he therefore advised his master to bring them 'to some real and infallible proofs' of their intention to assist England 'in

April 13.
Herbert's opinion on the policy of France.

[1] Kensington to Buckingham, Feb. 16, Feb. 26 (both letters printed without a date). *Cabala,* 290, 286. Kensington to Conway, March 4. *S. P. France.*
[2] We learn the Prince's opinion from Kensington's answer to Buckingham's letter of March 3. It is dated March 9. *S. P. France.*
[3] Kensington to the Prince, March 9. *Cabala,* 288.

CHAP. II.
1624.
April.

the recovery of the Palatinate at the same time or before' the marriage treaty was discussed. Otherwise they would 'want no excuse to keep themselves in peace of neutrality.' Herbert was the more confirmed in this view of the case by his knowledge that Lewis was anxious to send a diplomatic agent to the Elector of Bavaria. So unpalatable was the remonstrance made against this proposal by the English ambassador, that means were taken to induce James to recall him; and in fact the letter ordering him to return home had been already despatched before his last note of warning reached England.[1]

Was France likely to help in Germany?

Herbert had been guilty of seeing too clearly where the real difficulty lay. Whatever interest Lewis had in the matter lay in opposing Spain, and Spain alone. As a devout Catholic he would naturally wish to confine his operations in Germany within the narrowest possible limits. To send an embassy to the Elector of Bavaria was precisely the step likely to be taken by a man in his position. The victories of Tilly and the League would have been positively gratifying to him if only they could be dissociated from the formidable growth of the Spanish power. To join James in driving out Catholic rule and Catholic worship from the Palatinate might possibly be regarded by Lewis in the light of a political necessity, but it would never be considered by him as desirable in itself. The overtures which had been made to James in vain through Francesco della Rota, were certain to be acceptable to Lewis as placing the education of Frederick's children in Maximilian's hands, and leading almost certainly to a rivalry between him and the house of Austria.

[1] Herbert to Calvert, Jan. 26, Feb. 6, March 10. Herbert to the King, April 13. *S. P. France.* Tillières to Ville-aux-Clercs, $\frac{\text{March 30}}{\text{April 9}}$; *Harl. MSS.*, 4593, fol. 194, b.

THE STRUGGLE FOR THE VALTELLINE. 53

Nor was the divergence of the views of the two kings about the Palatinate the only difficulty in the way of a cordial co-operation between France and England. Lewis had a Palatinate of his own in the Valtelline, that long and narrow valley which, stretching from the Lake of Como to the Tyrolese mountains, offered the only way of communication by which Spanish armies could pass from Italy into Germany without encroaching upon the possessions of states more or less openly hostile. It was now in the grasp of Spain by a very questionable title. The Roman Catholics, who formed almost the entire population, had been treated with extreme harshness by the Protestant Grison Leagues, the masters of the whole valley. In 1620 the people of the Valtelline rose against their oppressors, massacred the few Protestants upon whom they could lay their hands, and called the Spanish governor of Milan to their help. In spite of the remonstrances of France, the Spaniards took the aggressive and carried fire and sword into the heart of the Grison mountains. At last a league of resistance was formed between France, Venice, and Savoy, and in the spring of 1623 Spain nominally relinquished its authority over the Valtelline and entrusted the valley to the Pope. But Spanish garrisons still occupied the principal fortified posts, and the King of Spain refused to withdraw them unless the right of passage through the Valtelline were secured to his soldiers by treaty. In 1624 matters were still unchanged, and French politicians were looking forward to a war for the recovery of the Valtelline as eagerly as English politicians were looking forward to a war for the recovery of the Palatinate. Here at least there was no risk that success would be attended with any danger to the interests of the Roman Catholic Church. If the Palatinate were reconquered

CHAP. II.

1624. April.

The French anxious about the Valtelline.

54   BUCKINGHAM'S ASCENDANCY.

CHAP. II.
1624.
April.

by the German Protestants, even with French aid, it would be very difficult for Lewis to secure the hold which the priests of his religion had taken upon the country. If the Valtelline were reconquered by the petty Grison states with the help of France, Venice, and Savoy, it would be easy enough for those who gave the assistance to take effectual steps for the cessation of persecution for the future.

Danger of too close an alliance with France.

Here then, as Herbert perceived, and Kensington did not perceive, lay the danger in the course which the English Government was bent on pursuing. The general direction of the policy of the two countries was the same, but the secondary objects at which they aimed were different. It was a case in which England had every reason to keep up a good understanding with its powerful neighbour, but in which an attempt to form too close an alliance would almost inevitably lead to mutual irritation, if not to an open breach.

Expectations in England.

Unhappily, great as was the difference of character of the three men at the head of affairs in England, they were all equally sanguine that others would do that which they wished them to do. The hesitating James, the reticent Charles, the hasty Buckingham, had no idea that they were in any respect unreasonable in asking the French Government to do precisely that which they wanted done, in the precise way in which they thought best. The French on their part nourished the deception. They too had their own ends to serve, and in the eagerness with which the English court was seeking their friendship they saw a ready means of gaining their own objects whilst giving as little as possible in return.

French view of the war in Germany.

To France then, for the present, the German war was secondary to the project for the recovery of the Valtelline. All that was wanted in Germany was to create a disturbance which would be sufficient to prevent the armies of Italy from coming to help the Spanish forces in the Italian valley. When the Valtelline was recovered, then, and not before, would be the time to consider what was to be done in Germany.

CHAP. II.
1624. April.

To any one with an eye to see it was obvious, from the shape which the first project of French co-operation with England took, that nothing more was meant. If there was a man in Europe who was unfit to stand at the head of any serious movement in Germany, that man was Mansfeld. That unscrupulous adventurer knew how to plunder friend and foe better than he knew how to conduct war. By the Catholics he was regarded with a well-deserved ferocity of hatred, whilst all Protestants who had anything to lose shrunk from him as they would shrink from the plague. He had not even the merit of success. To send Mansfeld into Germany was to invite defeat by the provocation which his mere presence would give to all peaceable citizens.

Mansfeld in Holland.

Early in the spring, Mansfeld was once more in Holland looking out for an employer. The great German war, for a moment, had sunk down into quietude, and it seemed as if the Emperor's authority would be acknowledged from the North Sea to the Alps. At this moment Du Maurier, the French ambassador in Holland, advised Mansfeld to go to France. Upon his arrival Lewis, for form's sake, refused to see him, but Mansfeld was informed that he might be employed in an attack upon Franche Comté in order to divert the Spanish troops in the Netherlands from sending reinforcements to the Valtelline.[1] As soon as Mansfeld's assent was gained he was sent over into

His visit to France.

[1] "Se non si trovasse modo d'aggiustare negotio della Valtellina dovera essere impiegato dalla Francia all' invasione della Borgogna Contesa." Siri, *Mem. Rec.* v. 526. Siri wrote from the despatch of the Florentine agent in Paris.

CHAP. II.

1624. April.

England in order to persuade James to take upon himself a share of the expenses of the undertaking. As the reconquest of the Valtelline would have an appreciable effect in diminishing the power of the house of Austria, it cannot be said that the scheme was one of purely French interest. But it is certain that neither James nor the English Parliament were likely to contemplate with satisfaction such a use of English troops or of English money.

April 5. Charles's pledge about his marriage.

The difficulties in the way of the French alliance were not confined to these military questions. On the 5th of April, when the Commons sent up to the Lords their petition against the Recusants, Charles went out of his way to swear that, ' whensoever it should please God to bestow upon him any lady that were Popish, she should have no further liberty but for her own family, and no advantage to the Recusants at home.'

The enforcement of the laws against the English Catholics was thus, in Charles's mind, a policy likely to be entirely unobjectionable to the French King whose alliance he was courting. On the 14th of April Mansfeld arrived in London. By the Prince he was eagerly received. He talked confidently of seizing Franche Comté and then falling upon the Austrian lands in Alsace and Swabia.[1] Apartments were assigned to him in St. James's Palace, the very room being given him which had been prepared for the Infanta. Whenever he appeared in the streets the people followed him with shouts of applause. On the 16th he was taken to see James at Theobalds. He touched the heart of the old King by the fluency with which he spoke of the recovery of the Palatinate as a

April 14. Mansfeld in England.

April 16.

---

[1] This must be meant by his offer ' d'attaquer les pais héréditaires de la Maison d'Autriche.' Tillières to Ville-aux-Clercs, April $\frac{20}{30}$. *Harl. MSS.*, 4523, fol. 239.

thing not so very hard to be accomplished. If his Majesty, he said, would give him 10,000 infantry and 3,000 horse, six guns, and 20,000*l*. a month, he would need no more. With such a force he would levy contributions to make up all deficiencies. France, Venice, and Savoy would assist if it were merely on account of the interest which they took in the Valtelline, but it was absolutely necessary that a commencement should be made in England.[1]

CHAP. II.
1624.
April 16.

James was evidently pleased. The Palatinate, he repeated for the hundredth time, must be recovered, whatever its recovery might cost. But he had not abandoned his usual caution. He entered into an engagement to furnish Mansfeld with the thirteeen thousand men, and the 20,000*l*. a month for which he asked. But he accompanied his engagement with a declaration that his promise would only be valid if the King of France would entrust the German commander with a similar force. The joint army would then be used " for the recovery and recuperation of the Palatinate and the Valtelline." [2]

April 18.
Engagement with him.

Ap l 25.

On the 25th Mansfeld left England. The few days which he spent in London had been passed in a whirl of popularity. Men pressed forward to have the honour of touching the edge of his cloak; the Archbishop of Canterbury received him as he stepped out of his boat on the Surrey side of the Thames, and the Earl of Carlisle conducted him in state as far as Rochester.[3]

Mansfield leaves England.

[1] D. Carleton to Elizabeth, April 24. *S. P. Dom.*, clxiii. 48.
[2] Mansfeld's engagements, April 18, 24; the King's Declaration, April 25. *S. P. Germany*. Rusdorf to Frederick, April; *Mémoires de Rusdorf*, i. 283.
[3] Rusdorf to Frederick, $\frac{\text{April 26}}{\text{May 6}}$; *Ibid.* i. 289. The estate granted to Mansfeld, according to some Continental writers, has no existence in reality.

He was able to take with him the news that preparations for war were being carried on in earnest in England. On the 15th, the day after his arrival, Commissioners had been at last appointed to treat with the Dutch about sending troops to their assistance. On the 18th orders had been given to fit out twelve ships of the Royal Navy.[1] On the 21st a Council of War had been appointed, and the names of its members were such as to give every assurance that its deliberations would be conducted with ability. Lord Grandison, who, as Sir Oliver St. John, had crowned a long military career by services as Lord Deputy of Ireland; Lord Carew, the Master of the Ordnance, and former President of Munster; Lord Brooke, the Fulke Greville of Sydney's days; Lord Chichester, the soldier and statesman; Sir Edward Conway, Sir Edward Cecil, Sir Horace Vere, Sir John Ogle, and Sir Thomas Button, formed a group which comprised all the available military knowledge of the time, whilst Sir Robert Mansel held a high place for acquaintance with maritime affairs.[2]

It would be some time before James could hear how his proposal to assist Mansfeld would be received in France. But two days before Mansfeld went away James had used words which were not likely to help on the negotiation. In answering the Commons' petition against the Recusants he expressed himself favourably to the request laid before him. He considered himself unfortunate, he said, to need a spur to do that which his conscience and duty bound him to do. His heart had bled when he had heard of the increase of Popery. If he had known any way better

---

[1] Commission, April 15; *S. P. Holland*; Warrant, April 18, *S. P. Dom.*, clxiii. 4.

[2] Warrant, April 21. *S. P. Dom.*, clxiii. 18.

than another to hinder its growth he would have taken it. Yet he had abstained from persecution, nothing being more likely to increase a religion. He was now ready to banish the priests, and to direct the Judges to put the penal laws in execution. His subjects should be forbidden to frequent the houses of foreign ambassadors, or to bring up their children in the Roman Catholic faith. As for the request that no immunity for the English Catholics should be included in any treaty for his son's marriage, he heartily assented to it. "Now," he said, "for the last part of your petition. You have therein given me the best advice in the world; for it is against the rule of wisdom that a king should suffer any of his subjects to be beholden and depend upon any other prince than himself; and what hath any king to do with the laws and subjects of another kingdom? Therefore assure yourselves that, by the grace of God, I will be careful that no such condition be hereafter foisted in upon any other treaty whatsoever; for it is fit that my subjects should stand or fall to their own lord."[1]

James most likely meant all this at the time. The increase which had lately taken place in the numbers of the Catholics, and which was doubtless in the main to be attributed to the readiness with which timid or half-hearted converts declare themselves as soon as persecution has ceased,[2] was as formidable to him as it was to the House of Commons, and he was especially disinclined to make concessions to France after his past experience of the Spanish treaty. The answer thus

CHAP. II.

1624.
April 21.

No condition for the Catholics to be in the treaty.

April 24.
His answer received as satisfactory.

---

[1] *Lords' Journals*, iii. 317.
[2] Mr. Peacock's *List of Roman Catholics in the County of York in 1604* is very instructive on this point. The recusancy of great numbers dates from James's accession; that is to say, from the time when the fear of the penal laws was for a time removed.

CHAP. II.
1624.
April 24.

given was generally regarded as satisfactory. The adoption by James of his son's promise about the French marriage treaty was especially grateful, though most of those who heard him would have been better pleased if he had announced that there would be no French marriage at all. 'In a wondrous fine speech,' Eliot proposed that the thanks of Parliament should be given to the King and the Prince; and, though the motion was not adopted, the House gave a practical form to Eliot's expression of feeling by pushing on the subsidy bill as fast as possible.[1]

Inojosa's fresh complaints against Buckingham.

At that very moment a fresh attempt was being made by Inojosa to shake the constancy of James. Seeking an audience, the Spanish ambassador repeated with his own mouth the charges against Buckingham which had formerly been brought by Lafuente and Carondelet. It was true, he insisted, that the favourite had conspired with Parliament to dethrone the master to whom he owed everything, in case of his refusal to make war upon Spain. If the King wished to test the truth of the assertion, let Buckingham's friends be asked, upon their oath, whether he had not made the proposal in their hearing.

Buckingham's ill-humour.

The words so confidently spoken could not fail to make an impression upon the King. As soon as Inojosa left him he set out for Windsor, stopping at St. James's on his way, where Charles came out to meet him with Buckingham at his side. The tears stood in James's eyes as he repeated what the Spaniard had said. Charles accompanied his father. But Buckingham, though invited, remained behind. He must have justice, he said, against his slanderers. Till his innocence had been acknowledged, Windsor was no

[1] Nethersole to Carleton, April 25; *S. P. Dom.*, clxiii. 50.

place for him. He would rather betake himself to the Tower, and deliver himself up as a prisoner.[1]

Inojosa next presented a paper to the King, in which he admitted that his charges were 'not such as could be made to appear by legal and judicious proofs.' Men, he said, were too much afraid of Buckingham to tell the truth. Then followed a long tirade against the misdeeds of the favourite, which, even if it contained no exaggeration, was entirely irrelevant to the point at issue.[2]

Inojosa had not improved his position. On the 2nd of May the members of the Privy Council were called upon to answer a series of interrogatories which had been prepared in order to sift the matter to the bottom. One by one the councillors swore that they had never heard any traitorous expression proceed from Buckingham's mouth. Inojosa's attempt to conjure with the wand of Gondomar had failed entirely. When he came the next day to present his letters of recall, James refused to accept them. He must see him again, he said, before he left England. Some who were present hinted that there were precedents for calling ambassadors to account before the House of

[1] *Valaresso's Despatch,* $\frac{April 30}{May 10}$; Conway's Note, April 25; *S. P. Dom.*, clxiii. 51; Rusdorf to Frederick, $\frac{April 26}{May 6}$, May $\frac{9}{12}$; *Mémoires,* i. 289, 294. Tillières to Ville-aux-Clercs, $\frac{April 26}{May 6}$; *Harl. MSS.,* 4593, fol. 2, 65.

[2] Amongst Valaresso's despatches is a copy of this paper in Latin, probably the language in which it was presented. Copies in different languages are to be found almost everywhere in Europe. In the *Cabala* there is an English translation (ed. 1691, 252). In 1813, Mr. Lysons printed it again in the *Archæologia,* xviii. 280, fancying that it was probably drawn up by Robert Carr, Earl of Somerset, for the very insufficient reason that he found it amongst other papers connected with Somerset, and there may have been people who have been under the impression that there is, in this way, evidence in existence to show that Somerset was at this time trying to oust Buckingham from the King's favour. The paper is ascribed by a contemporary to Lafuente, who probably drew it up. D. Carleton to Carleton; *S. P. Dom.* clxiv. 12.

CHAP. II.
1624.
May 2.

Middlesex supports the Spaniards.

Lords. But to these rash advisers James turned a deaf ear. Such precedents, he answered, had been found to cut off his mother's head. But he would not let the Spaniard go till he had enquired whether his conduct was approved of by his master. Inojosa complained in vain of the treatment to which he was subjected. James told him that he must either prove his case or eat his words.[1]

Inojosa's information was believed at the time to have been derived from Middlesex, who was supposed to have hazarded this desperate step to save himself from ruin.[2] Of the five Privy Councillors who in the beginning of the year had taken the most determined stand against a breach with Spain, Lennox was dead; Williams had made his peace with Buckingham; Arundel, though doubtless holding the same opinions still, was maintaining a prudent silence; whilst Calvert was only waiting for a fit opportunity to declare himself a Roman Catholic, and to retire from public life. Middlesex stood alone in attempting to stem the torrent. To the economical administrator of the finances Buckingham's lavish expenditure had never been congenial. The Lord Treasurer, whose business it was to think how money could be saved, had often winced under the pressure put upon him by the Lord Admiral, whose pleasure it was to think how money could be spent. Unless men were much mistaken, he had attempted, just as the Prince was starting for Madrid, to supersede Buckingham in the Royal favour with the help of his brother-in-law, Arthur Brett. The young man was ordered to travel on the Continent, and a seeming

[1] Locke to Carleton, May 8; D. Carleton to Carleton, May 21; *S. P. Dom.*, clxiv. 53, clxv. 12; *Salvetti's Newsletter*, May $\frac{7}{17}, \frac{14}{24}$.
[2] D. Carleton to Carleton, May 3; *S. P. Dom.*, clxiv. 12.

reconciliation was effected. But now Buckingham's enormities had reached their height. To the careful guardian of the Treasury, who had built up a surplus out of a deficit by the unremitting labour of years, a war with Spain opened visions of distress which were not to be counterbalanced by any prospect of national glory. He had no faith in the popular belief that the certain expenditure might easily be recouped by the capture of Spanish treasure-ships. Whilst Buckingham and the Commons were discounting the chances of the future, the old City merchant prudently shook his head and expressed his doubt of the value of the security offered.

To the Prince, Middlesex had given special offence. When the question of the Spanish marriage was being considered after Charles's return from Spain, all the other councillors who objected to seeing it broken off, qualified their opinions by saying that, if the Prince had taken any dislike to the person of the lady, it would be a sufficient reason for putting an end to the engagement. Middlesex alone expressed himself otherwise. Whether his Highness, he argued, wished to marry the Infanta or not, it was his duty to do so 'for reason of state and the good that would thence redound to all Christendom,' for 'he supposed that the Prince ought to submit his private distaste therein to the general good and honour of the kingdom.' 'Whereupon,' said Williams, who told the story long afterwards, 'the Prince bid him judge of his merchandises, if he would, for he was no arbiter in points of honour.'[1]

And now Middlesex had the King's ear. If James had listened to Lafuente or to Inojosa, if he had sunk back from time to time into his old dislike of war, Buckingham attributed it all to Middlesex. Before

Dillon's Articles against Williams, 1634 (?) ; *S. P. Dom.* cclxxx. 77.

the end of March the return of Arthur Brett to England brought matters to a crisis. Buckingham resolved that Middlesex and the King should be separated.

CHAP. II.
1624. March.
Charges against Middlesex.

In a moment, charges sprung up against the Lord Treasurer, whose economy had made him many enemies, and who had doubtless committed some faults. He had been harsh and imperious in his bearing, and had neglected on some occasions to observe the due formalities of his office. In taking care of his master's fortunes he had not forgotten to think of his own; and at a time when the practice of high officials was very loose, he had probably done enough fairly to expose himself to the charge of malversation.

As it had been with Bacon, so it was now with Middlesex. Many things said against him were exaggerated. Some of his actions might be palliated as being in accordance with the usual practice. Some things which formed the subject of accusation were even to his praise. But after all allowances have been made, there remains enough to show that he had done things which he ought never to have done.[1]

April 15. His impeachment.

On the 15th of April the charges against Middlesex were laid before the Peers by Coke and Sandys. In Bacon's case complaints made by individuals had merely been sent up for investigation. This time the Commons took a higher tone. Reviving in all its fulness the old

---

[1] Part of a letter, in the possession of Lord Buckhurst, is thus abstracted in the fourth report of the Historical MSS. Commission:—'Two days since, the Committee of Twelve being in examination what the Duke hath gotten out of the King's revenue, Sir Robert Pye took occasion to inform them that Middlesex had gotten from the King in a short time 120,000*l.*, and therefore moved that he might be likewise examined; to which Sir J. Eliot, being in the chair, answered that it might be true for ought he knew to the contrary; but that it was true that Middlesex had merited well of the King, and had done him that service that few had ever done, but they could find no such matter in the Duke.' Harman to Middlesex, May 3, 1626.

practice of impeachment, they asked for justice as the grand jury of the nation, 'the inquisitors-general of the grievances of the kingdom.'

The Lords were not likely to put a favourable construction upon the faults of the merchant's apprentice whose abilities had carried him to the height of power. Arundel, indeed, is said to have approved of his conduct in assisting the Spanish ambassadors.[1] But Arundel, whatever he may have felt, did not venture to support the Lord Treasurer openly, and contented himself with raising his voice from time to time in favour of moderation.[2]

During the long enquiry the Treasurer showed no lack of courage. But it was in vain that he fought his accusers point by point. On the 13th of May sentence was delivered against him. He was to lose all his offices, to be incapable for the future of holding any office in the State, to be imprisoned in the Tower during the King's pleasure, to pay a fine of 50,000*l.*, to be prohibited from taking his seat in Parliament again, or from coming within the verge of the Court.[3]

Whatever may be thought of the special faults of Middlesex, the practice of bringing criminal charges against men whose chief offence lay in their political convictions might easily lead to the grossest abuses, and could scarcely fail to turn to the damage of the heedless young men who had been the main instigators of the proceedings. To the old King their conduct appeared as foolish as it was unintelligible. "You are a fool," he said bluntly to Buckingham. "You are making a rod with which you will be scourged yourself." Turning to his son, he added a special word of

[1] *Valaresso's Despatch*, April $\frac{2}{30}$.
[2] *Elsing's Notes*.
[3] *Lords' Journals*, iii. 383.

CHAP. II.

1610. May.

March. Bristol's return.

Buckingham's designs against him.

April.

warning. "You," he said, with prophetic sagacity, "will live to have your bellyful of impeachments."[1] Before the trial was at an end Buckingham was prostrated by a severe illness. But Charles took up the cause with characteristic impetuosity. Again and again he thrust himself forward in the debate, ever painting the character of the friend of Spain in the blackest colours.[2]

Middlesex had been thus removed from the King's side. But a greater, more persuasive counsellor than Middlesex was at hand. When Bristol was recalled from Spain, it was only by pawning his plate that he was able to obtain the means needed for his journey. He was coming in the most dangerous of all tempers for Buckingham; full of the conviction that he had been hardly dealt with, and yet with all his irritation mastered by the most complete self-control. All he asked was the fulfilment of a promise which James had given him never to condemn him without first hearing what he had to say. He had no intention of throwing himself into opposition, open or secret. Like Bacon he held that the King's resolution, whatever it might be, was to be accepted as final.

That James should grant a hearing to Bristol was the last thing that Buckingham would approve of. If once the two men were brought together, there would probably be an end of the King's new anti-Spanish policy, and Buckingham's own insolence and folly at Madrid would be revealed on more credible evidence than that of the Spanish ambassador. Buckingham's first thought, therefore, was to send Bristol to the Tower. He talked over the plan with Pembroke and Hamilton. But Pembroke and Hamilton, opposed as they were to Spain, would not hear of so ill-advised a measure.

[1] *Clarendon*, i. 44. [2] *Elsing's Notes*.

Buckingham accordingly persuaded James to issue an order to Bristol to place himself in confinement in his own house. Yet, though Bristol was thus cut off from seeing his master, James had no intention of placing him under permanent restraint. Some little enquiry there must be for form's sake, and then he should be taken into favour. Meanwhile James was hopefully busying himself in bringing Buckingham to lay aside his rancour.

Chap. II. 1624. May. He is confined to his house.

Bristol was a difficult man to deal with in this manner. If at any time he had chosen to acknowledge that everything done by himself had been wrong, and that everything done by Buckingham had been right, he would probably have been welcomed, like Weston and Williams, amongst the Duke's train of penitents. But to this Bristol refused to stoop. He would hold his tongue if the King pleased. But unless he were convinced, he would never admit himself to be in the wrong. Loyalty to his sovereign ceased to bind him when he was required to prove it by declaring that to be true which he believed to be untrue.

He accordingly asked for a trial in Parliament, such as that which had been fatal to Middlesex. But the session was nearly at an end, and James shrunk from exposing him to his political opponents. For a little time longer, therefore, Bristol must remain under restraint.[1]

That Parliament must come to an end before the great business of the day, the French negotiations, could be seriously entered upon, was tacitly admitted at Court. One result of the alliance between Buckingham and the Commons had been the production of a large amount of legislation on matters of

The Monopoly Act.

---

[1] Preface to the Earl of Bristol's defence in the *Camden Miscellany*, vi. pp. i.-vii.

everyday importance. No statute had come into existence for fourteen years, and it was understood that James was willing to give his assent to the passing of many bills which had been prepared in 1610 and 1614, with the object of limiting the prerogative of the Crown in pecuniary matters. Above all, the question of the monopolies was by this time ripe for legislation. The Lords were ready to withdraw their objection against tying the King's hands for the future, upon which the Monopoly Bill of the last session had been wrecked, and the Commons, on the other hand, agreed to except from the operation of the Bill some of the principal monopolies already in existence.

Changes effected by it.

Great as the importance of this Act has been, it cannot be said to have been founded on any principle not recognised before. That a monopoly for a limited time should be granted to those by whom new processes of manufacture were introduced had long been accepted as the general rule. The great change effected was the rendering the rule more definite, and the entrusting its application to the Common Law Judges, who would be far more likely than Privy Councillors or Commissioners to apply a strictly judicial solution to any question which might arise, without being drawn aside by political or economical considerations.

Impositions not touched on.

On the question of impositions the Commons had maintained a discreet silence, although there had been debates on commercial matters which might fairly have suggested it to them.[1] Under these circumstances it

---

[1] Mr. Forster (*Sir J. Eliot*, 2nd edit. i. 89) has printed extracts from a speech of Eliot's on this subject, alleged to have been delivered in this session. From enquiries which he has kindly made for me at Port Eliot, it appears that the speech is not to be found in this place, and therefore, if spoken at all, it must have been spoken at some other time. There is no trace of it in any reports that I have seen of any of the four Parliaments with which this work is concerned. On the 20th of May,

might have been expected that the King and the Lower House would have parted in kindness. But James was no longer in a kindly mood. He had parted with some of his prerogatives, and he knew that he had been little better than a cypher in the resolutions which had been taken. On May 28 he listened with composure to the grievances presented to him, and answered that the lawyers must consider them before he could give an answer. Then he began to scold the House for the bills which they had laid before him. His tone was so exasperating that the Commons refused to enter the Royal Speech on their journals.

margin: CHAP. II. 1624. May. May 28. The grievances.

The next day Parliament was prorogued. James had fresh criticism for the bills presented for his consent. He made merry over one, for 'the better observance of the Sabbath,' as allowing 'no recreation to the poor men that labour hard all the week long, to ease themselves on the Sunday,' and he entirely refused to pass the bill for enforcing more strictly the penalties on recusancy. He then proceeded to express his annoyance at the impeachment of Middlesex, which he had not been bold enough to prevent. It was for him, he said, to re-examine the evidence, and to remit the penalties if he saw fit. No one in future was to complain in Parliament of any of his servants, without first asking his leave. He was master in his own household, and was well able to redress any grievance arising from the conduct of his Ministers.

margin: May 29. Prorogation of Parliament.

It was not by words unaccompanied by deeds that the rising power of Parliament was to be beaten back. For the present, however, all questions about the

margin: James threatens to amend the Subsidy Bill.

Conway (*S. P. Dom.*, clxv. 4) writes to Calvert that the House might probably fall upon 'questions concerning impositions,' and Calvert replies (*ibid.* 11) that all had gone well.

CHAP. II.
1624.
May 29.

extent of the prerogative were subordinate to the great question about the management of the war. At the beginning of his speech James had protested his continued care for the Palatinate, and had assured the Houses that if they met again with the same resolution as they had cherished in the past session, it would be the happiest Parliament known in history. Before he ended he remembered that he had attempted in vain to induce the Commons to insert into the Subsidy Bill a clause naming the recovery of the Palatinate as one of the objects of the grant.[1] Whereas, he said, they 'had made the preamble without his advice, and so as it might be prejudicial to him for some reasons of state, he must be forced to alter it, and set his marginal note upon it.' At this extraordinary and unexpected declaration the usual respect for the Royal person was for an instant forgotten, and those who were present gave vent to their dissatisfaction in murmurs and gesticulations.

Dissatisfaction of the Commons.

"And thus," wrote an eye-witness of the scene, "parted we from his Majesty, with much more discontent and fear of the success of this Parliament than when we came together at the beginning with hope and good and happy prosecution."[2]

Proceedings against Bristol.

James's intemperance was always greater in word than in action. The Subsidy Act was left untouched; and Middlesex, though his fine was subsequently reduced to 20,000*l.*, never saw the King's face again. Nor did James, in the face of the opposition of his favourite and his son, venture to admit Bristol to his presence. Both Buckingham and Charles, indeed, were preparing future difficulties for themselves by their conduct to the man whose influence with the King

---

[1] Locke to Carleton, May 17; *S. P. Dom.*, clxiv. 92.
[2] Report by E. Nicholas; *ibid.* clxv. 61.

they most dreaded. A long series of interrogatories were sent to Bristol bearing on the whole of his past diplomacy. Bristol answered them all with care. He was able to show that on all doubtful points he had acted by his master's orders, and that he had given such advice as he believed at the time to be the best for the King's service. Many of the Commissioners appointed to conduct the investigation expressed themselves fully satisfied, and James too sent word to Bristol that he was now ready to see him.

An interview between Bristol and the King was the very thing to which Buckingham most strongly objected. Hinting that there were further questions still to be put, he made use of the delay thus obtained to convey a suggestion to Bristol that he should surrender his Vice-Chamberlainship, and retire to his country-house at Sherborne, on the condition that all further proceedings against him should be dropped. Buckingham little knew the character of the man with whom he was dealing. Bristol's reply was that if his honesty and fidelity were declared to be unquestioned he was quite ready to acknowledge that he might have erred from weakness or want of ability. If not, he was ready to answer any further questions that might be sent to him. "For," he wrote, "in matter of my fidelity and loyalty towards his Majesty, the Prince, and my country, I hope I shall never see that come into compromise, but shall rather lose my life and fortunes than admit the least stain to remain upon me or mine in that kind."

Bristol's position was logically unassailable. If he was supposed to have done anything worthy of punishment, let his case be investigated. If not, why was he under restraint? Buckingham could not answer an argument like this. But he could continue to act in

CHAP. II.
1624.
July 10.

Buckingham suggests a compromise.

July 24.
Bristol refuses it.

Bristol at Sherborne.

defiance of it. Bristol was left at Sherborne untried and uncondemned. If he came into the King's presence he might say things about Buckingham's connexion with the Prince's visit to Madrid which would not conduce to raise him in his master's opinion. But, to do Buckingham justice, it was not mere personal enmity by which he was actuated. If Bristol was to be kept at a distance, it was that James, and England through James, might be kept from falling back into the evil Spanish alliance. Even when Buckingham was engaged in an apparently personal quarrel, he had usually great public ends in view. The interests of his country were so completely bound up with his own preferences and jealousies, that he came to think of himself and England as inextricably combined.

The disregard, not only of legal forms but of common justice, which had been shown in Buckingham's treatment of Bristol, marked another proceeding in which the King had to take a far more active part, and for which no pretext of public good could be alleged. In the far East as in the far West, it was almost, if not quite, impossible to bring the relations between European merchants under the laws which regulated commerce in the settled societies of Europe. In pursuit of the dazzling prize the subjects of each nation struggled and fought with their rivals, careless of treaties made at home. An attempt made by the English East India Company in 1620 to open a trade with Persia had been met with fierce opposition from the Portuguese subjects of Spain established at Ormuz, who regarded the whole commerce of that part of the world as their own. The English, beaten at first, had returned with superior forces, and had established a station at Jask. The report of the prowess of the newcomers was not thrown away upon the Shah, who had a quarrel with the Portuguese. He assured the English merchants that he would not allow them to place a bale of goods on board their ships unless they would join him in an attack upon Ormuz. With real or affected reluctance, the English consented, and Ormuz was soon reduced to capitulate.¹

CHAP. II.
1621.
1622. Capture of Ormuz.

To the complaints of the Spaniards preferred whilst the Prince was still at Madrid,² James does not seem to have paid much attention. But there was another side of the question to which he was more alive. Sending for the governor of the East India Company, he told him that it would be a graceful act to make a present to Buckingham in his absence for his services in the negotiation with the Dutch of the year before. The Company, thus urged, and considering that 'this business of Ormuz may find a strong opposition,' voted 2,000*l*. for the purpose.³

1623. April. Spanish complaints.

July. The East India Company's present to Buckingham.

When Buckingham returned, with his heart full of ill-will towards all Spanish subjects, there was of course no thought of satisfying the Portuguese. But, much to the surprise of the Company, the Duke began to make claims upon them on his own account. The machinery of the Court of Admiralty was put in motion to collect evidence that by the capture of Ormuz and by the seizure of Portuguese vessels in the East, they had realised, or ought to have realised, 100,000*l*.—a calculation which, as far as can be at present ascertained, appears to have been grossly exaggerated.⁴

His claims against the Company.

¹ Bruce, *Annals of the East India Company*, i. 229; *Purchas*, ii. 1785.
² Consultas of the Councils of Portugal and of State, April $\frac{16}{26}$, $\frac{17}{27}$, 1623; *Egerton MSS.*, 1131, fol. 169.
³ *East India Company Court Minutes*, July 23, 1623, vi. 24.
⁴ Bruce, *Annals of the East India Company*, i. 242; Examinations, *S. P. East Indies*.

CHAP.
II.

1624.
February.

As soon, however, as the preliminary enquiry was complete, Buckingham demanded 10,000*l*., a tenth of the sum named, as due to him as Lord High Admiral, as it would be due to him from captures made by privateers sailing under ordinary letters of marque in European waters.

The Company remonstrates.

The Company was at first disposed to resist the Duke's claim. They obtained a legal opinion to the effect that, as no letters of marque had been granted, no tenths were due. But they were 'not willing to contend with my Lord.' Yet what to do they hardly knew. A petition was drawn up, then abandoned as likely to give offence, and at last a committee was appointed to remonstrate as cautiously as possible.[1]

Feb. 28.

March 1.
Stay of the East India fleet.

It was dangerous to remonstrate, however cautiously, with Buckingham. The day after his interview with the committee he drew the attention of the House of Lords on behalf of a committee of which he was the reporter, to the fact that the Company's fleet was about to sail to the East Indies, and proposed that it should be detained for service against Spain. On the same day a similar motion was made in the Commons by Sir Edward Seymour, a member who was supposed to possess the confidence of Buckingham.

A deputation from the Company at once waited on the Duke. He received them graciously, and assured them that the stay of the ships had not originated with him. 'Having heard,' he said, 'the motion with much earnestness in the Upper House of Parliament, he could do no less than give the order.' He would only be too happy to advocate their cause with the Lords, and would, upon his own responsibility, allow the ships to drop down as far as Tilbury.[2]

---

[1] *East India Company Court Minutes*, Feb. 18, 23, 27, 28, vi. 412, 425, 430, 435.

[2] *Elsing's Notes; Commons' Journals*, i. 676; *East India Company*

It is possible that the first suggestion that the fleet should be arrested had proceeded from some independent member of the Lords' Committee. But the coincidence of the motions in the two Houses made it hard to persuade the Company that this was the case. And a few days later he struck another blow in the quarrel. To the argument that no tenths were due because there had been no letters of marque, the rejoinder was easy that if there had been no letters of marque there had been an act of piracy. A suit was accordingly commenced against the Company in the joint names of Buckingham and the King. The damages were laid at 15,000*l*., and that too without prejudice to further claims.¹

In vain the Company begged for mercy. "Did I deliver you," said James, "from the complaint of the Spaniards, and do you return me nothing?" He was no tyrant, and they might have the benefit of the law if they pleased. But if they did not wish to try their case against him, he must have 10,000*l*. for himself, as well as 10,000*l*. for Buckingham. To justify his demand he proceeded to propound a dilemma. The goods, he said, were taken either justly or unjustly. If unjustly, the whole was forfeited. If justly, the Lord Admiral's tenth must be paid. Apparently the inference was that the Company was to pay the King on the ground that they had been taken unjustly, and Buckingham on the ground that they had been taken justly.

The Company were in great straits. Their ships were still under embargo in the Thames. A few more days' delay would lose them the monsoon, and ruin

CHAP. II.

1624.
March 10.
The Company charged with piracy.

March 22.
James's dilemma.

He demands 20,000*l*.

Court Minutes, March 5, vi. 439. The motion made by Buckingham is given by Elsing as part of a report from a committee. The notice of the fleet may therefore have been taken in the committee by some other person.
¹ *Admiralty Court Records*, No. 158; *Book of Acts*, fol. 204.

their prospects for a year. Necessity had no law, and 10,000*l.* was offered to the King 'to shut up all businesses.'

The money paid.
But this would not do. James said that he must have as much for Buckingham. There was nothing for it but to submit. The whole 20,000*l.* was paid, and the fleet was allowed to sail. It seemed, as some one observed at the Company's meeting, as if 'ships stayed upon pretence of state might be released for money.'[1]

Such was the mode in which Buckingham, this time with the full co-operation of the King, exercised the duties of his office. Something, no doubt, was to be said against the Company on every count. The siege of Ormuz and the capture of the goods was an act of violence. The ships sailing to the East Indies might doubtless be called upon before they went to contribute their fair proportion to the defence of the realm. That which admits of no justification is the way in which every argument was pushed just so far as suited the immediate purposes of the men in power and no further. There was enough legality about the

[1] *East India Company's Court Minutes*, vi. 466–555. The receipt drawn up for Buckingham's signature was 'for 10,000*l.* to the Lord Admiral, in full satisfaction for all pretences of right as Lord Admiral, for all actions past in the Indies, by sea or land, to the 30th of April last.' The King's receipt was—'for 10,000*l.* now to be paid to the King, much challenged by his Majesty for freeing the Company's servants out of prison, and the Company from the complaint of the Spanish ambassador, and the Company's ships outward bound released, which were secured by order of Parliament, until upon promise thereof they were afterwards released." Buckingham afterwards stated that he had lent 9,800*l.* of the money for the equipment of the fleet, and this is corroborated by a letter written by him to Conway on the 14th of June in which he says, "I hope this morning will put an end to the business of the East India merchants for the moneys to be disposed to Mr. Oliver for the Navy.' *Tanner MSS.*, lxxiii. 447. Besides, the exact sum appears on a warrant from the Council of War, dated July 31, and was then probably repaid to Buckingham.

capture to extort one sum of money; enough illegality to extort another. The Portuguese, who were the main sufferers, were never thought of, save that the English ambassador was directed to inform the government at Madrid that the assailants at Ormuz had acted under compulsion from the Shah.[1]

CHAP. II.
1624.
June.

It was probably only by coming to some understanding with the other European powers for a territorial limitation between the trading grounds of the various nations, that such collisions as that which had taken place at Ormuz could be avoided for the future. Further to the East the experiment of a close combination with the Dutch, which had been tried under the treaty of 1619,[2] was already breaking down. Never had the feeling between the merchants of the two nations been more embittered than it was when they were bound to live at the same ports, and to share between them the same commerce in certain fixed proportions. As the most numerous and powerful body, the Dutch treated the English with studied unfairness, and the English gave vent to their feelings in such language as Englishmen are wont to use when they discover that they are being cheated.

1623.
The Dutch in the East.

Early in 1623 the slumbering hatred burst into a flame. The castle of Amboyna, the main seat of the clove trade, was guarded by the Dutch with peculiar jealousy. The English factory was only permitted to establish itself outside the fortifications; and a body of Japanese soldiers in the Dutch service were equally excluded. On the night of the 11th of February, however, one of the Japanese approached the Dutch sentinel, and asked some questions about the state of the defences. He was at once seized and put to the

Feb. 11.
The massacre of Amboyna.

[1] Conway to Acton, June 27; *S. P. Spain.*
[2] *Prince Charles and the Spanish Marriage,* i. 232, ii 292.

CHAP. II.
1624.
May.

torture. In his agony he confessed that his countrymen designed to surprise the castle. They, too, were tortured, and declared, or were made to declare, that the English were privy to the conspiracy. A drunken English surgeon, also under torture, acknowledged the truth of the charge. Nine other Englishmen, almost the whole of the English population of the town, were next subjected to the most horrible torments, and six others, residing at more distant stations, were subsequently sent for to be dealt with in the same barbarous manner. Of course some of them gave way before their tortures, and confessed anything that was required of them. In the end ten of the sufferers were set aside for execution, and were beheaded without further evidence.[1]

The news received in England.

News in those days was long in reaching England from the East. The massacre of Amboyna remained unknown till May 1624. At the meetings of the East India Company the tale gave rise to the greatest indignation. The story, as it was received from the Dutch, was in the highest degree incredible. The whole English population inculpated amounted to no more than twenty men, who were hardly likely, in the face of past experience, to attempt to right themselves against the overwhelming forces of their opponents. But the case of the Company against its Dutch rival did not end here. Even if the unfortunate men had been guilty of all that they had admitted under torture, the governor of Amboyna would not have been justified in touching a hair of their heads. By the treaty of 1619, all disputes between the nations were to be referred to the mixed Council of Defence; and, if they could not be settled in this way, were to be referred

[1] Brockedon and others to the Company; *E. I. C. Orig. Corr.*, 10, 11, 30; *Purchas*, ii. 1853.

home for negotiation between the two Companies, or, in the last resort, for negotiation between the two Governments.¹

There has seldom been a moment in our history when such an outrage would not have roused England from one end to the other. But, when the news arrived, the nation was in no mood to listen to charges against the enemies of Spain. At first, indeed, there seems to have been some little excitement. But it quickly died away.² The time had not yet come when the commercial differences with the Netherlands would seem greater than the religious differences with Spain; and by the middle of July revenge for the massacre of Amboyna appears to have been no longer thought of by the mass of men.

The King was more deeply affected by the sad story than any one else. He was the author of the treaty which, by bringing his subjects into such close neighbourhood with the Dutch, had made the massacre possible. He now told Caron, the Dutch ambassador, that, if justice were not done by the 12th of August, he would take his own measures to enforce it.³

Yet how was England, at such a moment, to quarrel with her neighbours in Holland? The alliance with the Dutch had been the corner-stone of the policy of the House of Commons, and, though

Marginalia: CHAP. II. 1624. May. Comparative apathy in England. July. James demands justice. June 5. Treaty with the Dutch.

¹ The treaty must be interpreted by the agreement between the Companies appended to it.
² Chamberlain to Carleton, June 5, June 19; D. Carleton to Carleton, June 26: *S. P. Dom.* clxvii. 16, clxviii. 8, 48; Dutch Commissioners to the States General, June ⁶⁄₁₆; *Add. MSS.*, 17, 677, k, fol. 369. But, as early as the 31st of May, we have a statement that 'it is said that the Company is much blamed by some, for that now, in a time when his Majesty had resolved to aid the Dutch, the Company had published the putting of ten Englishmen to death;' *E. I. C. Court Minutes,* x. 541.
³ Caron to the States General, July 16; *Add. MSS.*, 17, 677, k, fol. 576.

CHAP. II.

1624.
May 19.

James was unwilling to limit the war within the narrow bounds which seemed sufficient to the Lower House, he had fully accepted its designs, so far as they went. On the 19th of May an order had been given to equip thirty merchant vessels in addition to the twelve ships of the Royal Navy which were already in an advanced stage of preparation.[1] Directly after the prorogation the negotiation with the Dutch Commissioners was taken up warmly, and on the 5th of June a treaty was signed by which England agreed to pay, for two years, a body of six thousand volunteers to be sent over to aid the States General in defending their independence.[2]

June 5.

James seemed to be going fairly on in the way in which Buckingham would lead him, and there is no reason to suppose that he was in any way half-hearted in what he was doing. But he was less able than ever to perceive the necessary consequences of his actions. He thought that he could send troops to the aid of the Dutch, and fit out his navy, without breaking absolutely with Spain.

Coloma's protests.

Of course the Spanish ambassadors could not see things in this light. Coloma protested warmly against the levies as an infraction of existing treaties. On the other hand Inojosa intimated that he had fresh proposals to make about the restitution of the Palatinate. He was told that James would not see him, but that he might tell his secret to any Privy Councillor he chose. Inojosa refused to address himself to any one but the King; upon which he was informed that the sooner he and Coloma left England the better it would be. Coloma replied that he was under orders to remain till his successor arrived. Inojosa was only too glad to escape.

[1] Signet Office Docquets, May 19.
[2] Treaty, June 5; *S. P. Holland.*

There were fresh insults in store for him. No carriages were provided to take him to Dover. Even his request for the protection of a Royal ship against the Dutch cruisers was refused, and it was only after a delay of some days that he was allowed to take his passage in one of the merchant vessels which had been recently taken into the King's service, and which was consequently entitled to carry the Royal colours. On the day of his departure James wrote to complain to Philip of his ambassadors' conduct, requesting that they might be punished for their misdemeanour.[1]

CHAP. II.
1624. June 26. Inojosa leaves England.

Coloma had indeed a thankless task in remaining in England. Every day some new cause of offence was brought before his notice. At sea, so at least it was believed in England, Spaniards were already engaged in plundering English vessels. In Spain an embargo had been laid upon the goods of English merchants, and their ships were being confiscated, on the charge of having Dutch goods on board. Nearer home the Dunkirk privateers were making prize of English vessels engaged in trade with Holland; and, pushing up towards the mouth of the Thames in search of their enemies, had committed hostilities as high as Queenborough. Nor was it only from private and unauthorised attacks that danger was apprehended. A large fleet was fitting out in Spain, the destination of which was carefully concealed.[2] Part of this fleet, however, was placed by accident in the hands of the English government. A squadron setting out from Dunkirk to join the rendezvous in Spain was chased by the Dutch, and four of its galleons took refuge in the

Bickerings between Spain and England.

The Dunkirk ships in the Downs.

[1] Coloma to the King, May 23/June 2; The King to Aston, June 26; *S. P. Spain*; Conway to Carleton, June 12; *S. P. Holland*; Salvetti's *Newsletters*, June 11/21, 18/28.
[2] Conway to Acton, June 27; Acton to Conway, July 1; *S. P. Spain*.

VOL. 1.   G

CHAP. II.

1624.
Oct. 2.
Three of them escape.

Downs. James refused to treat them as enemies. But neither would he accede to Coloma's request that he would grant them the usual privileges of neutrality, and would allow them to sail with the advantage of two tides.¹ For three months the weary crews waited for deliverance till the equinoctial gales at last set them free. Putting to sea in the height of the tempest, three of the ships succeeded in regaining Dunkirk. The fourth was attacked by a Dutch vessel, and blew up, together with its assailant.²

June.
The programme of the House of Commons carried out.

Short, therefore, of an actual declaration of war with Spain, Buckingham had succeeded in carrying James with him in the fulfilment of the programme laid down in the Subsidy Act. The reinforcements to the Dutch and the equipment of the fleet had received prompt attention. The repair of the forts and the sending of reinforcements to Ireland waited only till money came in. Even the King's hesitation to declare war against Spain was at this time ascribed by one who had good opportunities of knowing the truth, not so much to any hankering after his old alliance with Philip, as to his high estimate of the risks of such a war if it were entered upon without allies. "The King," wrote Nethersole a fortnight after the prorogation, "is resolved not to break with Spain, nor to give them any occasion to break with him, until he be secure that France will join very close with him, and other Catholic Princes and States which have the same interest against the greatness of Spain; as being of opinion that all the Protestants in Europe would be too weak a party to oppose it, and that if they should

¹ Many of Coloma's letters on the subject are in the State Papers (*Spain*), and there are frequent notices of it in the Domestic series, and amongst *Salvetti's Newsletters*.
² *Salvetti's Newsletters*, Oct. $\frac{8}{18}, \frac{15}{25}$.

join against Spain without the drawing of other Catholic Princes into the action, it would be understood to be a war of religion, which would leave no Catholic Prince neuter, but cause them all to join with Spain."[1]

CHAP. II.
1624. June.

No one who has seriously studied the course which history took during the next quarter of a century will be inclined to doubt the wisdom of James's hesitation. The power to which he was opposed was too firmly rooted in the ideas of men to be overthrown by such means as seemed sufficient to the House of Commons. If Protestantism was to defend itself it must be by ceasing to be aggressive, and by appealing to the political sympathies of Catholic States. The policy of James was in the main the policy which, in after years, crowned Richelieu with glory. Yet to the one man it had brought nothing but defeat and shame, to the other it was to bring success and honour. Where James knew but how to dream, Richelieu knew how to act.

Policy of James.

Of the various parts of the enterprise upon which James had embarked the negotiation with the Protestant powers presented the least inherent difficulty. In the beginning of June Sir Patrick Spens was despatched to the King of Sweden, and Sir Robert Anstruther to the King of Denmark and the North German Princes.[2] If, when Parliament met in the winter, assurances could be given to it that a strong Protestant force was ready to take the field, the House of Commons might perhaps be induced to reconsider its determination against sharing in the German war; and, should this prove not to be the case, James would be clearly absolved from any engagement to carry on

Embassies to Denmark and Sweden.

[1] Nethersole to Carleton; *S. P. Dom.*, clxvii. 28.
[2] Instructions to Spens, June 6; *S. P. Sweden*. Instructions to Anstruther, undated; *S. P. Denmark*.

further a war which, with insufficient means, could only end in disaster.

Far more difficult was the task of treating with the Catholic opponents of Spain. For in nothing is diplomatic skill so necessary as in a negotiation between governments whose general interests coincide, whilst each has particular objects in view. James was anxious to recover the Palatinate. France was anxious to recover the Valtelline. The danger was great lest the French Government should use England for its purposes, and then kick away the ladder by which it had risen. And yet the offer of French aid was too tempting to be rejected. The wisest policy was doubtless that which was laid down not many months afterwards by Gustavus Adolphus. The great Swedish King held, that the attack upon the house of Austria should be made by a Protestant alliance. Those who had a common cause would be able without difficulty to stand shoulder to shoulder in the fight. There was no reason, however, that advantage should not be taken of the divisions amongst the Catholic States. Let France, Venice, and Savoy be invited to join, if they would, against Spain and the Emperor. But let not the union be too close. Rather let France and its Catholic allies be invited to fight in Italy or the south of Germany, whilst England and its Protestant allies were fighting in the north of Germany.[1]

If such a plan as this had been adopted, it is possible that the French alliance might have ended less disastrously than it did. The military situation would have corresponded with the political situation. Account would have been taken of the prominent fact that the King of France and the Protestant sovereigns were

[1] Oxenstjerna to Camerarius, Aug. 24; Moser, *Patriotisches Archiv* v. 42.

only half agreed. The friction certain to ensue upon such co-operation would have been diminished to a minimum. But unhappily the three men who directed the course of affairs in England were notoriously inclined to close their eyes to unpleasant facts. Already Mansfeld had been despatched to France with proposals for a joint military undertaking. Then followed Sir Isaac Wake, on his way to Italy to stir up Venice and Savoy. On May 17 Carlisle set out for Paris to tie the knot between the two kingdoms by the flowery bonds of a matrimonial alliance. James, Charles, and Buckingham agreed in looking for the closest possible unity of action between France and England.

CHAP. II.
1624.
May 17.

Carlisle sent to France.

CHAPTER III.

THE FRENCH MARRIAGE TREATY.

<small>CHAP. III.
1624.
May.
Carlisle as a negotiator.</small>

JAMES HAY, Earl of Carlisle, has been chiefly known in modern times as a spendthrift and a lover of the pleasures of the table. Yet he was in many respects well qualified to conduct the delicate negotiation with which he was entrusted. Compared with the courtly and volatile Kensington, with whom he was ordered to act, he may well rank as a statesman. His tried courtesy, and his special friendliness towards France, made him an acceptable person in the Court to which he was accredited, whilst he had a strong regard for his master's dignity, and a sympathy for the Protestant feeling in England, which would prevent him from becoming, as his colleague had become, a mere echo of the sentiments to which it might please the Queen Mother and her ladies to give utterance. When he arrived he was received with open demonstrations of satisfaction from all, with happy glances from the bright eyes of the Princess, and with friendly words from the King.[1]

<small>June.
Herbert's doubts.</small>

Herbert, however, who was still in Paris, doubted whether all this meant much. ".They do not spare," he wrote to James, "to profess openly that they have no disposition to come to a manifest rupture with Spain. Notwithstanding which, they have promised thus much already, that, in all that can be done by other means

---

[1] Carlisle and Kensington to Conway, May 27; *S. P. France.*

than coming to an entire breach they will not fail to give your Sacred Majesty contentment."[1]

The first difficulty of the negotiation, however, turned upon the marriage treaty. Both James and Charles had assured Parliament that there would be no article in favour of the English Catholics, and for the present both James and Charles intended to keep the promise which had been given. Carlisle was instructed by James to say that 'the constitution of our estate cannot bear any general change or alteration in our ecclesiastical or temporal laws touching religion for so much as concerns our own subjects.' Even for the Catholics themselves it would be better that they should rely on his own clemency than on a treaty with any foreign power. "For when," he added, "they shall have the reins loosed to them, they may, by abuse of favour and liberty, constrain us, contrary to our natural affections, to deal with them with more rigour than we are inclined to; so as we may not article for dispensation and liberty to our Roman Catholic subjects, but hold the reins of those laws in our own gracious hands. And you may assure that King and his ministers that, in contemplation of that marriage, we shall be the rather inclined to use our subjects Roman Catholics with all favour, so long as they shall behave themselves moderately; and, keeping their consciences to themselves, shall use their conversation without scandal."[2]

The first meeting between the ambassadors and the commissioners named by Lewis took place on May 31. As was often the case in those days the progress of business was stopped by a question of precedence. Richelieu was one of the commissioners, and claimed

CHAP. III.

1624. May. The marriage treaty and the English Catholics.

May 31. Refusal of the French to treat without mentioning the English Catholics.

[1] Herbert to the King, June 2; *S. P. France.*
[2] Instructions to Carlisle and Kensington, *Harl. MSS.*, 1584, fol. 10.

CHAP. III.
1624.
May 31.

honours as a cardinal, which the representatives of Protestant England were unwilling to concede. At last the difficulty was got rid of by Richelieu's taking to his bed under pretence of illness. He would thus cease to enter into competition with those who were seated round a table in the sick man's chamber.

The next dispute was more serious. The English ambassadors offered to take up the treaty which had been sketched out in 1613, when a marriage had been contemplated between Charles and the Princess's elder sister Christina, and in which there was no mention of toleration except for the bride and her household. The French commissioners at once replied that this would not do. On their side they had drawn up articles framed upon the model of the Spanish treaty, and one of them contained an express engagement on the part of the King of England that no Catholic in his dominions should be molested on account of his religion.

Further discussion did not tend to remove the difficulty. "No man," said the ambassadors, "shall be persecuted for being a Catholic. But if he goes to mass he will be punished for disobeying the law." After this it is not strange that an assurance that James should give a verbal promise of his intention to show favour to the Catholics made but little impression on Lewis. Nothing less than a written engagement, he informed Carlisle, would be satisfactory. James might keep this engagement secret if he pleased. But it was indispensable that it should be in writing.[1]

June, Charles draws back.

Whatever might be the value of the French alliance, it ought to have been evident that it was not worth purchasing on these terms. It was better to go to war without the help of France than to go to war without

[1] Ville-aux-Clercs to Tillières, June $\frac{1}{11}$; Lewis XIII. to Tillières, June $\frac{9}{15}$; *Harl. MSS.* 4594, fol. 41, 64, b.

the help of the English Parliament. And if the promises solemnly given by King and Prince were to be heedlessly flung aside, it would be hopeless to expect the support of the House of Commons. Not indeed, that, at first, it seemed likely that these promises would be broken. Tillières, as soon as he was apprised of the difficulties raised in Paris, reported that, though James's scruples might perhaps be overcome, nothing was to be expected from Charles. The Prince was 'very hard,' having 'little inclination to satisfy France in these essential points.' He was surrounded by Puritans, and would soon be a Puritan himself.[1]

If Lewis's demand had been pressed in the harsh terms in which it was originally couched, the negotiation would probably have been strangled at its commencement. But La Vieuville, with wisdom beyond that of his master, was little solicitous for an engagement which it was as impolitic to exact as to give, and he was very anxious to secure the practical co-operation of England in his resistance to Spain. But La Vieuville's wisdom was for others rather than for himself, and in pursuance of his own objects he allowed himself to use words which Lewis was certain to disavow as soon as they came to his ears. "Give us," he said to the English ambassador, "some stuff with which we may satisfy the Pope, and we will throw ourselves heart and soul into your interests." "They do here," wrote Carlisle, "let fall unto us that though they are bound to make these high demands for their own honour, the satisfaction of those of the Catholic party, and particularly for the facilitating of the dispensation at Rome, yet it will be always in your Majesty's power to put the same in execution according to your own pleasure; and they do also with strong protestations labour to persuade us

CHAP. III.
1624.

June. La Vieuville hints that the demand was only made to please the Pope.

June 14.

[1] Tillières to Ville-aux-Clercs, June $\frac{6}{16}$; *Harl. MSS.* 4594, fol. 59.

CHAP. III.
1624. June.

that when the articles of marriage shall be signed, they will enter into treaty for the making of a strict conjunction with your Majesty for the redress of the general affairs of Christendom, and will declare themselves to espouse your Majesty's interests, so as both the treaties shall be ratified together."[1]

French preparations for war.

To give weight to these words the French preparations for war were hurried on. Already on the 31st of May a treaty had been drawn up by which France engaged to assist the Dutch with large sums of money, and immediately afterwards Venice and Savoy were asked to join in the support of Mansfeld. On the 19th of June three French armies were ordered to prepare themselves for active service. Two of these were posted respectively in Picardy and at Metz, whilst the third, being stationed on the frontier towards Franche Comté and Savoy, would be equally available for an attack upon the Palatinate, or for an attack upon the Valtelline.[2]

[1] Carlisle to the King, June 14; *S. P. France.* The person from whom the idea about the Pope came is not mentioned in this letter. But in a later despatch (Carlisle and Holland to Conway, Oct. 9, *S. P. France*), the words given above are quoted as La Vieuville's—" Donnez nous de faste pour contenter le Pape, et nous nous jetterons dans vos intérêts à corps perdus." At a time when Charles had the greatest interest in showing that Lewis or Richelieu had encouraged the idea that the engagement was only offered to satisfy the Pope, with the express understanding that it might be disregarded in England, no one ever ventured to state that they personally had done so. The charge was always made impersonally, and had its foundation, I believe, upon these overtures of La Vieuville. Richelieu, indeed, when pushed hard, may have said, that without the engagement the Pope would not consent, and may have made civil speeches about his readiness to oblige the King of England if it were not for the Pope; or even said that the King would not be bound in case of actual danger to the State from the Catholics. But I do not believe that he ever used words to imply that the whole engagement was a sham one, got up for the purpose of deceiving the Pope.

[2] Siri, *Mem. Rec.*, v. 603; Kensington to Conway, June 15; *S. P. France.*

As far as it is now possible to ascertain the truth, these measures made little impression on James. He ordered the Judges to see to the execution of the penal laws.[1] The French alliance suddenly ceased to form the staple of conversation at Court, and those who were behind the scenes began to make inquiries about the good looks of marriageable Princesses in Germany.[2]

CHAP. III.
1624.
Dissatisfaction in England.

La Vieuville saw that something more must be done if the negotiation was to be saved. He begged Kensington to return to England to propound a middle course. If James objected to sign an engagement, he would perhaps not object to write a letter containing the promise required.

La Vieuville's middle course.

To give greater effect to this proposal, Tillières, who had never given more than a half-hearted support to the marriage, was recalled. His successor was the Marquis of Effiat, a man endowed with much of the tact and ability of Gondomar. He had not been in England many days before he found his way to the heart of James by eagerly listening to his long stories about his triumphs in the hunting field. But he was too clear-sighted not to perceive that his chief effort must be made in another direction. Buckingham, now recovered from his illness, was again at Court, and whoever could gain the ear of Buckingham had gone far to secure the approbation of his master.

Effiat sent as ambassador to England.

The French demands which had startled James and his son, had not startled Buckingham. To embark with all his heart upon some darling scheme, to cast aside all obstacles as not existing, was the course dictated to Buckingham by his sanguine and energetic nature. He was now bent on chastising Spain and reconquering the Palatinate. These objects he believed

July. Buckingham gained by Effiat.

[1] *Salvetti's Newsletter*, June 18/28.
[2] Nethersole to Carleton, June 25; *S. P., Dom.* clxviii. 40.

CHAP. III.
1624.
July.

could only be attained with French aid; if so, we may imagine him arguing, the terms laid down by France must be complied with. When Europe was at his feet, who would think of reminding him of the Royal promise that those terms should not be granted? He assured Effiat that he would stake his personal reputation on the success of the marriage negotiations. He was ready to row in the same boat with him. If the marriage did not take place it would be his ruin.¹

La Vieuville's proposal accepted by James.

It was a momentous resolution—how momentous for himself and for England, Buckingham little knew. Before Effiat's courteous flattery all difficulties faded away, and though the ambassador had not himself been entrusted with the secret of La Vieuville's suggestion, his presence was none the less favourable to its reception. And after all, to write a letter could hardly be a breach of the Royal promise. When Kensington returned to Paris he carried with him the news that James was ready to embody in a letter his already declared resolution to show favour to his Catholic subjects.

Aug. 2.
Disgrace of La Vieuville.

James had taken but a little step in advance; he doubtless intended that the letter should not contain any binding engagement, but he had left the firm ground on which he had hitherto stood, and if he once began to discuss with a foreign sovereign the administration of the English law, it would be hard for him to know where to stop. Before long, he had to face the alternative of going further or of drawing back altogether. When Kensington reached Paris he found that he had toiled in vain. La Vieuville's proposal about the letter had been made without his master's knowledge, in the belief that the thing when once done would be accepted

¹ Effiat to Lewis XIII., July 6/16; *Harl. MSS.*, 4594, fol. 115.

with gratitude. As soon as the truth came to the ears of Lewis, he dismissed his too independent minister and placed the direction of the government of France in the hands of Richelieu.

CHAP. III.
1624. August.

Whether Richelieu concurred in the stringent demands which he was now instructed to put forward, it is impossible to say. In the memoirs which he left behind, it was his studied object to falsify history in order to show that everything actually done proceeded from his own deliberate judgment. The real facts can often be shown, and still oftener suspected to have been very different from the representation which he has given of them. Instead of being the author of all that was done in his name, he was in these early years of his ministry the servant of a jealous master, who was careless indeed of details, and ready to leave high authority in the hands of one capable of exercising it, but who took good care to exact submission to his general views. And for the present Lewis had made up his mind to demand from England, as the price of his sister's hand, concessions to the English Catholics which would make that alliance thoroughly unstable. This was the mistaken policy of which Richelieu, willingly or unwillingly, made himself the mouthpiece. It is possible that, unversed as he was in English Parliamentary politics, he may have believed that the relaxation of the penal laws would be more easily attainable than it really was. At all events he had hardly any choice. If he refused his concurrence in the designs of Lewis he would fall as La Vieuville had fallen before him. The clergy, backed by a powerful party at Court and in the country, would have stood up as one man to advocate the resumption of the old friendly relations with Spain. Richelieu, therefore, if he was to hold his ground, must speak plainly to the English ambassadors. He would preserve all forms of

Richelieu's policy only to be known by conjecture.

Aug. 4. Richelieu demands an article for the English Catholics.

CHAP. III.
1624.
August.

courtesy, but they must understand that the concession demanded was a serious matter.

Richelieu, in fact, was not likely to fall into La Vieuville's mistake of fancying his power greater than it was. He understood that the need of satisfying the Pope should still be pleaded for the unwelcome requirements of Lewis. But he would take care that the Pope should be really satisfied. The King assured the ambassadors with studied politeness that the word of his dear brother would content him as well as either article or oath. But it would not content the Pope. The ambassadors betook themselves to the Cardinal. Was this the reply, they asked, which they were to deliver to their master. "Assuredly," answered Richelieu, "if the King said there must be an article, an article there must be." "Is this, then," they asked again, "the answer we are to give?" "Yes," he replied, "for you will find no other." The next day he spoke with the same resolution. "On my salvation," he said, "we must have either an article or a writing—baptize it by what name you will—signed and sworn to, so as to oblige the good faith of your King."

Aug. 5.

Carlisle and Kensington betook themselves to the Queen Mother. "We let her know," to use the words of their own narrative, "the impossibility of it, both in regard of the engagement of his Majesty's Royal word to his Parliament to the contrary, and that upon the motion and prayer of the Prince his son; and of the necessity of keeping himself free in that point to entertain good intelligence betwixt him and his subjects for the better enabling him to the common good." The ambassadors further reported that the Queen answered not a word, though she contrived, with all the grace of her southern breeding, to look as if she would gladly have satisfied them if she could.[1]

Both James and Charles, who were together at Rufford when the despatches announcing the new proposal reached them, agreed in rejecting the demand of an article. A letter, they probably argued, would simply announce their intention of showing favour to the Catholics; an article constituted an obligation. Conway was therefore directed to inform Effiat that if the arrangement made with La Vieuville was to be disavowed, the negotiation must be considered as broken off.[2] Charles was as decided as his father. "If," he wrote to Carlisle, "you perceive they persist in this new way that they have begun, in making an article for our Roman Catholic subjects, dally no more with them, but break off the treaty of marriage, keeping the friendship on as fair terms as you can. And, believe it, ye shall have as great honour with breaking upon these terms as with making the alliance. Yet use what industry you can to reduce them to reason, for I respect the person of the lady as being a worthy creature, fit to be my wife; but as ye love me, put it to a quick issue one way or other."[3]

Effiat felt that his diplomacy would be tested to the uttermost. His only hope lay in Buckingham, who was drinking the waters at Wellingborough, the curative properties of which had recently come into repute. Buckingham's aid was easily obtained, and he offered at once to accompany the Frenchman to the Court, which had by this time removed to Derby. On their way they met a courier with despatches for the ambas-

CHAP. III.

1624.
Aug. 12.
Refusal of James and his son to agree to the change.

Aug. 13.

Effiat appeals to Buckingham.

Aug. 14.

[1] Carlisle and Kensington to Conway, Aug. 7; *S. P. France*.
[2] Conway to Carlisle and Kensington, Aug. 12; *Hardw. St. P.*, i. 523.
[3] Charles to Carlisle, Aug. 13; *S. P. France*.

sadors in France. At Effiat's suggestion, Buckingham asked for the packet, broke the seal, and, having ascertained its contents, carried it back with him to James to demand its alteration. When he reached Derby, the whole Court was astir. The news that the marriage had been broken off was in every mouth.

All that evening Buckingham was closeted with the King and the Prince. What passed between them we have no means of knowing, but the result was that Buckingham sent back the despatch to Effiat with about two-thirds marked for omission. Yet the Frenchman was far from having everything his own way. James still positively refused to concede the article which Richelieu demanded. He told Effiat that in the face of Parliament such an article could never be admitted. But the promise which he would give in his letter should be so worded as to guarantee the Catholics against persecution.[1]

Would a mere alteration in the wording of the proposed letter be sufficient to satisfy the French Government? Buckingham at least hoped so, and wrote to Lewis, assuring him that his master could yield no further, and adding that, in his poor opinion, more could not reasonably be asked of him.[2]

To fancy, however, that such concessions would content the French Government was to mistake the meaning of the late change of ministry. La Vieuville's policy had been the policy of Protestant alliances in Germany, and he had fallen because neither the Queen Mother nor Lewis himself was ready for so startling an innovation. What Mary de Medici aimed at by favouring her daughter's marriage with the Prince of

---

[1] Effiat to Lewis XIII., Aug. $\frac{18}{28}$; *Harl. MSS.*, 4595, fol. 134; Nethersole to Carleton, Aug. 19; *S. P. Dom.*, clxxi. 60.

[2] Buckingham to Lewis XIII., Aug. $\frac{18}{26}$; *Harl. MSS.*, 4595, fol. 160.

Wales was the acquisition of influence which would ameliorate the lot of the English Catholics. Besides this Lewis aimed at the creation of a diversion against Spain which would enable him to secure his own interests in the Valtelline, and it was Richelieu's business to carry both these wishes into effect.

CHAP. III.
1624.

As soon, therefore, as the conferences in Paris recommenced after La Vieuville's fall, Richelieu proposed an engagement drawn up in the strongest possible terms. In the form which had been agreed upon with La Vieuville, James was to write to Lewis that, in contemplation of the marriage, he would permit his Roman Catholic subjects ' to enjoy all suitable favour, and would preserve them from all persecution, as long as they continue to live without scandal, and keep themselves within the limits of the obedience of good subjects; and he will also permit them to enjoy in trust upon his word and promise as much favour and liberty as they would have had in virtue of any articles granted to Spain.' The wording, as Richelieu proposed it, ran as follows :—" The King of Great Britain will give the King a private engagement signed by himself, by the Prince his son, and by a Secretary of State, by which he will declare that, in contemplation of his dearest son and of the Princess, the sister of the Most Christian King, he will promise to all his Roman Catholic subjects, on the faith and word of a king, and in virtue of his word and oath given on the holy Gospels, that they shall enjoy all the liberty and freedom which concerns the secret exercise of their religion which was granted by the treaty of marriage made with Spain, as he does not wish his Catholic subjects to be disquieted in their persons and goods on account of their secret profession of the Catholic religion, provided that they behave

Aug. 10.
He draws up an article.

VOL. I. II

modestly, and render the obedience and fidelity which good and true subjects naturally owe to their King."[1]

CHAP. III. 1624. Aug. 14. Anger of Carlisle.

Carlisle, when he became aware what the proposal was, was in the highest degree indignant. Whether these words were placed in the actual contract or not, there was no doubt, in Carlisle's mind, that their acceptance would involve an infraction of the promise given to Parliament. He refused even to reply to the French commissioners, and recommended James, if the proposed engagement were shown him by Effiat, 'to express some indignation and not to yield a whit till he heard from' his ambassadors again.[2]

Aug. 18. Kensington gained by the French.

Carlisle's colleague was made of more yielding stuff. Dissatisfied with Carlisle's attempt 'to carry all with a high hand,' and careless of any considerations beyond the success of the marriage, Kensington entered into secret communications with Richelieu, and was able, before many days were over, to paint the condescension and affability of the Cardinal in the most glowing colours. Richelieu, in fact, was loud in his professions of friendship, and threw the blame of his strictness upon the necessity of satisfying the Pope. But, though he consented to some verbal alterations, he was firm on the main point. The engagement need not form part of the contract, but it must be a binding obligation. "The signing by the Prince and Secretary," wrote Kensington, "was next questioned, because that made it a public act, whereas before we were made believe that a private promise of his Majesty's should serve the turn. It was answered that La Vieuville had therein transcended his commission, and that it was that brake his neck; that the treble signing was only to make it

---

[1] *Harl. MSS.* 4595, fol. 42, b, 55.
[2] Carlisle to Conway, Aug. 15; *S. P. France.*

more specious, that they could not think the King my master would press to change it."¹

Having thus secured an advocate in one of the English ambassadors, Richelieu was all the more confident of gaining his point. When James's draft and Buckingham's letter arrived, they were both thrust aside as offering no basis of agreement.² Some further modifications were made in the wording of the French draft, but that was all.

To support the demands of Lewis, the French Government made a great show of eagerness to give help to Mansfeld's expedition. The ambassadors were informed that the Count should be supported by France as long as he was supported by England. Nor is it altogether impossible that at this moment Lewis may have been inclined to do something in this direction. Though the mere fact of his sending Marescot to treat with the Elector of Bavaria had given umbrage to Spain,³ his plan of raising up a central party in Germany under French influence had broken down completely. Marescot, who had spent the summer in passing from one Prince to another, had just come back to report the entire failure of his mission. Many of the Princes had refused even to look at his credentials. The Elector of Saxony had treated him with the greatest rudeness, asking him 'whether there were any such King as the King of France.' On the ambassador's gravely replying 'That he could not be so ignorant as he pretended of a Prince so great and powerful,' "That is strange," said John George, mockingly, "that there should be a great and mighty King in France, and we for four years together never heard of him." To Marescot's rejoinder, that

CHAP. III.

1624.
Aug. 28.
The French demands insisted on.

Aug. 29.
Lewis promises to support Mansfeld.

Aug. 29.
Marescot in Germany.

¹ Kensington to Conway, Aug. 18; *S. P. France.*
² Lewis XIII. to Effiat, $\frac{\text{Aug. 28}}{\text{Sept. 7}}$; *Harl. MSS.*, 4595, fol. 219.
³ Philip IV. to the Infanta Isabella, March $\frac{8}{18}$; *Brussels MSS.*

VOL. I. *H 2

CHAP. III.
1624.

Sept.
The concessions to the Catholics discussed in England.

Buckingham supports Effiat.

this answer savoured too much of the Spanish faction,' the Elector's reply was prompt. "If I had been of the French," he said, "I had likewise perished, as I have seen those other Princes that depended upon that crown do before me."[1]

Such scorn flung openly in the face of a French ambassador was likely to provoke Lewis to more decided action, and the knowledge that this was the case may well have had weight with the English Government in their consideration of the amount of concession to be made on the subject of the English Catholics. When once James had agreed to put his promises upon paper at all, it was difficult for him to know where to stop. Each new alteration proposed seemed to involve but a little step of retreat from his original position, and it was not till the whole was yielded that the full extent of the ground lost could be measured. Yet on this occasion James was by no means inclined to yield. Buckingham, indeed, threw himself at once upon the side of the French. To him, the immediate object at which he aimed, the success of the marriage and the acquisition of French aid in the war, was the one thing visible. He knew that his close alliance with Effiat was regarded with suspicion at Court. Pembroke and Hamilton had raised objections to his policy, and he had good reason to believe that, when Parliament met, their objections would be urged far more strongly, and that he would be openly reproached for abandoning the position which he had taken up about the Catholics.[2] He now comported himself more as an agent of France than as an English minister. With Effiat he held long and secret consultations, placing without scruple in the French-

[1] Carlisle and Kensington to Conway, Aug. 29 / Sept. 8 ; S. P. France.
[2] "Où" i.e. in Parliament, "il se trouve à présent en ombrages, pour n'avoir pas tenu ses paroles contre les dits Catholiques."

man's hands the despatches of Carlisle and Kensington almost as soon as they were received. And it was not long before he gained over the Prince, whose mind was always fertile in excuses for doing that which at the moment he wished to do.

CHAP. III.
1624.
Sept.
The Prince gained over.

The old King was thus isolated. For two whole days he resisted the united pleadings of his favourite and his son. On the third day he gave way so far as to accept the formula offered by the French. But he saved his conscience by insisting that it should take the shape of a letter and not of an engagement, either in the contract or out of it.[1] "The business," wrote Charles to Carlisle, forgetful of his decision taken less than a month before, "is all brought to so good an issue that, if it is not spoiled at Rome, I hope that the treaties will be shortly brought to a happy conclusion, wherefore I pray you warn your Monsieur that the least stretching more breaks the string, and then Spain will laugh at both."[2]

Sept. 7. Decision of James.

Sept. 9. Satisfaction of the Prince.

One formality remained to be fulfilled. It was the custom in England, as Buckingham explained to Effiat, to submit treaties either to the Privy Council or to a select committee of its members. It was the more necessary to take this course now as he had little doubt that in the approaching session of Parliament an attack would be made upon him for advising the King to stop the execution of the Recusancy laws. If the Privy Councillors could be made partakers in the offence, they would be unable to open their mouths against him[3] as members of either House.

The treaty submitted to the Council.

What passed in the Council we do not know. Such a consultation, invited only after the King's mind had

[1] Effiat to Ville-aux-Clercs, Sept. $\frac{11}{21}$; *Harl. MSS.*, 4595, fol. 317; Conway to Carlisle and Kensington, Sept. $\frac{14}{24}$; *S. P. France.*
[2] The Prince to Carlisle, Sept. 9; *S. P. France.*
[3] Effiat to Ville-aux-Clercs, Sept. $\frac{11}{21}$; *Harl. MSS.*, 4595, fol. 317.

been made up, can scarcely have had any real value except for the purpose indicated by Buckingham. The resolution taken was conveyed to the ambassadors in Paris. "His Majesty," wrote Conway to them, "cannot be won to any more in largeness of promise or any other form, it being apparent to all this kingdom what promise the Prince hath made and the King approved, not to enter into articles or conditions with any other Prince for the immunities of his subjects Roman Catholics, that being indeed to part his sovereignty, and give a portion to another king."[1] It was a poor shred of comfort for James to wrap himself in. A letter engaging that the English Catholics should have as much freedom in the secret exercise of their religion as they would have had by the treaty with Spain might not form part of the contract, but its difference was not great, excepting that a promise given in a letter might be broken with a little less reluctance than a promise given in a contract.

James began to act on the assumption that everything was settled. Kensington, whose facile compliance with the French demands had endeared him more than ever to Buckingham, was raised to the Earldom of Holland in approbation of his conduct.

The Privy Council had consented, not merely to the form of the treaty, but also to that which was its necessary consequence, the suspension of the laws against the Recusants.[2] The immediate result was most disastrous to a good understanding between the King and his people. Whether the promise given by James

---

[1] Conway to Carlisle and Kensington, *Harl. MSS.*, 1593, fol. 266. The letter is undated, but was probably written on Sept. 5.

[2] Effiat to Lewis XIII., $\frac{\text{Sept. 26}}{\text{Oct. 6}}$; *Harl. MSS.*, 1596, fol. 17, b. Effiat speaks of a *supersedeas* under the great seal, of which no trace is to be found on the Patent rolls. Probably there is some mistake arising from a foreigner's ignorance of legal forms.

and his son about the Catholics had been broken or
not, it was certain that the promise about summoning
Parliament in November could not now be kept. How
would it be possible to face the Commons? When
once the bride was in England it would be too late to
remonstrate on the conditions on which she had come.
But if Parliament met before the step had been irrevocably taken, who could answer for the consequences?
The Houses were therefore prorogued to the 26th of
February, on the transparent pretext that London had
become too unhealthy to be a safe place of meeting.
Care was taken to insert in the proclamation a statement that this course had been adopted in pursuance
of the advice of the Council.[1]

CHAP. III.

1624.
Oct. 1.
Parliament prorogued.

The chances of winning over the hard heads of the
House of Commons to an unpopular domestic policy
with the aid of the charms of the young Queen were
not very great. Unless Buckingham could escape the
consequences of his actions in a blaze of military glory,
he was plainly doomed to be taunted with apostasy
from the cause which he had voluntarily adopted. To
some extent the news which reached him from the
Continent sounded hopefully in his ears. The Kings
of Sweden and Denmark were bidding against one
another for English support, and the Duke of Savoy
was eager to make use of the English navy for designs
of his own against Genoa. It was true that Buckingham

Buckingham's war policy.

[1] Proclamation, Oct. 1, *Rymer*, xvii. 625. The prorogation was really ordered 'for many weighty considerations, but principally this, that the respect of the Princess of France, and the reverence which will be given to her person when she shall be here, for those graces and virtues that shine in her, as likewise for the love and duty borne to the Prince, being all joined in her, will not only stay the exorbitant or ungentle motions that might otherwise be made in the House of Parliament, but will facilitate in his Majesty's proceedings those passages of favours, grace, and goodness which his Majesty hath promised for the ease of the Roman Catholics.' Buckingham to Nithsdale, Oct. (?); *Ellis*, ser. 1, iii. 179.

CHAP. III.
1624. Oct.

had no money with which to pay the fleets and armies which he was busily organizing in his imagination. The supplies voted in the last session had been devoted to special objects, and he had just cut off for five months all possibility of obtaining more from a legitimate source. But financial considerations seldom obtruded themselves upon Buckingham. If the war were only once begun on a scale large enough to dazzle the world, he might safely, he fancied, throw himself upon the patriotism of the English nation.

July. Refusal of the Council of War to supply Mansfeld.

It was a hazardous policy. Armies set on foot upon the chance of future supplies are apt to be less dangerous to the enemy than to their own commanders. And yet what else was to be done? An attempt had been made in vain to divert some of the subsidy money to the support of Mansfeld. The Council of War had replied by asking whether the King would give them a written declaration that he needed the money 'for one of those four ends mentioned in the statute.' Weston, who had been sent to ask for the money, could not say that, but he knew 'that it was both his Majesty's and the Prince's pleasure.' He was told distinctly that without 'some particular warrant in writing nothing could be done.'[1]

Questions arising out of Mansfeld's employment.

And even if Buckingham had been able to raise the money which he needed, was it likely that Mansfeld's armament would gain for him the good will of the House of Commons? If the force which it had been proposed to levy had been directed towards the Palatinate, such an employment would have been entirely outside the circle of ideas within which the Lower House had been moving. But by this time Buckingham had reason to question whether France was

[1] Weston to Conway, July 31; *S. P. Dom.*, clxx. 82.

disposed to give even that amount of satisfaction to the wishes of the King of England. On the 26th of August a league was signed between France, Venice, and Savoy for the recovery of the Valtelline; and in order to prevent the Spanish Government from bringing up fresh troops to resist the attack, it was arranged that the Duke of Savoy, with the aid of a French force, should make an attack upon Genoa, and that Mansfeld should throw himself upon Alsace and the Austrian possessions in Swabia.[1]

CHAP. III. 1624. Aug. 26. The League for the recovery of the Valtelline.

Whilst James and Buckingham, therefore, were fondly hoping to make use of Richelieu for the reconquest of the Palatinate, Richelieu was planning how to make use of James and Buckingham for the reconquest of the Valtelline. Although the result of Marescot's embassy to Germany had been discouraging, Richelieu had assured the Elector of Bavaria that he need have no fear of an attack from France for at least a year, and Effiat was instructed to lay before James a plan for the pacification of Germany which bore a very close resemblance to those unsatisfactory overtures which had been made by Francesco della Rota in the preceding winter.[2]

Richelieu and Germany.

Richelieu was probably right in judging that this was as much as he could persuade his master to do for some time to come; perhaps also in judging that it would be unwise for France to embark in open war till it was clear that she could find allies who could be trusted. But when Buckingham passed his neck under the yoke of the imperious Cardinal, he had certainly expected more than this.

Towards the end of September Mansfeld was once

Sept. Mansfeld again in England.

[1] Siri, *Mem. Rec.*, v. 639, 680.
[2] Richelieu, *Mém.*, ii. 405; Lewis XIII. to Effiat, Sept. $\frac{7}{17}$; *Harl. MSS.*, 4595, fol. 307.

CHAP. III.
1624.
Sept.

more in England, to ask again for men and money. His English troops, if he persuaded James to entrust him with any, would be allowed to land between Calais and Gravelines close to the Flemish frontier.¹ The King of France, he announced, was ready to allow him to levy thirteen thousand men, and would, in conjunction with his allies, supply him with money for the purpose.² But the French ministers, who had so pertinaciously demanded the strictest acknowledgment of the rights of the English Catholics, refused to bind themselves to any definite course in their military operations by a single line in writing. In the meanwhile, Lewis wrote to Effiat informing him that what was given to Mansfeld was given 'for the affairs of our league,' that is to say, for the support of his operations in the Valtelline. If the men could also be useful to the King of England and his son-in-law, he should be glad. After the marriage had been agreed upon, he would be able to deliberate further.³

Oct.
A written engagement demanded from France.

Such was the position of affairs at the time when the English Parliament was prorogued. Buckingham, it would seem, had sold his master's honour for naught. To his thinking, indeed, the only course left to him was to push blindly on. If he had had his way, 20,000*l.* would have been placed at once in Mansfeld's hands. James listened, well pleased, to the talk of the adventurer, and amused him by recommending him to ask leave of the Infanta to pass through the Spanish Netherlands on his way to the Palatinate.⁴ But there was still some prudence left in the English Court. The Council recommended a short delay till Lewis had

¹ Lewis XIII to Effiat, $\frac{\text{Sept. 24}}{\text{Oct. 4}}$; *Harl. MSS.*, 4595, fol. 369.
² Effiat to Lewis XIII., $\frac{\text{Sept. 26}}{\text{Oct. 6}}$; *Harl. MSS.*, 4596, fol. 17, b.
³ Lewis XIII. to Effiat, $\frac{\text{Sept. 30}}{\text{Oct. 10}}$; *Harl. MSS.*, 4596, fol. 33.
⁴ Rusdorf to Frederick, Oct. $\frac{2}{12}$; *Mém.*, i. 377.

given a written promise to allow Mansfeld's troops to enter France, and to permit their employment for the recovery of the Palatinate. In the meanwhile Mansfeld was to go to Holland to muster some Germans who were to take part in the expedition.¹

In a few days James learned that he had reckoned without the French in respect both of the marriage and of Mansfeld's army. Carlisle and Holland were plainly told that their master's letter, even if countersigned by the Prince and a Secretary of State, would not suffice, and were informed at the same time that there could be no offensive league for the present. "To capitulate in writing," said the French ministers, " would but cast rubs in the way of their dispensation, and make it altogether impossible ; since it must needs highly offend the Pope to hear they should enter into an offensive league with heretics against Catholics, and was like so far to scandalize the Catholic Princes of Germany, as this King should lose all credit with them, whom yet he hoped to win to their better party." In vain the ambassadors remonstrated. Not a line in writing could be drawn from the French ministers. 'They could not,' they said, ' condescend to anything in writing ; but if the King's faith and promise would serve the turn, that should be renewed to us here, and to his Majesty likewise by their ambassador in England, in as full and ample manner as we could desire it.' A long altercation followed, and the English ambassadors broke off the interview in high dudgeon, saying that ' they knew not whether when the King their master should hear of this their proceeding he might not open his ear to new counsels, and embrace such offers as might come to him from other parts, and leave them

¹ Rusdorf to Frederick, Oct. $\frac{5}{15}$, $\frac{6}{16}$; *Mém.*, i. 379, 381 ; Conway to Carlisle and Holland, *Hardw. St. P.*, i. 532.

CHAP. III.
1624.
Aug. 13.
Carlisle's opinion.

perhaps to seek place for repentance when it would be too late.'[1] In a private letter to the Prince, Carlisle expressed his opinion strongly. "It may therefore please your Highness," he wrote, "to give your humblest servant leave, out of his zeal and devotion to your Highness' service, to represent unto your Highness that our endeavours here will be fruitless unless you speak unto the French ambassador in a higher strain, and that my Lord of Buckingham also hold the same language unto him. It is true that they do offer the King's word for their assistance, and that their ambassador shall give his Majesty the like assurance; but what assurance can be given to the verbal promise of this people, who are so apt to retract or give new interpretations to their former words, . . your Highness, out of your excellent wisdom, will easily discern."[2]

The French plan supported by Buckingham.

With respect to the marriage treaty, so much had been yielded already that a point or two further hardly mattered much. Buckingham had before him the vision of an angry Parliament, incensed with him, as he told Effiat, because he 'had so far departed from the promises that had been made.'[3] Startling news, too, reached him from Spain. Inojosa, as might have been expected, had, after a mock investigation, been fully acquitted of the charge of conspiring against Buckingham. But the party opposed to Olivares had sufficient weight in the Council to make one more effort to avoid a breach with England, and a resolution was taken to send Gondomar once more to England in Coloma's

[1] Carlisle and Holland to Conway. [Oct. 9]; *Hardw. St. P.*, i. 536; date from copy in *S. P. France.*
[2] Carlisle to Charles, Oct. 7; *ibid.* i. 535.
[3] "À cause qu'ils disent que le Duc s'est fort éloigné des promesses qui leur avoient été faites." Effiat to Ville-aux-Clercs, Sept. 26/Oct. 6; *Harl. MSS.* 4596, fol. 25.

room. The prospect of seeing the winning Spaniard again whispering his words of command in James's ear was very terrible to Buckingham. What would be the result if Gondomar should find new and unexpected allies in the House of Commons?

If it was to be a question whether the King should give way to Spain or to France, Charles was sure to place himself on Buckingham's side, and he joined in urging his father to make the required concession. "Your despatch," he wrote to Carlisle, "gave us enough ado to keep all things from an unrecoverable breach. For my father at first startled very much at it, and would scarce hear reason, which made us fear that his averseness was built upon some hope of good overtures from Gondomar, who, they say, is to be shortly here, though I believe it not; which made me deal plainly with the King, telling him I would never match with Spain, and so entreated him to find a fit match for me. Though he was a little angry at first, yet afterwards he allowed our opinions to be reason, which before he rejected."[1]

It was like Charles to suppose that his father could not be really influenced by the motives he professed, and to fancy that it was impossible for any one to differ from himself with any semblance of reason. Yet if the concession which he was now recommending had been laid before him six months before, he would doubtless have started back with amazement and horror. He had directly engaged that his marriage should bring 'no advantage to the Recusants.'[2] As for James, a loop-hole was still left to him. He had promised that 'no such condition' should be 'foisted in upon any other treaty whatsoever.'[3] He was not asked to do precisely that.

[1] The Prince to Carlisle, Oct. 19; *S. P. France.*
[2] P. 56.   [3] P. 59.

He was to keep his word in the letter, whilst breaking it in its spirit. The article, separate from the treaty, was to be called a private engagement. But it was to be made as binding as possible by his own and his son's signature, attested by that of a Secretary of State. Surely this was enough to startle James without its being necessary to seek for an explanation of his reluctance to give his assent in some imaginary overtures from Gondomar.

To his own disgrace Charles had his way. James had not strength of mind enough to break up the alliance on which he had counted for the restoration of the Palatinate. Orders were sent to the ambassadors to accept the French proposals. But what was James to gain in return? The verbal promise of support to Mansfeld, which was all that Lewis offered, was plainly not worth having. "We think it not fit," wrote Carlisle and Holland, "to express by writing the sense we have of the proceedings of the French."[1] Lewis, in fact, had agreed to declare his intention of continuing his contribution to Mansfeld for six months, and of allowing it to be used for the recovery of the Palatinate. If, however, 'the affairs of the Palatinate were not settled within this time, his Majesty would continue in every way which he might consider most fitting, to testify to his brother the King of Great Britain his desire that he might receive contentment in the matter of the Palatinate.'[2] Against this wording the ambassadors protested. Instead of declaring that he would aid 'in every way which he might consider most fitting,' Lewis might at least say that he would aid in every way that was most fitting. They were told that this could not

---

[1] Carlisle and Holland to Conway, Oct 28; *S. P. France.*
[2] Ville-aux-Clercs to Effiat, $\frac{Oct. 25}{Nov. 4}$; *Harl. MSS.*, 4596, fol. 45.

be. In that case, they replied, they would rather not listen at all to so illusory a promise. Acting, no doubt, in pursuance of orders from England, they said that they would be content with a simple promise to pay Mansfeld for six months. To this Lewis cheerfully consented, and, in giving the promise, added a few words still vaguer than those to which objection had been taken. "As to the continuance of my assistance for the Palatinate," he said, "let my good brother the King of Great Britain confide in my affection, which I will show by my deeds and acting rather than by my words and promises."[1]

On these terms the marriage treaty was signed by the ambassadors on November 10. It needed only the ratification of the King of England and the grant of the Papal dispensation to be carried into effect.

What was now to be done for Mansfeld? Was he, without any real understanding with France, to be launched into the heart of Germany? And if a scheme so rash was to be persisted in, where was the 20,000*l*. which James would be called upon to pay month by month. The exchequer had not in it a farthing applicable to the purpose. The Council of War had shown by its former answer that its members did not believe that the subsidies were intended to be expended in such a way, and without an order from the Council of War the Parliamentary Treasurers could give nothing. But for the turn which the marriage arrangements had taken, Parliament would by this time have been in full session, able either to grant the sum required or to give the King plainly to understand that no further subsidies would be forthcoming for the purpose.

[1] Carlisle and Holland to Conway, Oct. 28, Nov. 12; *Hardw. St. P.*

CHAP. III.

1624. Nov.

Where was money to be found?

In default of Parliament, application had again been made to the Council of War. Payments for such an expedition as Mansfeld's were perhaps covered by the letter of the Subsidy Act, as being intended to assist 'other his Majesty's friends and allies,' but they were certainly in contravention of its spirit. Besides, even if this had not been the case, there was no money really applicable to the purpose. It would tax all the powers of the Treasurers to meet the demands made upon them for the four points expressly named in the Act, and it was only by neglecting one or other of them that it would be possible to divert something for Mansfeld.

By what arguments the Council of War was swayed we do not know. But on October 4 a warrant,

Nov. 24. Payments out of the subsidies.

followed up by another on November 24, was issued by that body to empower the Treasurers to advance 15,000*l*. for the expenses of levying troops for Mansfeld, and 40,000*l*. to pay his men for two months.[1]

Oct. 29.

Nov. 4. Mansfeld in England.

On October 29 orders had been given to levy 12,000 pressed men for this service.[2] On November 4 Mansfeld landed at Margate on his return from Holland. On the 7th he received a comission empowering him to take command of the troops. He was to use them for the recovery of the Palatinate, doing nothing against the King's friends and allies,

He is not to touch Spanish territory.

especially doing nothing against 'the lands and dominions of which the King of Spain our very dear brother, and the Infanta, have a just and legitimate possession.'[3]

---

[1] Abstract of the warrants of the Council of War, June 1625; *S. P. Dom., Charles I.*, Addenda.

[2] *Signet Office Docquets*, Oct. 29.

[3] Rusdorf to Frederick, Nov. 5: The King to Mansfeld, Nov. 7; *Rusdorf's Mem.*, i. 390, 392.

The troops, in short, were to be used for the purposes for which they were intended, and for nothing else. If a war with Spain must come, let it come after due deliberation, and not as the result of one of those raids which Mansfeld knew so well how to plan and to execute.

Assuredly reasons were not wanting to justify James in the policy of carrying the war into Germany rather than against Spain. But there is nothing to be said for the means which he adopted to secure his end. Mansfeld himself was a man upon whom no dependence could be placed. Even in the little Court which gathered round the exiles at the Hague, he was no longer regarded with favour. Camerarius, one of the ablest of Frederick's counsellors, predicted that no good would come of his employment. "From this," he wrote, "the restoration of the Palatinate is not to be expected. Indeed I see many other objections; and if Mansfeld has with him foreign soldiers, instead of an army for the most part composed of Germans, the whole Empire will be leagued against him. I fear, too, that Duke Christian[1] may combine with him, and he is alike hateful to God and man. The time requires not such defenders."

Broken and divided as Germany was, there was still some national feeling left. To fling a couple of adventurers with an army of foreigners into the heart of the country was not the way to conciliate this feeling. And as yet no arrangement had been come to with the German Princes. It was not upon any understanding with them that Mansfeld's projects were based. Nor, even if the chances of a foreign invasion had been greater than they were, was this invasion one which

[1] *i.e.*, Christian of Brunswick, the late Administrator of Halberstadt.

could be regarded hopefully. For, of the two governments by which it was to be supported, one was anxious to employ the troops against Spain, whilst the other was anxious to employ them in Germany.

There were, in fact, two policies, each of which was not without its merits. A close alliance with France to attack Spain would probably not have been without its fruits in lightening the weight which pressed upon the German Protestants. On the other hand a close alliance with Sweden, Denmark, the Dutch Republic, and the Princes of North Germany would probably have been more directly effectual for the recovery of the Palatinate. In the first case the co-operation of the Northern Protestants; in the second case the co-operation of France, would have to be regarded as of secondary importance.

The course which was actually taken was the result of the several faults of James and Buckingham. It satisfied the King's caution by the appearance of strength which he saw in an alliance reaching from Stockholm to Paris. It satisfied Buckingham's impetuosity, because England in reality stood alone, and was preparing to throw her only army into the midst of Europe without any trustworthy or ascertained alliance on any side.

James's notion that it was possible to treat the question of the Palatinate apart, without giving offence to Spain, was one which could hardly bear the test of conversion into practical action.[1] He had thought to mingle in a strife in which the passions of men were deeply engaged, without taking account of anything but their reason, and he had fancied that he could measure their reason by his own. He had expected his son-in-law to forget his injuries, and to consent to

[1] The impossibility of Spain remaining neutral if the Palatinate were attached, is clearly put in a letter from the Infanta Isabella to Philip IV., April $\frac{9}{19}$. *Brussels MSS.*

take his place again at Heidelberg as a peaceable subject of the Empire. He had expected the King of Spain, in spite of the deep distrust which he entertained of Frederick, to help him back into his old position. And he now expected the Infanta Isabella to surrender Frankenthal to an English garrison according to the treaty made in the spring of the preceding year.[1] The Infanta replied that she was quite ready to give up the town to an English garrison if James would send one to the gates; but she declined to assure that garrison against the probable danger of an attack from the Imperialist forces in the neighbourhood. Clearly the Spaniards were not about to assist in the recovery of the Palatinate.

CHAP. III.
1624.
Nov.
Frankenthal demanded from the Infanta.

Would France be more likely to help than Spain had been? For a moment James and Buckingham were able to flatter themselves that it would be so. On November 18 it was known in London [2] that, when the marriage treaty was signed, Lewis had promised with his own Royal mouth that Mansfeld should have liberty to land at Boulogne or Calais; that the letters of exchange for the French share of his expenses had actually been seen by the ambassadors; and that Richelieu had assured Carlisle and Holland that 'they had not so much linked together two persons as two Crowns, and that the interest of the Palatinate was as dear to them as to the English.'[3]

France gives hopes of aid.

At the news that the treaty had been signed the bells of the London churches rung out their merriest peals, and healths were drunk to the future Queen of England around bonfires in the streets.[4] And yet the

Nov. 21.
Rejoicings in London.

[1] *Prince Charles and the Spanish Marriage*, ii. 367.
[2] Rusdorf to Frederick, Nov. 20; *Mem.*, i. 394.
[3] Carlisle and Holland to Conway, Nov. 12; *S. P. France.*
[4] *Salvetti's Newsletter*, Nov. 26/Dec. 6.

CHAP. III.

1624.
Nov. 17.
French view of Mansfeld's expedition.

French Court had already made up its mind to draw back from the slight engagement into which Lewis had entered a few days before. The preparations for the attack upon the Valtelline were now complete; and, though it could not be known in Paris that the French force which had started from Coire on November 15 would sweep all opposition before it, there could be no doubt that the result would be determined long before Spanish troops could reach the scene of action from Flanders. So far as the Valtelline was concerned, therefore, there was no further need of Mansfeld's assistance.

What steps Lewis and Richelieu intended to take with respect to Germany in the next summer's campaign it is impossible to say. Most probably they did not know themselves. But we may be quite sure that they never seriously entertained the idea of allowing Mansfeld to pass through France to attack the Imperial garrisons in the Palatinate, whilst England remained at peace with Spain.

To those who are desirous of abandoning their engagements a good excuse is seldom wanting. The Spanish Government at this time combined a full appreciation of the benefits of peace, with a firm determination not to make those concessions which would alone make peace possible. In the past winter and spring Philip and Olivares had been quite in earnest in desiring to make peace in Germany, upon terms which would have secured the triumph of their own religion; and in the spring they had been equally in earnest in desiring to make a final peace with the revolted Netherlands, if only they could secure the opening of the Scheldt to the commerce of Antwerp, by which means, as the Infanta Isabella assured her nephew, the trade of Amsterdam would be entirely ruined. On July 3, the

THE SIEGE OF BREDA. 117

day after her letter was written, news arrived in Brussels that her overtures had been rejected at the Hague, and that the Dutch had entered into a league with France on the 11th. Spinola, who had remained inactive since his failure at Bergen-op-Zoom in 1622, marched at the head of his army[1] to lay siege to Breda.

CHAP. III.
1624.
Nov. 17.
The siege of Breda.

To the Prince of Orange, Breda was no common town. In it was the house in which his ancestors had dwelt whilst as yet the seventeen Provinces reposed peacefully under Spanish rule. Its recovery from the enemy had been his own earliest military exploit. Upon the ramparts and inundations by which Breda was guarded, he had lavished all the resources of his own consummate skill as a military engineer. "Have you seen Breda?" he used to say to travellers who spoke boastfully of this or that fortress which they had visited. And now, as he was himself wasting away with enfeebled health and forced inaction, this town, so dear to him as a man and as a soldier, was in danger. The forces of the Republic were not sufficient to justify him in running the risk of an attempt to save it.

During his last visit to Holland, Mansfeld had suggested to Maurice that the English troops entrusted to him might be employed in relieving Breda.[2] Lewis, too, who was sending over the secretary Ville-aux-Clercs to receive James's oath to the engagement he was to take about the Catholics, instructed him to argue that Mansfeld would be far better employed in succouring Breda than he would be in Alsace or Franche-Comté, especially as it would be impossible for him to march into the Palatinate in the winter.[3] In fact, if

The French wish to employ Mansfeld at Breda.

[1] The Infanta Isabella to Philip IV., July $\frac{2}{12}, \frac{3}{13}, \frac{19}{29}$; *Brussels MSS.*
[2] Villermont, *E. de Mansfeldt*, ii. 240.
[3] Instructions to Ville-aux-Clercs, Nov. $\frac{17}{27}$; *Harl. MSS.*, 4596, fol. 106.

CHAP. III.
1624.
Nov.

Unwillingness of James.

Mansfeld was not to be used at Breda, it was difficult to say how he could be used at all.[1] Even if the French had been more than half-hearted in the matter, it would have been premature to send him into Germany without any previous arrangement with the German Princes. And why, the French ministers might well argue, should James object? Six thousand soldiers were already serving in his pay under Maurice against Spain, and why should not twelve thousand under Mansfeld do the same? It was perhaps hard to meet the logical difficulty. But James drew a line between assisting the Dutch against Spain, and sending an independent force with the same object. He had fallen back upon the belief that he could escape a war with Spain after all. The fleet, which in the beginning of the summer had been gathering in the Spanish harbours, had been called off across the Atlantic by the news that San Salvador, in Brazil, had been captured by a Dutch force, and there had, in consequence, been the less necessity for proceeding hastily with the equipment of the English navy. Lest Spain should take umbrage at what little had been done, James explained to the Infanta's agent that the ships which he was preparing were intended to convoy the French Princess to England, and to make reprisals on the Dutch East India Company for the massacre of Amboyna. At the same time he repeated his assurance that Mansfeld should not attack Spanish territory.[2]

[1] The Infanta Isabella, writing to Philip IV., Nov. $\frac{19}{29}$, argued that the troops must be intended for Breda, for it was not the season of the year to begin war in Germany. The greater part of the troops would perish before they could reach that country. *Brussels MSS.*

[2] This was probably said about Nov. 19. The declaration is printed without a date by Villermont, *E. de Mansfeldt*, ii. 242. The order for reprisals on the Dutch had really been given. Conway to Carleton Nov. 4; *S. P. Holland.*

When Ville-aux-Clercs arrived, his first task was to obtain the ratification of the marriage treaty. The King was at Cambridge, suffering from a severe attack of the gout. His hands were so crippled that, like Henry VIII. in his old age, he had been obliged to make use of a stamp from inability to sign his name. On December 12, however, though still suffering, he was sufficiently recovered to be able to join his son in ratifying the articles of marriage. Much to the discontent of the Privy Councillors, not one of the number, excepting Buckingham and Conway, were allowed to be present at the ceremony.

CHAP.
III.

1624.
Dec. 12.
The marriage treaty ratified.

There remained the private engagement to be signed : " I the undersigned Charles, Prince of Wales," so ran the words finally agreed upon, " after having seen the promise of the Most Serene King of Great Britain, my very honoured Lord and father, and in conformity with it, promise on the faith and word of a Prince, both for the present and the future, in everything that is and shall be in my power, that, in contemplation of the Most Serene Princess Madame Henrietta Maria, sister of the Most Christian King of France, I will promise to all the Roman Catholic subjects of the Crown of Great Britain the utmost of liberty and franchise in everything regarding their religion, which they would have had in virtue of any articles which were agreed upon by the treaty of marriage with Spain, not being willing that the aforesaid Roman Catholic subjects should be disquieted in their persons and goods for making profession of their aforesaid religion, and for living as Catholics, provided, however, that they use the permission modestly, and render the obedience which as good and true subjects they owe to their King. I also promise, through kindness to them, not to constrain them to any oath contrary

The private engagement.

to their religion, and I wish that my engagement, which I now sign, should be attested by a Secretary of State."[1]

Then followed the signatures of Charles and Conway. It was not a transaction upon which they had any reason to be proud. The edifice of toleration, founded upon a breach of one promise, might easily be overthrown by the breach of another. But in truth neither Charles, nor Buckingham, who was the main instigator of his offence, cared about toleration at all. What they wanted was to make the French marriage and the French alliance possible, and we may well believe that they swallowed the necessary conditions without enquiring too closely into the possibility of fulfilling them. The explanation which Charles afterwards gave, that he had signed the engagement without intending to keep it, because he was aware that the King of France wished him to do so in order to deceive the Pope, finds no countenance from any source of information now open to us.

Whatever Charles's motives may have been, the French ministers required him to act at once upon the engagement he had taken. On December 24 the Courts were forbidden to admit any further prosecution of the Recusants under the Penal laws.[2] On the 26th an order was issued to the Lord Keeper to set at liberty all Roman Catholics in prison for offences connected with their religion. At the same time the two Archbishops were directed to stop all proceedings against them in the Ecclesiastical Courts, and the Lord Treasurer was commanded to repay all fines which had been levied from them since the last Trinity Term. For the future the fines, instead of passing into the Exchequer in the ordinary course, were to be paid over to two

---

[1] Secret engagement, *Harl. MSS.*, 4596, fol. 144.
[2] Conway to Williams, Dec. 30; *S. P. Dom.*, clxxvii. 39.

persons especially appointed for the purpose, who would of course repay the money at once to those from whom they received it. In this way it would look as if the fines were still being paid, whilst nothing of the kind was really being done. Nor was this the only deception practised upon the nation. These special orders were only made known to those specially interested in them. But another order directing the banishment of the priests then in prison, which, as there was now nothing to prevent them soon returning in security as soon as they had crossed the sea, can only have been intended to throw dust into the eyes of the world, was passed under the great seal, and enrolled on the Patent Rolls for all who chose to examine.[1]

If Charles had not strengthened his position by the step which he had taken, Richelieu had still less cause to congratulate himself. He had indeed gained a great diplomatic success. All that he had asked for had been conceded to him. But the very concession was fraught with future evil to France as well as to England. If neither he nor Lewis had aimed at so much as had been aimed at by Olivares and Philip; if France had been content with the protection of the English Roman Catholics, whilst Spain aimed at the restoration of the Papal authority in England, even the lesser demand was more than one sovereign could wisely make to another. It introduced an element of discord between the two nations which would more than counterbalance the family connection which was about to join the two kings. The marriage treaty was the first link in the chain of events which in two short years was to lead to war between France and England.

[1] The King to the Archbishop of Canterbury, Dec. 26; The King to the Lord Keeper, Dec. 26; the King to the Lord Treasurer and the Chancellor of the Exchequer, Dec. 29; *S. P. Dom.*, clxxvii. 25, 29, 37; Banishment of Priests, Dec. 24; *Rymer*, xvii. 644.

CHAPTER IV.

THE LAST DAYS OF JAMES I.

<small>CHAP. IV.
1624.
Dec. 1.
Ville-aux-Clercs to ask that Mansfeld might pass through Flanders.
Dec. 14.
James consents.</small>

To obtain from James the ratification of the marriage treaty was only part of Ville-aux-Clercs' mission. He had also to obtain permission for Mansfeld to attempt to succour Breda, and to contrive if possible to embroil James in open war with Spain.[1] James, indeed, had already taken one step in the direction in which the Frenchman wished to guide him. On the 14th of December he had issued an exposition of his former prohibition to Mansfeld. 'That commander was to ask leave from the Infanta to enter Flanders, but, in the event of a refusal, he was to force his way through the Spanish territory.'[2]

<small>Further demands of France.</small>
As yet the name of Breda had not been mentioned either by Ville-aux-Clercs or James, though the relief of Breda was plainly intended by the French. James's difficulties were only beginning. He had been given to understand that Mansfeld would land in French territory, and that he was to march at once to the French frontier in order to demand a passage. But now Richelieu took alarm, or pretended to take alarm, at James's former declaration that Mansfeld should not enter the Spanish Netherlands. Before the interpreta-

---

[1] Ville-aux-Clercs and Effiat to Lewis XIII., Dec. $\frac{1}{11}$, *Harl. MSS.*, 4596, fol. 144.

[2] Explanation by the King, Dec. $\frac{14}{24}$? *Ibid.* fol. 187.

tion had been given on the 14th, orders had already been issued in the name of Lewis to Ville-aux-Clercs and Effiat to inform James that Mansfeld could not be permitted to land in France unless the English Government distinctly authorised his passage through the Spanish Netherlands. The alternative offered was that Mansfeld should go by way of Holland. Mansfeld would certainly not be permitted to march a hundred miles on French territory.[1]

CHAP. IV.
1624. Dec.

As usual, the French ambassadors applied to Buckingham, for support. The exact nature of the conversation between them cannot now be discovered. The Frenchmen were under the impression when they left him, that Mansfeld, if the passage through Flanders seemed undesirable, might take any other route he pleased, on the sole condition that the French cavalry, which was to take part in the expedition, should accompany the English infantry. They therefore wrote at once to Mansfeld, strongly urging him to convey his men through Holland,[2] instead of through France and Flanders.

Dec. 18. Misunderstanding between Buckingham and the French.

Such, however, was not the understanding of Buckingham. Perhaps, as Ville-aux-Clercs thought afterwards, he was so confident of his influence over Mansfeld that he assented to the proposal that the commander might take any route he pleased, without duly considering all that might be implied in those words.[3] Perhaps, when he came to speak to the King,

[1] Lewis XIII. to Ville-aux-Clercs and Effiat, *Harl. MSS.*, 4596, fol. 200 b.
[2] They told Mansfeld that the English would give him entire liberty ' de prendre tel parti que vous estimerez le plus avantageux sans demander de nous autre condition que la cavallerie Français prendra même route, et sera embarquée pour passer avec leur infanterie.'—Ville-aux-Clercs and Effiat to Mansfeld, Dec. $\frac{18}{29}$, *Harl. MSS.*, 4596, fol. 212 b.
[3] *Mémoires de Brienne*, i. 394.

124   THE LAST DAYS OF JAMES I.

CHAP.
IV.
1624.
Dec. 18.

and to find how reluctant James was to give his consent to the course proposed, he may have found it expedient to disavow the promise which he had heedlessly given, and it is certain that he afterwards assured Ville-aux-Clercs that he had never mentioned the possibility of Mansfeld's passing through Holland to the King. In fact something very different from a mere military question was at issue. James wished to obtain the open complicity of France in the coming war. Lewis wished to involve James in hostilities with Spain whilst himself remaining at peace. If English troops landed at Calais, and then, accompanied by French cavalry, crossed the frontier into Flanders or Artois, it would be very difficult for Lewis to wash his hands of the whole matter; whereas if a small body of cavalry joined Mansfeld's army in Holland, whatever Mansfeld chose to do might be set down to his own wrong-headedness, or to the orders of his English superiors.

The rendezvous at Dover.

In the meanwhile, the unlucky men whose destination was the object of such contention, were gathering to their rendezvous at Dover. The aid of English troops was not to be despised. The Prince of Orange, who knew them well, used to say that when Englishmen had got over their first sufferings, they were the bravest men in his motley army. The ten thousand who had gone out in the summer had been received by the Dutch with open arms. But they had advantages which Mansfeld's troops would never have. They were volunteers, not pressed men. They had been incorporated in the Dutch army, and had gradually learned their work in the strictest school of discipline then existing in the world. They would be well clothed and well fed. There may have been an exaggeration in the popular saying that an Englishman could not fight without his three B's, his bed, his beef, and his beer, but it was exaggeration which contained a certain amount of truth.¹

All that went to the making of an army was wanting to Mansfeld's compulsory levies. His men, pressed against their will, had little heart for the service. The county officials, whose duty it had been to select them, had too often laid their hands upon those who were most easily within reach, rather than upon those who were fittest for the work. "Our soldiers," wrote one who saw a number of them pass on their way, "are marching on all sides to Dover. God send them good shipping and success; but such a rabble of raw and poor rascals have not lightly been seen, and go so unwillingly that they must rather be driven than led." "It is lamentable," wrote another in the same strain, "to see the heavy countenances of our pressed men, and to hear the sad farewells they take of their friends, showing nothing but deadly unwillingness to the service; and they move pity almost in all men in regard of the incommodity of the season, the uncertainty of the employment, and the ill terms upon which they are like to serve, whereof I know not how discreetly I should do to tell you all that I hear spoken; but it may suffice that I say the whole business is generally disliked, and few or none promise either honour to our nation by this journey, or anything but wretchedness to the poor soldiers." ²

Chap. IV. 1624. Dec. Wretched condition of the men.

Whether a real army could ever have been constituted out of such unpromising materials may admit of doubt. As it was, the men had not fair play. Mansfeld, accustomed as he was to live at free quarters, was not in the habit of paying much attention to his

They are irregularly paid.

¹ Relazioni Venete. *Inghilterra*, 75, 233.
² Chamberlain to Carleton; D. Carleton to Carleton, Dec. 18; *S. P. Dom.*, clxxvi. 65, 66.

CHAP. IV.
1624.
Dec.

commissariat. Money difficulties, too, were not long in presenting themselves to him. He had received 15,000*l*. for the expenses of levying and arming the men, and 40,000*l*. for their payment during the months of October and November. He now, though the men were only just gathering at Dover, asked for another 20,000*l*. for the current month of December. But the resources of the Parliamentary Treasurers were exhausted, and it was only after some delay that the Prince was able to borrow the money on his own personal security.[1] What chance was there that the further sum, which would soon become due for January, would ever be forthcoming?

Dec. 25.
Mutiny of the soldiers.

Whilst Mansfeld was disputing with the Government over the accounts, the men were left to shift for themselves. When they reached Dover they found that but few vessels had been collected to carry them over, and that the state of the tides was such that even those few were unable to enter the harbour. Neither food nor money awaited the troops. As a natural consequence the men roamed about the country, stealing cattle and breaking into houses. Their ranks were thinned by frequent desertions, and those who remained at Dover threatened to hang the mayor and burn the town.[2]

1625.
Jan. 1.
Martial law.

To send down a commission for putting martial law in force was the first thought of the Council. To those who were on the spot it seemed a very insufficient remedy. "If there be not order to pay the soldiers," wrote Hippesley, the Lieutenant of Dover Castle, "all

[1] Burlamachi's accounts, 1625; *S. P. Germany.* Chamberlain to Carleton, Jan. 8; *S. P. Dom.*, clxxxi. 29.
[2] Hippesley to the Privy Council, Dec. 25; the Mayor of Dover and Hippesley to the Privy Council, Dec. 26; Wilsford to Nicholas, Dec. 27; *S. P. Dom.*, clxxvii. 17, 18, 33.

the martial law in the world will not serve the turn." When the commission was read, one of the mutineers shouted out, " If you hang one you must hang us all." The man was seized and condemned to death. But the officers, who knew how much the men were to be pitied, were not anxious to carry out the sentence, and they contrived to find an excuse for setting the prisoner free.[1]

CHAP. IV.
1625.
Jan.

In order to obtain vessels in greater numbers, an embargo was laid on several Hamburg ships which were lying in the Downs.[2] But the removal of the physical difficulty in the way of the passage only served to bring the political difficulty into greater prominence. James and Buckingham, whatever may have been the real nature of their communications with the ambassadors, still flattered themselves that whether the troops passed through the Spanish Netherlands or not, they would at least be allowed to make a French port the starting point of their enterprise, so as to establish the complicity of Lewis in the undertaking.

Jan. 3. Transport ships put under embargo.

This was, however, precisely the thing which the French had determined should not be. Ville-aux-Clercs and Effiat had gained over Mansfeld, and Espesses, the French ambassador at the Hague, was busily employed in urging the States General to consent to the landing of Mansfeld somewhere near Bergen-op-Zoom. In spite of the advocacy of the Prince of Orange, who was ready to risk anything to save his beloved Breda, Espesses found it hard work to gain the consent of the States General. Mansfeld was better known than liked by them. Their towns, they said, in which there was neither forage nor victual,

French negotiations with the Dutch.

---

[1] Hippesley to Nicholas, Jan. 2; Hippesley to Buckingham, Jan. 3; *S. P. Dom.*, clxxxi. 10, 11.
[2] Embargo by the Council, Jan. 3; *S. P. Germany.*

could not receive his troops, and to quarter them on the peasants could not be suffered. If, indeed, they were regularly paid by the King of England, and commissioned by him to serve against Spain, and if the promised French cavalry were allowed to accompany them, it would be another matter.[1]

Before this hesitating acceptance of the plan reached England, Mansfeld had taken it for granted that it would be adopted by the Dutch. He sent orders to the German troops which were waiting for him in Holland, to remain where they were, and he began to drop mysterious hints of his intentions. When his shipping was ready, he informed Conway, he would take the course which the winds allowed him, and which was most proper and suitable to his designs, mentioning also certain vessels which would be required for the embarkation of the French cavalry. Conway replied that he did not understand his meaning. He thought it had been arranged that the army should land in France, and march by land.[2] Upon this Mansfeld spoke out plainly, and declared his intention of carrying his army to Flushing.[3]

Buckingham, perhaps with some uneasy remembrance of a consent half given in his conversation with the ambassadors, attempted to argue with Mansfeld. The winds would be contrary, the rivers would be frozen, the States General would be quarrelsome; there were no ships to bring over the French cavalry, so that his Majesty would be obliged to make war alone, and to this he would never consent. The sooner

---

[1] Carleton to Conway, Jan. 6; *S. P. Holland.* Villermont, *E. de Mansfeldt*, ii. 26. Rusdorf to Frederick, Dec. $\frac{18}{28}$; *Mem.* i. 399.

[2] Mansfeld to Conway, Jan. 2; Conway to Mansfeld, Jan. 4; *S. P. Germany.*

[3] This is implied in Buckingham's letter of the 7th.

Mansfeld sailed for Calais the better. A few days later Buckingham spoke more impatiently. The Prince chimed in, "What he wishes," he said, "is impossible. The best thing he can do is to land at Calais, or France will not be engaged. From Calais he can go by any way he likes. What has he to do at Flushing?"[1]

"France will not be engaged." There was the root of the matter now. Two thousand French horse, and such shadow of a French alliance as might rest upon the expedition by its being permitted to land at Calais, was all that remained of the grand scheme for the co-operation of the two nations in the recovery of the Palatinate. James's displeasure was still more outspoken. He sent Sir John Ogle and Sir William St. Leger to Dover, to enquire into the condition of the troops. If they found Mansfeld bent on taking ways of his own, they were to dismiss the transports which had been collected with so much difficulty, and to send the men back to their homes.

The men had no such good fortune before them. Mansfeld, well aware that any attempt to land in France would be fruitless, replied that he would do his best to place his troops on French soil, and that he would allow himself to be stopped by nothing short of a direct prohibition from Lewis. Such a prohibition was of course forthcoming, and on the 19th of January was placed in Mansfeld's hands, in the presence of Ogle and St. Leger. By this time his men were on board, and he talked of crossing over to Calais, though it was St. Leger's opinion that 'a very small matter would send him back.'[2]

CHAP.
IV.

1625.
Jan. 10.
The Prince angry.

Jan. 19.
Mansfeld forbidden to land in France.

[1] Buckingham to Mansfeld, Jan. $\frac{9}{8}$; Rusdorf to Mansfeld, Jan. $\frac{10}{20}$; *Harl. MSS.*, 4596, fol. 230, 231.
[2] Ogle and St. Leger to Conway; St. Leger to Conway, Jan. 19; *S. P. Dom.*, clxxxii. 15, 16; Mansfeld to Buckingham, Jan. 19; *S. P. Germany.*

VOL. I. K

1625.
Jan. 19.
Buckingham gives way.

The experiment was not made. Buckingham was anxious to get Mansfeld off on any terms. He told Effiat that, if the prohibition to land were persisted in, James would allow him no choice but to disband the army. Would it not be possible, he asked, to allow Mansfeld to go on shore at Calais only for a few hours? If this could not be, if only he could be assured that the French cavalry would really join the expedition, he would do his best to satisfy the King.[1]

Jan. 23.

To the Prince Buckingham gave his reasons for consenting to the passage through Holland. The opposition to the landing, he said, doubtless proceeded from the Jesuit party in France. Was it, however, worth while to strive against it? Would it not be better, as matters stood, to send Mansfeld through Holland to the ecclesiastical territories on the Rhine? If the French cavalry were with him, Lewis would be as much engaged in the quarrel as if Mansfeld had landed in France. Such an arrangement as this would in all appearance advance more the main ends of recovering the Palatinate, having the States at their back, and the Princes of Germany about to move if they were encouraged.[2]

The march to the Palatinate therefore, not the relief of Breda, was uppermost in Buckingham's mind.

Jan. 26.
Mansfeld forbidden to go near Breda.

On the 26th he wrote to Mansfeld that, against his own judgment, he accepted his opinion in favour of the march through Holland, whilst on the same day Conway issued directions from the King to the colonels of the army, forbidding them to obey their general if he attempted to employ them at Breda.[3]

[1] Effiat to Lewis XIII. $\frac{\text{Jan. 23}}{\text{Feb. 2}}$; *Harl. MSS.*, 4596, fol. 2956.
[2] Buckingham to the Prince, Jan. 23; *S. P. Dom.*, clxxxii. 96.
[3] Conway to the Colonels, Jan. 26; Minute in Conway's letter-book, p. 688; *S. P. Dom.*

At last, on the 31st of January, the sorely tried army was able to leave Dover. As had been foreseen, the port of Calais was closed against them. The French cavalry, which had been placed under the command of Christian of Brunswick, was not ready to start. Mansfeld passed on his way without any accession of strength, and on the 1st of February the vessels which bore the English army cast anchor off Flushing.[1]

What good could come of an armament of which the commander was bent upon one line of action, whilst the officers were under strict orders to pursue another? But even before this difficulty could be faced there were many hardships to be endured. The provisions brought from England would only last for four or five days, and who could say how soon the scanty stock would be replenished? Mansfeld knew full well that not a single penny would be forthcoming from the English exchequer for some time to come. And even if, by some strange good fortune, the men succeeded in reaching Germany without being starved on the way, what possibility was there that these raw levies, without food or money, could stand against Tilly's veterans for a day?

Mansfeld, however, had plainly no intention of leading his men against Tilly. And even if he had wished to do so, a plan which would have left Breda unrelieved was not likely to find favour with the States General, and without the good will of the States General there was no obtaining the means of transport which he needed. In Holland at least, it was firmly believed that the relief of Breda was the first step needful to success in Germany. It was "the common

CHAP. IV.

1625. Jan. 31. He sails at last.

Feb. 1. Anchors at Flushing.

Hardships of the men from want of food.

Want of transport.

[1] Carleton to Conway, Feb. 3; *S. P. Holland.* Villermont, *E. de Mansfeldt,* ii. 283.

CHAP. IV.
1625.
Sickness breaks out.

opinion that if the Palatinate be only fought in the Palatinate, it would never be recovered."

Yet the troops could ill support delay. The men were 'poor and naked.' At Flushing they had remained for some days closely packed on board the vessels which brought them over. Then they were transferred to boats which were to carry them to Gertruidenberg, a town not far from Breda. Three regiments reached the place of their destination. The other three had gone but a few miles when the frost came down upon them and made further passage impossible. Exposed to the cold blasts and the driving snow, sickness broke out amongst them. The exhaustion from which they had already suffered unfitted them to bear up against fresh hardships. When they left Flushing they had not tasted food for eight and forty hours. But for the aid of the Dutch Government they would all have perished from starvation.

Great mortality.

At Gertruidenberg matters were no better. No preparation had been made to provide food for such a multitude. "All day long," wrote Lord Cromwell, who had come out in command of a regiment, "we go about for victuals and bury our dead."[1] Forty or fifty deaths were recorded every night. At last Count Frederick Henry, the brother and heir of the Prince of Orange, came to the relief of the suffering Englishmen. He sent them meat and bread, and provided them with straw to cover their freezing limbs as they lay in their boats. The account which Carleton gave of their sufferings ended in a cry for money. Mansfeld had brought with him merely 2,000*l*. He was not a man, the English ambassador thought, to care much for the welfare of his troops. He would prefer filling up the

[1] Cromwell to ——— ? Feb. 26; *S. P. Holland.*

vacancies with new levies to taking reasonable care of the old ones.[1]

What possible use could be made of this ill-starred force? The way to the Palatinate was barred against them by Imperialist armies hurried up to oppose them, and James persisted in his refusal to allow of their employment at Breda. If they were able to march up the Rhine, the diversion might be useful to the Dutch. But James had no money to send. He argued that the French, who had caused all the mischief, ought to supply the deficiency. If this could not be done, the States might perhaps advance the 20,000*l.* a month which he had bound himself to pay to Mansfeld.[2]

The Dutch were not quite inexorable. They allowed their credit to be used to raise a loan of 20,000*l*.[3] They perhaps hoped that James would get over the difficulty by accepting a proposal which had been made for placing Mansfeld under Frederick's orders, who would not be bound by the King of England's engagement. "His Majesty," they were told, "cannot yet be moved to think it fit to break it by equivocations, or by changing of forms and names."[4]

James's last words in this matter—for they were his last—were entirely in consonance with his earlier ones. The Palatinate, and the Palatinate alone, was the object at which he aimed. War with Spain was to be avoided as long as possible. Impartial posterity will perhaps be inclined to think that he was wise in looking to the recovery of the Palatinate, rather than to vengeance upon Spain, as the true object of the war. But his mind, indolent in itself, and becoming more in-

[1] Carleton to Conway, Feb. 14, 18, March 1; *S. P. Holland.*
[2] Conway to Carleton, March 4; *ibid.*
[3] Memorial of Money raised for Mansfeld, Aug.? *Ibid.*
[4] Rusdorf, *Mem.*, i. 498-510. Conway to Carleton, March 21; *S. P. Holland.*

CHAP. IV.

1625.
March.

dolent as years rolled by, shrank from the fatigue of planning a large scheme of foreign policy as a whole, and he did not see that the enmity of Spain was the inevitable result of any serious attempt to recover the Palatinate. And even if he had been right in thinking it possible to interfere in Germany without provoking Spain, it would have been a grave mistake to pursue this object in so close connection with France and Holland. For the first interest of France and Holland was to diminish the power of Spain, and not to recover the Palatinate.

The army wastes away.

Whilst the Governments were disputing, the soldiers were dying. In little more than a week after James's last refusal was given, out of a force of 12,000 men, barely 3,000 were capable of carrying arms. The French cavalry was equally thinned by sickness and desertion. When at last Christian of Brunswick brought his troops from Calais only a few hundreds out of the two thousand men originally under his orders were disembarked on the Dutch coast.[1]

Negotiations in Germany.

Whilst Mansfeld's prospects of finding his way into Germany were becoming more hopeless every day, where were those allies upon whom James ought to have been able to reckon before he allowed a single Englishman to take part in an enterprise for the recovery of the Palatinate? What had been done to engage the assistance of the North German States, or with the Kings of Denmark and Sweden?

1624. Aug.
Anstruther's mission.

When Anstruther unfolded his master's plans in August to Christian IV. of Denmark, the King answered that he was quite ready to take arms, but that he must first be assured of the support of England and of the Protestant States of North Germany. It was therefore arranged that Anstruther should visit

[1] Villermont, *E. de Mansfeldt*, ii. 285.

the Princes who had most to fear from the progress of the Imperialists, and that Christian would give him a final answer on his return.[1]

CHAP. IV.
1624.
Aug.

The position of the King of Denmark was a typical one. Like the other Princes of North Germany he had looked with disfavour upon Frederick's Bohemian enterprise. But he looked with equal disfavour upon the establishment of a strong Imperial authority, and his zeal for Protestantism was quickened by the knowledge that whether the secularised ecclesiastical possessions held by his house in Germany were held legally or not, no doubt existed in the Emperor's mind that they were still rightfully the property of the Church. His personal interest in the great question of the ecclesiastical lands was by no means slight. His younger son Frederick had the dioceses of Bremen, Verden, and Halberstadt either in possession or reversion.

Christian IV. and the ecclesiastical territories.

As usual, personal and political objects were closely intertwined with objects which were neither personal nor political. These North German Sees were occupied by Protestants, who though they called themselves Bishops, or sometimes more modestly Administrators, were simply lay Princes, like the Dukes and Counts around them, the only difference being that, instead of holding their rank by hereditary right, they were elected for life by the Chapters of the dioceses, the Chapters themselves often consisting, at least in part, of aristocratic sinecurists like themselves. It was quite

The North German bishoprics.

---

[1] Anstruther, in his account of his negotiations, March? 1625, S. P. Denmark, says 'that the King did ingenuously advise me, and did not forbear to second me by invitation of the Electors of Saxe and Brandenburg and others, by his own particular letters by me sent, and since again by letters of the King of Great Britain.' Droysen (Gustaf Adolf, i. 207-224), not being aware of this evidence, fancied that Christian assented to take part in the war at a later period through jealousy of Gustavus.

natural that Catholics should regard such an arrangement as wholly indefensible, and, if no more had been at stake than the loss by the neighbouring Princes of so rich a provision for their younger sons, the sooner a change came the better for Germany.

The results of the forcible dispossession of the Protestant Administrators would, however, have been far more widely felt. Their lands were inhabited by a Protestant population which would at once have been doomed to compulsory reconversion. Their fortresses would have been occupied by troops hostile to the order of things established in the neighbouring territories, and their revenues would have served as a bait held out to those Protestants who were anxious to make provision for their families, and who might perhaps not be slow to learn that Canonries and Bishoprics would fall into the lap of any ardent convert to the doctrines of the Emperor and the Pope.

Were the North German Princes so very steadfast that they could be trusted to withstand the temptation? It is hardly too much to say that the fate of German Protestantism was at stake. And with the fortunes of German Protestantism would come at last to be involved the fortunes of German nationality. The intellectual giants who since the days of Lessing and Göthe have overshadowed Europe, have all sprung up on Protestant soil; and men of the generation which has only just passed away could tell of the peaceful conquest over the ignorance of Catholic Germany which was achieved at the beginning of this century by the men of the Protestant North,[1] and which paved the way for that political unity which is at last healing the wounds inflicted in the great war of the 17th century.

[1] See especially the life of Friederich Thiersch, by his son, Dr. H. Thiersch.

The Emperor had accepted the agreement made at Mühlhausen in 1620, by which the Protestant Administrators were declared safe from attack as long as they remained obedient subjects. But doubts were freely expressed whether he would keep, in the days of his prosperity, the promise which he had made in the hour of adversity. And even if scant justice were probably done to Ferdinand in this surmise, he might fairly be expected to urge that the diocese of Halberstadt was no longer under the protection of the agreement of Mühlhausen. Its Administrator, Christian of Brunswick, had certainly not been an obedient subject to the Emperor. He had now abdicated in the hope that the Chapter would choose a Protestant successor. But in the eyes of the Emperor such an election would have no legal basis. Christian's treason, he would argue, had replaced the See in the position in which it was before the agreement of Mühlhausen, and the Chapter was therefore bound to elect a real Catholic Bishop, instead of a cavalry officer who called himself a Bishop in order that he might enjoy the revenues of the See. And there were other ways, besides that of force, by which Protestantism could be undermined in the Bishoprics. If a majority of a Chapter could be gained over, a Catholic Bishop would be chosen at the next election. Many of the Canons were Catholics still, and, with the help of an armed force, it was easy to find legal grounds for turning the minority into a majority. In this way Osnabrück had lately been won from Protestantism, and other Sees might be expected, unless something were done, to follow soon.[1]

At such a time Anstruther had not much difficulty in gaining the ear of most of the Princes to whom he

CHAP. IV.
1624. Aug.
Was the Emperor likely to reclaim the bishoprics.

Anstruther's successful negotiation.

[1] On the position of these Bishoprics, and of Halberstadt especially, see Dr. Opel's *Niedersachsische Dänische Krieg.*

138 THE LAST DAYS OF JAMES I.

CHAP. IV.
1624. Aug.

addressed himself. The Elector of Saxony, indeed, continued to stand aloof. But in other quarters the English ambassador found no lack of readiness to stand up against the Emperor, if he could engage to bring into the field a force large enough to give promise of success.

Gustavus Adolphus.

Whilst Anstruther was passing from one German state to another, Spens was engaged in making similar advances to the King of Sweden. Gustavus Adolphus was bound by every conceivable tie to the Protestant cause. He had to fear a Catholic pretender to the Swedish Crown in the person of his cousin Sigismund. If the Emperor extended his authority to the shores of the Baltic, the throne of Gustavus and the national independence of Sweden would be exposed to serious danger. The dominion over the Baltic was for him a question of life or death. Yet it would be in the highest degree unjust to speak of him as taking merely a selfish or even a national view of the work of his life. Politics and religion were closely intertwined in the minds of the men of his generation. To him, the consummate warrior and statesman, the defence of Protestantism was no empty phrase. It filled him with the consciousness that he was sent forth upon a high and holy mission. It taught him to believe that in prosecuting the aims of his own policy he was a chosen instrument in the hands of God.

His position in 1624.

For Sweden he had already done much. Succeeding to his father in an hour of desperate trial, when the armies of Christian of Denmark were sweeping over the desolate land, the youthful hero had stemmed the tide of invasion at its highest, and had wrung from the invader a peace which had preserved the independence of the country. He had since driven back the Russians from the coast of the Baltic, and was able to boast that the subjects of the Czar could not launch a boat on its waters without the permission of the King of Sweden. He had struggled not unsuccessfully against his Polish rival. But his eye had never been removed from the strife in Germany. To drive back the Imperial armies from the North, if not to overthrow the House of Austria altogether, was the object of his ambition. But no man was less likely than Gustavus to interpret the conditions of success by his wishes; and it was certain that he would never throw himself, as Frederick of the Palatinate had done, into the labyrinth of a desperate enterprise, on the complacent assurance that what he was desirous of doing was certain to obtain the approval and the support of Heaven.

CHAP. IV.

1624. Aug.

Already, the year before, Gustavus had made proposals to the exiled Frederick for a general Protestant league. Those proposals had been, with the consent of the States General, communicated to the Prince of Wales, and when Spens arrived at Stockholm in August 1624, he brought with him, in addition to his public instructions from James, verbal directions from Charles and Frederick to come to an understanding with Gustavus respecting the proposed alliance. Gustavus was not long in sketching out his programme. The time for half measures he held to be passed. There must be a common understanding between all Protestant states. He, if properly supported, would make his way, through Poland and Silesia, into Bohemia. England and Holland could do much to help. Spain would have to be kept in check as well as the Emperor to be beaten back. The assistance of Catholic powers, France, Venice, and Savoy, was not to be despised. But let them find their own field of operation for themselves. They might attack Bavaria, or might make war in Italy at their pleasure.[1]

Mission of Spens.

Plan of Gustavus.

[1] Oxenstjerna to Camerarius, Aug. 24; Moser's *Patriotisches Archiv*, v. 42.

CHAP. IV.
1624.
Aug.
Its merits.

The view taken of the war by the Swedish King was certainly very different from that taken by James. Moderation, fairness, and conciliation, admirable as they are whilst a friendly settlement is still possible, or when it once more becomes possible after victory has been won, must be flung aside when hostilities have been once commenced. The spirit must be aroused which alone gives endurance to the warrior. The watchword must be spoken for which men's hearts will beat. To place poor, vacillating Frederick once more in his Electoral seat was not an object for which nations would care to fight, least of all if it were to be accomplished with the aid of a marauder like Mansfeld. But if it once came to be believed that Protestantism was in danger, it would be a very different thing. Then, indeed, an irresistible force could be gathered to make head against Imperial aggression. And with strength would come again the possibility of moderation. The leader of an army such as Gustavus would have gathered under his standards would enforce discipline and spare the towns and fields of Germany from indiscriminate plundering. More than this, if he could give assurances that he was fighting in defence of his own religion without any intention of proscribing that of his opponents, he might gain help from those who from political motives were hostile to the House of Austria.

Was it not premature?

All this Gustavus was one day to accomplish. Was it not premature in 1624? Until men have actually felt the weight of evil, they are hard to rouse to a course so revolutionary as that which, in the opinion of Gustavus, would alone be of service to them. The Lower Saxon circle was threatened by Tilly. But it had not yet been invaded. The fertile plains of Northern Germany had not yet been wasted by the armies of the South. The mischief was threatening enough. But the bolt had not yet fallen. The iron had not yet entered into the soul of the peasants of Pomerania or the burghers of Magdeburg.

CHAP. IV.
1624.
Aug. 24.

There was another risk, too, not unforeseen by Gustavus himself. If he was not at war with Denmark the fires of the old rivalry still smouldered on. What if Christian should fall upon Sweden when the King was in the heart of Silesia or Bohemia? And Denmark was not then the petty realm which modern events have made it. Its king reigned in Norway, ruled in Schleswig, and in part of Holstein, and held lands beyond the Sound which are now counted as the southern provinces of Sweden. So certain was Gustavus that no good could come from Denmark, that he demanded that his allies should join him in forming a fleet to guard the Baltic against a Danish attack in his absence.

Risk from Denmark.

Before long Gustavus was compelled to modify his plan in a way which was certain to give offence to Christian. The Elector of Brandenburg sent an ambassador, Bellin, to Stockholm, to offer to the King of Sweden his aid in placing him at the head of a league of North German Princes. But the Elector coupled his offer with the condition that the war should be carried on as far as possible from Brandenburg. Instead of directing his course through Silesia into Bohemia, Gustavus was to ascend the valley of the Weser, and to cut his way to the Palatinate.[1]

Sept. Bellin at Stockholm.

Before these representations Gustavus consented to abandon his original plan. But though he was ready to act in any way which might, at the time, seem advisable, he was not ready to act at all excepting

[1] Oxenstjerna to Camerarius, Sept. 10; Moser's *Patriotisches Archiv*, v. 56, 58.

CHAP. IV.

1625. Jan.

Demands of Gustavus.

under conditions which would give him a fair prospect of success. When therefore Spens and Bellin presented themselves in England to declare the intentions of the King of Sweden, those who heard them were fairly astonished at the magnitude of their demands. Gustavus, the ambassador said, was ready to lead an army of 50,000 men to the Palatinate. Of these he would furnish 16,000 himself, leaving the remaining 34,000 to be provided by his allies. He was ready to meet one third of the expenses of the war, but another third must be borne by England, and the remainder by the German Princes. There must be something more than mere talk of finding money. Gustavus had no intention of throwing himself upon a friendly country, like Mansfeld or Christian of Brunswick, on the mere chance of being able to pay his way. Four months' wants must be supplied in hard cash before he would stir. When he did stir, he would not encounter the dangers of a divided command. The whole direction of the war must be placed in his own hands. That he might be secured against a possible attack in the rear from Poland or Denmark, a fleet of twenty-five ships must be stationed in the Baltic, and the German ports of Wismar and Bremen must be temporarily surrendered to him to give him a firm basis of operations. In order to discuss these propositions, a congress of the powers friendly to the operation was to be held as soon as possible.[1]

Jan. 2.
James shrinks from the expense.

If there was to be war at all, the best policy for the English Government would probably have been to place itself unreservedly in the hands of Gustavus. But Gustavus was as yet but little known in England; and as matters stood, with Mansfeld's expedition swallowing up

[1] Rusdorf, *Mémoires*, i. 438, 439.

all the little money which remained in the exchequer, and with no Parliamentary grant possible for many a month to come, the magnitude of the Swedish demands only inspired alarm. "I am not so great and rich a Prince," said James, "as to be able to do so much. I am only the king of two poor little islands." The yearly expense in fact, which he was asked to meet, would have exceeded 400,000l., and he had already engaged to pay nearly 100,000l. a year for the troops which he had sent to the help of the Dutch, and 240,000l. a year for Mansfeld's army.

<small>CHAP. IV.
1625.
Jan. 5.</small>

As the discussion went on, a natural anxiety was expressed by the English Government to see Sweden and Denmark acting in concert. Why, said Conway, should not Christian be asked to bear part of the burthen? If neither of the kings would serve under the other, might not the supreme command be given to the Elector of Brandenburg?[1]

<small>Denmark to be asked to join.</small>

Day by day the financial difficulties appeared in a stronger light. At last Buckingham assured Bellin that though he would spare neither life nor honour in the cause, he must first hear what the Kings of Denmark and France would do. Bellin had better go on to Paris to consult Lewis. As he had done in the case of Mansfeld, James was at last brought to promise that he would do as much as the King of France would do. Christian might be asked to leave the direction of the war to Gustavus, and a congress could meet at the Hague on the 20th of April.

<small>Jan. 17. France to be consulted.</small>

On his arrival at the French Court, Bellin found no difficulty in obtaining a promise of assistance. A French emissary, La Haye, had visited the coasts of Copenhagen and Stockholm, and, though he does not

<small>Bellin in France.</small>

[1] Rusdorf to Frederick, Jan. $\frac{3}{12}$, $\frac{8}{18}$ (probably misprinted $\frac{18}{28}$); *Mémoires* i. 420, 430.

seem to have had any definite overtures to make,[1] it is probable that Richelieu was now hoping to obtain his sovereign's consent to a more active intervention in Germany. But Bellin was told that help would be given only on the understanding that the conditions of peace to be demanded after the war were to be settled by the Kings of France and England. Whether Gustavus would have consented to take money on such terms may reasonably be doubted.[2]

Before Bellin returned to England, important despatches were received from Anstruther.[3] Christian, encouraged by the reports which the English ambassador had brought from the North German Courts, and possibly urged to exertion in the hope of outbidding the King of Sweden, now professed himself ready to embark on the war with less extensive preparations than those which seemed indispensable to Gustavus. Instead of asking for 50,000 men, he thought that 30,000 would be sufficient. If England would support 6,000 foot and 1,000 horse at the expense of 170,000*l.* or 180,000*l.* a year, he would be perfectly satisfied. As his own dominions lay on the south side of the Baltic, he could secure a basis of operations without asking for the surrender of German ports. Finally, he made no request for the provision of payment in advance.[4]

To a Government without money in hand these considerations were decisive. But in England it was not understood that the acceptance of Christian's offers

---

[1] Notes of a letter from Anstruther to Carlisle, Jan. ; *Mémoires de Rusdorf*, i. 478. Oxenstjerna to Camerarius, Jan. 23. *Moser*, v. 94.
[2] Rusdorf to Frederick, Feb. 12/22 ; *Mémoires de Rusdorf*, i. 480.
[3] They arrived between the 9th and 20th of Feb., as I judge from two letters written by Conway on those dates ; *S. P. Denmark*.
[4] Substance of Anstruther's despatch, Jan. 13. *Mémoires de Rusdorf*, i. 472.

involved the rejection of the Swedish plan. The rivalry between the two Kings, it was thought, would be put an end to by the decision of the Congress when it met at the Hague.¹ In the meanwhile Spens was to go back to persuade Gustavus to enter upon the stage in conjunction with Christian. The offer of Denmark, he was directed to say, 'stood upon shorter ways and less demands, and if not so powerful, yet feasible, and held sufficient for the present.'²

CHAP. IV.
1625. March 15. Gustavus invited to co-operate.

The task of reconciling the two Kings was not so easy as it seemed to the English Government. There was jealousy of long standing between Sweden and Denmark. Nor was the enterprise to which Christian and Gustavus were invited, one to be lightly undertaken. Though the North German Princes were alarmed for the future, they were not yet reduced to desperation. But there can be no doubt that Gustavus alone perceived the conditions indispensable to success. In the first place, a military force strong enough to defy opposition must be brought together. In the second place, within the larger league of the political opponents of the House of Austria, there must be a narrower league of those who specially aimed at a Protestant restoration in Germany, which would be able to speak with the authority of conscious strength if any attempt were made by France to snatch from them in the hour of victory the object on which their hearts were set.

Aims of Gustavus,

In England, for different reasons, neither James nor Buckingham were capable of taking so broad a view of passing events. James, wishing to recover the Palatinate with as little cost as possible to his impoverished exchequer, was drawn on, half against his will, from one step to another, always selecting that

Of James,

---

¹ Rusdorf to Frederick, March 19; *Mémoires de Rusdorf*, i. 510.
² Instructions to Spens, March 19; *S. P. Sweden.*

VOL. I.   L

CHAP. IV.
1625.
March.
And of Buckingham.

policy which would involve him as little as possible in the war, and which would spare him something at least of those terrible demands upon his purse which even the most economical mode of conducting military operations was certain to make. Buckingham, on the other hand, with Charles following in his wake, desired a vigorous and all-embracing war. Yet for the very reason that he had no idea of the strength gained by the concentration of effort in one direction, he shrunk almost as much as James had shrunk from the large demands of Gustavus. If war was to be carried on here, there, and everywhere, it must of necessity be starved in each separate locality. If Gustavus stood alone in perceiving the way to victory, he also stood alone in resolutely refusing to take part in a war in which the probabilities of victory appeared to him to be small. As soon as the English resolution was reported to him, he informed Spens that he would take no part in the German war on such conditions. Those who thought it so easy a task to overpower the resistance of the House of Austria might do their best.[1] The negotiation was thus brought to a close. When the spring came to an end, Gustavus embarked to carry on his hereditary feud with the King of Poland, hoping at least to prevent the Poles from coming to the assistance of the Emperor.

Gustavus turns against Poland.

Buckingham's further schemes.

Even if Buckingham's policy had been far surer of a favourable reception in Parliament than it was, the demands for money for Mansfeld, for the Netherlands, and for Germany, would have strained his late popularity to the uttermost. But these projects, involving as they did an annual expenditure of more than 500,000*l*. formed only a part of the magnificent schemes upon which Buckingham was launching the English nation.

[1] Gustavus Adolphus to Spens, March 13; *S. P. Sweden.* This characteristic letter will be published in the next volume of the Camden Society's Miscellany.

After all, if he was not a great military commander, even in his own eyes, he was Lord High Admiral of England, and the war would be sadly incomplete if the navy were to take no part in it. Though the armament of the fleet had been postponed from want of money, and on account of the cessation of any fear of an attack from Spain, orders had been given which pointed to the employment of the ships in the following spring.[1]

CHAP. IV.
1624.

What was the exact use to which these ships were to be put was still undecided. When Wake had set out in May for Turin, he had carried with him instructions to sound the Duke of Savoy on the subject of the co-operation of an English fleet with a French and Savoyard army in an attack upon Genoa similar to that which had been suggested by Raleigh before he started on his expedition to Guiana. When Wake arrived at his destination, he found Charles Emmanuel already prepared with a design of his own. Let the King of England, he said, lend him twenty ships of war, and pay twenty thousand soldiers for three months. The whole expense would be about 126,000*l.* In return for this, James should have a third part of the booty; or, if he preferred certainties to uncertainties, the Duke would engage to pay him 900,000*l.* after the surrender of the city.

May. Proposed attack upon Genoa.

Aug.

Genoa had so notoriously merged its interests in those of Spain, that it could hardly claim the privilege of neutrality. But as soon as the Duke's proposition reached England, doubts were expressed, from a financial point of view, of the soundness of the proposed investment. Wake was told to ask the Duke what were his grounds for thinking the enterprise an easy

Oct. Hesitation in England.

---

[1] Survey of the Fleet, Aug. 31, 1624; *S. P. Dom.*, clxxi. 36.

one, but at the same time to assure him that it would be seriously taken into consideration if he could succeed in showing it to be feasible.[1]

By this time, however, a French army under the command of old Marshal Lesdiguières was preparing to take part in the attack upon Genoa, as a diversion in favour of the troops invading the Valtelline, and Lesdiguières, sorely in need of a naval force, had despatched agents to England and Holland to recommend the plan in another shape. He now proposed that the fleet should sail in the name of the King of France, though it was to be composed of English and Dutch vessels. They would simply be hired by Lewis as he might hire them from a merchant, and if neither James nor the States General would be able to lay claim to any share of the splendid profits which the Duke of Savoy had held up to the English Government, neither would they have been called upon to take any part in the expense.

To this plan the Dutch at once gave their consent, and agreed to lend twenty ships for the purpose.[2] In England Buckingham warmly supported Lesdiguières' agent, and persuaded James to follow the example set by the States General. It was therefore understood that the French commander would have twenty English ships at his disposal.

Merely to lend a few vessels, however, was a trifle hardly worth mentioning in the midst of Buckingham's far-reaching schemes. In the course of a conversation with Ville-aux-Clercs and Effiat on the subject of this arrangement, he flashed before their eyes the grand project which, in the following summer, was to occupy so large a space in the thoughts of men. Another fleet, he

---

[1] Wake to Conway, Aug. 9; Conway to Wake, Oct. 20; *S. P. Savoy.*

[2] Treaty with M. de Bellujon, Dec. 14; *S. P. Holland.*

said, there must be. It should be sent to sea in the name of the King of Bohemia. It would carry a land army strong enough to seize some fortified post on the Spanish coast, after which the ships could look out for the treasure ships which annually returned to Spain with their precious freight from the mines of America. When that was taken—and there could be no real difficulty in the way—the power of Spain would be crushed. Mansfeld and the Prince of Orange—at the time when Buckingham was speaking, Mansfeld was still in England—would have an easy task; France and England would be the joint arbiters of Europe.[1]

Truly it was a bright and glorious vision. When Genoa had been taken, when Mansfield had won his victorious way into the heart of Germany, when city after city of the Spanish Netherlands was surrendering to the armies of the Dutch Republic, then, even if the wealth of the Indies had not been there to pay for all, Buckingham would have had small need to fear the persistent opposition of the House of Commons. It was true that he had made no allowance for difficulties or even for accidents. But how could difficulties or accidents be thought of when he was there to guide the State?

Buckingham's vainglorious forecast had been uttered in the middle of December. A month later he learned that even his path was beset by obstacles. By that time he knew that Gustavus at least did not think victory so very easy of attainment. He knew that the French had ideas of their own about Mansfeld's employment. And he knew, too, that if they liked to control the march of English troops according to their own convenience, they were quite ready to appeal to England for the aid which they needed in their own domestic difficulties.

[1] Ville-aux-Clercs and Effiat to Lewis XIII., Dec. $\frac{19}{29}$; *Harl. MSS.*, 4596, fol. 208, b.

CHAP. IV.

1624.
Dec.
The French Huguenots.

For a long time the condition of the Huguenots had been such as to forebode a catastrophe. Too weak to trust themselves to the protection of the common laws of the realm, they had yet been strong enough to wrest from their sovereign the right of maintaining garrisons in certain strong places, so as to secure at least a local independence. Such a situation was full of danger. To surrender their privileges was to place their religion at the mercy of a jealous, perhaps of a bigoted, master. To keep them, was to exist as a state within a state, and to flaunt the banners of a group of urban republics in the face of the growing popularity of a monarchy which had undertaken the task of founding the unity of France upon the ruins of a self-seeking aristocracy.

Encroachments of the French Government.

Whatever may have been the right solution of the problem, the French Government, before Richelieu's accession to power, made no attempt to discover it. The Peace of Montpellier, by which the last civil war had been brought to a conclusion, had been violated again and again. Amongst other promises the King had engaged to pull down Fort Louis, a fortress erected during the war to command the entrance to the port of Rochelle. But the Rochellese knew only too well that the walls and bastions thus solemnly devoted to destruction in word, were being strengthened under their eyes. Marshal Lesdiguières is reported to have said that either the Rochellese must destroy the fort, or the fort would destroy Rochelle. Richelieu, there is little doubt, would have counselled the fulfilment of the terms of the treaty in order that France might have her arms free to operate against Spain. But Richelieu had to consult his master's mood, and he would find it hard to wring from Lewis a consent to an act which looked like the abandonment of all control over a French city.

THE FRENCH HUGUENOTS.

At last, whilst the more prudent among the Huguenots were still counselling submission, two brothers, the Dukes of Rohan and Soubise, both of them alike ambitious and incompetent, resolved upon once more trying out the old quarrel in arms. On the 26th of December Soubise sailed into the harbour of Blavet in Brittany, and, capturing six vessels of war, carried his prizes safely to Rochelle. The seafaring population of the great city welcomed him as their deliverer, and the civil war once more began.

<small>CHAP. IV.
1624.
Dec. 26.
Soubise seizes the French fleet.</small>

Great was the indignation at the French Court when the news was told. Yet how was Lewis to take vengeance on the rebels without a larger navy than that which, after Soubise's captures, he had at his disposal? Richelieu as usual came to the rescue in the hour of difficulty. Whether he wished to see the demands of the Huguenots conceded or not, he was not the man to deal lightly with rebellion. If England and the States General, he argued, had been ready to lend ships to Lesdiguières for an attack upon Genoa, why should they not lend ships to Lewis to be used against that perfidious city which was holding him back from the fulfilment of his obligations to favour their interests against Spain.

<small>Richelieu asks aid from England and the Netherlands.</small>

The Dutch Government had scarcely a choice. They could not afford to offend the sovereign with the help of whose subsidies they were making head against their oppressor. Richelieu's request, therefore, was at once granted at the Hague.

<small>1625. Jan. Consent of the Dutch,</small>

In England the preparations for the great naval expedition against Spain were in full swing. Twelve ships of war and a hundred transports were being prepared for sea,[1] and Buckingham was only waiting to

<small>And of the English Government.</small>

---

[1] The King to the Council of War, Dec. 1624; *S. P. Dom.*, clxxvi. 58, i.

152   THE LAST DAYS OF JAMES I.

CHAP.
IV.
———
1625.
Jan.

hear once more from Lesdiguières in order to get ready the ships intended for Genoa. To him, therefore, news which made it likely that there would be any obstacle in the way of the French co-operation on which he counted was most unwelcome. He at once informed Effiat that the demand made by his master should be complied with, and, without going through the form of consulting James, he gave orders that the ships required should be fitted out immediately.[1] Not that James was likely to throw any obstacle in the way. When he first heard what had taken place, and before Effiat had had time to ask for the use of his ships, he expressed himself strongly on the subject. "If Soubise," he said, "or any one else takes upon himself to commit such follies in your master's dominions, I will give every kind of assistance against him, in men, in ships, and in any other way in my power." When he heard what Effiat wanted, he had no objections to make. "If those rascally Huguenots," he said, "mean to make a rebellion, I will go in person to exterminate them."[2]

Buckingham to go to France.

The French alliance was still regarded at the English Court as worth making sacrifices for, in spite of the misunderstanding which had by this time arisen about Mansfeld's destination. It was known in December that the dispensation for the marriage had been granted at Rome; and, as it was believed that the Princess would be in England before the end of January, Buckingham, who was to hold the Prince's proxy at the ceremony, began his preparations for the journey. Charles indeed had been eager to go in

---

[1] Effiat to Lewis XIII., Jan. $\frac{11}{21}$, $\frac{17}{27}$, $\frac{18}{28}$; *Harl. MSS.*, 4596, fol. 258, b, 277, b, 290, b.

[2] Effiat to Ville-aux-Clercs, $\frac{\text{Jan. 23}}{\text{Feb. 2}}$; Effiat to Lewis XIII., $\frac{\text{Jan. 23}}{\text{Feb. 2}}$ Feb. $\frac{14}{24}$; *Harl. MSS.*, 4596, fol. 295, b, 298, b, 327.

person to Paris, as he had gone to Madrid; but, upon a note from Lewis that his presence in France was not desired, he had been forced to abandon the idea.¹

January, however, passed away without the arrival of the dispensation; and with the delay came the necessity for a further prorogation of Parliament,² a prorogation which deferred for a yet longer time the possibility of obtaining money with which to meet the wants of Mansfeld's starving soldiers.

Richelieu had taken every means in his power to induce the Pope to grant the dispensation. Immediately upon the fall of La Vieuville, he had despatched Father Berulle to Rome to expound to the Pope the advantages which would accrue to the Catholic Church from the English marriage. But he had taken care to reinforce the pleadings of the gentle enthusiast by plain speaking at Paris. He declared openly that if the dispensation did not come quickly, they would proceed to the marriage without it.³

Richelieu's attitude had the desired effect. The dispensation was granted on the 21st of November. But when it arrived in Paris it appeared that the Pope had only given way conditionally upon certain changes being made in the wording of the agreement between the two Kings. Amongst other demands, he asked that, instead of the private engagement taken by James and his son, there should be a public instrument assuring

CHAP. IV.

1625. Jan. 19. Prorogation of Parliament.

1624. Aug. Richelieu and the dispensation.

Nov. Alterations in the contract are demanded by the Pope.

---

¹ Chamberlain to Carleton, Dec. 4, *S. P. Dom.*, clxxvi. 15; Ville-aux-Clercs and Effiat to Lewis XIII., Dec. 13/22; Lewis XIII. to Effiat, Jan. 10/20; *Harl. MSS.*, 4596, fol. 157, 262.
² Proclamation, Jan. 19; *Rymer*, xvii. 648.
³ Richelieu, wrote Langerac, the Dutch ambassador at Paris, on Aug. 8/18, 'verclaert dat indien deselve dispensatie niet haest en compt, dat men daerom niet laeten en sal met het huwelick voorts te procederen.' I owe this quotation, taken from the despatch at the Hague, to the kindness of Dr. Goll, of Prague.

freedom of worship to the Catholics, of which all the world might take cognisance.¹

Some of the French ministers fancied that even this concession might be wrung from James. But they forgot that publicity had never been required before, and Effiat soon convinced himself that the Pope's wishes had no chance of being complied with in England. And this time James had Richelieu on his side. On the 21st of March a promise was signed on behalf of the King of France to the effect that if the Pope's demands were not withdrawn within thirty days, the marriage should take place without any dispensation at all.²

Whether the French alliance would be able to stand the strain which the divergent views and interests of the two nations were certain to put upon it might perhaps be doubted. But there could be no doubt that as far as position at Court went, both Buckingham and Richelieu were the stronger for the successful termination of the controversies which had sprung out of the marriage treaty. Of Buckingham it might truly be said that he held the government of England in his hands. Whatever wild scheme crossed his brain was accepted with docility by the Prince, as if it had been the highest effort of political and military wisdom; and, when Charles and Buckingham were agreed, James was seldom capable of offering any serious opposition to their impetuous demands.

Until Parliament met, therefore, Buckingham had nothing to fear. It is true that there had been murmurs in high places at his tergiversation with respect to the English Catholics, and there can be little doubt

---

¹ Carlisle to Buckingham, Feb. 16; *Hardw. St. P.*, i. 551.
² Carlisle and Holland to Buckingham, Feb. 24; *S. P. France.* Effiat to Lewis XIII., March $\frac{21}{11}$; *Harl. MSS.*, 4596, fol. 359, b.

that the greater part of the old nobility regarded him with aversion as an upstart. But such opposition he could afford to disregard. The Privy Council and the government offices were filled with his creatures, or with men who found it expedient to bear themselves as though they were his creatures. No man except Middlesex and Bristol had ventured to stand up against him. Middlesex, though upon his humble submission he had been liberated from the Tower, and had been excused the payment of a large part of his fine, was hopelessly excluded from public life. Bristol was less yielding than Middlesex. To a fresh demand that he should acknowledge that he had been guilty of errors in judgment in his embassy at Madrid, he replied by a re-statement of his own view of the matter, accompanied by a letter which, though humble enough, did not contain any acknowledgment that he had been in the wrong.[1] An acknowledgment that he had been in the wrong was however the one thing upon which Buckingham insisted, and unless Bristol was much mis-

CHAP. IV.
1625. Jan.

Middlesex and Bristol.

Feb. 2.

---

[1] "Hoping that your nobleness and equity will be such as a true and clear answer will be more acceptable to your Grace than an unjust acknowledgment, I have entreated Sir Kenelm Digby to deliver unto your Grace my answers unto the propositions which he brought unto me from you, and humbly beseech your Grace to cast your eyes over them, and if there shall be anything wherein your Grace shall rest unsatisfied, I entreat your Grace to give me leave to attend you, where I shall endeavour not only to satisfy you in these particulars, but that I truly and unfeignedly seek your Grace's favour, to which, if I may upon fair and noble terms be admitted, your Grace shall find me for the future a faithful and real servant to you to the utmost of my power. But if I must be so unhappy as these my humble seekings of your Grace may not find acceptance—although I conceive my ruin an easy work for your greatness—I shall with patience and humility endeavour to bear whatsoever God shall be pleased to lay upon me as punishments for other sins committed against him, but not against my master, whom I take God to record I have served both with exact fidelity and affection."—Bristol to Buckingham. *Earl of Bristol's Defence*, Pref. xxiii. *Camden Miscellany*, vi.

CHAP. IV.

1625. Jan.

taken, he was debarred from appearing at Court by an order issued by the favourite in the King's name, without the consent of James. The Duke, said Bristol, in the account which he subsequently gave of the matter, 'moved his Majesty that I might first make an acknowledgment of my fault, which his Majesty refused to compel me unto ; saying he might then be thought a tyrant to force a man to acknowledge that which he was not guilty of; and his Majesty sent me word that I should make no acknowledgment unless I would freely confess myself guilty. Yet the Duke caused a message to be sent me that his Majesty expected that I should make the said acknowledgment, and confess myself guilty.'[1]

Williams, Weston, and Calvert.

Others were more supple than Bristol. Williams and Weston had convinced their patron that they would be ready to carry out his wishes ; whilst Calvert, who was secretly a convert to the Church of Rome, and had long been anxious to escape from the entanglements of office, had laid his secretaryship at the Duke's feet, telling him plainly that he intended to live and die in the religion which he professed. Buckingham, who had spoken hard things of Calvert a few months before, was always inclined to deal gently with opposition of this submissive kind, and assured the secretary that he should come to no harm by his avowal. He was therefore allowed, according to the custom of the time, to bargain with his successor for 6000*l*. to be paid to him as the price of his withdrawal from office, and he was soon afterwards created Lord Baltimore in the Irish peerage.[2]

Calvert's successor was Wotton's nephew, Sir

[1] *Ibid.* xxiv.
[2] *Salvetti's Newsletter*, $\frac{\text{Jan. 27}}{\text{Feb. 6}}$; Chamberlain to Carleton, Feb. 12; *S. P. Dom.*, clxxxiii. 43.

Albertus Morton. He had formerly been secretary to Elizabeth, when she was still at Heidelberg. For the first time since the office had been divided, both the secretaries were thoroughgoing opponents of Spain; and though neither of them was likely to be more than an exponent of Buckingham's policy, the indication of the views now prevailing at Court is not to be neglected. A few weeks later, the other secretary, Sir Edward Conway, received the reward of his obsequious devotion to Buckingham, 'his most gracious patron,' as he always called him, and was raised to the peerage as Lord Conway. The treasurership, which had been in commission since the fall of Middlesex, had recently been placed in the hands of Chief Justice Ley, who acquired a peerage with the title of Lord Ley. If he knew nothing of finance, he has at least Milton's high testimony to his personal integrity. After all, if Buckingham was to spend money at anything like the rate he was inclined to do, it hardly mattered much whether Ley knew anything of finance or not. A Colbert or a Peel would under the circumstances have failed in guarding the exchequer against an enormous deficit.

CHAP. IV.
1625. Feb. 9. Morton secretary in Calvert's place.

March 23. Conway made a peer.

1624. Dec. 20. Ley treasurer.

In the course of the past year, Buckingham had added another office to those which he already held. Having received the reversion of the Wardenship of the Cinque Ports, he persuaded the Warden, Lord Zouch, to surrender the post to him at once, by an offer of 1000*l.*, and a pension of 500*l.* a year.[1] Such arrangements were too common at the time to call forth much remark, and but for subsequent events it is probable that we should have heard no more of it

Buckingham Warden of the Cinque Ports.

---

[1] Agreement between Buckingham and Zouch, July 17, 1624. Statement relating to the Cinque Ports, Nov. 11. *S. P. Dom.*, clxx. 16, clxxiv. 71. Grant of Office, Patent Rolls, 22 Jac. I.

THE LAST DAYS OF JAMES I.

CHAP. IV.
1624. Dec.

than we have heard of the very similar transaction between Calvert and Morton, or than we heard, till within the last few years, of the sums of money which passed from hand to hand whenever an officer in the army thought fit to sell his commission.

His defence of his conduct.

Buckingham afterwards declared that in accepting this office he was solely actuated by consideration for the public welfare. In the approaching war, it would be highly inconvenient if one part of the coast were to be under the jurisdiction of the Lord High Admiral, and another part under the jurisdiction of the Warden of the Cinque Ports; and future generations, by reducing the Warden's office to a dignified sinecure, were to afford testimony to the Duke's foresight in this particular. But however this may be, there is no reason to doubt his sincerity. For, about the same time Buckingham refused to accept an office of still greater dignity which James pressed upon him.

He declines the Lord-Lieutenancy of Ireland.

It was proposed that he should be named Lord Lieutenant of Ireland, and should execute the functions of government by deputy. It is said that his refusal to decorate himself with the title caused great annoyance to his enemies, who hoped to profit by the disrepute into which his acceptance of the offer would have brought him.[1]

1625. March 2. Advice of Williams.

In truth, it was not so much from the number of offices which he held that Buckingham was likely to lose the popularity which he had gained in the preceding spring, as by the superiority which he assumed over the holders of all offices. Williams, whose cautious prudence always led him to avoid extreme follies, but whose want of tact was continually leading him to forget that good advice is not always palatable, contrived

[1] *Pesaro's despatch*, Nov. $\frac{19}{29}$, Dec. $\frac{13}{23}$, 1624.

to give dire offence to his patron by recommending him to retire from his dangerous prominence. The Marquis of Hamilton, the Lord Steward of the Household, had just died, and Williams at once wrote to Buckingham advising him to give up the Admiralty and to become Steward of the Household. In time of war, it was a necessity for the Admiral ' either to be employed abroad personally, or to live at home in that ignominy and shame as' his Grace ' would never endure to do.'[1]

CHAP. IV.
1625. March.

It was good advice enough, but hardly likely to commend itself to a man who fancied himself equally capable of commanding a fleet and of governing a state. Williams had only succeeded in injuring himself.

Hamilton was but one of the many men of note who had fallen victims to that sickly winter. In the Low Countries, Southampton, the patron of Shakespeare in early life, sunk under the fatigue of his duties as colonel of one of the regiments which had gone out in the summer to maintain the cause of Dutch independence. At home Caron, for thirty years the representative of the States in England; Chichester, the soldier statesman, who had ruled Ireland so wisely; and Nottingham, the Admiral whose flag had floated over the fleet which drove the Armada to its destruction, sunk one after another into the grave.

Deaths of men of note.

Rife as disease had been, no apprehension had been entertained of any danger to the King's life. At the beginning of the year he had recovered from the severe attack of the gout from which he had suffered at the time of Ville-aux-Clerc's visit in December, and he

Illness of the King.

[1] Williams to Buckingham, March 2, 1625; *Cabala*, 280. This is the true date. Hacket, fancying the letter related to the death of Lennox, supposed it to have been written the year before.

CHAP. IV.
1625.
March.

was again able to take his usual interest in current affairs.[1] On the 1st of March he was at Theobalds, in his favourite deer park. On the 5th he was attacked by a tertian ague, and, although those around him did not think that anything serious was the matter, he was himself prepared for the worst. Hamilton's death affected him greatly, the more so as there were wild rumours abroad that he had been poisoned, or that he had been converted on his death-bed to the Roman Church, rumours which, however destitute of truth, made some impression at the time on the popular mind. To James the loss of Hamilton was the loss of a personal friend. 'I shall never see London more,' he said, as he gave directions for the funeral; and he gravely reproved his attendants who sought to cheer him with the popular saying, 'An ague in the spring is physic for a king.' He had never been a good patient, and he now refused to submit to the prescriptions of his physicians, who would consequently be all the more likely to take offence if irregular treatment were applied.[2]

March 12. His apparent recovery.

On the 12th James was believed to be convalescent, and was preparing to move to Hampton Court for change of air. Anxious to improve his condition still further, he remembered or was reminded that when Buckingham had been ill in the spring, he had been benefited by some remedies recommended by a country doctor living at Dunmow. Under the directions, it

Lady Buckingham's doctoring.

would seem, of Buckingham's mother, a messenger was despatched to Dunmow, and the result was a posset drink given by the Duke himself, and some plaster applied to the King's stomach and wrists by the Countess, with all the zeal which elderly ladies are apt to throw

---

[1] Chamberlain to Carleton, Feb. 26; *S. P. Dom.*, clxxxiv. 47.

[2] Chamberlain to Carleton, March 12; *ibid.* clxxxv. 48. Chambermayd to Elizabeth, March 27; *S. P. Dom., Charles I.*, i. 2.

THE KING'S LAST ILLNESS. 161

into the administration of remedies suggested by themselves. The remedies may have been, and probably were, harmless. But they were given just as the hour came round for the returning fit, and this time the fit was worse than ever. The regular physicians found out what was going on, and were highly indignant. They refused to do anything for the patient till the plasters were removed. After this fit the King's condition again improved. But on the 21st he again asked for Lady Buckingham's remedies, and, though Buckingham appears to have remonstrated, the wilful patient insisted on having his way. The next fit was a very bad one. Again the physicians remonstrated. One of the number, Dr. Craig, used exceedingly strong language, and was ordered to leave the Court. But Craig's tongue was not tied, and it soon became an article of belief with thousands of not usually credulous persons that the King had been poisoned by Buckingham and his mother.[1]

CHAP. IV.

1625. March 14. The King worse.

The next day, when the fit was over, Pembroke was about to leave Theobalds. But James could not bear to part with him. "No, my lord," he said, remembering the rumours that had been spread of Hamilton's change of religion; "you shall stay till my next fit be passed; and if I die, be a witness against those scandals that may be raised of my religion, as they have been of others."

March 22.

The King had asked for Bishop Andrewes. But Andrewes was too ill to come, and Williams had been sent for to administer spiritual consolation to the sick man. On the road he met Harvey, the discoverer of

March 23. Williams sent for.

---

[1] *State Trials,* ii. 1319; Fuller, *Church History,* v. 568. The evidence is worthless in itself, and the only ground for supposing it to have any value is cut away when once it is understood that Buckingham had no object in poisoning the King. Except in the single matter of the relief of Breda, he had had his way in everything.

VOL. I. M

CHAP. IV.
1625.

the circulation of the blood, who expressed his fears that the patient would not recover. Williams found the King's spirits low; and the next morning he obtained the Prince's leave to tell his father that his end was near. James bore the tidings well. "I am satisfied," he said; "and I pray you assist me to make ready to go away hence to Christ, whose mercies I call for, and I hope to find them." Till the end came, Williams was by the sick man's side whenever he was awake, 'in praying, in reading, most of all in discoursing about repentance, faith, remission of sins, and eternal life.' On the 24th, James, after making at some length a confession of his faith in the presence of his son and the principal attendants on his person, received the Communion from the hands of Williams. After this his strength gradually sunk, and on the 27th he died.[1]

March 24. James receives the Communion.

March 27. His death and character.

James was in his fifty-seventh year when, already an old man in constitution, he was taken away from a world which he had almost ceased even to attempt to guide. The last years of his life had not been happy. Nor was the promise of the future brighter. He had raised expectations which it would be impossible to satisfy, and it was certain that any credit which might accrue to him would be attributed by the popular voice to others than himself. It is but just to ascribe to him a desire to act rightly, to see justice done to all, to direct his subjects in the ways of peace and concord, and to prevent religion from being used as a cloak for polemical bitterness and hatred. But he had too little tact, and too unbounded confidence in his own not inconsiderable powers, to make a successful ruler, whilst his constitutional incapacity for taking trouble in thought or action gave him up as an easy prey to the passing feelings of

[1] *Hacket*, i. 222. Conway to Carleton, March 31. *Court and Times of Charles I.*, i. 1.

the hour, or to the persuasion of others who were less enlightened or less disinterested than himself. His own ideas were usually shrewd; and it is something to say of him that, if his ideas had been realised, both England and Europe would have been in far better condition than they were. The Pacification of Ireland and the Colonisation of Ulster were, together with the effort which he made to effect a more perfect union with Scotland, the acts which did him most credit. And if in late years his attempts at pacification in Germany had covered him with ridicule, and his attempts at forming a great continental alliance as the basis of war seemed likely to end in failure, it was not because his views were either unwise or unjust, but because either the obstacles in his way were too great, or he was himself deficient in the vigour and resolution which alone would have enabled him to overcome them. Keenness of insight into the fluctuating conditions of success, and firmness of will to contend against difficulties in his path, were not amongst the qualities of James.

CHAP. IV.
1625.
March 27.

The irony of flattery which in his lifetime had named him the British Solomon, was continued after his death. Williams, to whom the best points of the late King appeared so admirable in contrast with the rash, headstrong violence of his successor, proclaimed in his funeral sermon the comparison between James and the wisest of the Hebrew kings; and, either by the wish of Charles or by James's own desire, the body of the first of the Scottish line in England was not to lie apart as Elizabeth lay in her own glory. The vault in which reposed the remains of Henry VII. and Elizabeth of York was opened. The occupants of the tomb were thrust aside, and room was made for the coffin in which was the body of him who was proud of being their descendant. To unite England and Scotland in

His funeral

peace justly seemed to James to be as great an achievement as to unite the rights of York and Lancaster, and to close the long epoch of civil war. But the comparison which was thus invited could not but bear hardly upon the memory of the late sovereign. Henry, by his mingled vigour and prudence, laid the foundation of the strong monarchy of the Tudors; James sowed the seeds of revolution and disaster.[1]

[1] There is an account of the opening of the tomb in Dean Stanley's *Memorials of Westminster Abbey*. Curiously enough, James was defied even in the tomb. Close by the coffin of the author of the 'Counterblast to Tobacco' was found a pipe, probably dropped by a workman.

CHAPTER V.

MILITARY AND DIPLOMATIC PROJECTS OF THE NEW REIGN.

THE news that Charles had succeeded to his father was received with general satisfaction. "The joy of the people," as a contemporary expressed it, "devoured their mourning."[1] Of the character of the new King, silent and reserved as he was, little was known, and still less had reached the public ear of his questionable proceedings in the negotiation of the marriage treaty. It was enough that, ever since his return from Madrid, he had been the consistent advocate of war with Spain.

CHAP. V.
1625. March 21.
General satisfaction with the new reign.

When Ville-aux-Clercs went back to France with the marriage treaty, Richelieu asked him what he thought of Charles. "He is either an extraordinary man," was the shrewd reply, "or his talents are very mean. If his reticence is affected in order not to give jealousy to his father, it is a sign of consummate prudence. If it is natural and unassumed, the contrary inference may be drawn."[2]

Ville-aux-Clercs' opinion of Charles.

The extreme reserve of the young King was doubtless closely connected with that want of imaginative power which lay at the root of all his faults. With all his confidence in his own thoughts, he failed to give to his ideas an expression which was satisfactory to others

His reticence.

[1] Tilman to D'Ewes, April 8; *Ellis*, ser. 2, iii. 243.
[2] *Mémoires de Brienne*, i. 399.

or even to himself. His father's rapid utterance had swept his slow conceptions away as with a torrent before he could find out what he really meant to say, and he did not like to be contradicted. The man who is too vain to bear contradiction and not sufficiently brilliant or wise to overpower it, must of necessity take refuge in silence.

Unfortunately the defect which hindered him from being a good talker hindered him also from being a good ruler. The firm convictions of his mind were unassailable by arguments which he was unable to understand, and unaltered by the impression of passing events which slipped by him unnoticed. The wisest of men, the most decisive of facts, were no more to him than the whistling of the storm is to the man who is seated by a warm fireside. They passed him by; and, if he heeded them at all, it was only to wonder that they did not conform to his own beneficent intentions. "I cannot," he said on one occasion, "defend a bad, nor yield in a good cause."[1] Conscious of the purity of his own motives he never ceased to divide mankind into two simple classes—into those who agreed with him, and those who did not; into sheep to be cherished, and goats to be rejected. Such narrowness of view was no guarantee for fixity of purpose. Whenever the moment came at last for the realities of life to break through the artificial atmosphere in which he had been living, when forms unknown and unimagined before crowded on his bewildered vision, it was too late to gain a knowledge the acquisition of which had been deferred too long, or to exercise that strength of will which is only to be found where there is an intelligent perception of the danger to be faced.

The same explanation will probably in a great

[1] *Laud's Diary*, Feb. 1, 1623.

measure account for the special fault which has more than any other cost Charles the respect of posterity. The truthful man must be able to image forth in his own mind the effect which his words have upon others. He must be able to represent to himself the impression his engagements leave upon those with whom they were made; and he must either keep them in the sense in which they are understood by others, or he must openly and candidly show cause why it is wrong or impossible so to keep them. The way in which Charles gave and broke his promises was the very reverse of this. He looked too much into his own mind, too little into the minds of those with whom he was bargaining. When he entered into an engagement he either formed no clear conception of the circumstances under which he would be called to fulfil it, or he remembered too clearly this or that consideration which would render his promise illusory, or would at least, if it had been spoken out, have prevented those with whom he was dealing from accepting his word. When the time came for him to fulfil an engagement he could think of nothing but the limitations with which he had surrounded it, or with which he fancied that he had surrounded it, when his word had been given. Sometimes he went still further, apparently thinking that it was lawful to use deception as a weapon against those who had no right to know the truth.

Of the defects in Charles's character, the nation was as yet profoundly ignorant. All that was known of him was to his advantage. James died a little before noon. After some hours spent in private, the young King—he was but in his twenty-fifth year—came up from Theobalds to St. James's. The next morning he gave orders that all his father's officers of state should retain their places. With the exception of the

CHAP. V.
1625.
March 28.

Catholic Lords, Wotton and Baltimore, who were excluded, the new Privy Council was identical with that which had existed at the close of the last reign. For though the names of Suffolk, Wallingford, Middlesex, Bristol, and Bacon were also removed, those who bore them had long ceased to appear at the board. The only addition to the number was Sir Humphrey May, the Chancellor of the Duchy of Lancaster, a man of some ability and of a very conciliatory disposition.[1]

Charles and Buckingham.

The remainder of the week was passed by Charles in seclusion at St. James's. Buckingham, who was alone admitted to share his privacy, 'lay' on the 'first night of the reign in the King's bedchamber, and three nights after in the next lodgings.'[2] There is nothing to show that this was any way unpopular at the time. The transactions relating to the French treaty were as yet involved in mystery. Of all men living Eliot was least open to the charge of undue subserviency. Yet Eliot wrote to Buckingham that he hoped to become 'wholly devoted to the contemplation of' his 'excellence.'[3]

Williams objects to the preparations for war.

If the outer world was satisfied for a time, there were those at Court who knew too much to be at ease. Williams had instinctively shrunk from the unpopularity

---

[1] Proceedings of the Privy Council, March 28; Chamberlain to Carleton, April 9; *S. P. Dom.*, i. 5, 46. *Council Register*, March 29.

[2] Neve to Hollonde, April 5; *Court and Times*, i. 3.

[3] Eliot to Buckingham, April 1; Forster's *Eliot*, i. 111. Eliot had been coming to London to attend Buckingham on his visit to France, and Mr. Forster regards the order, which met him, to remain in the West, as evidence of some intrigue countenanced by the Duke. But the order (*Council Register*, March 28) was plainly a *bond fide* one, giving him special duties to fulfil. In fact, Eliot was not wanted to accompany Buckingham, simply because Buckingham's journey was indefinitely postponed. When the Duke went it was under other circumstances, and the suite which he proposed to take was left behind. There was no slight whatever put upon Eliot. As I shall hereafter show, the breach between Eliot and Buckingham cannot be proved to have taken place till much later than Mr. Forster supposes.

which was sure to result as soon as the concessions made to the Catholics were known, and he had too much common sense to look with favour on Buckingham's military projects, which he knew to be far too extensive for the means at his disposal. When he was first admitted to the Royal presence, he found Charles bent upon summoning Parliament immediately, to enable him to go on with his preparations by sea and land. The King even asked why the old Parliament of the preceding year might not be called without the delay of fresh elections. Williams told him that this would be distinctly illegal, and hinted that it would be well to afford time to canvass the constituencies in favour of candidates of the right sort. But Charles was in no mood to hear of difficulties. Let the writs, he said, be despatched forthwith. Let not a day be lost. The fleet was to go forth in the summer. War with Spain must be carried on vigorously. Williams did not venture to argue with his new master. But the few words which he spoke were not sufficiently enthusiastic. The King turned his back upon him and dismissed him.[1]

CHAP.
V.
1625.
March 28.

In the Council too voices were raised against proceeding with the marriage treaty as it stood. But matters had gone too far to admit of hesitation now, and all opposition was put down by Buckingham with a high hand.[2]

March 29
Objections
to the
marriage.

A week after his father's death, Charles removed to Whitehall, walking without state across St. James's Park. His demeanour gained general approbation. His face was serious and pale. His attention to the services of religion was the object of almost universal remark. Men told one another with satisfaction that the new King was ' very attentive and devout at prayer

April 3.
Charles at
Whitehall.

[1] *Hacket*, ii. 4.
[2] Effiat to Lewis XIII., April $\frac{18}{28}$; *Harl. MSS.*, 4597, fol. 36.

CHAP. V.
1625.
April 9.

and sermons,' and were especially pleased to hear that he had refused to make the customary present of mourning to a single recusant. A few weeks later the newsmongers reported that, as an Irish Earl was talking in a loud voice in a room next to that in which the King was at prayers, Charles sent to him to leave off prating and come to prayers. "His Majesty," said the Irishman, "knows well enough that I do not come to his prayers." "If he will not come to my prayers," replied Charles, "let him get out of my house."[1]

Order at Court.

Such anecdotes were sure to be favourably received. Nor was the restoration of the state which had been observed at Court in the days of Elizabeth likely to injure him in the popular opinion. Almost any one with a courtier's introduction could gain access to James; Charles directed that no one should be admitted to his presence without special directions from himself.[2] Amongst those who were thus excluded was one who might have hoped for better treatment. Sir Francis Cottington had been Charles's secretary when he was Prince of Wales, and had served him faithfully in that capacity. But it was well known that, having fallen sick at Madrid, he had declared himself to be a Roman Catholic, at least till his recovery, and he had since protested, as Bristol had protested, his belief that the restoration of the Palatinate was to be hoped for from the Spanish ministers. He was now not only stripped of his official position and emoluments, but forbidden to appear at Court. Cottington, like a man of the world as he was, went straight to the Duke, asking him 'whether it could not be in his power, by all dutiful application and all possible service, to be restored to the

[1] Neve to Hollonde, April 5; Chamberlain to Carleton, April 9; Meade to Stuteville, May 6; *Court and Times*, i. 3, 6, 20.
[2] *Salvetti's Newsletter*, April $\frac{15}{25}$.

good opinion his Grace had once vouchsafed to have of him, and to be admitted to serve him?' Buckingham had at least the merit of speaking out his thoughts. He told Cottington 'that he would deal very clearly with him; that it was utterly impossible to bring that to pass which he had proposed; that he was not only firmly resolved never to trust him, or to have to do with him, but that he was and would be always his declared enemy; and that he would do always whatsoever should be in his power to ruin and destroy him, and of this he might be most assured.'

CHAP. V.
1625. May 26

Cottington, seeing that all chance of advancement was at an end, replied that 'he hoped from his justice and generosity, that he would not suffer himself to gain by his loss,' adding that he had not only by the Duke's command laid out money in jewels and pictures, but had once 'in hope of his future favour' made him a present of a suit of hangings worth 800*l.* Buckingham told him that he should be at no loss. If he would send in his account, every penny should be repaid.[1]

Such an anecdote as this points to the special danger of the new reign so far as it was to be influenced by Buckingham. Generosity there would be above mere personal meanness. But whether any one was to be treated as a friend or as an enemy would depend entirely on the accordance of his political views with those prevalent for the time at Court. There would be no largeness of mind, no readiness to hear all sides of disputed questions.

Charles's heart was set upon greater things than on the restoration of etiquette. On the 9th he directed the formation of a Committee of the Privy Council to advise him on foreign affairs. Buckingham, of course, was one of the selected number. Of the other four

Committee of foreign affairs.

[1] *Clarendon,* i. 33.

172   PROJECTS OF THE NEW REIGN.

CHAP. V.
1625.
April.

members, Pembroke, Brooke, Ley, and Conway, Pembroke was the only one who had ventured to differ from Buckingham, and even he had never differed from him for any length of time.¹

Mansfeld allowed to assist the Dutch.

The first result of the consultations of this body was the removal of the bar to the employment of Mansfeld at Breda. The States General were again applied to for money, and they consented to give their security to a loan of 40,000*l.* raised at Amsterdam. The English Government hoped that this sum would be sufficient to enable Mansfeld to take his way towards the Palatinate as soon as the fate of the besieged town was decided.². The demands of the Northern Powers were next taken into consideration. It appeared that the Congress at the Hague could not be brought together as soon as was expected, and Charles therefore entered into a separate agreement with the King of Denmark. He offered to furnish him with 30,000*l.*³ a month, and before May was at an end he paid over 46,000*l.* on account. He did not, however, abandon the hope that the co-operation of Gustavus might still be secured.⁴

May 26.
Money sent to the King of Denmark.

April.
The fleet got ready.

If Charles was anxious for the success of Mansfeld and Christian, he was still more anxious for the success of his own fleet, which, thanks to a timely loan of 30,000*l.* from Buckingham, was being rapidly prepared for sea. His first recorded appearance in public after his father's death was on the occasion of a visit to the shipping at Blackwall.⁵ It had been finally settled that

¹ The King to Ley and others, April 9; *S. P. Dom.*, i. 43.
² Conway to Carleton, April 19; Carleton to Conway, April 19; *S. P. Holland.*
³ *Enrolments of Privy Seals*, May 26; Anstruther to Carleton, May 28; *S. P. Holland.* Ley to Conway, June 11; *S. P. Dom.*, iii. 52.
⁴ Declared Accounts, Treasurer of the Navy. *Audit Office.*
⁵ Meddus to Mead, April 22; *Court and Times*, i. 11.

twelve ships of the Royal Navy, twenty armed merchantmen, and fifty colliers, to act as transports, should rendezvous at Plymouth in June. Something more than ordinary sea service was intended, and on May 1 the Privy Council ordered that 10,000 landsmen should be pressed to accompany the fleet as soldiers. Of these, 8,000 were to be at Plymouth on May 25. The remaining 2,000 were to be sent over to the Netherlands there to be exchanged, if the consent of the States General could be obtained, for the same number of disciplined men from the English regiments in the Dutch service. By this means some steadiness might be imparted to the raw levies who were but too likely to be the mere offscouring of the streets sent by justices of the peace to serve his Majesty because they were troublesome to their neighbours at home.[1]

CHAP. V.

1625. May 1.

Land soldiers to be pressed.

The application made at the Hague for disciplined soldiers had been accompanied by a proposal that the Dutch should take an active part in the expedition itself. When the demand reached the Netherlands the soldier who had guided the Republic since the death of Barneveld had died after a lingering illness. In his brother, Frederick Henry, who succeeded him as Prince of Orange, and as Stadtholder of five out of the seven Provinces, the States were eventually to find a soldier of a quality equal to that of Maurice. But he was as yet untried in his high post, and, with the fate of Breda trembling in the balance, the States General naturally demurred to Charles's request to be allowed to select two thousand picked men from all the English regiments in their service. Whatever men he took, they said, he must take by whole companies, the good and the bad together. But they had no objection to his

April. The Dutch asked to take part.

April 13. Death of the Prince of Orange.

[1] *Enrolments of Privy Seals*, Dec. 23, Feb. 2; Reply to Carleton's Memorial, April 17; *S. P. Holland*. Council Register, May 1, 16.

CHAP. V.

1625.
April 17.
Reply of the Dutch.

invitation to share in a maritime attack upon Spain, and they agreed to furnish twenty ships to the proposed expedition. At the same time they expressed their desire to bring to trial the perpetrators of the massacre of Amboina, and, for the time at least, this cause of dissension was removed.[1]

May.
Buckingham to command the expedition.

The discussion then turned on the further arrangements to be made for the expedition. For some reason or another, perhaps to avoid subjecting England to reprisals from Spain,[2] Charles was unwilling actually to declare war, and it was arranged that Buckingham should take the command in person, but that he should receive his commission from Frederick, the titular King of Bohemia.[3]

Where was the thunderbolt to fall? The intention had originally been to direct it towards the coast of Spain, to occupy some fortified town there, and to watch for the treasure-ships returning from Mexico. But an idea dropped in conversation by some one in authority at the Hague was now taken up by Buckingham with characteristic warmth. The fleet and army might, he thought, be more usefully employed in an attack upon the ports of Flanders in combination with the Dutch forces. If those nests of privateers were taken and destroyed, both England and the Netherlands would be the better for the operation.[4]

Plan of a campaign in Flanders.

Necessity of consulting France.

Before such a scheme as this could be finally adopted it was necessary to obtain the approbation, if not the co-operation, of the French Government. Up to this

[1] Reply to Carleton's memorial, April 17; *S. P. Holland.*
[2] That there was any wish to avoid attacking Spain, is a theory impossible to maintain in the face of the evidence of the French ambassadors and others, who were watching Charles from day to day.
[3] Buckingham to Carleton, May 4; *S. P. Holland.*
[4] Compare Richelieu, *Mémoires,* ii. 461-4, with Morton's instructions, June 14; *S. P. Holland.*

time Charles had scrupulously carried out his engagements to Lewis. By mutual consent the term within which the marriage was to be celebrated had been prolonged for a month as soon as James's illness was known to be serious, and before the month came to an end, the Pope, discovering that no attention would be paid to his remonstrances, ordered his Nuncio at Paris to deliver up the dispensation without waiting for further concessions from the English. The marriage was accordingly celebrated by proxy on May 1, in front of the great west door of Nôtre Dame, after the precedent set at the marriage of Margaret of Valois with the Huguenot Henry of Navarre.[1]

On the same day Charles gave directions to the Lord Keeper to carry out the engagement which he had taken as Prince to remove the burdens weighing upon the Catholics in England. "We will and require you," he wrote, "to give order to all such our officers to whom it may appertain, that all manner of prosecution against the said Roman Catholics, as well on their persons as goods, for the exercise of the said religion, be stayed and forborne, provided always that they behave themselves modestly therein, and yield us that obedience which good and true subjects owe unto their King."[2]

Charles was represented at the marriage ceremony by the Duke of Chevreuse, a distant kinsman of his own,[3] who had attached himself warmly to the English alliance. As soon as the death of James had opened a prospect of greater political activity in England, Buckingham abandoned the idea of visiting Paris as proxy for his sovereign, and, setting himself down to the work

[1] Siri, *Memorie Recondite*, v. 835, 847.
[2] The King to Williams, May 1; *S. P. Dom.*, ii. 1.
[3] Through his great-grandmother, Mary of Guise.

CHAP. V.
1625.

May 1. Doubts around the French alliance.

April 21. Carlisle's warnings.

before him, looked forward, at the most, to sailing across the Straits in command of the fleet which was to fetch home the young Queen.[1] It is not likely that either Charles or Buckingham, in their sanguine optimism, foresaw the storm which they were raising in England by their concessions to the Catholics. But they were beginning to doubt whether they would have anything except the person of the bride to show in return for what they had done. The league offensive and defensive between England and France, once promised as the crowning ornament of the marriage, had vanished amidst a cloud of compliments. And now, before the end of April, had come a letter from Carlisle, arguing that, for Charles's own sake, the less he said about such a league the better. No one could tell on which side the weight of the French monarchy would ultimately be thrown. On the one hand French troops were co-operating with the Duke of Savoy against Genoa. On the other hand, no peace had yet been made with Soubise and the Huguenots of Rochelle. The Pope had despatched his nephew, Cardinal Barbarini, to Paris to mediate an agreement between France and Spain. Under these circumstances Carlisle doubted the wisdom of urging a stricter alliance upon the French. "I am infinitely apprehensive," he wrote, "of adventuring my gracious young master's virgin reputation to a refusal." The French, he argued, would break a treaty as easily as they would break their word. If they continued adverse to Spain they would of their own accord seek aid from England. If they made peace with Spain they would expect

[1] *Salvetti's Newsletters*, April 1, 29, May 6. That his final resolution to go to Paris was a sudden one, is plainly stated in a letter from Conway to Carleton, May 24; *S. P. Holland*. This explains why Eliot was not and could not be asked to attend. *See* p. 168, note 3.

England to aid them against the Huguenots, a thing to which it would be impossible for the King of England to consent.[1]

CHAP. V.
1625.
April 4.

It was excellent advice, such as Carlisle, mere courtier and spendthrift as he is generally represented, was usually accustomed to give. But how was it possible for Buckingham to follow it? This policy of waiting till France made up her mind which side she would take, he had long ago impetuously dashed aside. For the sake of the closest union with France he had sacrificed his own consistency; and with it, though as yet he knew it not, his popularity with the English nation.

Buckingham cannot abandon hope.

Buckingham could not bear that doubt should be thrown upon the hopes on which he had buoyed himself up so long. One chance yet seemed to remain to him. Forgetting how little his personal presence in Spain had availed him, he would try whether his personal presence in France would not clear all difficulties away. It was certain that he would not come empty-handed. The great English fleet and army was not to be despised. If he offered to attack the Spanish Netherlands by sea and land from the north in conjunction with the Dutch, whilst Lewis, taking up in earnest his father's last enterprise, directed his armies upon them from the south; if he promised that the Spanish province of Artois should be surrendered to Lewis as his share of the spoils, what French heart could turn away from so much glory, combined with so much solid advantage to the monarchy? For the sake of such an alliance as this, Lewis could hardly object to grant acceptable conditions to the Huguenots.[2]

He determines to go to France.

[1] Carlisle to Buckingham, April 21; *S. P. France.*
[2] There are no despatches from Buckingham giving an account of his mission. But its main objects are to be found in Richelieu's *Memoirs*,

VOL. I.   N

178 PROJECTS OF THE NEW REIGN.

CHAP. V.
1625. May.
The English vessels for Rochelle.

With these hopes and fears Buckingham had ceased to wish to give English aid to France against Rochelle. He would rather, as far as we can judge from his acts, see Lewis pardon the Huguenots in order that he might make war, than help Lewis to subdue the Huguenots with the same object. A few days before James died, the contracts had been signed which made over to the King of France the 'Vanguard,' a ship of the Royal Navy, together with seven merchant vessels hired for the purpose from their owners. They were to be placed under the command of Pennington, the companion of Raleigh in his last voyage to Guiana, and were to be at the service of Lewis for a time varying at his discretion from six to eighteen months. It was expressly stated that the vessels might be used 'against whomsoever except the King of Great Britain.'[1] On the 8th of May the ships were ordered to cross the Channel, but on the 18th, a few days after Buckingham had left England, Sir John Coke, who was the leading spirit amongst the Commissioners of the Navy, and was deep in Buckingham's confidence, wrote to Pennington directing him in no way to meddle with the civil wars of France, or to take part in any attack upon Protestants there or elsewhere. The true intention of his employment was to serve against

They are not to serve against the Huguenots.

(ii. 459), and his statement is confirmed, so far as relates to the proposed league, by Rusdorf (Rusdorf to Frederick, $\frac{\text{May } 22}{\text{June } 2}$; *Mémoires*, i. 578); and as far as relates to the attack upon Flanders, we know, from Morton's instructions referred to at p. 186, that such a project was in contemplation. The proposal about the Huguenots is noticed in Langerac's despatch of May $\frac{20}{30}$, an extract from which has been communicated to me by Dr. Goll.

[1] Contracts, March 25; *S. P. France*. When Glanville afterwards stated that the vessels had been pressed, he probably meant, not that they had been pressed for the King of France, but that they had been first pressed for the service of the King of England, and then transferred to France.

'the foreign enemies of France and England.' These orders, in flagrant contradiction with the letter and spirit of the contract, were said to be for its 'better understanding.'[1]

CHAP. V.
1625.

This change of front in the matter of the ships was accompanied by a change of front in the matter of the Recusancy laws. On the 11th of May the English Catholics were full of hope. The order sent to Williams on the 1st[2] was, as they believed, to be carried out. Three thousand letters to the Judges, the Bishops, and other official personages, commanding them to desist from any further execution of the penal laws, were ready to be sent out. Before the 23rd the Catholics were told that they must wait a little longer. It would be unwise to fly so openly in the face of the coming Parliament. When the session was at an end their demands might be attended to.[3]

May. Change in the treatment of the Catholics.

It was hardly wise of Buckingham to offer so openly to the French Government the alternative between a complete alliance with England and an open rupture. For Richelieu, anxious to lead his sovereign in the path in which Buckingham desired him to tread, the advent of the impetuous young man must have been a sore trial. He knew that Lewis, balancing as he was between two opinions, loathing the domination of Spain and the independence of his own Protestants almost equally, would be thrown off his balance by the slightest semblance of a threat on either side. And how was it to be expected that the headstrong English-

Danger of Buckingham's visit to France.

[1] Warrant from Buckingham, May 8; Coke to Pennington, May 18; *S. P. Dom.*, ii. 37, 74. I must ask those who think that Coke's letter was written to throw dust in the eyes of Pennington, to suspend their judgment till I have told the whole story.
[2] P. 175.
[3] The English Catholics to Ville-aux-Clercs, May 11, 23: *Harl. MSS.*, 4597, 140, b, 170, b.

man, whose whole political position was endangered, should abstain from threats?[1]

1625. May 14. He arrives at Paris.

On the 14th of May, Buckingham arrived in Paris. To the world in general he appeared to have set his whole soul on displaying his handsome person and his jewelled attire at the Court festivities.[2] But those who knew that he was accompanied by the new secretary, Sir Albertus Morton, might suspect that he had more serious work in hand.[3]

Peace to be offered to the Huguenots.

Of his negotiations at Paris we merely learn that, with Richelieu's warm support, the King sent a nobleman to Rochelle to invite the Huguenots to send deputies to Paris to treat for peace.[4] After some delay caused by the state of the King's health, the Court set out for Compiegne, where Lewis was to take leave of his sister. Buckingham employed the two days which were spent there in urging the French Government to

[1] Richelieu's position is clearly defined in Langerac's despatch of $\frac{June\ 23}{July}$. He was always urging the King to war without and peace within. The same ambassador, writing on June $\frac{17}{27}$, says that Buckingham told the Queen Mother that the Huguenots must seek peace on their knees, with rapiers in their hands. As far as I can gather Buckingham's intentions, he seems to have come over in much the same spirit, though probably he thought less of the rapier at the beginning, and more at the end, of his mission.

[2] The list of his clothes and attendants, printed in *Ellis*, ser. 1, iii. 189, of which so much use has been made by Buckingham's biographers, is not a list of what he really had with him, but of what he intended to take if he had gone as proxy at the marriage. Instead of the long train there set down, only Montgomery, Morton, and Goring accompanied him (*Salvetti's Newsletter*, May $\frac{13}{23}$). He left England in such haste that he had to send back a gentleman "pour lui apporter ses nouveaux riches habits, afin qu'il se puisse montrer en ses vanités' (*Rusdorf*, i. 579). Under these circumstances Eliot, of course, did not accompany him. The story told by Wotton how he dropped a diamond in Paris which he subsequently recovered, is, I suspect, the origin of the incredible tale that he purposely left his diamonds so loosely fastened on as to fall off, and that he then refused to take them back from those who picked them up.

[3] *Salvetti's Newsletter*, May $\frac{13}{23}$.

[4] *Langerac's Despatch*, May $\frac{20}{30}$.

join England in a declared war against Spain. But either the Duke's manner was distasteful to Lewis, or he shrunk from taking so decided a part. He would neither bind himself to reject any pacific overtures which might come from Spain, nor would he engage to take open part in a war for the recovery of the Palatinate. Even the proffered bribe of the annexation of Artois to France was not enough to move him. He would give 100,000*l*. towards the expenses of the King of Denmark, and he would continue his share of Mansfeld's pay for seven months longer, and would reinforce the Count's shattered army with two thousand additional French horse.[1] More than this he would not do.[2]

CHAP. V.

1625. May. Buckingham demands a strict alliance.

By a statesman accustomed to take hard facts as they were, the result of Buckingham's mission would not have been regarded as so very pitiful. It was something that the French Court should show a disposition to treat with the Huguenots and to oppose Spain in its own time and its own way. But Buckingham had staked his reputation on far more than this. Nothing but the most brilliant success would save his conduct with respect to the Catholics and Mansfeld's expedition from the gravest animadversion in the coming Parliament. He went to France with

Buckingham's failure.

---

[1] The destination of the French horse is not mentioned in the despatch of Chevreuse and Ville-aux-Clercs which refers to the offer ($\frac{\text{June 27}}{\text{July 7}}$; *Harl. MSS.*, 4597, fol. 193). But Lorkin tells Conway, in a letter of June 22 (*S. P. France*), that Richelieu had informed him that 'he had offered further a new succour of 2,000 horse for Count Mansfeld.' In his letter of Aug. 18, Lorkin further says that Richelieu, in conversation, told him 'that at Compiegne they had offered a million towards the King of Denmark's entertainment, 2,000 horse towards the setting up of Mansfeld's army again, and to continue their wonted pay for seven months longer, but could never, in all this time, get answer from England.' *S. P. France.*

[2] Richelieu, *Mémoires*, ii. 461.

inflated hopes of unbounded success; he returned bitterly disappointed. It is hardly too much to say that his visit to Paris in 1625 cut the ground from under his feet as completely as his visit to Madrid in 1623 had cut the ground from under the feet of James. He had yielded much, and had nothing to show for it in return.

Is it wholly impossible that Buckingham's vexation at his political failure may have vented itself in the extravagance of which he was guilty a few days later? Though Lewis went no further than Compiegne, his mother and his wife accompanied the young Queen of England some stages further. At Amiens Buckingham spoke bitterly to Mary of Medici. The Huguenots, he said, might come to Paris to ask for peace upon their knees, but they must bring their swords in their hands.[1] Queen Anne he addressed in terms of such passionate devotion as they were walking together in the shades of evening, that she was forced to call her attendants to her help. That the handsome Englishman had made an impression upon the poor young wife who had been treated with complete neglect by her husband, there can be no doubt whatever. And Buckingham was not the man to restrain himself from taking advantage of her weakness. After he had taken leave, he met a courier at Abbeville with directions to impart certain information to the French Government. Hurrying back to Amiens, he informed Mary de Medici of the State secret confided to him, and then asked for an audience of the young Queen. Being introduced, as was the fashion of those days, into the chamber in which Anne was in bed with her attendant ladies around her, he threw himself on his knees, and kissing the coverlet

---

[1] *Langerac's Despatch*, as quoted at p. 180.

over her, poured forth a torrent of impassioned words such as would have beseemed a lover restored after long separation to the sight of his plighted mistress. Vanity and licentiousness were deeply rooted in Buckingham's nature. But were vanity and licentiousness sufficient to account for conduct so strange? May there not have mingled with unchastened desire some feeling of pleasure at the affront which he thus put upon the man who had thwarted his policy, by paying his addresses thus publicly to his wife?[1]

Whilst Buckingham was making love or weaving political schemes at Amiens, the innocent pledge of the tottering alliance was continuing her journey. On June 12 she landed at Dover. Charles, at the urgent entreaty of his mother-in-law, had retired to Canterbury, in order that he might not set eyes on his bride till she had recovered from the effects of sea-sickness. The next morning he rode over to Dover and took her by surprise. Running down stairs as soon as she heard that he had come, she offered to kiss his hand. He caught her in his arms and kissed her. "Sire," she said, as soon as she was able to speak, "I am come to this country to be used and commanded by Your Majesty." By-and-by, seing that she reached to his shoulder, Charles, who had heard much of her shortness of stature, glanced downwards to see if her feet were raised by artificial means. "Sire," she said with

---

[1] The scene is described substantially in the same way in the *Memoirs of Madame de Motteville*, and in the *Memoirs of Brienne*. There is no very clear account of the despatch which reached Buckingham at Amiens. It seems to have been connected with the Duke of Savoy (Ville-aux-Clercs to Lewis XIII., $\frac{\text{June } 27}{\text{July } 7}$, and the subsequent correspondence: *Harl. MSS.*, 4597, fol. 192, 213, b.). Buckingham appears to have added a request that the 2,000 horse, instead of being placed under Mansfeld, should be lent to Charles to do what he pleased with them, probably to use them for the attack upon Flanders.

the ready wit of her nation, "I stand upon my own feet; I have no helps by art. Thus high I am, and am neither higher nor lower."[1]

Such passages between a sharp, bright-eyed girl of fifteen and a husband of twenty-four could not do more than gloss over the inherent difficulties of the situation. The young wife had been taught to regard herself as entrusted with the mission of comforting and protecting the persecuted members of her own Church. She had not crossed the sea forgetting her own people and her father's house. Nor was Charles likely to fill a large space in her imagination. Affectionate himself towards her, he was eager for her affection in return. But he expected to be obeyed without showing that superiority which secures voluntary obedience. He was punctilious, harsh when contradicted, and without resource in moments of emergency. Petty difficulties soon arose. Henrietta Maria had grown up under the care of Madame de St. Georges, and she could not bear to be separated from her as she drove with her husband from Dover to Canterbury. But she was told that the lady's rank was not high enough, and Buckingham's mother and sister, together with the Countess of Arundel, were allowed to seat themselves in her stead in the Royal carriage. The first matrimonial conflict, rising at times almost into the dignity of a diplomatic dispute, arose out of this question of precedence. The French ladies of the Queen's suite took good care to keep the quarrel open, and to teach her to regard everything English with contemptuous dislike.[2]

On the 16th the King and Queen entered London by the highway of the river. The rain was falling

[1] Mead to Stuteville, June 17; *Ellis*, ser. 1, iii. 196, 197.
[2] Chevreuse and Ville-aux-Clercs to Lewis XIII., undated; *Harl. MSS.*, 4597, fol. 181.

THE KING AND QUEEN IN LONDON. 185

fast. But they kept the windows of their barge open, so that they might be seen by the multitude which awaited them. They were received with the utmost enthusiasm. The tops of the houses, the decks of vessels and lighters, were covered with a shouting crowd. Deeply laden wherries gave life to the surface of the river. The ordnance of the fleet at Blackwall, and after that the Tower guns, discharged a thundering welcome. The Queen, as she landed at Denmark House—the Somerset House of an earlier and a later generation—seemed to be well pleased with her reception. The London crowd knew no ill of her, and those who gathered to see her as she passed had it not in their hearts to be uncivil to one so young and fair. It was rumoured too that there were hopes of her conversion. Perhaps she had herself unwittingly given rise to the report. Some one had impertinently asked her whether she could abide a Huguenot. "Why not?" she quickly replied; "was not my father one?"[1]

CHAP. V.
1625.
June 14.

Charles might well look merrily around him as he led his wife to his home. But for those terrible religious and political questions behind, he had no need to be alarmed at the little disagreement about Madame de St. Georges' precedence, or the important discovery of the French ladies in waiting that their mistress had to sleep in an old-fashioned bed which had done service in the days of Queen Elizabeth. But already, two days before the royal entry into London, the first stroke had been aimed at the French alliance of which Henrietta Maria was the living symbol. On June 14 Morton was despatched to the Netherlands to urge the Dutch to co-operate with England in the attack upon

Morton's missions to the Netherlands.

[1] —— to ——, June 17; *Court and Times*, i. 30.

CHAP. V.
1625.

May 26.
Surrender of Breda.

June.
Deplorable condition of Mansfeld's troops.

Flanders, which Lewis had refused to share.[1] If this project should be adopted, the war would assume a more exclusively Protestant character, and poor Henrietta Maria's marriage would, politically at least, have lost its meaning.

For the moment, however, this risk was averted. It was by no means a propitious time for inviting the States General to take part in so hazardous an enterprise. On May 26 Breda had surrendered, and there was nothing so stable in the military or financial strength of England as to induce the cautious Dutch Government to abandon its defensive policy for an attack upon the enemy in the very centre of his power, especially as there was every reason to suppose that the project was not regarded with favour at Paris. If indeed a warning were needed to keep the Dutch from placing too great confidence in the overtures of England, it was not far to seek. The condition of Mansfeld's troops was more deplorable than ever. As soon as Breda was lost, the States, anxious to be rid of him without delay, had done their best to forward him on his way towards the Palatinate. But the attempt was no sooner made than its impracticability appeared. Beyond the frontier 19,000 of the enemy's troops were waiting to swoop down upon him the moment that he abandoned the protection of the Dutch fortresses. In spite of the money which Carleton had succeeded in raising upon the security of the States, the men had, as usual, been infamously neglected. Four days passed after their arrival at the frontier before even a piece of bread was served out to the famished soldiers. The peasants, fearing the consequences of the irruption of a starving mob, had fled at their approach. Of the whole force,

[1] Instructions to Morton, June 14; *S. P. Holland.*

English, French, and Germans together, but 6,000 marching men were left. "Our General," wrote Lord Cromwell on June 1, "studies his profit and how to ruin us, I think; else he would give us that which might make us live like poor Christians, and as the King's subjects. ..... I desire nought in this world but an honest life, and so doth my Lieutenant-Colonel, your servant. Let us but command men that may not die as if we had killed them by giving them neither meat nor money, and we will go anywhere where our noble conductor dare send us; but to command a regiment starved, now not 220 men, I scorn it."[1]

{.sidenote}
CHAP.
V.
1625.
June 7.

Such was the position of England on the Continent when, on June 18, Parliament met at last. The only diplomatic effort and the only military effort which had been seriously taken up had ended in failure. The French alliance had produced no visible results. The men who had followed Mansfeld in January were either lying under the green sod in the fields of Holland and Brabant, or were cowering for shelter under the guns of the Dutch forts. The projects for the future were uncertain, hazardous, and enormously expensive. In the course of the next year 360,000*l*. would be required for the King of Denmark, 240,000*l*. for Mansfeld, 100,000*l*. for the regiments in the Low Countries, and some 300,000*l*. for the fleet, making in all a sum of 1,000,000*l*., or more than three times the amount of the subsidies which had been granted in 1624 as an unprecedented contribution.

{.sidenote}
June 18. Military and diplomatic failure.

{.sidenote}
Necessities of the future.

Yet it is probable that the mere extent of the demand would not have stood in the King's way if the hearts of the Commons had been with him. But, unless the new Parliament abandoned the position taken up

{.sidenote}
Probable state of feeling in the House of Commons.

[1] Cromwell to Carleton, June 7; *S. P. Holland*.

by the old one, this was more than unlikely. At all events, in 1624 neither the close alliance with France, nor the embarkation of England upon a Continental war on a large scale, had been approved of by the Lower House. It remained to be seen whether the Commons of 1625 would be of a different opinion.

CHAPTER VI.

THE FIRST PARLIAMENT OF CHARLES I. AT WESTMINSTER.

NEVER within living memory had there been such competition for seats in the House of Commons. Never had the members chosen attended so numerously on the first day of the session. Something there was doubtless of a desire to welcome the young King, of whom nothing but good was as yet known; something too, it may be, of curiosity to learn the secret of the destination of the ships which were gathering, and of the diplomatic messages which had been speeding backwards and forwards over Europe. Nor is it at all unlikely that many at least were anxious to hear from the King's lips some explanation of the way in which his promise had been kept to the former Parliament, some assurance, if assurance were possible, that the English Catholics had not benefited by the King's marriage.

CHAP.
VI.
1625.
June 18.
Numerous attendance at the opening Parliament.

The presence of the members in London was not without risk to themselves. The Plague, that scourge of crowded and ill-ventilated cities, had once more settled down upon the capital. In the first week of April twelve deaths from this cause had been recorded. By the middle of June, just as Parliament was meeting, the weekly mortality was one hundred and sixty-five.[1]

The Plague in London.

Seldom has any sovereign had a harder task before him than was before Charles when he stood up to per-

Charles opens Parliament.

[1] Salvetti weekly records the numbers. The number last given is from a letter from Mead to Stuteville, June 18; *Court and Times*, i. 32.

suade the Commons to vote him unheard-of sums of money in order that he might carry out a policy on which their opinion had never been asked, and of which they were almost certain to disapprove. But it is very unlikely that Charles felt at all embarrassed, or that the idea that any reasonable man in that great assembly could possibly disagree with him, even entered into his mind.[1]

The business to be treated of, said the King, needed no eloquence to set it forth. He had nothing new to say. The advice which the Houses had given to his father had been taken, and he had but to ask for means to carry it still further into execution.

"My Lords and Gentlemen," he then went on to say, "I hope that you do remember that you were pleased to employ me to advise my father to break both those treaties that were then on foot, so that I cannot say that I come hither a free, unengaged man. It is true that I came into this business willingly, freely, like a young man, and consequently rashly; but it was by your entreaties, your engagements... I pray you remember that this being my first action, and begun by your advice and entreaty, what a great dishonour it were both to you and me if this action so begun should fail for that assistance you are able to give me." After a few more words urging his hearers to haste on account of the plague, and protesting his desire to maintain true religion intact, he left it to the Lord Keeper to signify his further pleasure.[2]

---

[1] Of course some will take the view that the speech was deliberately drawn up so as to avoid mention of the difficulties of the case. What I have said above, however, seems to me far more in consonance with Charles's character.

[2] In addition to the scanty notices in the Journals, we have for this Parliament Eliot's *Negotium Posterorum*, and the Fawsley MS. belonging to Sir R. Knightley, which I have edited for the Camden Society. I

Williams had not much to say,[1] and his hearers were doubtless thinking more of the young King's first appearance than of the Lord Keeper's rhetoric. If we can trust to the subsequent recollection of Eliot, the impression made by Charles was pleasing. It was natural that he should not himself go into details, and the House might reasonably expect to hear more, in due course of time, from the Lord Treasurer or from a Secretary of State. Men were tired of the long speeches of the late King, and there was a general disposition to trust to the good intentions of his successor.

CHAP. VI.
1625.
Impression made by the speech.

There was one point, however, on which the Commons had made up their minds. Whatever Charles or his ministers had yet to tell them about the war, they meant to hold him to his promise about the Catholics. Any concession to them they regarded as dangerous to the security of the realm.

Feeling about the Catholics

When the Speaker, Sir Thomas Crew, was presented to the King, he took the opportunity of expressing the general opinion of the House on this subject. The King, he trusted, would be able to recover the Palatinate, and also 'really to execute the laws against the wicked generation of Jesuits, seminary priests, and incendiaries, ever lying wait to blow the

expressed by the Speaker.

---

shall refer to the latter as *Camden Debates.* Unless there is any special necessity for referring to one particular source, it will be understood that what I say in the text is founded on these authorities. The further volume of notes taken by Eliot I shall give as *Eliot Notes.*

[1] I am unable to discover the enormity of Williams's suggestion, that if subsidies were too slow in coming in, Parliament might find some other way of hastening their grant, as that could not "be unparliamentary which is resolved by Parliament." Eliot's account of this session is so interesting that one is apt to forget that it was written some years after the event, and coloured by the recollection of all that had passed since. I may say at once that I do not believe that there was no feeling against the King till after the second application for supply.

coals of contention.' To this exhortation Williams, by the King's command, replied vaguely that speedy supplies were urgently needed, and that the House might trust his Majesty to choose the proper means of defending his religion.

On the 21st the Commons proceeded to business. There could be no doubt that precedent as well as ordinary courtesy demanded an explicit statement on the King's behalf of the amount of the proposed expenditure and of the reasons upon which the demand was founded. With the last Parliament James had entered into a direct engagement to take the Commons into his confidence when they next met. Whether, if Charles had told the truth, he would have satisfied the Houses, may well be questioned. It is certain that he did not tell them anything at all. Not a minister rose in his place in Lords or Commons to say how much was wanted, or to explain in what way the surplus voted would be spent. Charles threw the reins about the neck of Parliament, and expected it to follow his call.

Silence such as this, whether it was the result of a deliberate purpose, or, as is more likely, of mere youthful inexperience and ignorance of human nature, was in itself the worst of policies. Above all things assemblies of men ask to be led; and to this assembly no guidance was offered. Whilst the House was still hesitating what to do, an unexpected motion was brought forward. Mallory, the member for Ripon, proposed that the King should be asked to adjourn the session to Michaelmas on account of the prevailing sickness. The motion was warmly supported by Sir Thomas Wentworth. It is easy to understand why it should have found favour in his eyes. To him the war with Spain was sheer folly. King and Parliament, he thought, had gone mad together the year before. The duty of

England, he considered, was to attend to its own business, to amend its laws, and improve the administration of justice, leaving the Continent to settle its troubles in its own way. When he had heard of the prorogation of Parliament in October, he had been beyond measure delighted. "For my part," he had written to a friend, "I take it well, and conceive the bargain wholesome on our side, that we save three other subsidies and fifteenths."[1] An adjournment to Michaelmas now, which would save more subsidies still, would, we may readily conjecture, be equally agreeable in his eyes.[2]

That Yorkshire members, whose antagonism with Spain was less pronounced than that of the counties, and above all, of the port towns of the south, should wish to dispose for three months of the King's demand for subsidies, is easily intelligible. It is far more significant that Phelips, to whom Spain was as hateful as the principle of evil itself, should have risen in support of the proposal. There was matter of fear, he said, in every part of the State. Before they thought of giving, they ought to take an account of that which was last given, and as by reason of the plague there could not possibly be found time enough then for such an enquiry, they should ask his Majesty that it might be referred to some other time.'[3]

CHAP. VI.

1625. June 21.

The adjournment supported by Phelips,

---

[1] *Strafford Letters*, i. 24.
[2] Eliot ascribes Wentworth's support of the motion to his desire to postpone an impending enquiry into the validity of his election. But Eliot could know nothing of Wentworth's motives; and, even if it were worth Wentworth's while to put off an investigation which must have taken place whenever the House met again, his was the character to court rather than to shun enquiry.
[3] *Camden Debates*, 7. The omission of all reference in Eliot's narrative to the part taken by Phelips, is enough to put us on our guard against trusting it too implicitly as a complete authority. Phelips's speech is mentioned in the Journals, though not in a satisfactory manner,

VOL. I. O

CHAP. VI.

1625.
June 21.
And rejected by the House.

June 22.
Committee for grievances not appointed.

Petition on the Recusancy laws proposed by Seymour.

How far these words of the impetuous orator expressed the floating opinion of the House, must be left to conjecture. But, whatever members might think, they were not prepared to drive the King to extremities, and Mallory's motion was without difficulty rejected.

Something, however, must be done, if it were only to occupy the time of the House. If the Commons had voted ten or twelve subsidies without asking questions, they would have given great pleasure to Charles and Buckingham, but they would have pleased no one else. At the next sitting, therefore, after a proposal for the appointment of the usual Committee for grievances, came a motion from Alford[1] for a Committee 'to consider of what course we shall take in all business this Parliament.' To these motions Rudyerd rose. After a studied panegyric on the King, he adjured the House not to be led away into enquiries which might lead to contention so early in the reign. Sir Edward Coke professed himself content that there should be no Committee for grievances, on the understanding that an answer would be given to those which had been presented the year before; and Coke's suggestion was ultimately adopted.

A new turn to the debate was given by Sir Francis Seymour.[2] Their duty to God, he said, must not be forgotten. Let them ask the King to put in execution the laws against priests and Jesuits. After an animated discussion, in which member after member expressed himself in accordance with Seymour's proposal, the

and the *Eliot Notes* have the following after Mallory's motion: 'Seconded by Sir Ro. Phelips, in consideration of the dangers, either for adjornment to another time or place.' We have therefore Eliot's own handwriting in favour of the correctness of the *Camden Debates* on this point.

[1] Doubtless the old member, who again sat for Colchester in this Parliament, though his name is omitted by Willis.

[2] Mr. Forster ascribes this to Pym; but Eliot does not give his name and the Journals and the *Camden Debates* agree on Seymour.

question was referred to a Committee of the whole House.

The most remarkable feature of this debate was the complete silence of the Privy Councillors in the House. It was only at its close that Heath, the Solicitor-General, promised that an answer should be given to the grievances of 1624. On the general policy of the government, it would seem, no man was commissioned to say a word.

The next day the House went into Committee on religion and supply, 'wherein religion was to have the first place.' The key-note of the debate was struck by Eliot. "Religion it is," he said, "that keeps the subjects in obedience, as being taught by God to honour his vicegerents. A *religando* it is called, as the common obligation among men; the tie of all friendship and society; the bond of all office and relation; writing every duty in the conscience, which is the strictest of all laws. Both the excellency and necessity hereof the heathens knew, that knew not true religion; and therefore in their politics they had it always for a maxim. A shame it were for us to be less intelligent than they! And if we truly know it, we cannot but be affectionate in this case. Two things are considerable therein—the purity and the unity thereof; the first respecting only God, the other both God and man. For where there is division in religion, as it does wrong Divinity, so it makes distractions among men. It dissolves all ties and obligations, civil and natural, the observation of heaven being more powerful than either policy or blood. For the purity of religion in this place I need not speak, seeing how beautiful the memories of our fathers are therein made by their endeavours. For the unity, I wish posterity might say we had preserved for them that which was left to us."

CHAP. VI.

1625.
June 22.
Silence of the Privy Councillors.

June 23.
Eliot's speech on religion.

To this lack of unity Eliot now addressed himself. Arguing that those who had fallen away from it were a constant danger to the State, he urged that, if necessary, the Recusancy laws should be amended, or, if that could not be, that the existing laws should be put in execution.

Meaning of the speech.

Eliot's speech is the more noteworthy as it announced the complete adhesion of a man who was no Puritan to the Puritan opposition against Rome. In Eliot's composition there was nothing of the dogmatic orthodoxy of Calvinism, nothing of the painful introspection of the later Puritans. His creed, as it shines clearly out from the work of his prison hours, as death was stealing upon him—'The Monarchy of Man'—was the old heathen philosophic creed, mellowed and spiritualised by Christianity. But between such a creed and Rome there was a great gulf fixed. Individual culture and the nearest approach to individual perfection for the sake of the State and the Church, formed a common ground on which Eliot could stand with the narrowest Puritan. All superstitious exaltation of the external ordinances of the Church, of human institutions which gave themselves out to be divine, was hateful to both alike. The Calvinist creed he could ennoble to his own uses; the Roman creed he could have nothing to do with. For the sake of the English nation it was to be proscribed and trodden under foot. There must be unity and purity of faith, and that faith must be one which brought man face to face with his Maker.

Recusancy petition drawn up.

The result of this debate was a petition drawn up by Pym[1] and Sandys, and altered to some extent in committee. The King was asked to execute the penal laws in all their strictness, and to take other measures

[1] Mr. P. in the *Camden Debates* is surely Pym.

to prevent the spread of the doctrines of the Roman Catholic Church. Nor did the Commons trust only in coercive measures. They desired that silenced ministers, who would engage not to attack the government of the Church, should again be allowed to preach; that a restraint might be put upon non-residence, pluralities, and other abuses; and that some scheme might be drawn up for increasing the income of the poorer clergy.

CHAP. VI.
1625.

It is easy for us to condemn the readiness with which Eliot and Pym called in the authority of the State to repress a religion of which they disapproved. But it is impossible to use their shortcomings as a foil for Charles's virtues. He, at least, had no more idea than they had of opposing religious error by moral force. But for the disturbing influence of his marriage, he would have been quite as ready as they were to put the laws in force against the Recusants. His difficulty was not that of a man who is asked to do what he thinks wrong, but merely that of a man who is entangled by two contradictory promises, and who sees the time approaching when one, if not both of them, must be broken.

Charles not opposed to persecution.

When on June 30 the petition was sent up to the Lords for their approval, it had been still further modified. The request that the silenced ministers should be readmitted to their pulpits had given place to a request that a fresh effort would be made to reduce them to conformity.

June 30. The petition sent up.

It would still be some time before the petition on religion reached the throne. What Charles expected the Commons to do as soon as they had relegated their religious grievances to the House of Lords, it is impossible to say. Supply stood next in order to be treated of; but though twelve days of the session had passed away, giving him time to reflect on the attitude of the

Seymour's motion for a small supply.

CHAP. VI.
1625.
June 30.

Importance of the motion.

Consistency of Seymour.

The Court party taken by surprise.

Commons, he had taken no steps to explain to them the real meaning of the vague demands which he had made in his opening speech.

If he expected that, when once the petition on religion was cleared out of the way, the Commons would lay at his feet the vast treasures which he needed, but the amount of which he had not ventured to specify, he was soon bitterly undeceived. Scarcely had the petition left the House, when Sir Francis Seymour rose and proposed the grant of one subsidy and one fifteenth, or about 100,000*l.* Seldom has a motion more simple in appearance been more momentous in its consequences. The vote proposed was as nearly as possible one tenth of the sum which Charles required to fulfil his engagements. It therefore implied, under the most courteous form possible, a distinct resolution of the House to give no adequate support to the war in which the King was engaged.

Seymour gave no reasons for his abrupt intervention. As far as he is personally concerned, it is not difficult to find an explanation of his conduct. He had been one of the most eager in the last Parliament to engage England in a war with Spain, one of the most decided in protesting against any attempt to involve Parliament in extensive military operations on the Continent.[1] He was therefore only consistent with himself in refusing the supply necessary to carry out a policy of which he disapproved.

The Court party was taken by surprise. Many of its members were absent from the House: all of

[1] On the 19th of March, 1624, he had said that he had heard 'wars spoken on and an army; but would be glad to hear where. The Palatinate was the place intended by his Majesty. This we never thought of, nor is it fit for the consideration of the House, in regard of the infinite charge.'

them had been left without instructions how such an emergency was to be met. Rudyerd alone, facile speaker as he was, was prepared to say something, and he dwelt at some length upon the recent expenses of the Crown, the sums of money which would be required for the payment of debts incurred in burying King James, for the entertainment of foreign ambassadors, for the approaching coronation, and for the war. The navy was to be got ready; the Dutch, the King of Denmark, Mansfeld, to be assisted. But whatever Rudyerd might say, he had not been empowered to ask for any definite sum of money, and the combined vagueness and magnitude of his demands was not likely to conciliate men who felt themselves drifting into a war the duration and extent of which were beyond calculation. The most dangerous temper in which an assembly can be found is that which arises when it believes that it has not been treated with confidence; and though we have no means of knowing whether the House was in such a temper when Seymour rose, it certainly was not for want of a cause, if no such feeling existed.[1]

marginal: CHAP. VI. 1625. June 30.

The existing dissatisfaction, whatever may have been the extent to which it had spread, found full expression in Phelips. Now, it would seem, he was less isolated than when at the beginning of the session he had risen to support the motion for an immediate adjournment. After a few words, which to Charles at least must have sounded like bitter irony, in which he described the proposed grant as an expression of the affections of the subject, he went on

marginal: Speech of Phelips.

---

[1] I am sorry to say that I am forced to treat the situation as though the *Negotium Posterorum* had never been written. Eliot was so little able to place himself back in past days, that he reasons as if the vote passed were an adequate supply.

CHAP. VI.
1625.
June 30.

to complain, in somewhat exaggerated terms, of the state of the kingdom as it had been left by James. Then, coming to the point at issue, he aimed straight at the argument upon which Charles had relied in his opening speech. It was not true, he said, that Parliament was bound by any engagement to the King. "The promises made," he explained, "were in respect of a war. We know yet of no war, nor of any enemy." Then, touching on still more delicate ground, he referred to the late disasters. No account had been given of the expenditure of the last subsidies. But even if that were in readiness, "What account is to be given of twenty thousand men, and of many thousand pounds of treasure, which have been expended without any success of honour or profit."[1] Such failures, he added, had not been usual in the days of Elizabeth. Let them press upon the King the necessity of taking these things to heart, and beg him 'to proceed in his government by a grave and wise counsel.' He would vote, however, for rather more than Seymour had proposed. He thought they might give two subsidies without any fifteenths, that is to say, about 140,000*l*. He hoped no man would press for more. If any man put forward the King's merit as a reason for a higher grant, he missed the right way. "For other argument," he ended, "we know what can be said, and hope that at the return of the navy there will be better inducements." In the end Phelips's amendment was carried, and two subsidies were voted.

Grant of two subsidies.

Charles's want of confidence in the House was thus

[1] The 20,000 men are either a slight oratorical exaggeration, or include the French and Germans who were with Mansfeld. Eliot makes Phelips speak of millions of treasure, which is too absurd, one would think, even for an orator. I have followed the *Camden Debates*.

met by a vote which was practically a vote of want of confidence in his advisers. Phelips's main position was unassailable. It was not true that even if the existing Parliament were bound by the vote of the last one, it was under any engagement to the King, except to take into consideration his proposals relating to the war. When he came before the Houses without any definite demands, they could but judge him by the result of his actions, and those actions had been so thoroughly unsuccessful that they furnished no inducement to trust him blindly in the future.

Yet though the step taken by the House under the guidance of Seymour and Phelips was certainly justifiable, it is impossible not to regret the manner in which the thing was done. An event of such historical importance as a breach between the Crown and the House of Commons should not have been allowed to take place upon a sudden and unexpected motion, followed by a hasty vote. The House, in all probability, would have failed in any case to establish satisfactory relations with Charles. But it would have spared itself much obloquy in the future and would have conciliated much popular feeling at the time, if it had condescended to put its views and intentions into an address which would have vindicated its thoroughly legitimate position. That there was no ill intention is probable enough. Men who disliked voting money for questionable objects would be glad enough to escape from the necessity of entering into controversy with their sovereign, and would doubtless flatter themselves that, in voting two subsidies, they had done the King considerable service.[1]

[1] This view of the case is that which finds a reflection in Eliot's narrative. As a key to the situation it is quite worthless, but I do not doubt that it is not without foundation in the feeling which existed at the time.

CHAP. VI.
1625.
Charles thinks of remonstrating.
July 4.
But promises to end the session.

The vote of so inadequate a supply was a bitter pill for Charles to swallow. His first impulse was to remonstrate against the measure which had been dealt out to him. Instructions were given to one of the Ministers to press the Commons to increase their vote.[1] But the intention was soon abandoned. The Solicitor-General was ordered to lay before the House the answer to the grievances of the last Parliament, and the Lord Keeper at the same time informed the House that the King was sorry 'for the great danger they were in by reason of the sickness, and that' he was prepared to end the session as soon as they were ready.[2] In these words the Commons naturally discovered an intimation that they were to hear no more of the demand for money. The plague

[1] One is always loth to challenge any assertion of the late Mr. Bruce, but it is clear to me that the provisional instructions calendared under July 8 (*S. P. Dom.*, iv. 26) must have been written before July 4, as they contain a direction that the person to whom they are addressed should, if the main object failed, urge the House to turn their resolution into a Subsidy Bill, which was what they did on the 4th of July, without pressing.

[2] Eliot says that the message was "that his Majesty received great satisfaction and contentment in their gift, both for the form and matter, it coming as an earnest of their love." On this Eliot founds an argument, that the King having accepted the gift was precluded from asking for more. We have, however, three separate reports of the message: that of the *Lords' Journals*, that in Coke's statement in the *Commons' Journals*, and that in the *Camden Debates*. In none of these do any such words occur. Something of the sort may be implied from the fact that the King did propose to close the session, and Eliot may have taken that which was implied as actually said. The Lord Keeper may, on the other hand, have said something which, as not forming part of his message, may not have been formally reported. At all events, Eliot cannot be relied on for details. He says that the Subsidy Bill "being passed the House of Commons, and that intimated to the King, it produced a message." As a matter of fact the Bill had not even been read a first time when the message was delivered. Since this note was written, I am able to bring Eliot's own testimony against the *Negotium*. The report in the *Eliot Notes*, like that in the *Camden Debates*, is silent on any word in the message about accepting the subsidies.

was raging terribly in London. Men were counting up the growing death-rate with perplexed faces. The members, believing that all serious business was at an end, slipped away in crowds to their homes, leaving less than a fourth part of their number to bring the session to a close.

CHAP. VI.
1625.
Members go home in crowds.

Already, in spite of the preoccupation of the House with other matters, a question had been decided of some interest in itself, and of still greater interest as bringing into collision two men who more than any others were to personify the opposing views of the parties in the approaching quarrel, and who were both to die as martyrs for the causes which they respectively espoused. At the beginning of the session Sir Thomas Wentworth took his seat as member for Yorkshire. But his rival, Sir John Savile, accused the sheriff who had returned him of conducting the election so irregularly as to make a fresh appeal to the electors a matter of necessity. According to Savile, the sheriff, being a friend of Wentworth, interrupted the polling when he saw that it was likely to go against the candidate whom he favoured. The sheriff, having been summoned to give an account of his proceedings, explained that when the poll was demanded it was past eleven in the morning, and that he had doubted whether it could legally be commenced at so late an hour. He had, however, given way on this point, but he believed that no one who had not been present when the writ was read had a right to vote, and consequently when some of Savile's men broke open the doors in order to force their way to the poll, he had put a stop to the voting and had declared Wentworth to be duly elected.

June.
Wentworth's election.

In the discussions which followed in the House, not only were the facts of the case disputed, but there was

CHAP. VI.
1628.
June.
Wentworth's advocacy of his own case.

considerable difference of opinion as to the proper procedure at elections. Wentworth himself bore himself as haughtily as usual. Not only did he state his case proudly and defiantly, but, in opposition to the rules of the House, he omitted to withdraw when it was under investigation, and rose again to answer the arguments which had been urged against him. Eliot at once rose to denounce the offender, comparing him to a Catiline who had come into the senate in order to ruin it. Before this invective Wentworth was compelled to leave the House, though he was afterwards permitted to return and to state his case once more.[1]

Comparison between Wentworth and Eliot.

It was no mere personal rivalry, no casual difference, which divided Wentworth and Eliot. With Wentworth good government was the sole object in view. Everything else was mere machinery. Conscious of his own powers, he was longing for an opportunity of exercising them for the good of his fellow countrymen. But, excepting so far as they could serve his ends, he cared nothing for those constitutional forms which counted for so much in the eyes of other men. The law of election was there, one may suppose him to think if not to say, for the purpose of sending Sir Thomas Wentworth to Parliament. He was himself arrogant and overbearing to all who disputed his will. It is certain that in private he expressed the utmost contempt for his fellow members,[2] and it is not likely that he had

[1] Mr. Forster (*Sir J. Eliot*, i. 160), after giving Eliot's speech from the *Negotium*, proceeds as follows: "'Yet hear me first,' cried Wentworth, as with a general feeling unmistakeably against him, he rose to leave. He spoke briefly and without interruption." This implies that Wentworth succeeded in setting the rules of the House at defiance. The *Eliot Notes* do not agree with this view of the case. After referring to Eliot's appeal to the privileges of the House, they say " W. sent out again. After, the motion being renewed upon question, W. admitted to be heard." Wentworth therefore was specially authorised to speak.

[2] *Strafford Letters.* i. 24.

any higher respect for his constituents. He was an outspoken representative of that large class of politicians who hold that ability is the chief requisite for government, and who look with ill-concealed contempt upon the view which bases government upon the popular will.

CHAP. VI.
1625.
July 4.

Eliot stood at the opposite pole of political thought. To him the attempt to convert Parliamentary elections into a sham was utterly abhorrent. In them he saw the voice of the nation speaking its mind clearly, as he saw in the representatives of the nation once chosen the embodiment of the majesty of England. Out of the fulness of his heart he reproved the man who held both the House and its constituents in contempt.

Eliot's reproof.

The majority sided with Eliot. Glanville, whose authority was great on all questions of this nature, produced precedents to show that a poll when demanded must be granted, whether it was after eleven or before, and that electors had a right to vote even if they had not heard the writ read. Wentworth's election was declared void, and the doors of the constitution were opened more widely than they had been before.[1]

July 5.
The election declared void.

Few as were the members remaining at Westminster during the last days of the session, they had still matters of unusual importance to discuss. Some three years before, Richard Montague, the Rector of Stamford Rivers, in Essex, found in the hands of some of his parishioners a paper drawn up by a Roman Catholic missionary, which contained the usual arguments against those Calvinistic tenets which, at the close of the preceding century, had been the accepted doctrines of the great majority of the clergy, and which were therefore attacked as if they formed the accepted

1622.
Montague at Stamford Rivers.

[1] Forster, *Sir J. Eliot*, i. 153; *Camden Debates*, 13, 36, 44.

doctrine of the English Church. Montague, who belonged to a different school, and who found support for his opinions in those formularies of his Church which reflected the belief of an earlier generation, determined to frame a reply which should base its repudiation of the Roman doctrine upon grounds very different from those which were popular amongst the clergy and laity. He was not unversed in controversy, having already entered the lists against Selden himself, whose History of Tithes he had unsparingly condemned.

The result of Montague's meditations was that The Gag for the new Gospel—such was the quaint name of the paper which had aroused his indignation—received a reply under the equally quaint name of A New Gag for an old Goose. It is unnecessary to say that it was deformed with that scurrility from which few controversies in that age were free. But, as far as the matter of the volume is concerned, an impartial judgment will probably consider it as a temperate exposition of the reasons which were leading an increasing body of scholars to reject the doctrines of Rome and of Geneva alike. To the Calvinistic doctrine of predestination Montague entertained an insuperable objection. He refused to speak of the Roman Church as indubitably Antichrist, or of the Pope as the man of sin.[1] Those

---

[1] The passage about the Roman Church is a quotation from Cassander: "Et quamvis præsens hæc ecclesia Romana non parum in morum et disciplinæ sinceritate, ab antiquâ illâ unde orta et derivata est, discesserit, tamen eodem fundamento doctrinæ, adde etiam in doctrinæ sinceritate et sacramentorum a deo institutorum firma semper constitit, et communionem cum antiquâ illâ et indubitatâ Christi Ecclesiâ agnoscit et colit. Quare alia et diversa ab illâ non potest, tametsi multis in rebus dissimilis sit. Manet enim Christi Ecclesia et sponsa, quamvis multis erroribus et vitiis sponsum suum irritaverit, quamdiu a Christo suo sponso non repudietur, tametsi multis flagellis ab eo castigetur." *New Gag*, 53.

who remained under his authority formed a part of the Church of Christ, corrupt and unsound in the highest degree, but not utterly apostate. Of the more peculiar doctrines sanctioned by Papal authority he spoke in a way very different from that in which the majority of Protestant Englishmen were accustomed to express themselves. He denied the right of the clergy to enforce upon the people the practice of compulsory auricular confession.[1] But he held that in cases where the mind was perplexed or the conscience burthened with sin, the person so troubled might be invited, or even exhorted, to come voluntarily to the Christian minister, and to seek for advice and consolation, and for the declaration of divine pardon to the repentant offender. He denied that the bread and wine in the Lord's Supper underwent any substantial change. But he asserted that Christ was therein present to the faithful receiver in some mysterious way which he did not venture to define.[2] Pictures and images, he said, might not be made the object of worship or even of veneration. But there was no reason why they should not be used, even in churches, to bring the persons and actions of holy men of old before the minds of the ignorant, and so to excite devotion in those upon whose ears the most eloquent sermon would fall flat; if, in short, they could be used much in the same way as the pictures in illustrated Bibles, or in painted church windows, are used in our own time.[3] Finally, Montague argued that prayers to the saints were to be rejected,

---

[1] *New Gag*, 83.   [2] *Ibid.* 258.
[3] " Images have three uses assigned by your schools. Stay there, go no further, and we charge you not with idolatry! *Institutionem rudium, commonefactionem historiæ, et excitationem devotionis.* . . . Not the making of images is misliked, not the having of images is condemned, but the profaning of them to unlawful uses in worshipping and adoring them." *New Gag*, 300, 303.

CHAP. VI.
1624.

not because he doubted that the holy dead retained a loving sympathy with those who were yet living, but because he was unconvinced that there was any way of reaching their ears so as to excite their pity, and further, because 'we may well be blamed of folly for going about, when we may go direct; unto them, when we may go to God.'[1]

The Commons refer the book to Abbot.

Such opinions were not likely to pass long unchallenged. Two clergymen, Yates and Ward, complained to a Committee of the Commons in the last Parliament of James, and, as the session was drawing to a close, the Commons referred their complaint to the Archbishop of Canterbury.

Abbot's proceedings.

With the objections taken to the New Gag, Abbot warmly sympathised. But he did not much like the responsibility thrust upon him by the House of Commons. If the idea, prevalent with modern writers, that he was still under disgrace in consequence of the accidental homicide committed by him in Lord Zouch's park, finds little countenance from contemporary evidence, it is certain that James far preferred the chatty, secular-minded Williams, to the Calvinistic, clerical Archbishop. Abbot therefore thought it best, as soon as he had read the book, to ask James what he had better do, and was recommended to send for the author.

He remonstrates with Montague.

Abbot took the hint. "Mr. Montague," he said, "you profess you hate Popery, and no way incline to Arminianism. You see what disturbance is grown in the Church and the Parliament House by the book by you lately put forth. Be occasion of no scandal or offence; and therefore this is my advice unto you. Go home, review over your book. It may be divers things

[1] *New Gag*, 229.

have slipped you, which, upon better advice, you will reform. If anything be said too much, take it away; if anything be too little, add unto it; if anything be obscure, explain it; but do not wed yourself to your own opinion, and remember we must give an account of our ministry unto Christ."

Such advice, which might perhaps have been of some avail with a young man whose opinions were as yet unformed, was of course thrown away upon a practised writer who was simply asked to cast the whole treasure of his intellect in a new mould. Montague too went to the King, and found in James a sympathising auditor. "If that is to be a Papist," said James, "so am I a Papist." By the King's permission he prepared a second book, entitled *Appello Cæsarem*, in which he vindicated more fiercely than ever his claim to be the true exponent of the doctrine of the Church; and this book, having been referred by James to Dr. White, Dean of Carlisle, was by him declared to contain nothing but what was agreeable to the public faith, doctrine, and discipline of the Church of England, and was accordingly licensed for the press. Before it was ready for publication, James died, and it was issued with a dedication to his successor.

And now, on July 1, as soon as the question of supply had been settled, the Commons sent a deputation to Abbot to know what steps he had taken. The deputation found him much vexed. After telling them all that had happened, he complained that he had not even been informed of the intended publication of the second book till it was actually in the press. But he had no legal jurisdiction over Montague on the mere complaint of the House of Commons. All that he could say was that he would gladly give his judgment upon the *Appello Cæsarem* whenever he should be 'orderly directed to it.'

The attempt of the Commons to obtain the unofficial support of the Archbishop having thus fairly broken down, they referred the whole subject to the Committee by which the petition on Recusancy had been prepared.

That the report of the Committee would be adverse to Montague was clearly to be foreseen. His opinions had made but little way amongst the lawyers and country gentlemen—the two most conservative classes in the nation—of whom the House was mainly composed. Nor indeed was it to be expected that the prevailing Calvinism would surrender its ground without a struggle. It had done great things for Europe. At a time when the individual tendencies of Protestantism threatened to run riot, it had given to men a consistent creed and an unbending moral discipline, which was yet Protestant to the core, because it was built upon the idea of the divine choice resting upon the individual soul, without the intervention of any priest or ecclesiastical society. Wherever the struggle with Rome was the deadliest, it was under the banner of Calvinism that the battle had been waged. Wherever in quiet villages, or in the lanes of great cities, any one woke up to the consciousness that a harder battle with sin was to be waged in his heart, it was in the strength of the Calvinistic creed that he had equipped himself for the contest. Alone with his God, the repentant struggling sinner entered the valley of the shadow of death. Alone with his God he stepped forth triumphantly to hold out a hand to those who had passed through the like experience with himself.

The strength of the English Calvinists lay mainly in the humble peaceable men who found in it a safeguard against a life of sin. Such a one was the father of Richard Baxter. Around his Shropshire home, in the last ten years of James's reign, there was but little preaching at all. In one village there were 'four readers successively in six years' time,' ignorant men, and two of them immoral in their lives! In another 'there was a reader of about eighty years of age that never preached.' He said the Common Prayer by heart, and got a day-labourer or a stage-player to read the psalms and lessons. These were succeeded by others, one of whom obtained a living in Staffordshire, and, after preaching for twelve or sixteen years, was turned out on the discovery that his orders were forged. Then came an attorney's clerk who was a drunkard, and who took orders, or pretended to have done so, because he could not make his living in any other way. On Sundays and holidays these men read prayers, 'and taught school and tippled on the week days,' often getting drunk and whipping the boys. The villagers did not prosper under such shepherds. As soon as the hasty service was over on Sunday morning, they gathered round the maypole on the green and spent the rest of the day in dancing and jollity. To take no share in these riotous amusements was to incur the mockery of the little community, and to be called a Puritan, a word which then carried the deadliest reproach. Not that the elder Baxter had any wish to separate himself from the Church. He 'never scrupled Common Prayers or ceremonies, nor spoke against Bishops, nor ever so much as prayed but by a book or form, being not ever acquainted then with any that did otherwise ; but only for reading Scripture when the rest were dancing on the Lord's Day, and for praying —by a form out of the end of the Common-Prayer Book—in his house, and for reproving drunkards and swearers, and for talking sometimes a few words of

CHAP. VI.

1625. July 1.

CHAP. VI.
1625.
July 1.

Scripture and the life to come, he was reviled commonly by the name of Puritan, Precisian, and hypocrite.'[1] For most of those who took part in the conflict with Rome and the conflict within themselves, there was no disposition to shake off the Calvinistic doctrine. They felt it as a support rather than an incumbrance. They had no wish to probe it to its depths or to search out its weak points. Its moral strength was enough for them.

Reaction against Calvinism.

Yet this could not last for ever. There was sure to come a time in every land when this feeling that religion was a conflict would die away, at least with some; when those who grew up strengthened by the surrounding influences of habitual piety would look to their religion rather as an intellectual framework to the quiet morality of their lives than as a struggle or an effort. In England it had come when men like Laud and Montague set themselves free from the bonds of Calvinistic dogmatism. They claimed to think for themselves in cases in which no decision had been pronounced, and to search for goodness and truth on every side. They were offended not merely by this or that doctrine of Calvinism, but with its presumption in repelling half the Christian Church of the present, and almost all the Christian Church of the past, from participation in the divine favour. They were offended with its dogmatism, with its pretensions to classify and arrange men's notions of mysteries which eye hath not seen nor ear heard, and they claimed the right to say that there were things on which the popular religion had pronounced clearly, which were nevertheless beyond the domain of human knowledge.

Not a popular movement.

Even if, like the Arminians of the Netherlands, the rebellion against Calvinistic dogmatism had taken a

[1] *Baxter's Life*, 1.

merely doctrinal form, the supporters of that rebellion would have had but little chance of taking hold of the popular mind. The objections which they felt were only likely to occur to men of culture and education. It was alike their weakness and their strength that the movement was emphatically a learned movement, a movement springing from those who had outgrown the leading strings which were necessary to guide the steps of others, and who could look without shrinking at the fact that religion was a subject upon which human reason could, to a very limited extent, exercise its powers. They were intellectually the liberal churchmen of the age. They stood between two infallibilities—the infallibility of Calvinism and the infallibility of Rome—asking for evidence and argument at each step which they took, and daring to remain in uncertainty when reason was not satisfied.[1]

CHAP. VI.
1625.
July 1.

Evidently such a standing point as this was not likely to be received with popular applause; and the difficulty before these men was considerably increased by the fact that they did not content themselves with merely doctrinal differences. It is a necessity of human nature that for every plunge which it makes forward into the untried sea of free thought, it must attach itself all the more closely in some other direction to the firm ground of orderly systematic belief.

Necessity of system to the party.

[1] There is a passage in the conference held in the following year on Montague's books, which seems to me to embody the spirit of the movement more than any other which I have seen. The question asked was whether General Councils could err. To this Buckeridge and Cosin replied: "All assemblies of men *in sensu divino*, and confederated merely as men, may err in the weightiest matters of faith: but all assemblies of men *having sufficient ability of learning to judge*, and who with prayer and pious affection endeavour to understand heavenly truth by the rule of God's Word, all such assemblies of men shall not err, because God hath promised the assistance of His Heavenly Spirit to deliver them from fundamental error." *Cosin's Works*, ii. 24.

CHAP.
VI.
1625.
July 1.

Luther, as he struck boldly out from the Church institutions of his day, saved his creation from falling into chaos by clinging with almost convulsive grasp to the institutions of the State. Calvin, in fixing his eyes upon the individual salvation of the man predestined to glory, took care to surround the future saint with the strictest discipline and with the iron bonds of a theology which was for him to be ever unquestioned. In our day those who trust most to their own powers of reason are the loudest in proclaiming the forces of universal law, and in expounding the necessities of a fixed order in the universe.

Position taken by it.

For men like Montague and Laud the order of Rome and the order of Calvinism were alike impossible. Never again would they bend their necks under either yoke. But in the earlier days of the English Reformation, in the days when Calvinism was but stealing in, they found exactly what they needed. The theology of Cranmer, fixing itself upon the principle that all practices were to be maintained, all doctrines held, which could not be proved false by the authority of Scripture and the custom of the early Church, suited them exactly. It gave them a rational ground on which to stand. It gave employment to minds to which the history, especially the ecclesiastical history, of the past was an attractive study. It appealed to the poetic and artistic instincts which were almost smothered under the superincumbent weight of dogmatic theology. It fenced them in with memories of the past, and ceremonial forms in the present. Their life was more sympathetic, more receptive of a higher culture, but at the same time weaker, and less fit to take the lead in any crisis through which the nation might be called upon to pass, all the more so because these ideas were not originally arrived at by themselves, but partook to a great extent in the weakness which attends the revival of the system of an earlier age. That which in Cranmer was the forward movement of the present, became in Laud a looking back to the dry bones of the past.

CHAP. VI.
1625.
July.

It was natural that the outward ceremonialism of the men should attract more notice than that principle of intellectual liberalism which, though yet in its germ in their minds, brings them into connexion with modern thought. And it was natural too that they should be accused of inclining towards Rome. They attached weight to external acts and ceremonies, which they venerated in common with the Roman Church. Their whole way of regarding the spiritual life of man was, if not Roman, distinctly not Protestant. Luther and Calvin, differing in much, had agreed in this, that the relation between the individual soul and God came first, and that all Church arrangements were secondary matters. The new school of English Churchmen brought forward the Church arrangements into fresh prominence. Uniformity was to be maintained as the surest preservative of unity. From the cradle to the grave man's life was to be surrounded with a succession of ecclesiastical acts influencing his soul through the gates of the senses. The individual was cared for by the Church. He stepped from the first to the second place.

How far it was inclined towards Rome.

It is impossible to deny that even the modified permission to men to think as they pleased on matters on which the Church had not pronounced her decision arose rather from a feeble grasp of speculative truth than from any broad view of the necessity of liberty to its cultivation. When they repudiated, as most of them did, the epithet of Arminian which was hurled in their faces by their opponents, they were guilty of no.

hypocrisy. They did not much care whether any particular view of predestination were true or false. What they did care for was that men should be honest and virtuous, and live peaceable and orderly lives under the care of the proper authorities in Church and State. And if it is true that this view of life deserved to be held in due regard, it is also true that without the stern self-denying striving after truth which was the characteristic of the opposite party, life tends to become more like a stagnant pool, breeding all manner of foulness and corruption.

Such a system might be regarded as holding a middle place between Rome and Calvinism. But it might also be regarded as a mere feeble copy of Rome. Those who valued the independent reasoning and the freedom of enquiry upon which it was based would take the more favourable view. Those to whom freedom of enquiry was an object of terror, would have nothing to say to it. They would desert it for the infallibility of Rome, or they would attack it in the name of Calvinism. Between the negation of individual religion and the assertion of individual religion, a compound of free thought and ceremonial observance was likely to have a hard time before it could establish itself in the world.

As yet, however, the ceremonial part of the controversy had hardly engaged the attention of observers. It was with Montague's doctrinal positions that the Commons' Committee was principally engaged. However orthodox a Committee of the House of Commons might be, it was certain to be influenced by thoughts which would have no weight with a Synod of Dort or a Scottish General Assembly. Those who drew up its report did their best to conceal from themselves the fact that they were advising the proscription of certain theological opinions. They said that 'though there be tenets in that first book contrary to the Articles of Religion established by Act of Parliament, yet they think fit for the present to forbear till some more seasonable time to desire a conference with the Lords that course may be taken to repair the breaches of the Church and to prevent the like boldness of private men hereafter.' All direct action against the opinions contained in the book, therefore, was to be postponed for the time. But the author was not to be allowed to escape so easily. The powers of the House in dealing with theological belief might be doubted. Its right to interfere in matters of State could not be doubted. Montague was accordingly accused of dishonouring the late King, of disturbing Church and State, and of treating the rights and privileges of Parliament with contempt.

Of these three charges the first was absolutely ludicrous. To accuse a man of treating James with disrespect by publishing a book of which James had expressed his approbation, simply because certain opinions were controverted in it which James had advocated in early life, was not only absurd in itself, but would have led to conclusions which the Commons would have been the first to repudiate. For if a man was to be prosecuted for disagreeing with James on a point of theology, why might he not much more be prosecuted for disagreeing with Charles?

The real weight of the accusation, however, fell upon the second head. The unity of religion which Eliot had so enthusiastically praised had its advantages. Statesmen as well as theologians might look with apprehension on the day when Protestantism was to embark upon the raging waves of internal controversy, and when, as it

CHAP. VI.
1625.
July 7.

Montague accused of differing with King James.

Of sowing dissension.

CHAP. VI.
1625.
July 7.

Of treating the House of Commons with contempt.

Debate in the House.

might be feared, the Jesuits would be enabled to sing triumphant songs of victory whilst their antagonists were fleshing their swords in mutual slaughter. Even if that were not to be the case, the entrance of religious strife would open a sad and dreary perspective of bitterness and wrangling, of seared consciences, and of polemical ability rearing itself aloft in the place which should have been occupied by moral suasion. And it must be acknowledged that, if Montague was far less scurrilous than Milton was a few years later, his tone was by no means calm. He had used expressions which might occasionally give offence. Above all, he had spoken of his adversaries as Puritans, a term which is now generally applied to the whole Calvinistic party; but was then looked upon as a disgraceful epithet, only applicable to those who refused conformity to the Prayer Book.

The third charge carried the question into the region of law and privilege. Montague had presumed to print his second book before the Commons had concluded their examination into the first, and had attacked Yates and Ward, who, as complainants, were under the protection of the House.

As soon as the report of the Committee had been read a debate arose in which the charge of differing from King James seems to have been treated with silent contempt. The second charge found more ready acceptance. A small minority indeed argued that Montague's opinions had never been condemned by the Church of England. Even amongst those who scouted this view of the case there appears to have been a feeling that there was no wisdom in approaching so nearly to a theological discussion. Coke, however, had no such hesitation. To him the Common Law was all in all, and he quoted Fleta to prove 'that the civil courts ought to have a care of the peace of the Church.' Others again argued that the complaint was not made 'directly for the doctrine, but for the sedition;' that the meaning of the Articles was plain, and that they only asked that the law should be put in execution. In the end it was resolved that a committee should be appointed to examine Montague's books, and that when Parliament next met the whole subject should be brought before the Lords. There remained the question of privilege. Sandys indeed, with the support of Sir Humphrey May, took the common-sense view, that there had been no contempt of the House. All that had been done in the former Parliament, they said, had been to refer the case to the Archbishop; and as the Archbishop had not thought proper to treat Montague as a delinquent, he had not put him upon his trial. And it was well known that a man not upon his trial was not precluded from replying to his opponents. The House seems to have been divided between its respect for these arguments and its wish not to allow Montague to escape altogether. He was committed to the custody of the sergeant-at-arms, but a hint was given him that he would be allowed to go at liberty upon giving a bond to the sergeant for his reappearance when the Commons met again.[1]

A breathing time was thus afforded to Charles to consider what part he would take in the controversy. The importance of the question before him was more momentous even than that of the direction of the war. Whatever the Commons might think, it was clearly to the advantage of the nation that the men who thought

What was the King to do?

---

[1] The bond was to be given to the sergeant, because it was affirmed by Sir Ed. Coke 'that the House could not take a recognisance.' *Camden Debates*, 53. Subsequent practice has decided against Coke. *Hatsell's Precedents*, iv. 276.

CHAP. VI.
1625.
July 7.

with Montague should not be condemned to silence, and that there should be room found outside the pale of Rome for those who had revolted against the dogmatic tyranny which was supported by the House of Commons. For a great statesman like Barneveld the work would have had its attractions, though he would have known that he was treading on dangerous ground, in which a slip might be fatal to himself, even if his cause was certain of ultimate success. But difficult as the task of finding room for differences of opinion was, its difficulty was immeasurably increased by the tone of Montague and his friends. They did not ask for liberty of speech or for equal rights with others. They and they only were the true Church of England. Their teaching was legal and orthodox, whilst the opinions of their opponents had been cast upon the Church 'like bastards upon the parish where they were born, or vagabonds on the town where they last dwelt.'

Charles made no attempt to save these men from their own exaggerations. His own sympathies were entirely with those who resembled himself in their love of art, in their observance of ceremonial order, and in their reverence for the arrangements of Church and State. He listened to Laud as his father never had listened to him. That pushing, bustling divine was convinced even more clearly than Montague that his system was the only true system for all men and for all times. Scarcely had Charles ascended the throne when he applied to Laud to draw up a list of the principal clergy, suitable or unsuitable for promotion. A long catalogue was soon handed in, duly marked with O. and P., the Orthodox as fit for reward, the Puritan to be treated with neglect. It was the beginning of a fatal course. Calvinism had too much vitality in England, and was too thoroughly identified with the struggle with Rome

Laud's O. and P. list.

THE TONNAGE AND POUNDAGE BILL. 221

and Spain, to be borne down by a partial distribution of Court patronage. The power of the Crown counted still for much. But its strength had rarely been tried as Charles would try it, if he attempted to impose his own religious opinions upon an unwilling nation.

CHAP. VI.
1624.

Religion was to be Charles's main difficulty in the future. His main difficulty in the present was want of money. And he now saw questions stirred in the Lower House which might seriously impair even his existing revenue. Ever since the days of Henry VI. the duties on exports and imports known under the name of tonnage and poundage had been granted by Parliament for the lifetime of each successive sovereign in the first session of his reign. The grant now for the first time met with opposition. The usual formula was that the supply was offered to provide means for guarding the seas. Sir Walter Erle, who, as member for Dorsetshire, would know something of what was passing in the Channel, reminded the House that during the last few weeks English vessels had been captured off the Scilly Isles by rovers from Sallee, and that even the Channel itself was not adequately guarded. And Erle had more to say than this. In James's reign certain duties had been levied under the name of pretermitted customs, which were alleged by the Crown lawyers to be included in the Parliamentary grant, a view of the case which found no favour in the eyes of those who were called upon to pay them. Erle now proposed that in order to give time for the examination of the point, the grant should be limited to one year.

July 5. Tonnage and Poundage.

Proposal to limit the grant to a year.

Matters were not likely to rest here. Phelips, who succeeded Erle, carried the debate into another region. He moved that the bill 'might so be passed as not to

Question impositions.

exclude the question of other impositions.' The old quarrel which had been smothered in 1621 and 1624, when the Commons were looking forward to co-operation with the Crown in war, was certain to break out afresh when there was no longer any such prospect. And even if there had been no change in this respect, it is hard to see how the question could have been avoided when the beginning of a new reign opened up the whole subject by the introduction of a new bill for the grant of tonnage and poundage. Phelips took up a position which was logically unassailable. If the King, he said, possessed the right of imposing duties upon merchandise at his own pleasure, why was Parliament asked to grant that which belonged already to the Crown?[1] In spite of Heath's opposition, the House resolved to grant tonnage and poundage for one year only. There would thus be time to consider the questions which had been raised. The bill thus drawn was carried up to the House of Lords and was there read once. It is not necessary to suppose a deliberate intention to defeat it. But neither, it would seem, was there any desire to hurry it on, and the bill was swept away by the tide of events which brought the session to a hurried close.[2]

A few days more, and the members of the House would be dispersed to every part of England. With the plague demanding its victims in London alone at the rate of 370 a week, more than a third of the total death rate,[3] the Commons could afford to wait for a

---

[1] "Kings ever received it as a gift of the subject, and were therewith contented, without charging them with any other way of imposition. For if they had any such power it were altogether unneedful to pass." *Camden Debates*, 43. The speech is toned down in the Journals.

[2] The speeches in the *Camden Debates* seem to me to warrant the conclusion that far more than a mere adjustment of rates was at issue.

[3] Mead to Stuteville, July 2; *Court and Times*, i. 39.

more convenient opportunity to discuss the issues raised by Montague's book, or even to settle the vexed question of the impositions. But Charles could not afford to wait. In the full belief that the Commons would grant him, without hesitation, any sum for which he chose to ask, he had entered into the most extensive engagements with foreign powers. Was he now to acknowledge to the King of France and the King of Denmark that he had promised more than he could perform? Was he to disperse his fleet and send his pressed landsmen to their homes? And yet this and more than this must be done, if no more than a beggarly sum of 140,000*l.* was to find its way into the exchequer. If on the 4th of July he had submitted to hard fate, and had consented to end the session, further reflection did not render more endurable the rebuff with which he had been met. Who can wonder if he made one more effort to supply his needs?

CHAP. VI. 1625. July 7. The King's financial difficulties.

The King was at Hampton Court, whither he had fled in hot haste as soon as he learned that the plague had broken out amongst his attendants at Whitehall.[1] Late on the evening of the 7th Buckingham hurried up from York House, assembled his followers, and told them that an additional supply must be asked for the next morning.[2] It is said that on account of the lateness of the hour many of the leading members of the Court party were absent. At all events when Sir Humphrey May heard on the following morning what Buckingham's intentions were, he resolved to keep back the proposed motion till he had remonstrated with the Duke.

He determines to ask for a further grant.

[1] Locke to Carleton, July 9; *S. P. Dom.*, iv. 29.
[2] The authority for all this is Eliot's *Negotium Posterorum*. I do not see any reason to suppose that things happened in the main otherwise than he tells them, though his view of the position is evidently coloured by the misconception that the Commons had already done all that the King could reasonably ask, even from Charles's own point of view.

CHAP. VI.

1625.
July 8.
May sends Eliot to remonstrate with the Duke.

For the purpose of conveying this remonstrance May selected Eliot, as one who had stood high in Buckingham's favour, and who was likely to set forth the arguments against the step which the Duke was taking in the most persuasive manner. That Eliot had already seen reasons to distrust his influential patron is likely enough. But there had been nothing approaching to a breach between them, and there is no reason to suppose that, at this time, Eliot was inclined to go further than May, or that, though he must have thought Buckingham hardly capable of taking the lead in the national councils, he had any wish to bear hardly on him, or to deprive him of the confidence of his sovereign.

Eliot's interview with Buckingham.

What followed may best be told in Eliot's own words, written with such recollection of the scene as he was able to command after some years had passed.

"Upon this," he writes, speaking of himself in the third person, "he makes his passage and address, and coming to York House finds the Duke with his lady yet in bed. But, notice being given of his coming, the Duchess rose and withdrew into her cabinet, and so he was forthwith admitted and let in."

His arguments.

"The first thing mentioned was the occasion, and the fear that was contracted from that ground. The next was the honour of the King and respect unto his safety; from both which were deduced arguments of dissuasion. For the King's honour was remembered the acceptation that was made of the two subsidies which were passed and the satisfaction then professed; which the now proposition would impeach either in truth or wisdom. Again, the small number of the Commons that remained, the rest being gone upon the confidence of that overture, would render it as an ambuscade and surprise, which, at no time, could be honourable towards subjects, less in the entrance of the sovereign. The rule for that was noted. According to the success of the commencement, is the reputation afterwards.[1] The necessity likewise of that honour was observed without which no Prince was great, hardly any fortunate. And on these grounds a larger superstructure was imposed, as occasionally the consequence did require. For his own safety many things were said, some more fit for use than for memory and report. The general disopinion was objected which it would work to him not to have opposed it, whose power was known to all men, and that the command coming by himself would render it as his act, of which imputation what the consequence might be nothing but divinity could judge, men that are much in favour being obnoxious to much envy."

" To these answers were returned, though weak, yet such as implied no yielding :—That the acceptation which was made of the subsidies then granted was but in respect of the affection to the King, not for satisfaction to his business : that the absence of the Commons was their own fault and error, and their neglect must not prejudice the State : that the honour of the King stood upon the expectation of the fleet, whose design would vanish if it were not speedily set forth. Money there was wanting for that work, and therein the King's honour was engaged, which must outweigh all considerations for himself."

Evidently the arguments of the two men were moving in different planes. Buckingham believed the Commons to have been wrong in refusing to vote larger supplies. Eliot, whatever he may have thought, was content to avoid the real point at issue, and only

[1] " Ut initia provenient, fama in cæteris est."

CHAP. VI.
1625.
July 8.
Buckingham's avowal.

attempted to show that it would be inexpedient to ask the House to reverse the decision.

It may have been prudent in Eliot to avoid all mention of the opinion which the members were doubtless passing on Buckingham's qualifications as a war minister. But, on the other hand, to ask a man so self-confident as Buckingham to withdraw from a course of action merely on the ground of its inexpediency was to court failure. "This resolution being left," the narrative continues, "was a new way attempted, to try if that might weaken it. And to that end was objected the improbability of success; and if it did succeed, the greater loss might follow it by alienation of the affections of the subjects who, being pleased, were a fountain of supply, without which those streams would soon dry up. But nothing could prevail, there being divers arguments spent in that; yet the proposition must proceed without consideration of success, wherein was lodged this project,—merely to be denied."

Eliot's surprise.

"Merely to be denied." Whatever words Buckingham may have used—and he was open enough of speech—such was the inference which Eliot drew from them. And more too, it seems, was behind. "This secret," Eliot tells us, "that treaty did discover, which drew on others that supported it, of greater weight and moment, shewing a conversion of the tide. For the present it gave that gentleman some wonder and astonishment: who, with the seal of privacy closed up those passages in silence, yet thereon grounded his observations for the future, that no respect of persons made him desert his country."

What did Buckingham mean?

What did Buckingham mean when he proposed to press for additional supply, 'merely to be denied'? That he wished, from pure gaiety of heart, to engage in a struggle of prerogative against the popular representation of the country is an idea which needs only to be mentioned to be dismissed, especially as there is another interpretation of his words which exactly fits the circumstances of the case. If Buckingham really thought, as there is every reason to suppose that he thought, that he had been scandalously ill-treated by the House of Commons, that they had, without raising any open charge against him, deserted him in the midst of a war which he had undertaken on their invitation, he may well have believed himself justified in putting the question once more directly to them, with the distinct prevision that if they refused to help him he would stand better with the nation than if he allowed the war to languish for want of speaking a necessary word. Somehow or other the immediate crisis might be tided over, and the military operations on the Continent postponed. Somehow or another the equipment of the fleet might be completed. A great naval success, the capture of the Mexico fleet, or the destruction of some Spanish arsenal, would work wonders. Whatever blot attached to him through past failures—and Buckingham's failures were always, in his own eyes, the result of accident, his successes the result of forethought—would be wiped away. A second Parliament would gather round Charles of another temper than his first had been. The King who had done great things could ask, without fear of rebuff, for further means to accomplish things greater still.

CHAP. VI.
1625.
July 8.

If this was Buckingham's intention—and his subsequent conduct goes far to show that it was his intention—it is easy to understand how Eliot would have been shocked by it. Viewing, as he did, the House of Commons with almost superstitious reverence, and probably already inclined to doubt Buckingham's qualifications for rule, he must have regarded with extreme

His overtures distasteful to Eliot.

Q 2

228   FIRST PARLIAMENT OF CHARLES I. AT WESTMINSTER.

CHAP. VI.
1625.
July 8.
Buckingham badly represented in the House of Commons.

dislike both the attempt to deal disingenuously with the House, and the vaunting language in which Buckingham's confidences were doubtless conveyed.

Whatever the exact truth may have been about this conference with Eliot, Buckingham's immediate difficulty was to find a fit exponent of his policy in the House of Commons. Of the Secretaries of State, Conway was in the House of Lords, and Morton was absent on a mission to the Hague. Sir Richard Weston, the Chancellor of the Exchequer, would have been naturally selected to bring forward a financial proposal. But, as he was one of those who had originally objected to the war with Spain, Buckingham may have suspected that, supple as he was, his heart was not wholly in the matter. May and Heath, whose tact had hitherto been conspicuous in the debates, would evidently be useless as supporters of a proposal of which they were known to disapprove.

His demand entrusted to Sir J. Coke.

The man who had been selected as Buckingham's mouthpiece was Sir John Coke. Having been from the first a leading member of the Navy Commission, he had long taken into his hands the control over matters relating to the fleet. He was versed in the details of his office, and would probably in our days have made a very excellent permanent Under-Secretary. As far as he took any interest in politics at all, his principal characteristic was a fixed dislike of everything which savoured of the Papacy.[1] But in general he was a mere tool, ready to do anything or to say anything as he was bidden by Buckingham and the King.

Further supply asked for.

As soon as it was known to Buckingham's friends

[1] Thus he was one of the instigators of the complaint against Montague in the Conference at York House in 1626, and he did his best in 1628 to lead the House of Commons astray by an attack upon the Jesuits. In later years he opposed the Spanish alliance advocated by Weston, Cottington, and Windebank.

in the House that Eliot's mission had failed, Coke rose. For the hasty grant of two subsidies before any minister of state had been heard on behalf of the King, he found a convenient excuse in the eagerness of the House to satisfy his Majesty. He now explained the way in which the subsidies granted in the last Parliament had been expended, said what he could in defence of Mansfeld's failures, and stated that the fleet in preparation would cost 293,000*l*., or 133,000*l*. more than the subsidies already voted. Besides this would be needed 240,000*l*. a year for Mansfeld, and the same sum for the King of Denmark. Even this, though the needs of the King of Denmark were understated, was enough to frighten the House, and Coke went on to throw away whatever chance remained to him of persuading the members, by adding that this expenditure ' could not be supported without more help by Parliament, or else some new way.' After this last phrase, which was sure to grate upon the ears of his hearers, he made an appeal to the magnanimity of the House. " The King," he said, " when he was Prince, borrowed 20,000*l*. for these provisions. The Lord Admiral hath engaged his estate. Other ministers have furnished above 50,000*l*. Shall it be said that these men are left to be undone for their readiness to the public services? Shall we proclaim our own poverty by losing all that is bestowed upon this enterprise, because we cannot go through with it? What shall we say to the honour of the King? But that is not all. Even the establishment of his Majesty in his royal throne, the peace of Christendom, the state of religion, depend upon the fleet."

CHAP.
VI.

1625.
July 8.

Coke's estimates, underrated as they were, were larger than the House cared to face. And even now there was no attempt to convince the Commons that it was wise to enter so extensively upon a Continental war.

The Crown at issue with the Commons.

CHAP. VI.
1625.
July 8.

It was taken for granted that Charles and Buckingham had been in the right in entering into engagements with Mansfeld and the King of Denmark, and the House was merely asked to provide the means for so necessary an expenditure.

Nature of Coke's demand.

If the sixty members or so who still remained at Westminster to represent the Commons, cared to please the King without bringing any apparent responsibility upon themselves, the way was made easy before them. Coke did not ask them actually to vote the subsidies. They were only to express their affection to the business, and to give assurance, by some public declaration, that when they returned they would be willing to relieve his Majesty.

It falls flat on the House.

But they were not so easily entrapped. The whole display of military preparation flashed thus suddenly before their eyes, created astonishment rather than any other feeling. They did not wish to bind their fellow members to answer a demand which had been kept in the background as long as the House was full. Neither did they like to enter into a contest with the King. Scarcely a word was spoken for or against the motion. Heath, seeing that the discussion, if it once began, would take an angry turn, did the best he could for his master by smothering the debate. The House, he said, had already expressed its affection in its previous grant. No man ought to speak but as if the King of Spain were there to hear him. It would be enough if they made it appear that, whensoever they met again, they would bring the hearts of true Englishmen.

And is put aside by Heath.

The King takes up Montague's case.

In spite of this rebuff Charles kept his temper. To a deputation from the two Houses which carried the petition on religion to Hampton Court, he replied civilly that he would shortly give them an answer. He then called Heath aside and enquired about Montague's committal. Montague, he said, was now his chaplain, and he had taken the case into his own consideration. "Montague," replied the Solicitor-General, "did not allege so much for himself. It was hardly known but to very few in the House." "I believe," replied the King, "if they had known it, they would not have proceeded in that manner." He then expressed a hope that the prisoner would be set at liberty, in which case, he said, he would be ready to give them satisfaction. Montague's committal, Heath said, was not for his opinions, but for his contempt of the House. He then gave an account of all that had taken place. Charles 'smiled, without any further reply.'[1]

CHAP.
VI.
1625.
July 8.

The House, when it heard what had passed, determined to maintain its position. This recent nomination of Montague to a chaplainship looked very like a Court intrigue to screen his conduct from investigation, and the doctrine that the King's servants were responsible to the King alone was not likely to find favour amongst the Commons.

July 9.
The Commons maintain their position.

On the 11th of July the Houses were informed that their labours were to come to an end that day, and that they were to meet again shortly to hear more from the King. The Commons then proceeded to the Upper House to hear the Royal assent given to the few bills which had been passed. The word "shortly" was then explained to them by the Lord Keeper. There was to be an adjournment, not a prorogation. They were to meet again at Oxford on the 1st of August. They would then receive a particular answer to their petition on religion, and in the mean time his Majesty, 'by present execution of the laws, would make a real rather than a verbal answer to their contentment and the contentment of all the kingdom.'[2]

July 11.
The House adjourned to Oxford.

Execution of the Recusancy laws promised.

[1] *Camden Debates*, 62.   [2] *Ibid.* 67.

CHAP. VI.
1625.
The step taken opposed by Williams.

July 10.

The Lord Keeper had been an unwilling instrument in pronouncing the King's resolution for the adjournment to Oxford. Williams, with his usual good sense, saw that there was little prospect of success in an attempt to drive the Commons to vote supplies to which they entertained an apparently insurmountable objection. The day before the adjournment he had advised that the Houses should meet not in August but at Christmas. As Williams did not hope much from the fleet which was preparing for sea, the proposal came natural enough from him. To Buckingham it looked very like treachery. "Public necessity," he said, "must sway more than one man's jealousy."[1] Charles sided with his favourite, and the prescient Lord Keeper was reduced to silence. The Houses dispersed, hardly thanking Charles in their hearts for the modified promise which had been given them, and full of discontent at the prospect of meeting again, to be asked once more for those subsidies which they were so reluctant to grant.

[1] *Hacket,* ii. 14.

CHAPTER VII.

THE LOAN OF ENGLISH SHIPS TO THE KING OF FRANCE.

THE promise made at the adjournment that the penal laws should be put in execution, was a symptom of a change which was coming over the minds of the King and his minister. It was easy to suppose that because the House of Commons cared a great deal about repressing the Catholics they cared for very little else, and that if only the penal laws were put in execution the House, at its next meeting, would make no more difficulty about supply. Nor was Charles, in consenting to this course, doing any violence to his own wishes. Ever since Buckingham had reported the failure of his mission in France, there had been growing up at Court a carelessness about the value of the French alliance, and an increasing belief that England was being sacrificed to the separate interests of Lewis.

To these political grievances was added a personal grievance still more irritating. The dream of domestic happiness which had floated before Charles, in after life the most uxorious of husbands, was vanishing away. The dispute about the precedence of Madame St. George had embittered the early days of his married life. Other troubles were not long in coming. Henrietta Maria was impetuous and indiscreet. "The Queen," wrote one who had seen her, "howsoever little of stature, is of spirit and vigour, and seems of more than

CHAP. VII.
1625.
July 11.
Meaning of the promise to execute the penal laws.

June. Charles's domestic troubles.

ordinary resolution. With one frown, divers of us being at Whitehall to see her, being at dinner, and the room somewhat overheated with the fire and company, she drove us all out of the chamber. I suppose none but a Queen could have cast such a scowl."[1] It was a scowl which her husband sometimes experienced as well as her courtiers. He did not pay much respect to her priestly attendants. When she heard mass he directed that no Englishman should be present.[2] After the Royal pair had been a few days at Hampton Court, a deputation from the Privy Council was sent to instruct her about the regulations which the King wished to be observed in her household. " I hope," she replied, pettishly, " I shall have leave to order my house as I list myself." Charles attempted to argue the point with her in private, but the answer which she returned was so rude that he did not venture to repeat it to her own mother.[3] She regarded herself as in a foreign land, in which everyone was at war with her. Even the exhortations of Richelieu's kinsman, the Bishop of Mende, who had accompanied her as the head of her train of ecclesiastics, could not induce her to treat the highest personages of the English nobility with common civility.[4]

Such a misunderstanding between a spirited child and a punctilious young husband ten years older than herself, is only too easy to explain. Nor was the Queen without

[1] Mead to Stuteville, July 2; *Court and Times*, i. 39.
[2] —— to Mead, June 24; *ibid.* i. 33.
[3] Instructions to Carleton, July 12, 16, 26; *Ludlow's Memoirs*, iii. 305.
[4] " Il seroit apropos que la Reine traita le Roi et les grands de l'état avec plus de courtoisie, n'ayant personne de quelque qualité que ce soit à qui elle fasse aucun compliment, c'est ce que nous ne pouvons gaigner sur elle, et que peut-être les lettres de la Reine Mère gaigneront." Decyphered paper from the Bishop of Mende, inclosed in a letter from Ville-aux-Clercs, Aug. $\frac{15}{25}$; *King's MSS.* 137, fol. 52.

reason for complaint. She had come to England in the full persuasion that her presence would alleviate the lot of the English Catholics. She had scarcely set foot in the island when she learned how little had been gained for them. The orders which were to have saved them from the penalties of the law had been countermanded. Is it not probable that if the secrets of those early days of married life could be rendered up, we should hear of the young wife's stormy upbraidings of the man who had beguiled her into taking upon herself the marriage vow by promises which he now found it convenient to repudiate?

CHAP. VII.
1625.

At all events the French ambassadors, Chevreuse and Ville-aux-Clercs, who were in England on special business, protested loudly. At first they received nothing but evasive answers. A few days after Parliament met, they were asked to allow the King to hold out hopes to his subjects that he would put the laws in execution, and to shut their eyes if sentence were passed on one or two Jesuits, on the express understanding that the sentence would not be carried into execution.[1] At last the time was come when the fulfilment of Charles's contradictory promises was demanded of him. He would soon find that he must either break his word to his Parliament or his word to the King of France. For the present a way was found by which the difficulty might be postponed for a little time. Effiat was about to return to France, as well as Chevreuse and Ville-aux-Clercs. James had been in the habit of allowing foreign ambassadors who took leave of him to carry with them large numbers of priests on the understanding that they would not return

Difficulty of satisfying the French ambassadors.

July 12. Liberation of priests.

---

[1] Chevreuse and Ville-aux-Clercs to Lewis XIII., $\frac{\text{June } 23}{\text{July } 3}$, $\frac{27}{7}$.

236 LOAN OF ENGLISH SHIPS TO THE KING OF FRANCE.

CHAP. VII.

1625. July 12.

to England. Williams was accordingly directed to seal pardons for the priests in confinement at the time. But Williams objected, and it was only by the King's special command that the pardons were issued. That command was given at the Council held on the 10th of July to decide upon the adjournment of the Houses.[1] The way was thus cleared for the announcement made the next day that the laws would be put in execution. Though there was no real contradiction between the issue of pardon for past offences and the intention to carry out the law in the future, the sight of so many priests coming out of confinement, without any word of explanation being given, was likely to throw doubt on the honesty of the governing powers.

The impossibility of reconciling engagements made in opposite directions weighed no less heavily on Charles in the matter of the squadron which had been fitted out for the service of the King of France. As early as the 11th of April the 'Vanguard' and her seven consorts had been ready for sea,[2] but delays had supervened. As soon as the captains and owners of the merchant vessels discovered that they were to be employed against Rochelle, they hung back and did their best to find excuses. One of the captains, Sir Ferdinando Gorges, who was to go as Pennington's Vice-Admiral, kept away from the rendezvous till the end of May, and was only compelled by threats of imprisonment to take his place with the others.[3]

April. The ships for Rochelle.

May. Reluctance of the captains to take part in the enterprise.

Part taken by Charles and Buckingham.

The exact part taken by Charles and Buckingham in the affair must always be matter for conjecture. It is probably true that when the contract was signed by

[1] *Hacket*, ii. 14.
[2] Effiat to Ville-aux-Clercs, April $\frac{11}{21}$; *Harl. MSS.*, 4579, fol. 57.
[3] Conway to Coke, May 21 ? *S. P. France. Council Register*, May 29, 31.

which the merchant ships were offered to Lewis for service against anyone excepting the King of England, the owners were quieted by assurances that they would not have to fight against the French Protestants.[1] At all events, on the 18th of May Sir John Coke was employed to write to Pennington to that effect, and this letter of Coke's may be fairly taken as embodying the sentiments of the Lord Admiral. For Buckingham was already in France with the object of inducing the French Government to make peace with the Rochellese, and it was Buckingham's habit to regard as absolutely certain anything which he had strong reasons for desiring. That it would be to his interest that there should be no fighting at Rochelle there could be no doubt whatever. He was still looking hopefully for French co-operation, if not in his projected attack on the Flemish ports, at all events in some way or other in the Continental war. His original plan had been to lend the ships for the purpose of an attack upon Genoa, and nothing would please him better than to see it carried out.

Still the fleet had been offered to the French to be used against all enemies, and Charles found himself, as he had found himself in the matter of the English Catholics, in a strait between two engagements.

To find an issue from such entanglement Charles had recourse to that double dealing which was characteristic of him whenever he was driven into a difficulty. Through Conway he conveyed orders to the fleet to get ready instantly for sea. Through Coke he intimated to Pennington that he was not to give his ships up to the French till he had used them to convoy

[1] This was stated by Glanville in his speech at the impeachment of Buckingham.

the Queen to England.[1] Charles's intention was doubtless merely to delay the delivery of the vessels till he heard what turn Buckingham's negotiation had taken.

When Buckingham learned in France, that, though Lewis would not join England openly in the war with Spain, he had despatched a messenger to offer peace to the Huguenots, there seemed no longer any reason for delay. On June 9 Pennington sailed with his eight ships. On the 13th he was at Dieppe. Pennington was an honest sailor, sympathising doubtless with the unwillingness of the captains to fight against Protestants, but anxious, above all things, to carry out his instructions. His main difficulty was to know what his instructions were. He knew that by the contract he was bound to serve against the Huguenots if the French Government ordered him to do so. He knew that by Coke's letter he was prohibited from doing anything of the sort. When he arrived at Dieppe he found that every Frenchman whom he met told him that his ships were wanted for an attack upon Rochelle. In the midst of these distracting uncertainties he resolved firmly that he would not allow the command of the squadron to slip out of his hands. When, therefore, he was requested by the French authorities to take three hundred soldiers on board the 'Vanguard' and two hundred on board each of the smaller vessels,

[1] " His Majesty hath been much moved at the delays of Sir F. Gorges, and because it will be the utter overthrow of the voyage if it be not gone away presently, his Majesty hath commanded me to will and require you by all means to hasten it away, or else show the impossibility of it." Conway to Coke, undated, but written on May 20 or 21; *S. P. France.*

" Nevertheless, having received a command from his Majesty by Sir J. Coke to detract the time as much as I could for the wafting over of the Queen, for which service I was appointed, though with privacy, I could not depart without a discharge of that command." Pennington to Conway, May 22; *S. P. Dom.,* ii. 83.

he flatly refused compliance. His orders, he said, authorised him only to take the French Admiral on board his own vessel, 'with such convenient train as' he was able to accommodate, and not to admit into the merchant ships more than 'half of the numbers of each ship's company.'¹

CHAP. VII.

1625. Refuses to admit French soldiers on board.

Possibly these orders had been given by Buckingham to enable him to retain a hold upon the vessels. But the French refused to accept them on these terms. They had by this time learned enough of the temper of the English sailors to discover that, except under compulsion, they would never fight against their fellow Protestants. Officers and seamen alike, including Pennington himself, had spoken out their minds on this. But the French were aware that their demand was not justified by the letter of the contract. All that they could do was to exhort Pennington to take a broad view of the case instead of haggling over words, whilst they wrote at once to their ambassadors, who were still in England, to urge Buckingham to alter his instructions.²

The French try to get the ships into their power.

With Pennington there was nothing to be done. Montmorency, the Admiral of France, came in person to Dieppe to use his influence. But Pennington replied that he was ready to obey orders from his own Government, but that he would not go an inch beyond them. And he soon conveniently discovered that it was impossible to remain much longer in an open roadstead exposed to the violence of the winds. At midnight on June 27 the whole fleet weighed anchor and took refuge in Stokes Bay, leaving it to diplomacy to settle what was next to be done.

June 26. Montmorency at Dieppe.

June 27 The fleet returns to England.

¹ Pennington to Pembroke, June 15; *S. P. Dom.*, iii. 71.
² D'Ocquerre to Pennington, $\frac{\text{June 21}}{\text{July 1}}$; *S. P. France*, D'Ocquerre to Ville-aux-Clercs, June $\frac{20}{30}$; *Harl. MSS.*, 4597, fol. 198.

CHAP. VII.

1625.
June 27.
Remonstrances of the French ambassadors.

June 26.
Negotiations between Lewis and the Huguenots.

Charles's first impulse was to assert that Pennington had been in the right, and even to suggest that the ships were not bound to fight against Rochelle.[1] But it was impossible for him to maintain this view of the case in the face of the French ambassadors, who knew perfectly well that, whatever the letter of the contract might be, there had been a full understanding that the ships were originally offered for the object of overcoming the resistance of the Huguenots. The conclusion was very hard for him to accept. His feeling that the French had duped him was growing stronger. Just after Pennington arrived in England, however, news reached Charles which promised better things. Gondomar had visited Paris on his way to Brussels, had taken his leave on the 26th without venturing to make any direct overtures to the French Government, and on the same day the deputies of the Huguenots, who had come to treat for peace in consequence of the negotiations opened whilst Buckingham was in France, were formally received by Lewis. To Lorkin, who after the return of Carlisle and Holland represented Charles in France in the inferior capacity of agent, the French ministers spoke in the most friendly terms. " Peace will be made," said Richelieu; "assure yourself of that. If only the King of England will show that he means to assist the King against his rebels, peace will soon be made." [2]

According to Richelieu, therefore, a mere demonstration against Rochelle in order to help on that pacification which he and Charles alike desired, was all that was intended. Charles, obliged to trust him to some extent, and yet unwilling to trust him altogether,

[1] Chevreuse and Ville-aux-Clercs to Lewis XIII., $\frac{\text{June } 27}{\text{July } 7}$; *ibid.* fol. 207.

[2] Lorkin to Conway, $\frac{\text{June } 28}{\text{July } 8}$; *S. P. France.*

tried to steer a middle course. He informed Pennington, through Conway, that his proceedings had been well received on the whole. But he had been wrong in divulging the secret that his instructions bound him not to fight against the Protestants. As this had given rise to fresh demands, he must return to Dieppe, and take sixty Frenchmen on board the 'Vanguard,' and fifty on board each of the other vessels. He was then to sail against any enemy pointed out to him by the King of France.[1]

As the number of Frenchmen thus allowed to be taken on board was very similar to that to which the French authorities had already taken objection, renewed protests were made by the ambassadors. At last on July 10, the day of the Council on which it was resolved to promise the execution of the penal laws, Conway sent a warrant to Pennington to deliver over the ships to the French, and take on board as many Frenchmen as the King of France might order him to receive.[2]

As far as words could go the question might be regarded as settled. It may be that Charles trusted for the moment to Richelieu's assurances that there would be no war with the Protestants. But there were those at Court who were not inclined to put too much trust in these assurances. On the 11th Sir John Coke forwarded to Conway, with evident approval, a protest from the captains and owners of the merchantmen. The French, according to this protest, had threatened to take possession of the ships, and to place English sailors under French martial law. "And

CHAP. VII.

1625. July 3.

Pennington's further orders.

New objections of the French.

July 11. Statement of the case by Sir J. Coke.

---

[1] Conway to Pennington, July 3; *S. P. Dom., Addenda.*
[2] Ville-aux-Clercs and Chevreuse to Buckingham, July $\frac{7}{17}$; The same to Lewis XIII., July $\frac{9}{19}$; *Harl. MSS.* 4597, fol. 207 b, 218 b; Conway to Pennington, July 10; Pennington to the King, July 27; *S. P. Dom.,* v. 33, 132.

VOL. I.　　　　R

lastly," they said, "for serving against them of our religion, it is very well known that our seamen generally are most resolute in our profession; and these men have expressed it by their common petition that they would rather be killed or thrown overboard than be forced to shed the innocent blood of any Protestants in the quarrels of Papists, so as they will account any commandment to that end to be in a kind an imposition of martyrdom." Nothing could come of it, as Coke thought, but a quarrel between the two nations, "to which," he said, "if we add the discouragement of our party at home and abroad, the late murmuring against it in Parliament, and the open exclaiming made in the pulpits that this taking part against our own religion is one chief cause of God's hand that now hangeth over us, we can hardly balance these consequences with any interest or assistance we can have from the French."

The difficulty, Coke proceeded to show, lay in the King's promise and in the terms of the contract. It might be argued, he said, that the prohibition to serve against his Majesty included a prohibition to serve against the French Protestants who were his Majesty's allies. But it would perhaps be better to order Pennington to comply with the French demands, taking care, however, to instruct him that if he could not 'presently obey this direction by reason of any interruption whatsoever,' he was to 'acquaint his Majesty therewith, that he' might 'give order to remove it, and so take away all excuse for not accomplishing the intended gratification of his dear brother the French king.' In plain English, if the men were mutinous, Pennington was to represent his difficulties to the King. This would take up time, and it would be possible to spin matters out by retorting upon the French that they had not made their payments at the proper day, and had not kept their part of the contract. The blame would thus be thrown upon the French. " Only," added Coke, " some care would be taken after his Majesty's letters written, that Sir Ferdinando Gorges, who . . . purposeth to go aboard his ship to the rest of the fleet, may receive some directions for the carriage of their answers, that Captain Pennington by the unexpected style of his Majesty's letters may not be surprised." [1]

CHAP.
VII.

1625.
July 11.

It is hardly likely that Coke would have made so startling a suggestion unless he had been well aware that Charles was longing to be off his bargain. That it was well received is evident. But it was perhaps thought too hazardous to entrust either Pennington or Gorges with the secret, and at all events a more suitable person was at hand. Edward Nicholas, the Lord Admiral's secretary, was one of those useful men who are intelligent, busy, and subservient. To his pen we owe much information which would otherwise have been lost on the debates in the Parliaments in which he sat. When Coke was removed to another sphere, the business of the Admiralty, accounts, orders, information, all passed through his hands. He was now selected as the fittest instrument for a delicate mission, as likely to say and do no more than was necessary, whilst his official position would raise him above suspicion.

The proposal considered at Court.

July 15.
Mission of Nicholas.

Apparently the next move involved a complete surrender to the French. Effiat, who was now leaving England, was to pass through Dieppe on his way home. A letter was written to Pennington by Buckingham, ordering him to take the ships to Dieppe and there to give them up to the French, allowing them to 'put into them so many men as they shall think good, and

Orders for the surrender of the ships.

---

[1] Coke to Conway, July 11 ; *S. P. Dom.*, iv. 40.

CHAP. VII.
1625.
July 15.

dispose of them as ' the King of France might direct. He would receive in return security from the French for the restitution of the value of the ships in case of their coming to harm,¹ security which, as Nicholas thought, would be entirely valueless, seeing that it could not be enforced by anything short of war.²

July 16.
Buckingham at Rochester.

Buckingham, accompanied by Nicholas, went to Rochester to confer with the French ambassadors about the security to be given to the owners. He did his best to play a double part. To the Frenchmen he was all courtesy, and offered to do his best to satisfy them.³ At the same time he warned the shipowners not to 'deliver over their ships unless they had security to their content.'⁴ But if Buckingham counted on any dispute between the shipowners and the French he was disappointed. Security was offered to which Buckingham took no exception, preferring perhaps that objection should come from others rather than from himself.⁵

July 18.
Resistance of the enemy.

When he first arrived at Rochester Buckingham had reiterated his orders to Pennington to deliver up the ships at Dieppe.⁶ The reply which he received must have sounded like music in his ears. Pennington was at Stokes Bay with the ships. The other captains were away at Rochester with the Duke. The crews of the merchantmen refused to stir till their captains returned. If they would not come, Pennington wrote, he would obey orders, and go with only the ' Vanguard.'

¹ Buckingham to Pennington, July 15; *S. P. Dom.*, iv. 59.
² This does not seem conclusive, as it might be given through an English capitalist. But the objection shows what another of Buckingham's *entourage* thought of the surrender of the ships. Nicholas to Buckingham, July 16; *ibid.* iv. 58.
³ Chevreuse and Ville-aux-Clercs to Lewis XIII., July $\frac{17}{27}$; *Harl. MSS.*, 4597, fol. 220.
⁴ Statement by Nicholas, 1626 (?);*S. P. Dom.*, xliii. 43.
⁵ Burlamachi to Effiat, July 19; *S. P. France*.
⁶ Buckingham to Pennington, July 16; *S. P. Dom.*, iv. 67.

By doing so, he and his ship's crew would be as slaves to the French. The business was too difficult for him to understand, and he hoped a more competent person would be sent to take his place. "Moreover," he added, "your Grace may be pleased to take notice that I have a strange uproar in my ship amongst my own company upon this news of going over again, I having much ado to bring them to it, though I keep all from them, and make them believe we go over upon better terms than formerly."[1]

CHAP. VII.

1625. July 18.

Pennington's request to be relieved from his troublesome command was at once refused. Buckingham had taken his course, and before he left Rochester to return to the Court, Nicholas had been despatched to Dieppe with secret instructions.

The instructions, as Nicholas set them down long afterwards, were as follows:—

Secret instructions to Nicholas.

"To employ my best endeavour to hinder or at least delay the delivery of the ships to the French, but therein so to carry myself as that the ambassador might not discern but that I was sent of purpose, and with full instructions and command, to effect his desire and to cause all the ships to be put into his hands."[2]

On the 19th news arrived from France that the terms of peace had been agreed on between the King and the Huguenots. Upon this Buckingham wrote to Nicholas acquainting him with what he had heard, and enjoining upon him the duty of doing all that Effiat might ask, though he expressed a hope that the French would no longer need the ships.[3]

July 19. News of peace in France.

[1] Pennington to Buckingham, July 18; *S. P. Dom.*, iv. 78.
[2] Account by Nicholas of his employment, *ibid.* xxvii. 111. This and the statement formerly quoted were probably drawn up at the time of the Duke's impeachment in 1626. We have a letter written by him to Pennington, May 6, 1626, *S. P. Dom., Addenda* (1), corroborating these statements, and valuable as appealing to Pennington's knowledge of their truth. *See* p. 248, Note 5.
[3] "I having received advice lately from Lorkin that peace is con-

CHAP. VII.

1625.
July 20.
Secret message to Pennington.

The next day he had changed his mind. It may be that he wished to wait yet a few days, to see if the news was really true. Pembroke, who had been taken into Buckingham's confidence, despatched the following message to Pennington :—

"That the letters which Captain Pennington sent the Lord Duke of Buckingham's Grace, to himself and the Lord Conway was the best news that could come to the Court, and that the King and all the rest were exceeding glad of that relation which he made of the discontent and mutinies of his company and the rest; and that if such a thing had not fallen out, they should have been constrained to have sent him advice to have brought some such thing to pass. If the French should accept of the service of that ship alone without the rest, that he should carry it on fairly with them,[1] but still to keep himself master of his ship, and if they proceeded so far as to offer to take the possession of her, that then his men should take him prisoner and bring away the ship : and that the said Captain Pennington might believe him that he had thus much to deliver, it being the King's will and the rest,[2] that it was far from them that any of his ships should go against any of the Protestants."[3]

A mutiny to be got up if necessary.

cluded between the Most Christian King and those of the Religion, it may be the Marquis d'Effiat, upon hearing of the same, will easily put an end to all these questions, having not the use expected." Buckingham to Nicholas, July 19; *S. P. Dom.*, iv. 80.

[1] In the MS. we have—"to have brought such thing to pass if the French should accept of the service of that ship alone without the rest, and that he should carry it on fairly with them." The slight alteration above makes sense of it.

[2] Of Buckingham, Conway, &c., I suppose.

[3] Message sent from Pembroke by Edward Ingham, *S. P. Dom.*, iii. 120, undated, and calendared June 1? but the date is approximately fixed by the mention of "that ship alone," as coming soon after Pennington's letter of the 18th. The following letter from Pembroke to Pennington (*S. P. Dom., Addenda*), written on the 20th, gives it to that day:

If Pennington had before been anxious to surrender his command, what must have been his feelings when he received instructions in this underhand manner to get up a mutiny on board his Majesty's ship entrusted to his charge?

CHAP. VII.
1625.
July 20.

Pennington, when Pembroke's message reached him, was once more at Dieppe with the 'Vanguard,' having brought his own ship away in spite of the murmurs of his men. A day or two later the merchantmen followed, as soon as their captains came on board.[1] When the 'Vanguard' arrived, Nicholas was already in the town with Effiat. Pennington, although he had not been informed of the real nature of Nicholas's mission, was ready to fall back upon any excuse which would cause delay, and discovered that he had not sufficient warrant to deliver up the ships. He even refused at first to come on shore to confer with Effiat, and said that he could do nothing till he had fresh authority from England. Nicholas then took up his cue. He remonstrated with Pennington in accordance with Effiat's wishes, and arranged with him to send off a message to England. But to his disappointment Effiat would not allow him to go on board.[2] At last Pennington consented to land and to confer with Effiat, and in spite of the jealousy of the Frenchman, who did his best to prevent any communication between Nicholas and the Admiral, Nicholas contrived to whisper a few words of warning to him, bidding him take heed that he had

July 21.
Pennington ton again at Dieppe.

July 22.

" I must give you many thanks for your respect to me in so freely acquainting me with all particulars that have happened this voyage. You shall receive directions by this bearer from his Majesty and my Lord Admiral how to carry yourself in this business, which I know you will punctually obey. From me you can expect nothing but assurances of my love, &c."

[1] Pennington to Nicholas, July 21; *S. P. Dom.*, iv. 97.
[2] Pennington to Nicholas, July 21; Nicholas to Pennington, July 22; Nicholas to Buckingham, July 22; *S. P. Dom.*, iv. 97, 100, 104, 105.

CHAP. VII.
1625.
July 22. Appeal to the crews.
July 23. Mutiny beginning.
Double language of Nicholas.

sufficient warrant for delivering up the ships. He had but a letter from Conway, and, in such a case, the King's signature to a warrant might fairly be demanded.[1] Nicholas's next step was to address a letter to the officers and crew of the 'Vanguard.' Would they or would they not either deliver up the ship, or receive three hundred Frenchmen on board?[2] The answer was contained in a note from Pennington. "I pray," he wrote, "let me entreat you to come aboard, for my people are in a mighty mutiny, and swear they will carry me home per force. I know your words will do much amongst them, and I have a great desire to give satisfaction to my Lord Ambassador, so far as I may with safety of my life."[3] Upon this appeal Nicholas was permitted to go on board. Alike in the 'Vanguard' and the merchant ships he met with opposition. The crew of the 'Vanguard' would take on board 150 unarmed Frenchmen, would carry them to England, 'and there leave the ship to them, so as they may have a good discharge.' The captains of the merchantmen objected to the security agreed upon at Rochester, and said that they could not deliver the ships till this point had been better arranged.[4] Nicholas, in fact, had made use of this visit to do his master's bidding.[5] To

[1] Account by Nicholas of his employment, 1626 (?), *S. P. Dom.*, xxvii. 111.
[2] Nicholas to Pennington and the Ship's Company, July 22; *S. P. Dom.*, iv. 102.
[3] Pennington to Nicholas, July 23; *S. P. Dom.*, iv. 110.
[4] Answers to Nicholas, July 23; *S. P. Dom.*, iv. 102; *S. P. France*.
[5] When Buckingham was accused the next year of giving up the ships, Nicholas, who seems to have been quite proud of his part in the transaction, wanted to tell the whole truth. On the 6th of May, 1626, he wrote to Pennington (*S. P. Dom., Addenda*)—"The Vanguard and the six merchant ships are come to Stokes Bay, but you are to satisfy the Parliament by whose and what warrant you delivered them up to the French. The masters of the merchants' ships, have some of them said that it was by my Lord's command, and by reason

Pennington he repeated the warnings which he had addressed to him on shore. With the captains he of threatening speeches which I used to them by order from my Lord, but this will be, I doubt, disproved by many witnesses, and by some of them when they shall speak on their oaths. It is true that, before the Ambassador or his people, I did often charge them aloud to deliver them over according to my Lord Conway's letter and the King's pleasure; but I fell from that language when we were private with the masters; and you may remember how often I told you I had no warrant or order from my Lord for delivery over of those ships, and though I did not wish you to go over into England, yet I think you may well remember I told you, you had not warrant, nor could I give you any to deliver them, and that my Lord was absolutely against the delivery of them. But I pray keep it to yourself until you shall be called on oath and have leave from the King to declare that I told you I came over rather to hinder than further the delivery or loan of those ships."

CHAP. VII.
1625.
July 23.

In the statement already quoted, Nicholas writes, after giving the substance of his instructions :—

"Accordingly when the Vanguard came into the road of Dieppe, and that Captain Pennington sent for me to come aboard, I acquainted the Ambassador with it, and told him if I went to the Captain, I made no doubt but to persuade him to come ashore with me, notwithstanding he was—as the Ambassador had complained to me—so obstinate that he refused to come out of his ship to the Duke de Montmorency, who importuned him there by many kind invitations and noble messages; but the Ambassador would not permit me to go aboard, but commanded me to write to Captain Pennington to come ashore, which I did as pressing as the Ambassador desired, which took effect. When he was come, the Ambassador interposed still between us, so as I could not have a word in private with him, but was forced to let fall a word now and then as I purposely walked by him, to bid him look well whether he had sufficient warrant to deliver the ships : which I did lest the Ambassador, by importunity or artifice, shewing a letter under his Majesty's hand to the French king, which was much more effectual than the warrant from my Lord Conway, should draw a promise or engagement from the Captain to deliver the ships before I should have opportunity privately to advertise him to beware how and on what warrant he did surrender the fortresses of the kingdom into the hands of a foreign prince; for if the Ambassador should have found him more averse than before, it would have given his Lordship just occasion to be jealous of the intent of the instructions I had received from my Lord. And the Captain kept himself very warily from any engagement, and craved time to speak with the other Captains and his company before he could promise anything, and so got leave to return to his ship.

"Afterwards I seemed not forward to go aboard to him, though I much desired it, till the Ambassador wished, and, indeed, pressed me to held two languages. If there were any Frenchmen present, he charged them to give up the ships at once. When he could speak with them alone he charged them to do nothing of the sort without better warrant. After this Effiat had but little chance of getting possession of the ships. Nicholas continued to summon Pennington to do his duty and to surrender the vessels. But as he had previously warned Pennington not to take account of anything which he might write to please the French, his words naturally produced no effect. Pennington excused himself upon the notorious disaffection of his crews. If that was all, Effiat replied, he would place four hundred Frenchmen on board to put down the mutiny.[1] As soon as the sailors heard of

go and use means to work him and the rest of the Captains to effect his desire, and to deliver over the ships with all speed.

"I told Captain Pennington, as soon as I came aboard his ship and had an opportunity to speak privately with him, that I thought the warrant from the Lord Conway which he showed to me, and whereof I had before seen a copy, was not sufficient for the delivery of the ships.

"In all the time of my negotiating this business, I never plainly discovered to Captain Pennington what mine instructions were, because I saw he was of himself unwilling to deliver up the ships, and after I had told him I had no warrant for the delivery of them to the French, he was as adverse in it as I could wish him.

"I told him also I was by the Ambassador pressed often to write what I intended not, and therefore desired him not to be moved with whatsoever letters he should receive from me touching the delivery of the ships until he spake with me. My Lord, after I went over, never wrought (wrote?) to Captain Pennington or myself, but in every material and pressing point concerning delivery of the ships, his Lordship referred us to the instructions his Grace had given me for that service; and when the Captain came to demand a sight or knowledge of my instructions to warrant the surrender of the ships, I told him I had none.

"If I used any pressing course or language to the masters of the ships, it was either in the presence of the Ambassador, or some such of his servants as he sent aboard with me, or else when I perceived them far enough from yielding, thereby the better to disguise and keep unsuspected my instructions." *S. P. Dom.*, xxvii. 111.

[1] Nicholas to Pennington, July 24; Answer from Pennington, July 24; Demands and Answers on board the Vanguard, July 24; Nicholas

the threat, they took the matter into their own hands and stood out to sea. "And when," wrote Pennington, "I demanded their reason, they told me that they had rather be hanged at home than part with your Majesty's ship upon these terms. Yet however they did it without acquainting me, I must confess I knew of it and did connive, otherwise they should never have done it, and I live. For I had rather lose my life than my reputation in my command."[1] The merchant ships remained at Dieppe. But their captains refused to surrender them to the French.[2]

CHAP. VII.
1625.
July 25.
The 'Vanguard' puts to sea.

Charles and Buckingham had therefore, at whatever expense to their own honour, succeeded in staving off the immediate surrender of the ships.[3] And now at last it seemed that the object of all this trickery was within their grasp. The news from France had been growing brighter as each despatch arrived, and there was every reason to believe that the ships might now be safely delivered up without any risk of seeing them employed against the Protestants of Rochelle.

Prospects of peace in France.

The plea which Buckingham had put up for peace had been seconded by the Constable Lesdiguières, who was in command of the French troops which had gone to assist the Duke of Savoy in his attack upon Genoa. But it was hopeless to attack Genoa without the command of the sea, and Lesdiguières longed for the pre-

June.

to Pennington, July 25; Pennington to Nicholas, July 25; Nicholas to Buckingham, July 25; *S. P. Dom.*, iv. 106, 115, 117, 119, 120, 122.

[1] Pennington to the King, July 27; *S. P. Dom.*, iv. 132.
[2] Demands of Gorges and the Captains, July 27; *S. P. France.*
[3] When the first news of the difficulties at Dieppe reached Charles, he told Conway to inform Buckingham that he had nothing to change in his former orders. "I must," wrote Conway, "in the duty I owe your Grace, say that there is not anything so tender, and to be so dear to you, as the avoiding of that scandal, offence, and hazard of extreme inconstancy, as if his Majesty's ships should fight against those of the Religion." Conway to Buckingham, July 25; *S. P. Dom., Addenda.*

252   LOAN OF ENGLISH SHIPS TO THE KING OF FRANCE.

CHAP. VII.
1625.
June.

sence of the ships which Soubise had seized, reinforced if possible by Pennington's English squadron, which had been originally destined for that service.[1] At the French Court, however, there was a strong party urging Lewis to finish with the Huguenots now that he had a chance, and the French clergy were ready to offer large sums to support the holy war.

Richelieu and the Huguenots.

Richelieu himself wavered—perhaps he only saw that if he was to keep his hold upon the mind of Lewis, it was necessary to him to appear to waver. In the beginning of May he had declared that it was impossible to wage war with Spain and the Huguenots at once, and recommended, though in a somewhat hesitating tone, that peace should be made with Spain, and that the Huguenots should be compelled to submission. In June, when there was a prospect that the Huguenots might be brought to acknowledge their fault, he urged that they should be satisfied as far as possible, but that Fort Louis, at the mouth of the harbour of Rochelle, which had been kept up in defiance of the express words of the last treaty, should not be razed, on the ground that to destroy the fort would look as though the King had granted to rebellion what he had refused to do at the humble petition of his subjects.[2]

June 25. The Huguenot deputies at Fontainebleau.

On June 25 the Huguenot deputies arrived at Fontainebleau and threw themselves at the feet of the King. If they obtained the concessions which they considered indispensable for their security, they were quite willing to accept it as a Royal favour. Their demeanour seems to have made a favourable impression on Richelieu. If the Royal authority was to be acknowledged as the

[1] Lesdiguières to Lewis XIII., June $\frac{2}{12}$; *S. P. France*.
[2] The two discourses are printed by M. Avenel (*Lettres de Richelieu*, ii. 77, 98). They are assigned by him to the beginning of May and the middle of June.

source of all that was conceded, he would no longer bar the way to peace. In a splendid argument, he urged the advantages of making peace at home and of confirming the religious toleration granted by the Edict of Nantes, in order that France might turn its whole attention to war with Spain.[1] Difficulties hindered the final arrangement of peace for some days. At last came news that Soubise had inflicted some loss upon the French Admiral who, with the aid of twenty Dutch ships, was guarding the entrance to the harbour of Rochelle. The party of resistance at Court found that to overpower the great seaport was not so easy as they thought, and, on July 15, the conditions of peace were mutually agreed on. A form was drawn up in which the King was to engage out of his Royal goodness to dismantle Fort Louis within a year. As the deputies had no power to conclude the peace themselves, the conditions were at once forwarded to Rochelle for ratification.[2]

Such was the news which had reached Buckingham on the 19th, and which had caused him for a moment to think of ordering the delivery of the ships.[3] A few days later, Lorkin was able to send better news still. A council had been held at Fontainebleau, and it had been resolved to declare open war against Spain and to encourage the Duke of Savoy to attack the Milanese. In order that there might be no further danger of disturbance at home, couriers had been despatched to the French commanders in the south of France to order

---

[1] The anonymous discourse, which is evidently Richelieu's, is wrongly placed at the end of Jan. 1626 (*S. P. France*). A translation with notes will be found in *The Academy* for 1874.
[2] Lorkin to Conway, June 28, July 15; *S. P. France*. All this is completely ignored in Richelieu's Memoirs.
[3] P. 245.

254   LOAN OF ENGLISH SHIPS TO THE KING OF FRANCE.

CHAP. VII.
1625.

July 28. Final orders to Pennington.

Aug. 5. Surrender of the 'Vanguard.'

Aug. 6. And of six of the merchantmen.

them to abstain from all acts of hostility as soon as the treaty had been ratified by the Huguenots.[1] That the ratification would follow seemed hardly open to doubt. At all events neither Charles nor Buckingham doubted it. A formal order was issued to Pennington to take back the 'Vanguard,' and to deliver up the fleet at once, and Buckingham gravely informed him that the King had been extremely offended at his previous delay. A private letter from Pembroke explained the mystery. "The King," he wrote, "is assured that war will be declared against Spain for Milan, and the peace is made in France for the Religion. Therefore his pleasure is that you peremptorily obey this last direction without reply."[2]

Pennington had at last got orders which he could understand. On August 3 he was again at Dieppe, and on the 5th the 'Vanguard' was placed in Effiat's hands. Sir Ferdinando Gorges, who was in command of one of the merchant ships, continued to refuse to deliver his vessel till better security for its value had been given, and sailed for England in defiance of Pennington and Effiat alike. The other six captains submitted more readily. But if the French got the ships they did not get the men. One only of the whole number consented to accept a service in which

[1] Lorkin to Buckingham, *S. P. France*. There is no date; but it was received on, or just before, July 28. See Pembroke to Pennington, *S. P. Dom., Addenda*. The date of July 18 is given in an incorrect copy, *S. P. Dom.*, iv. 134. Lorkin's informant was the Abbot of Scaglia, the Savoyard ambassador in Paris. I have no doubt of the truth of the story, though, as I have said, Richelieu chooses to ignore it all, simply, I believe, because he did not like to acknowledge having furthered a negotiation which afterwards came to nothing.

[2] The King to Pennington, July 28; Buckingham to Pennington, July 28; *S. P. Dom.*, iv. 136, 137. Pembroke to Pennington; *ibid., Addenda*.

THE SHIPS GIVEN UP TO THE FRENCH. 255

they expected to be employed against their fellow Protestants, and it was believed in England that that one was not long afterwards killed by the accidental explosion of a gun.[1]

Buckingham therefore had reason to flatter himself that when Parliament met at Oxford he would be able to give a good account of Pennington's fleet. If he could not openly declare the means by which he had kept it so long out of the hands of the French, he could point to the fact that it had not been surrendered till peace had been secured. When the news came that France was at open war with Spain, and that the English vessels were on their way to Genoa, there would be little disposition to enquire too narrowly into the original engagement by which the ships had been offered to the King of France.

As far as their foreign policy was concerned, therefore, Charles and his minister had some ground for the expectation that they would meet with more favourable consideration for their proposals than they had met with at Westminster. But what was to be done about the English Catholics? The engagements which Charles had severally taken to the King of France and to his own Parliament were so flagrantly in contradiction with one another, that no double-tongued Nicholas could by any possibility help him out of this difficulty. The advice given by Williams was, that, seeing that promises had been made to Lewis, Charles should announce to the Commons that the execution and relaxation of the penal laws was entirely a matter for himself to judge of.[2] If he had been able to

CHAP. VII.
1625.

July 30. The English Catholics.

[1] Pennington to Nicholas, Aug. 3; Gorges to Buckingham, Aug. 5; S. P. Dom., v. 7, 10; Elliat's receipt for the Vanguard, Aug. 5; Agreement for the six ships, S. P. France.
[2] Hacket, ii. 17. See also the brief of depositions against Williams, June 16, 1637; S. P. Dom., ccclxi. 101.

CHAP. VII.
1625.
July.

inform the Houses at the same time that peace had been made in France with the Huguenots, and that there would be no longer any persecution of the Protestants there, it is just possible that, with a really effective French alliance to fall back upon, he might have stood his ground, even with the House of Commons. On the other hand, if Charles put the laws in execution to please the Commons he would give deadly offence to Lewis, and would probably render all active French co-operation impossible.

Aug. 1.
Reassembly at Oxford.

By this time the members of the House of Commons were unwillingly preparing to make their way to Oxford. The temper in which they were did not bode much success to the experiment which Charles was about to try. Even the difficulty of obtaining lodgings in a strange place was raised to the dignity of a practical grievance. History was ransacked for instances of unlucky Parliaments which had met at Oxford, whilst no one seems to have thought of the glories of that great assembly which gave birth to the Provisions of Oxford. Worse than all, the plague was already breaking out in the town, and there were not a few who shrunk from facing that fell disease away from their homes, and in the midst of a population swollen by so great a concourse.[1]

[1] Eliot in his *Negotium* speaks of cases of the plague as already occurring when the Houses were adjourned at Westminster. But the King on the 4th of August expressly stated that this was not the case, and the way in which he ran away from Whitehall may be taken as good evidence that for his own sake he would not fix upon an infected place in which to meet Parliament. On the 5th Whistler said there had then been only six deaths; a small number if the plague had been there more than three weeks.

CHAPTER VIII.

THE FIRST PARLIAMENT OF CHARLES I. AT OXFORD.

On August 1 Parliament met at Oxford. Upon the motion of Sir Edward Coke it was resolved that a Committee of the whole House should take an account of the expenditure of the subsidies granted in the last Parliament. He doubtless intended that investigation into the past should form the basis of a decision upon the course to be pursued in the future.

<small>CHAP. VIII.
1625.
Aug. 1.
The assembling of Parliament.</small>

If religion had not been first mentioned, the omission was soon repaired. The favours granted to the Catholics on the supplication of the French ambassadors were not likely to pass unnoticed, and Sir Edward Giles held up the copy of a pardon granted to a Jesuit expressed in terms of unusual latitude. The pardon, he observed, bore the date of July 12, the very day after the promise of a real compliance with their petition had been given.

<small>Pardon to the Jesuits complained of.</small>

The inevitable inference bore so hard on persons high in office, if not on the King himself, that for some time no one ventured to speak. At last Eliot rose, ever the first to throw himself into the breach. "I cannot think," he said, "that this pardon we have seen issued from the King; or, if it did, that he rightly understood it. I cannot believe he gave his pardon to a Jesuit, and that so soon upon his promise unto us." Some one must have abused his confidence.

<small>Eliot's speech.</small>

258   THE FIRST PARLIAMENT OF CHARLES I. AT OXFORD.

CHAP. VIII.
1625.
Aug. 1.

Let the Lord Keeper be asked who gave the warrant for the issue of the pardon. They might then discover who procured it.

The ministers present did their best to avert enquiry.

Defence of Heath.

Heath truly asserted that the promise of which the pardon was the fulfilment had been given before July 11, the date of the King's answer through Williams, and explained it as a concession to the French ambassadors. They had only to wait, he said, till they heard the King's answer to their petition on religion, which was certain to give them satisfaction.

Heath's mode of meeting the difficulty was the more noteworthy as he was known to be possessed of Buckingham's confidence. Buckingham, in fact, was making up his mind, if he had not made it up already, to cast to the winds his engagements to France, and to throw himself upon the popular sympathies of the House, by offering up to them the Catholics whom Charles had promised to protect. He did not see that it was too late; that a man who plays fast and loose with every principle, and who joins each party when it suits him, is certain to be mistrusted by all parties. As the members were arriving at Oxford one of the Duke's confidants told Sir Francis Seymour that if the Commons 'would set upon the Lord Keeper, they should be backed by the greatest men in the kingdom.' Seymour answered sharply, "I find nothing in the Lord Keeper but the malice of those great men."[1] Heath's appeal therefore met with but little response in the House. Phelips attacked the practice of complying with the demands of foreign ambassadors, although the presence of Charles himself at Madrid had not availed to release a single prisoner from the Inquisition. A further blow came from Sir Henry Marten, who,

Buckingham's intentions.

Answers of Phelips and Marten.

[1] Statement made by Williams to the King, Aug. 14; *Hacket*, ii. 18.

old as he was, sat now for the first time in Parliament. As Judge of the Admiralty Court, he was often brought into collision with Buckingham, and he may perhaps have had some cause for complaining of him at this moment. Even in former times, he said, when old ambassadors were employed, England had been more skilled in fighting than in diplomacy. Marten did not go further than this allusion. But his reference to the old ambassadors of former days was understood to imply a reflection upon the young ambassador who had talked so much and had done so little.[1] The whole discussion finally resulted in a petition to the King, in which the Lords were asked to join.

CHAP. VIII.
1625.
Aug. 1.

A petition to be prepared.

The first day at Oxford had been devoted to the Catholics. The second was devoted to the High Churchmen. The sergeant-at-arms reported that Montague had written to say that he was too ill to surrender on his bond. Coke at once rose to warn the House of its danger. The ancient Britons had been worsted, according to Tacitus, because there had been no unity in their mode of fighting. So it was now in matters of religion. Permission was given 'to every particular man to put out books of all sorts.' He wished that 'none concerning religion might be printed but such as were allowed by Convocation.'[2]

Aug. 2. Montague's case again.

Coke's attack upon liberty of printing.

[1] Mr. Forster makes Marten draw the contrast himself. "In former times (*Sir J. Eliot*, i. 199), when old ambassadors of wisdom and experience were employed, our treaties had *not* been unsuccessful," &c. The *Negotium* however makes Marten say that they had been unsuccessful. "He showed that in former times, when old ambassadors were employed, where wisdom and experience might give a promise for their works, success did prove it not the propriety of their nation," &c.

Success, as I understand it, here means 'the result' not 'success' in the modern acceptation of the word.

I may add that Eliot's description of Carlisle which follows, as 'so ceremonious and affected that his judgment and reality were in doubt,' is unfair to Carlisle. But then Eliot had not read Carlisle's despatches.

[2] *Camden Debates*, 69.

CHAP. VIII.
1625.
Aug. 2.

This was at least plain speaking. It was as well to know what Eliot's magnificent declamation about unity of religion meant in prose. Upon liberty, so far as it implied the right of each man to enjoy the freedom of person and property according to the law of the land and the decision of the judges, Coke placed the highest value. For liberty, so far as it meant intellectual freedom, he cared nothing at all. If Charles had possessed a mind of a higher order he might have entered the lists against the legal intolerance of Coke and the dogmatic intolerance of the Calvinistic clergy with a fair prospect of success. If he had failed, at least he would have failed in a noble cause. But Charles was not likely to take his stand upon so broad an issue; perhaps the time was not yet come when it was possible for any man to take so high a ground. At Hampton Court he had claimed to save Montague from the Commons by declaring him to be his chaplain, and Heath now warned the House against touching a man in his Majesty's service. The challenge was not allowed to pass unquestioned. "All justices of the peace, all deputy-lieutenants," said Alford, "are the King's servants." No man could by any possibility commit a public offence but by colour of public employment and service to the King. If all these were to be freed from Parliamentary enquiry, what would be the condition of future Parliaments?

Heath declares Montague to be the King's chaplain.

Claims of the Commons.

In spite of the tendency of some speakers to go off upon the merits of Arminianism and the doctrine of the fallibility of grace, the leading members had sufficient influence to keep the point raised by Alford in the foreground. Coke, who was allowed to speak a second time, expressly disclaimed any right in the House to meddle with points of doctrine. They had only to deal with Montague for his contempt of the House. They would inform the Lords of his evil doctrine, and, as the Bishops had seats in the Upper House, such questions might be resolved there. At the last the sentence would come before the King, who might execute it or remit as he thought fit. There were even precedents of cases in which Parliament had petitioned the King not to use his prerogative of mercy. Phelips closed the debate by reminding the House that in the last Parliament James had already put forth the claim 'that no servant of his should be questioned.' In the end, the sergeant was ordered to bring Montague to the bar, an order which took no effect, as it was discovered that Montague was really too ill to attend.

CHAP. VIII.
1625.
Aug. 2.

The question of the responsibility of the King's officers, when once stirred, was certain to recur sooner or later. Coke might strive hard to bring the desire of the House within the formulas of the past. But in itself the question of responsibility was the question of sovereignty. If all official persons were liable to complaint and punishment in Parliament, whether the King liked it or not, Charles might still have functions to perform which would be eminently useful to the Commonwealth. But he would not be a sovereign in the sense in which Henry VIII. and Elizabeth had been sovereigns. The impeachment of Middlesex and the threatened impeachment of Montague were the signs of a great change in the relations between the King and the House of Commons. The question was raised because the House had ceased to have confidence in the King. But the innovation was none the less striking for that.

Question of responsibility.

As far as the great religious dispute by which men's minds were agitated was concerned, it mattered little whether Montague was the King's chaplain or not. On the very day on which the Commons were pronouncing strongly against his opinions, the three Bishops by

View taken of Montague's book by the Bishops friendly to him.

whom these opinions were regarded with the greatest favour, were writing to Buckingham in their defence. 'The Church of England,' said Buckeridge, Howson, and Laud, 'when it was reformed from the superstitious opinions broached or maintained by the Church of Rome, refused the apparent and dangerous errors, and would not be too busy with every particular school-point. The cause why she held this moderation was because she could not be able to preserve any unity among Christians if men were forced to subscribe to curious particulars disputed in schools.' Some of the opinions for which Montague was attacked were 'yet only for schools, and to be left at more liberty for learned men to abound in their own sense, so they keep themselves peaceable and distract not the Church; and, therefore, to make any man subscribe to school opinions may justly seem hard on the Church of Christ, and was one great fault of the Council of Trent.'

Evidently the Bishops were more liberal than the House of Commons. Beyond the region of dogmatic teaching they saw a region of mystery into which the eye of reason could hardly pierce, and which might well be reserved for reverent investigation by learned and devout men, whilst it was utterly unsuited for the violent declamation of the popular rhetorician. Unhappily it is by slow steps that the world rises to the height of a great argument. Something had been done for liberty of thought when dogmatism was restricted by Laud and his fellows. But what the Bishops gave with one hand they took with the other. It is hard for men who look upon a creed from the outside to know by how many ramifications its dry propositions gather vital strength for the moral life of its believers. It was well to say that grace and predestination were fitter subjects for the schools than for the

THE PREDESTINATION QUESTION. 263

pulpit. But, for all that, the fact remained that there were thousands of men in England who thought otherwise, and who, if they were not to hear of grace and predestination, would find that their whole framework of spiritual thought had broken down. When therefore the Bishops went on to say, that they could not conceive what use there was 'of civil government in the Commonwealth, or of preaching and external ministry in the Church, if such fatal opinions as some which are opposite and contrary to those delivered by Mr. Montague are and shall be publicly taught and maintained,' they were calling upon the King to use his authority to silence opinions which had by long experience become dear to many a pious soul from one end of the land to the other. The Bishops were seeking to accomplish by force that which they might well have striven to accomplish by example.

CHAP. VIII.
1625.
Aug. 2.

conjoined with illiberality.

With this difference of opinion on Church doctrine was necessarily connected a difference of opinion on Church government. On this head Coke had been somewhat hesitating. He would have had books prohibited by Convocation. He would have had Montague judged by the House of Lords because it had Bishops amongst its members. The view of the Bishops was clear. " When the clergy," they said, " submitted themselves in the time of Henry VIII., the submission was so made that if any difference, doctrinal or other, fell in the Church, the King and the Bishops were to be judges of it in a National Synod or Convocation ; the King first giving leave, under his Broad Seal, to handle the points in difference." [1]

Who is to decide on Church questions?

Such was the ground thus early taken up by Laud, and maintained by him through the whole of his career.

The King and Convocation.

[1] Buckeridge, Howson, and Laud to Buckingham, Aug. 2; *Laud's Works*, vi. 244.

CHAP. VIII.
1625.
Aug. 2.

It was a claim hard to be met if it were once admitted that the clergy were a body separate from the rest of the nation, and able to bind the nation to the perpetual observance of any compact to which it has once assented. But if this be not the case—and the whole spirit of English history is opposed to such a view—then Laud was in the wrong. What was temporary in the settlement of Henry VIII. was the position taken by the King as the head of the clergy. What was permanent was that in so doing Henry VIII. represented the state and nation. Just so long as Charles represented the state and nation would Charles and the Bishops be able to lay down the law as to what was to be taught and what was not. Already the Commons were beginning feebly and incoherently to put in their claim to be the representatives of England. But they, too, would have to learn that the voice of numbers will not suffice to give permanent supremacy. The question of religious differences was coming to the front. Whoso could most wisely solve it, whether King or Commons, would lead the English nation in the ages which were coming.

Immense as was the ultimate importance of these religious disputes, they did not form the immediate question of the hour. But the feelings roused by the discussions of the first two days were not favourable to Charles's design of drawing fresh subsidies from the Commons. The third day, too, kept as a fast on account of the plague, was certain to bring with it thoughts and feelings which boded no good to the King who issued pardons to Jesuits and shielded Arminians from punishment.

Aug. 3. The fast.

Aug. 4. The King in Christchurch hall.

On August 4 Charles came in from Woodstock, where he was staying, and summoned the Houses to appear before him in Christchurch hall. He had indeed need of all the eloquence he could command. His exchequer was even at a lower ebb than it had been when he opened Parliament in June. It was only with the greatest difficulty that the necessary provisions for the Royal Household had been procured.[1] And now too, as in June, he had to balance the advantages of making a clean breast of it to Parliament, and telling all his plans and all his needs, or of contenting himself with asking only for as much as would be required for the equipment of the fleet, which, as it was to be directed against Spain, was more likely to stir the popular feeling than any combination in Germany.

CHAP. VIII.
1625.
Aug. 4.

As usual, he did not say much. He again reminded the Houses of their engagement to support him in the war, and begged them to think of the reputation of the kingdom even at the risk of danger to their own persons from the plague. His preparations had cost him great sums of money, and it would be better that half the ships should perish at sea than that they should remain at home. In two days, he ended by saying, they should have an answer to their petition on religion.

His speech.

Charles had dwelt entirely on the fleet. Conway, who followed, took a wider view of the situation. He said that 30,000*l*. or 40,000*l*. were wanted to enable the fleet to start. But he drew a picture in the background of the Continent in flames, and hinted at the large sums needed for keeping the Protestant forces on foot in Germany and the Netherlands.

Conway's address.

There was thus a discrepancy between the smallness of the sum named and the largeness of the expenditure hinted at. To fulfil his engagements, Charles wanted not 40,000*l*. but some 700,000*l*. or 800,000*l*. at

[1] Conway to Ley, July 24; *S. P. Dom., Addenda.*

the least. To make up his mind to forego this and to be content with the smaller sum would probably have been his wisest course, and if he had done this he might perhaps have avoided summoning Parliament at all. But this was precisely what he was unable to bring his mind to. He therefore, it may be supposed, whilst authorising Conway to mention the fact that no more than 30,000*l.* or 40,000*l.* was needed for the fleet, allowed his greater expenses to be expounded in the hope of stirring the liberality of the Commons to the uttermost.[1]

Originally, it would seem, it had been intended to reserve all further observations for a message which Sir John Coke had been directed to deliver to the Commons in their own House.[2] But it may have been that signs of impatience were seen amongst the members, or that Charles felt that a mistake had been committed in allowing Conway to say so much without saying it more plainly. At all events, he beckoned Coke to his side, and, after whispering a few words in his ear, sent him into the middle of the hall to do his work at once.

Coke at least did not start with asking for a paltry 40,000*l.* for the fleet. With all possible emphasis he enlarged upon the greatness of the work before them. 600,000*l.* a year would be wanted for Mansfeld and the King of Denmark. He argued that though Mansfeld's armament had not been so successful as could have been wished, it had shown that the King of England was in earnest. The German Princes had been encouraged. The Danes had taken the field. The

---

[1] Conway's speech seems to be very fully given in the *Camden Debates*, 73. I gather from it that there is no ground for saying that the King only asked for 40,000*l.* Conway seems simply to have spoken of that sum as that which was immediately needed for the fleet.

[2] Instructions for a message, *S. P. Dom.*, v. 14.

King of France was aiming at Milan, and had made peace with his Huguenot subjects. It now devolved on Parliament to consider whether they would yield his Majesty a convenient help. But even now Coke did not ask for all that was needed. Those who dreaded such an enormous expenditure were reminded of the importance of sending out the fleet. It would not be a constant drain on the nation. When once success had been obtained, that success would help to bear the charge. When the pride of Spain had been quelled, private adventurers could follow to sweep the seas at their own expense. The spirit of the people would be roused, and the whole land would be enriched at the enemy's cost.

CHAP. VIII.
1625.
Aug. 4.

Coke's hearers were thus left in uncertainty, an uncertainty which was doubtless shared by the King himself, how much they were really expected to grant. The small sum needed for the fleet was fixed and definite. All else was hazy and impalpable. The success of the fleet would perhaps enable Charles to dispense with almost everything that he now needed. But he did not come forward, as Gustavus had come forward in the negotiations of the past winter, with a definite demand which he himself recognised as indispensable. He tried to influence the minds of the members without first making up his own.

Coke was not popular amongst the Commons, and it was felt as a mark of disrespect that they should be addressed in the King's name by a man who was not a minister of state. Yet, as far as the fleet was concerned, he seems to have spoken the whole truth as completely as if he had been a Privy Councillor or a Secretary of State. The Prince of Orange had by this time rejected Morton's proposal for an attack upon the ports of Flanders, and Charles had reverted to his

Feelings of the Commons.

CHAP. VIII.

1625.
Aug. 4.

original scheme of sending his fleet to capture the Spanish ships returning from America.[1]

The Commons were fairly puzzled. Though Coke named no sum in particular, it seemed as if he had come round again to Conway's 40,000*l*. The wildest conjectures were hazarded as to what was really meant. Some thought that the fleet was not to go at all, and that the blame of failure was to be thrown on the House of Commons. Others even thought that a peace had been patched up with Spain. It needed the utmost frankness of explanation on the part of the ministers of Charles to do away with the ill-will caused by the long reticence of the King, followed by the involved and almost unintelligible demands which had been made at the close of the sittings at Westminster, and which were repeated in a form more involved and unintelligible still at the opening of the sittings at Oxford.

Aug. 5.
Proposal to confer with the Lords.

When the House met the next morning, Mr. Whistler opened the debate by a proposal which, if it had been met in the spirit in which it was made, might have changed the history of the reign. Let the Commons, he said, ask the opinion of the Lords upon the necessity of the action proposed. If they could not get satisfaction there, let them go to the King.

Objections raised to it.

Full and complete information upon the intentions of the Government was plainly the only condition upon which the Commons could be justified in acceding to the demands made upon them. But even if Charles had been willing to grant such information, it was one of the evils of the new system of government that there was no one in the House of sufficient authority to take

[1] The Prince's answer is unknown, as it was given by word of mouth (Morton to Conway, July 13; *S. P. Holland*), but it may be gathered from that officially made by the States General. Morton and Carleton to Conway, July 4; *S. P. Holland*.

upon himself the responsibility of meeting an unexpected proposal. It was probably from instinct rather than from any knowledge of the King's wishes that Sir George More replied, with courtier-like facility, that it was unconstitutional to apply to the Lords on a question of subsidy. But May, Weston, and Heath sat silent in their places, and before they had time to receive instructions the debate had taken another turn.

CHAP. VIII.
1625. Aug. 5.

If there was a man in the House who would be consistent with himself in attacking the foreign policy of the Crown it was Sir Francis Seymour, the proposer of the restricted supply which had been granted at Westminster. In itself the fact that the Government had entered into engagements with foreign powers so extensive that it did not venture directly to ask the Commons for the means of fulfilling them was calculated to give rise to the gravest suspicions, and Seymour, the old opponent of the system of Continental wars, was not likely to treat such suspicions lightly. This meeting of Parliament, he argued, had been the work of those who sought to put dissensions between the King and his people. It was absurd to suppose that it needed a Parliament to procure 40,000*l.* for the fleet. As for the rest that had been said, he had no confidence in the advisers of the Crown. He did not believe that peace had been made in France, and he hoped that English ships would not be used as abettors of the French king's violence against his Huguenot subjects. Then turning to the past, Seymour continued, " We have given three subsidies and three fifteenths to the Queen of Bohemia for which she is nothing the better. Nothing hath been done. We know not our enemy. We have set upon and consumed our own people." What he wished was that they might now ' do somewhat for the country,' and

Seymour attacks the foreign policy of the Crown.

CHAP. VIII.
1625.
Aug. 5.

May's answer.

200,000l. asked for by Edmondes. Speech of Phelips.

they would then give his Majesty a seasonable and bountiful supply.

Distrust of Buckingham's capacity, perhaps of his integrity, was imprinted on every word of Seymour's speech. When May rose to answer him, he knew that the whole foreign policy of the Government needed defence. And if he could not meet all attacks he was able to tell of much that had been overlooked by Seymour. It was something that the King of Denmark was on the move. It was something that France was no longer in friendship with Spain. May then went on to relate an anecdote from his own personal knowledge. When at the end of Elizabeth's reign Mountjoy had been sent into Ireland and was in great danger of defeat, Sir Robert Cecil had protested beforehand that if disaster followed no imputation could be brought against the Government at home. "My Lord Mountjoy," he had said, "cannot complain of us. He hath wanted nothing from hence. If things miscarry, the blame must be somewhere else." The application of the anecdote was obvious. It was the business of the House to vote supplies and to throw the responsibility off their own shoulders.

May had forgotten that the House courted responsibility, and that it was very far from feeling that confidence in Buckingham's powers as a minister which Cecil had in Mountjoy's powers as a soldier. He did not acknowledge that times were changed, and that those who supply the money for war must necessarily ask for a larger share in its management as soon as they have reason to think that the supplies are being squandered or misused. Nor did Edmondes, who followed, mend the position of the Government by asking directly for two subsidies and two fifteenths, about 200,000l., a sum far too great for supplying the immediate needs of the fleet, whilst altogether inadequate to meet Charles's engagements on the Continent.[1]

If Seymour had hinted at some things which he could have expressed more clearly if he had thought fit, Phelips, who rose next, was certain to speak out all that was in his heart. And speak out he did. For his part, he told the House, he saw no reason for giving. But neither was there any reason for leaving the work to which they had been so unexpectedly called. Let them stay to do something to make his Majesty glorious. Those who were now urging them to war—so far at least the person intended was suggested rather than expressed—were those who had been foremost in urging on the Spanish marriage, and who had for its sake broken up the Parliament of 1621, and had thrown members of the House into prison, himself being one of the sufferers, for refusing to hold their tongues. In the Parliament of 1624 three things had been desired.[2] They had asked that the Prince should marry a Protestant lady, that the Dutch Republic should be supported, and that religion in England should be

CHAP. VIII.
1625.
Aug. 5.

[1] Eliot, as is well known, believed that Buckingham wanted to be denied. I am quite unable to take this view of the case after a full consideration of Buckingham's whole proceedings, of which an historian is now able to know much of which Eliot knew nothing. It is likely enough, as I have before said, that he expected to be denied, and that he intended to make use of the impression caused by his being in the right and the Commons in the wrong, when success came. Nor can I see that he only asked for 40,000l. at first. I fancy he simply wanted that at least, and would take as much more as he could get; a frame of mind the very opposite to that of Gustavus, who at once refused to engage in war except on his own terms.

[2] Eliot makes Phelips say that they had been 'desired and promised.' Phelips was an impetuous orator and may have said this. But as it is not true that Charles promised to marry a Protestant lady, I have followed the *Camden Debates*, 81, giving Phelips the benefit of the doubt.

It was, indeed, not strictly true that the House had asked for a Protestant marriage. But the desire of the members can hardly have been a matter of doubt, and may have been taken oratorically as equivalent to an actual demand.

preserved. Had this been done? "What the Spanish articles were," he said, "we know. Whether those with France be any better it is doubted. There are visible articles and invisible. Those we may see, but these will be kept from us."

Then, after touching on the sore of the impositions, and of tonnage and poundage, still levied, though the Lords had not yet passed the bill, Phelips went to the root of the matter. "In the government," he said plainly, "there hath wanted good advice. Counsels and power have been monopolized." Then, with an allusion to the Parliament which, meeting at Oxford, had wrested authority from Henry III., he said that he did not love the disordered proceedings of Parliaments. In all actions, he cried, "there is a mixture of good and ill. So was it with their forefathers struggling with the prerogative. Let us," he cried, "avoid that which was ill, but not that which was good. They looked into the disorders of the time, and concluded with the King for a reformation. When kings are persuaded to do what they should not, subjects have been often transported to do what they ought not. Let us not come too near the heels of power; nor yet fall so low as to suffer all things under the name of the prerogative. Let us look into the right of the subject. I will not argue whether the fleet is best to go or stay, whether leagues abroad are apt to support such great actions. The match has not yet brought the French to join with us in a defensive war, or any longer than conduceth to their own ends. The French army, which they say is gone, we hear is upon return. In Germany the King of Denmark hath done nothing. The best way to secure ourselves is to suppress the Papists here. . . Let the fleet go on; and let us not part till his Majesty may see an ample demonstration of our affections. Let us look into the estate and government, and, finding that which is amiss, make this Parliament the reformer of the Commonwealth."

There was more in Phelips's words than even distrust of Buckingham's ability or honesty. Both Buckingham and Charles had failed to recognise the importance of the fact that neither the French alliance nor the intervention in Germany had ever received the approbation of the House of Commons. It was enough for them that they judged this policy to be right, and that they promised to themselves great results in the future from it. They would tell the House what they had done, and ask for the means to carry out their designs, but they would not so far demean themselves as to consult it upon the direction which their policy was to take.

To this Phelips's somewhat ironical answer was decisive. The responsibility must fall upon those by whom that policy had been originated. The Commons would give no support to a course of action which they were unable to understand. They would confine themselves to those internal affairs which were within the compass of their intelligence, and would content themselves with criticising the administration of the laws, and the financial and political arrangements of the Government.

Such a speech was an historical event. If Charles could not make up his mind to discuss with the Commons the policy which he had adopted with such headlong rashness, it was useless for Weston, who followed, to try to persuade them that success might still be looked for if money enough were voted, or to frighten them with a prospect of dissolution by saying that, if they refused to give, 'beyond that day there was no place for counsel.' Nor was the speech of Sir Edward Coke much more to the point, as he

VOL. I.   T

274   THE FIRST PARLIAMENT OF CHARLES I. AT OXFORD.

<small>CHAP.
VIII.
1625.
Aug. 5.
Heath's offers on the part of the Government.</small>

contented himself with calling attention to the minor causes of the financial embarrassment of the Treasury, without touching upon the question really at issue.

The House was all the more attentive when Heath, the Solicitor-General, rose to speak, because he had had time to receive instructions from Buckingham since Phelips sat down, and because he was far too able a man, and had too good an acquaintance with the temper of the House, to fail in giving full weight to any concessions which the Government might be disposed to make. He began by placing the engagement of the Parliament of 1624 on its proper footing. The House, he argued, was bound to follow the King unless he propounded anything to which it was impossible to consent. As they were not engaged to everything, let there be no misunderstanding. Let them ask the King against what enemy he was prepared to fight. He was sure that the King was ready to take measures against the Catholics, ' that they might not be able to do hurt.' It had been said that places were filled by men who wanted experience. He was under great obligations to the person to whom allusion had been made, but if there was anything against him he hoped that it would be examined in such a way as that the public good might not suffer. Let the blame, if blame there was, light upon himself, not upon the Commonwealth.

<small>Alford says the House never promised to recover the Palatinate.</small>

Heath had done his best to open the way to a better understanding. But the speaker who followed him, Edward Alford,[1] struck at once at the weak point of the case, the fact that objection was taken not merely to Buckingham's management of the war, but to the dimensions which the war was assuming in his hands. "We are not engaged," he said, "to give for the recovery of the Palatinate. For when it was in the Act

[1] *Camden Debates,* 88, 135.

of Parliament, as it was first penned, it was struck out by the order of the House, as a thing unfit to engage the House for the recovery of the Palatinate, and if possible, yet not without great charge and difficulty."

CHAP. VIII.
1625.
Aug. 5.

The full truth was out at last. The House did not mean to support Mansfeld and the King of Denmark, and Buckingham and the King would have to reconcile themselves to the fact.

That afternoon Buckingham's agents were busy amongst the knots of members who were gathering everywhere to discuss the morning's debate. The greater part had already taken sides, the majority against the Court. Some few alone were accessible to influence. But besides the scenes which were passing in the streets or in the members' lodgings, another scene, it can hardly be doubted, was passing in Buckingham's apartments. There were men who wished him well, whilst they disliked his policy, and who were anxious to induce him to give way to the strength of Parliamentary opinion. What was said we do not know, probably shall never know. But no one who reads with attention the course of the next day's debate can doubt that an effort was being made on the part of his friends to save him from the consequences of his own self-conceit.

Discussions in the afternoon.

The next morning, after a brisk passage on a protection accorded by Conway to a Roman Catholic lady in Dorsetshire, the great debate was resumed. The course which it took was altogether different from that of the preceding day. The 5th had been given up to a conflict between the ministers of the Crown and the men who, in modern political language, would be termed the advanced wing of the opposition. On the 6th all is changed. Phelips, Coke, and Seymour are as silent as Weston, Heath, and Edmondes. It looks

Aug. 6.
Suggested reconciliation between Buckingham and the House.

T 2

CHAP. VIII.
1625.
Aug. 6.

Mildmay's proposal.

Coryton's speech.

Eliot's argument.

as if both parties had come to a tacit agreement to allow a body of mediators to declare the terms on which an understanding might yet be effected.

Sir Henry Mildmay, who spoke first, was Master of the King's Jewel House, and was on friendly terms with Buckingham. He proposed that the House should ask what sum would be sufficient to complete the equipment of the fleet, and that that sum should be granted, not by way of subsidy, but by some other mode of collection, apparently in order that it might be at once brought into the exchequer. Such a course of raising money, he added, being taken in Parliament, will be a Parliamentary course.[1]

Mildmay had quietly thrown overboard all the King's continental alliances. He was followed by Coryton, Eliot's friend, who was ready to supply the King, 'if there was a necessity,' but suggested that the state of the King's revenue should be examined, the question of impositions sifted, and a Committee appointed to debate of these things,[2] 'and especially for religion.'

Eliot followed. It was his last appearance as a mediator. But it is plain that he had already ceased as completely as Phelips and Seymour to feel any confidence in Buckingham. The war, he said, 'extendeth to Denmark, Savoy, Germany, and France.' "If he shall deal truly, he is diffident and distrustful of these things, and we have had no fruit yet but shame and dishonour over all the world. This great preparation is now on the way; he prayeth it may have a prospe-

---

[1] This speech is substantially the same in the Journals and in the *Camden Debates*. But see especially the report in the appendix to the latter, 136.

[2] "And everyone may contribute his reasons which may do much good," probably means this. *Camden Debates*, 139.

rous going forth, and a more prosperous return." He did not believe there was any necessity for more money than had been voted at Westminster, and he could not see why, if the seamen were pressed in April and the landsmen in May, the fleet had not been at sea long ago. That the delay had been caused, in part at least, by Buckingham's project of diverting the enterprise to the coast of Flanders, was of course unknown to Eliot. But though he had spoken thus strongly of the proceedings of the Government, he went on to acquit Buckingham of all personal blame about the fleet. If anything had gone wrong it was the fault of the Commissioners of the Navy.

The attack upon the Commissioners called up Sir John Coke, who protested loudly against this imputation upon the office which he held. Strode then followed, supporting [1] Mildmay's proposal that the money should be raised in some other way than by subsidy, by asking how subsidies payable more than a year hence could supply a fleet which was to go out in a fortnight. After a few words from Sir John Stradling, Sir Nathaniel Rich, who even more than Mildmay represented in the House that section of the Duke's friends which objected to his late proceedings, rose to put Mildmay's proposal in a more definite form. He proceeded to lay down five propositions, which had probably been accepted by Buckingham the evening before. In the first place, he said they must ask the King for an answer to their petition on religion. In the second place, his Majesty must declare the enemy against whom he meant to fight, so that the object of the war might be openly discussed, though the special design

Rich's five propositions.

---

[1] This at least seems to me to be the obvious interpretation of Strode's question. Mr. Forster, if I understand him rightly (*Sir J. Eliot*, i. 226), regards it as an argument against the grant of supply.

CHAP. VIII.
1625.
Aug. 6.

ought properly to be kept secret. Further, he wished that 'when His Majesty doth make a war, it may be debated and advised by his grave council'—a proposal which in the most courteous terms expressed the general wish that the opinion of others than Buckingham should be heard. Besides these three demands, Rich asked that the King's revenue should be examined with a view to its increase, and that a permanent settlement of the vexed question of the impositions should be arrived at.[1]

Thus far the House had listened to men who, if they were friends of Buckingham, could speak in an independent tone. But other voices were now raised. Before we give more money, said some one, let us take account from Buckingham of the subsidies voted the year before.[2] Edward Clerke, a man trusted by the Duke as his agent in affairs of questionable propriety, rose to defend his patron. "Bitter invectives," he

Incident of Clerke's imprisonment.

began, "are unseasonable for this time." There was at once an outcry from all parts of the House, and Clerke was committed to the custody of the sergeant-at-arms. With this scene ended the day's debate. The House was adjourned at Seymour's motion, in order that at the next sitting they might go into committee on the great business. But the members did not

Rich's scheme approved by Phelips.

separate before Phelips had expressed his decided approbation of 'the platform of Sir Nathaniel Rich.'[3]

[1] I would refer those who doubt my view of this debate to what I have said in the Preface (xiii) to the *Camden Debates*.

[2] This speech, which gave rise to Clerke's unlucky words, is mentioned in a letter from the Bishop of Mende. *King's MSS.*, 137, fol. 84.

[3] *Camden Debates*, 140. Rich is mentioned by Williams in a paper given in to the King on Aug. 14, as one of those who were 'never out my Lord Duke's chamber and bosom.' *Hacket*, ii. 18. There may have been some exaggeration, but unless there had been friendship, Williams would not have said this to the King.

Thus ended the discussions of this memorable week. That Saturday afternoon pressure was put upon Buckingham to accept the terms offered by Rich, which would then without doubt be adopted by the House. "The advice he had," writes Eliot, "was much to endeavour an accommodation with the Parliament. The errors most insisted on were said to be excusable if retracted. That the disorders of the navy might be imputed to the officers; that the want of counsels might be satisfied by a free admission to the Board. The greatest difficulty was conceived to rest in religion and the fleet. For the first, the jealousy being derived from his protection given to Montague; for the latter, that it had so unnecessary preparation and expense; and yet in both there might be a reconciliation for himself. Sending the fleet to sea and giving others the command, was propounded as a remedy for the one; having these reasons to support it, that the design could not be known, nor, if there wanted one, that judged by the success, and the success was answerable but by those that had the action. For the other, it was said that the leaving of Montague to his punishment, and the withdrawing that protection, would be a satisfaction for the present, with some public declaration in the point, and a fair parting of that meeting. That the danger of the time[1] was a great cause of dislike—that the dislike had ushered in most of those questions that had been raised. Therefore to free them from that danger would dissolve the present difficulties, and facilitate the way to a future temper for agreement. The fleet must needs go forth to colour the preparation, and the return might yield something to

CHAP. VIII.

1625. Aug. 6.
Arguments used with Buckingham.

---

[1] i.e. from the plague.

CHAP. VIII.
1625.
Aug. 6.
How this would sound to Buckingham.

justify the work, at least in excuse and apology for himself, by translation of the fault."¹ If this account of the language used to Buckingham has not been distorted in its passage through the medium of other men's minds, it must have been beyond measure annoying to him. To have it hinted that the fleet which had been for so many months the object of his solicitude was never intended to sail, was not a suggestion to which he was likely to listen with equanimity. The wonder is not that the proposal was ultimately rejected by him, but that he should, even for a moment, have given any hope to his advisers. For he was called not merely to admit himself to be incapable of directing the state, by consenting to place himself under the control of a Council reinforced by men who looked upon him with distrust, but to renounce all those long-considered plans which he regarded as of such importance. Already war had broken out in Germany, and the King of Denmark, depending on English promises, was holding out with difficulty against Tilly. From France every post brought news of preparations for war, and a day or two, he firmly believed, would tell the world that the internal struggle with the Huguenots was at an end. And were Buckingham and his master, in the face of one adverse debate, to fling their engagements to the winds? Were they to tell Christian that in building on the word of an English king he had been building on the sand? Were they, by teaching Richelieu that English co-operation was unattainable, to throw France back into the arms of Spain, and to force her to pass once more into the bondage from which she had with such difficulty emancipated herself?²

¹ Eliot, *Neg. Posterorum.*
² All these considerations arise out of the facts as we know them, and

What wonder therefore if Buckingham resolved to make one more effort to win the Commons to his side? There was one point at least on which he was ready to give them satisfaction. Neither he nor the King cared really for the principle of religious toleration. They were both of them as ready to execute the penal laws against the Catholics, if anything could be gained by so doing, as they had been to remit the penalties. Yet how could this be done without risk to the French alliance? Would Lewis help Charles to recover the Palatinate, if Charles's promise to protect the English Catholics were treated as if it had been never given? That Charles and Buckingham should have found excuses for breaking their engagements is no matter for surprise. But no better proof can be found of their incapacity to understand human nature than the ease with which they persuaded themselves that the King of France would be quite content that the engagements, by which he set such store, should be broken openly.

CHAP. VIII.
1625.
Aug. 6.
He determines to make one more effort. The Catholics to be abandoned.

On Sunday, August 7, there was high debate at Court. From La Vieuville's unguarded language, from Richelieu's polite phraseology, Buckingham, with Carlisle and Holland to back him, drew the astounding inference that the promise, so solemnly signed and attested at Cambridge, had never been anything more than a mere form, adopted with the approval of the French Government, to deceive the Pope.[1] For impar-

Aug. 7.
The promise to France explained away.

---

as Buckingham knew them. Eliot's picture of Buckingham is drawn not merely in ignorance of them, but in the belief that things were true which we know were not true.

[1] The Bishop of Mende to Richelieu, received Aug. $\frac{19}{29}$; *King's MSS.*, 137, fol. 84. The Council is here by mistake dated Aug. 9, if this is more than a copyist's error. But the 7th is meant, as it is said to have taken place the day before Buckingham's speech at Christchurch.

CHAP. VIII.
1625.
Aug. 7.

tial judges it is enough to condemn so monstrous a proposition that it was now heard of for the first time, and that Charles had already acknowledged by his actions that, when his wife was on her way to England, he considered his engagement to her brother as a reality.

This view accepted by the Council.

From this time forward it was to become a cardinal principle at the English Court to disavow all obligation to the King of France in the matter of the Catholics, and to appeal to words spoken in conversation by the French ministers as if, even if they meant all that Buckingham asserted them to mean, they could outweigh an obligation formally contracted. The members of the Privy Council had not a word to say in opposition when the revelation, as they supposed it to be, was suddenly made. Williams, and perhaps Arundel, may have been displeased at the rashness of the affront offered to the King of France, but they were powerless to resist. Of the others, Pembroke and Abbot were probably in communication with the leaders of the Commons, and doubtless shared to a great extent the general dissatisfaction. But whatever their exact form of opposition may have been, when once Buckingham had taken his stand, with the King's support, it was useless to raise further questions.

Buckingham in Christchurch hall.

On Monday morning therefore Buckingham appeared, radiant with self-confidence, in Christchurch hall, and the Commons were summoned to hear from his lips a communication from the King. After a short preamble from Williams, the Duke stood up as he had stood up at Whitehall eighteen months before, to answer for the government which was in reality centred in his person.

The petition of religion granted.

First he directed the King's answer to the petition of religion to be read. All that the Commons had demanded was fully and freely granted. If they thought that the execution of the penal laws against the Catholics was an object worth striving for, they were to have their wishes.

CHAP. VIII.
1625.
Aug. 8.

Buckingham then proceeded to defend his foreign policy. He spoke of the dissolution of the anti-Spanish party in Europe at the time when he came back from Spain. Now it was far otherwise. "Now," he said, "the Valtelline is at liberty, the war is in Italy; the King of Denmark hath an army of 17,000 foot and 6,000 horse, and commissions out to make them 30,000; the King of Sweden declares himself; the Princes of the Union take heart; the King of France is engaged in a war against the King of Spain, hath peace with his subjects, and is joined in a league with Savoy and Venice. This being the state of things then and now, I hope to have from you the same success of being well construed which then I had; for since that time I have not had a thought, nor entered into any action, but what might tend to the advancement of the business and please your desires. But if I should give ear and credit, which I do not, to rumours, then I might speak with some confusion, fearing not to hold so good a place in your opinion as then you gave me, whereof I have still the same ambition, and I hope to deserve it. When I consider the integrity of mine own soul and heart to the King and State, I receive courage and confidence; whereupon I make this request, that you will believe that if any amongst you, in discharge of their opinion and conscience, say anything that may reflect upon particular persons, that I shall be the last in the world to make application of it to myself, being so well assured of your justice, that without cause you will not fall on him that was so lately approved by you, and who will never do anything to irritate any man to have other

Bucking-ham defends his foreign policy.

284   THE FIRST PARLIAMENT OF CHARLES I. AT OXFORD.

<small>CHAP.
VIII.
1624.
Aug. 8.
Declares
he has
acted by
counsel.</small>

opinion of me than of a faithful, true-hearted Englishman."

Then turning to the demand for more counsel and advice, he declared that he had never acted without counsel. All that he had done or proposed to do had been submitted to the Council of War or to the Privy Council. He himself, when he went to France, had advised the institution of a Committee to give advice on foreign affairs. If therefore the Commons thought that he took too much on himself, they were mistaken. The Council which they demanded was already in existence.

<small>The necessity of the fleet.</small>

Of the suggestion that the fleet was not intended to sail, Buckingham spoke scornfully. "For my part," he said, "I know not what policy my master should have to set out a fleet with the charge of 400,000*l.* only to abuse the world and lessen his people, and to put you to such hazard. What should my master gain? Would he do an act never to meet with you again? Certainly he would never have employed so great a sum of money but that he saw the necessity of the affairs of Christendom require it; and it was done with an intention to set it out with all the speed that may be."

<small>What was intended?</small>

After touching on other less important points, Buckingham spoke of his plans for the future. "Hitherto," he said, "I have spoken nothing but of immense charge which the kingdom is not well able to bear if it should continue: the King of Denmark, 30,000*l.* a month; Mansfeld's army, 20,000*l.*; the army of the Low Countries, 8,000*l.*;[1] Ireland, 2,600*l.*; besides twelve ships preparing to second the fleet.

" Make my master chief of this war, and by that

---

[1] 8,500*l.*, according to the Lord Treasurer.

you shall give his allies better assistance than if you gave them 100,000*l.* a month. What is it for his allies to scratch with the King of Spain, to win a battle to-day and lose one on the morrow, and to get or lose a town by snatches? But to go with a conquest by land, the King of Spain is so strong, it is impossible to do. But let my master be chief of the war and make a diversion, the enemy spends the more; he must draw from other places, and so you give to them."[1]

If they wished to know who was their enemy they might name him themselves. Let them put the sword into the King's hands, and he would maintain the war.[2]

Buckingham's declaration was followed by a statement by the Lord Treasurer, in which the King's debts and engagements were plainly stated. But the main interest lay in the reception which would be accorded to Buckingham's vindication of himself. That there was intentional deception about his words it is impossible to imagine. There is a ring of sincerity about them which cannot be mistaken, and those who are best acquainted with the facts will probably acknowledge that he said exactly what, under the circumstances, he might reasonably be expected to say. But it is one thing to hold that he was sincere; it is another thing to hold that what he said ought to have given satisfaction. Doubtless it was perfectly true that he had appealed from time to time to the Privy Council and to the Council of War. But had he done his best to fill the Privy Council with men of independent judgment? Had he not rather given away places at the Board to men who had risen by obsequiousness rather than by merit? In politics, as in all other actions of life, one or two questions, decided one way or another, carry

[1] i.e., to the King's allies.
[2] *Lords' Journals*, iii. 479; *Camden Debates*, 95.

286 THE FIRST PARLIAMENT OF CHARLES I. AT OXFORD.

CHAP.
VIII.
1625.
Aug. 8.

with them the settlement of all other points at issue. Buckingham may have asked advice whether the fleet was to sail against Cadiz or Dunkirk, but had he asked advice whether the secret engagement about the French Catholics should be signed, or whether the King of Denmark should be encouraged to take part in a fresh war in Germany by offers of aid from England?

His aim probably not clear to himself.

If Buckingham's defence against the charge of despising counsel was unsatisfactory, his account of his own future designs was more unsatisfactory still. The Commons wished him to abandon his continental alliances, and to be content with attacking Spain. It can surprise no one that Buckingham was unwilling so lightly to turn his back upon the efforts of the past year. But when he proceeded to sum up the King's engagements, and when he allowed the Lord Treasurer to restate them in fuller detail, it was only natural to expect that he would urge upon the Commons the absolute necessity of furnishing money to enable the King to carry out his undertakings. He did nothing of the sort. He suggested that if the fleet were successful it would do more good to the common cause than if 100,000*l*. a month were paid to the allies of England on the Continent.

The explanation doubtless is that, whilst he could not abandon the world of alliances and subsidies in which he had been living and moving during the past year without a word spoken in their favour, his sanguine mind seized upon the chance that the success of the fleet might make all these subsidies unnecessary. After all, why should he not pay Mansfeld and Christian with gold from the mines of Spanish America rather than from the purses of English citizens and landowners?

Such a solution would rid him of his difficulty. It would satisfy the King's allies and satisfy the House of Commons as well.

CHAP. VIII.
1625.
Aug. 8.

Buckingham's explanation, taken at its best, is fatal to his claims to statesmanship. Either he had promised too much before, or he was asking too little now. Was it likely that it would allay the suspicions which were so rife amongst the Commons?

The Commons not likely to be satisfied.

On Wednesday morning the Lower House was to go into committee on Buckingham's explanation of the King's demands. Before the Speaker left the chair a message from the King had been delivered by Weston, pressing for an immediate answer, which was demanded alike by the necessity of the case and by the danger to their own health. If the Commons would vote a supply at once, he would pledge his Royal word that they should meet in the winter, and should not separate till they had considered the plans which had been suggested for the reformation of the Commonwealth. He hoped that they would remember that this was the first request which he had ever made to them.

Aug. 10.
The King's message.

For some time the debate wavered to and fro. There were some who had been carried away by Buckingham's evident zeal in the cause which was their own. But there were others who disliked his assumption of almost regal dignity, and who mistrusted him too much to repose in him the confidence which he required. Even his concession of the execution of the penal laws offended some who had been displeased at the countenance before shown to the Recusants. Men whose religion, if of a somewhat narrow and uncharitable nature, was a reality very dear to their hearts, had no respect for the man who had attempted to prostitute a thing so high and holy to considerations

Feeling in the House.

of State policy, and had made use of religion to support a tottering minister.[1]

Such men, and they were doubtless many, found an apt spokesman in Phelips. He treated the question as altogether one of confidence. Reputation, he said, is a great advantage to a king, but it is not built on every action, but only on such as have a sure ground of advice preceding, and a constant application of good counsel, leaving as little as possible to chance. It was no honour to send forth the fleet if it was exposed to so hazardous a return. It was easy to say there was necessity. It was for those who had brought the King to such a necessity to take upon themselves the burthen of their own counsels. In old days there had been Parliaments which had demanded the reformation of abuses and the dismissal of favourites. "We," he said with striking force, "are the last monarchy in Christendom that retain our original rights and constitutions. Either his Majesty is able to set out this fleet, or it is not fit to go at all. We ought neither to fear nor to contemn our enemy. If we provide to set it out, we must provide to second it too, for without a second it will do nothing but stir a powerful king to invade us."

Everything, as Phelips clearly saw, turned on the question of confidence. Forty thousand pounds might be a little sum for them to give, but it was no light matter to embark on a war with a leader who could not be trusted. Nor was Phelips content with mere declamation. He had a practical solution of the difficulty to recommend. Buckingham had declared that the Council of War had authorised his proceedings. But not a single member of the Council of War had come forward to confirm his statement. One of them, Sir

[1] This seems to have been Eliot's view.

Robert Mansell, was a member of the House. Let Mansell be asked 'to declare his knowledge with what deliberation and counsel this design hath been managed.' A Committee might also be appointed to inform his Majesty that, though supply would not at once be granted, the House would in due time 'supply all his honourable and well-grounded actions.'[1]

It would perhaps have been well if Mansell had responded at once. The King's claim to be judge of the grounds upon which he demanded supply had been met by the counter-claim of the House to judge the sufficiency of those grounds before they gave the money. But Mansell held his peace, and the debate went on. The King's cause was feebly defended by May. No one had been authorised to join issue with Phelips. Then came Seymour, still more personal in his attack than Phelips, complaining of peculation in high places, and of the sale of honourable preferments at Court.[2]

CHAP. VIII.
1625.
Aug. 10.

Continuance of the debate.

[1] *Camden Debates,* 109; *Commons' Journals,* i. 814.

[2] With respect to the alleged speech of Eliot I had better repeat what I have said in the preface to the *Camden Debates:*—

"In the first place I shall have to ask my readers to abandon the notion that the great speech prepared by Eliot in conjunction with Cotton for the debate of the 10th of August, was ever really spoken. Mr. Forster was, indeed, perfectly justified in inserting the speech, for not only does it bear throughout the impress of Eliot's mind, but Eliot has inserted it both in the *Negotium* and in his own collection of speeches, and though he does not use his name, he says, after reporting May's speech :—

But the esteem of precedents did remain with those that knew the true value of antiquity, whereof a larger collection was in store to direct the resolution in that case, which thus contained both reason and authority.

" Then after giving the speech in the Eliot, not in the Cotton form, he goes on :—

This inflamed the affection of the House, and pitched it wholly on the imitation of their fathers; the clear demonstrations that were made of the likeness of the times gave them like reasons who had like interests and freedom. But the courtiers did not relish it, who

CHAP. VIII.
1625.
Aug. 10.

The debate was kept up for some time longer. Amongst the speakers was Wentworth, who had been at once forsook both their reason and their eloquence; all their hopes consisting but in prayers and some light excuses that were framed, but no more justification was once heard of, in which soft way the Chancellor of the Exchequer did discourse, &c.

"This certainly is strong evidence, and in the face of it Mr. Forster was quite justified in treating with disdain the fact that nothing of this speech is to be found in the Journals. But the Journals do not now stand alone. We have three reports completely independent of one another, but all agreeing in omitting Eliot's speech, and in substituting one spoken by Sir Francis Seymour. If this were all, those who think Eliot's statement enough to counterbalance those of three independent witnesses might still hold that it had not been rebutted. But there is another argument far stronger. Sir Richard Weston, according to all four authorities, followed. He does not even allude to one of the arguments which are supposed to have been pouring out from Eliot. He utters no word of remonstrance against his tremendous personal attack upon Buckingham; but he applies himself very closely to Seymour's argument, and carefully answers it. I cannot believe that anyone who will take the trouble of reading Weston's speech at p. 112, can doubt that Seymour really spoke before him. And if so, where is there any room for Eliot's speech, which is substituted for his in the *Negotium*?

"The two forms of the speech which have come down to us are, as Mr. Forster has pointed out, substantially the same, but the one is the speech of an orator, the other of an antiquary. Mr. Forster argues, that in the case of Cotton's speech, 'some one finding at the same time,' i.e. after 1651, when the speech was published by Howell in his *Cottoni Posthuma*, 'a manuscript copy of the speech purporting to have been spoken by Eliot, was misled by Howell into a marginal indorsement of it as "not spoken but intended by Sir John Eliot," and the preservation of the copy in the *Lansdowne MSS.*, so indorsed, adds to the confusion.'

"The argument is probably based upon the fact that, at the head of the speech (*Lansd. MSS.*, 491, fol. 138) is written in a different hand from the rest of the paper 'Sir John Eliot's: this speech was not spoken but intended.' But any argument drawn from the difference of handwriting falls to the ground when it is observed that this is merely a copy of a heading which was originally at the top of the page, and the greater part of which has been cut off in the process of binding; enough, however, remains to show that the heading was originally in the same writing as the body of the document. My own belief is that it was a copy taken from Cotton's notes at the very time by some one who knew that Eliot intended to use them but did not. For, in after years, who was likely to call to mind the mere intention to deliver a speech, especially as it was known amongst Cotton's friends as his production?

re-elected for Yorkshire during the vacation. He had promised to take no part in any personal attack upon the Duke.[1] He took no interest in the Duke's projects, and the slight put upon the House of which he was a member stung him to the quick. 'He was not,' he said, 'against giving, but against the manner.' He did not like to hear the threat that they must either give or adjourn. 'The engagement of a former Parliament,' he added, 'bindeth not this.' Not that he seems to have cared much whether the House had confidence in the Duke or not. As far as he was concerned, we may safely conjecture, if the subsidies were

CHAP. VIII.
1625.
Aug. 10.

In a letter written by Sir S. D'Ewes, on the 4th of February, 1626 (*Ellis*, ser. 1, iii. 214), the writer, speaking of the omission of the King to land on his way to his coronation at Sir R. Cotton's stairs, says :—' I conceived the Duke had prevented that act of grace to be done him, by reason of that piece I shewed you, which began, " Soe long as thou attendedst our master, now with God," framed by him. You may remember how I told you that I doubted him the author, by reason of the style and gravity of it.'

" Curiously enough, the first words here given are not the first words of Cotton's work as it stands in the *Cottoni Posthuma* and the *Lansdowne MSS*. The paper which D'Ewes saw must have omitted the introduction relating to Clerke's censure by the House. On the other hand it was Cotton's, not Eliot's work which he saw. For Eliot began with a verbal difference : ' While thou remainedst in the service of King James.'

" The most probable explanation is that the speech is by Cotton; that Cotton shrank from making use of it, and that Eliot, catching it up, breathed into it the fire of his own magnificent imagination, and converted the result of the antiquary's laborious investigation into words inspired with life.

"It is easy to find reasons why, after all, Eliot should have preferred silence. In the first burst of his indignation at finding Buckingham had broken away from his compact, nothing would seem too hard to say. But when it came to the point, we should only be inclined to think more highly of Eliot if he shrunk back and refused to strike the first blow."

Since these words were written I have an additional witness to call, and that is no other than Eliot himself. In the notes in his own handwriting which, through Lord St. Germans' kindness, I have before me, Seymour's speech is given, and not a word is said of any speech of Eliot's own.

[1] Wentworth to Weston ; *Strafford Letters*, i. 34.

to be spent in war with Spain, it mattered little whether Buckingham or some more trusted councillors were to have the disposal of them. The internal affairs of England were the prime object of his solicitude from the first day on which he opened his mouth in Parliament. " Let us first," he said, " do the business of the Commonwealth, appoint a Committee for petitions, and afterwards, for my part, I will consent to do as much for the King as any other."[1]

Other speakers followed with various opinions, Coke strangely enough suggesting a benevolence as the best way out of the difficulty. As a private man he was ready to give 1,000*l.*, and that willingly, notwithstanding all his crosses. He hoped those of the King's council would do as much. Then at last Mansell rose. Since February, he said, he had not been at any debate of the Council of War. When the proposition had been made for the levy of 10,000 landsmen to go on board the fleet, he ' thought that proposition to no purpose, being such as would gall the enemy rather than hurt him.' He had a plan of his own which would be far more useful. Conway had told him that the resolution would admit no debate. The advice of the Council was asked only concerning the arms for 2,000 men. He had answered that he protested against the business itself.

Upon this the Committee was adjourned to the next morning. It would be hard for Buckingham to wipe away the impression made by Mansell's words. By this time, too, Pennington and his sailors were back in England. The tale of the delivery of the ships by special orders from Buckingham must have been in every mouth. It was known that the French boasted that they would use them against Rochelle. The un-

[1] *Camden Debates*, 113; *Eliot Notes*.

confirmed assertion of Buckingham that there was peace in France was entirely disbelieved.

CHAP. VIII.

1625.
Aug. 11.
The Sallee rovers.

Before the debate recommenced on Thursday morning a letter was read from William Legg, a prisoner to the Moorish pirates at Sallee. He was one, he said, of eight hundred Englishmen captured at sea. Enormous ransoms had been demanded, and those who refused or had been unable to pay had been treated with the utmost cruelty. Some of them had been tortured by fire, some were almost starved, and one poor wretch had been compelled to eat his own ears. Witnesses, too, who had escaped from the pirates were actually in attendance. One had been captured but eight leagues from the Land's End. It appeared that great spoil had been committed on the English coast, so that vessels scarcely ventured from port to port. If the West of England cried out against the rovers of Sallee, the East cried out against the Dunkirk privateers. Even the Huguenots of Rochelle had forgotten the respect due to English commerce. They had seized some ships of Bristol for service against the King of France, and had turned the sailors adrift on shore without money or provisions.

Indignation was fast coming to a head. It was known that orders given by the Council for the employment of some of the King's ships against the pirates had been countermanded by the Navy Commissioners. It was replied that the Duke had given directions to Sir Francis Steward, one of the commanders of the fleet, to clear the seas of pirates. The answer was that Sir Francis Steward had looked calmly on whilst a capture was being made near the French coast, on the plea that he had no orders to act in foreign waters. At last Seymour spoke out what was in the mind of all. " Let us lay the fault where it is," he

Anger of the House.

said. "The Duke of Buckingham is trusted, and it must needs be either in him or his agents." "It is not fit," cried Phelips, "to repose the safety of the kingdom upon those that have not parts answerable to their places." A Committee was appointed to frame a petition embodying these complaints.

For the first time the Duke had been attacked by name. It was a fitting answer to his assumption of almost regal dignity in Christchurch hall. The man who had assumed to direct all things must bear the responsibility of all things.

When the House at last went into committee, Sir Henry Marten [1] made one more effort to obtain a grant of supply. But he, at least, was not likely to make much impression on the House. Rightly or wrongly, it was believed that he was trying to wipe off the offence given by his reference to Buckingham as a young ambassador. He produced so little effect that Seymour, in repeating his advice not to give, did not care to put forward any fresh reasons. After a few more words on both sides, Sir Robert Killigrew advised that the question should not be put. It would be a greater disgrace to the King to be in a minority than to have the whole House against him.[2]

That afternoon [3] the Council met to consider whether the House should be allowed to sit any longer. Once more Williams pleaded hard against the fatal error of opening the new reign with a quarrel with the House of Commons. And for once Buckingham was

---

[1] He, and not Sir J. Coke, is the 'old artist' of the *Negotium*, as appears from what Eliot says, 'Some did imagine that an act of expiation for the former trespass he had done.'

[2] *Camden Debates*, 120.

[3] Bishop of Mende to Richelieu, received Aug. $\frac{19}{29}$; *King's MSS.*, 137, 99. Nethersole to Carleton, Aug. 14; *Camden Debates*, 162.

on the same side. Throwing himself on his knees he entreated the King to allow the Parliament to continue. But Charles was immovable, and the dissolution was irrevocably determined on.

CHAP. VIII.
1625.
Aug. 11.

Buckingham's petition was naturally described by his opponents as a mere piece of acting.[1] It may have been so, but it was not in his nature to shrink from opposition. His temper always led him to meet his detractors face to face, certain of the justice of his own cause and of his own ability to defend it. In truth it was Charles's authority as much as Buckingham's which was at stake. The course which the Commons were taking led surely, if indirectly, to the responsibility of ministers to Parliament. And the responsibility of ministers to Parliament meant just as surely the transference of sovereignty from the Crown to the Parliament.

The next morning, before the fatal hour arrived, an attempt was made by Heath to answer Mansell. The Council of War, he said, had often been consulted. Chichester, who was dead, had left papers to show how far he agreed with the plans proposed. Carew was absent from Oxford; Harvey had only recently joined the Council. But Lords Grandison and Brooke, the Sir Oliver St. John and Sir Fulk Greville of earlier days, would come, if they were invited, to tell the House what they knew. As for Mansell, he had a scheme of his own to which no one else would listen, and had consequently refused to attend the Council.

Heath replies to Mansell.

This account of what had taken place was very likely true, but Heath had not met Mansell's assertion that he had been told that he was not to speak on the scheme itself, but only on its execution. And Mansell, who rose in self-defence, did not deny that there had been

Mansell's answer.

[1] Eliot's *Negotium*, in *Forster*, i. 252.

personal ill-will between himself and Buckingham, but he said that when he laid his own proposal before the Council, he was told that he must go to Buckingham, 'who only had permission from the King to consider of new propositions.' To this, which was only what the Commons suspected, no reply was vouchsafed; the testimony of Brooke and Grandison was neither demanded on one side nor pressed on the other.[1]

By this time it was known in the House that they had but a few minutes more to sit. The Black Rod was already at the door to summon them to dissolution. Some wished to petition for delay. But what good would delay do them unless they were prepared to abandon their ground? "Rumours," said Phelips, "are no warrant for such a message. Let them go on with business. When they had notice of the King's pleasure, it was their duty to obey it."

The House went at once into committee, and adopted a protestation prepared by Glanville, who had taken a prominent part in the debates of the past days. In the following fashion the Commons approached the King:—

"We, the knights, citizens, and burgesses of the Commons' House of Parliament, being the representative body of the whole commons of this realm, abundantly comforted in his Majesty's late gracious answer touching religion, and his message for the care of our healths, do solemnly protest and vow before God and the world with one heart and voice, that we will ever continue most loyal and obedient subjects to our most gracious sovereign King Charles, and that we will be ready in convenient time and in a parliamentary way freely and dutifully to do our utmost endeavour to discover and reform the abuses and grievances of the

[1] *Camden Debates,* 122.

realm and State, and in the like sort to afford all necessary supply to his Majesty upon his present and all other his just occasions and designs; most humbly beseeching our ever dear and dread sovereign, in his princely wisdom and goodness, to rest assured of the true and hearty affections of his poor Commons, and to esteem the same—as we conceive it indeed—the greatest worldly reputation and security a just king can have, and to account all such as slanderers of the people's affections and enemies of the Commonwealth that shall dare to say the contrary."

One last effort was made by Sir Edward Villiers to induce the House to reconsider its determination. "We are under the rod," answered Wentworth, "and we cannot with credit or safety yield. Since we sat here, the subjects have lost a subsidy at sea."[1]

The protestation was hurried through the necessary forms. Whilst Black Rod was knocking at the door, some one moved that there should be a declaration 'for the acquitting of those who were likely to be questioned for that which they had spoken.' If any one was likely to be questioned it was Phelips. But Phelips would hear nothing of it. "There hath been little effect of such declarations," he said. "The last Parliament but one [2] some went to the Tower, some were banished to Ireland, notwithstanding just acquittals. For my part, if I am questioned, I desire no other certificate but the testimony of my conscience, in confidence whereof I will appeal from King Charles misinformed to King Charles rightly informed."

At last the doors were opened. The Commons

CHAP. VIII.
1625. Aug. 12.

The last scene.

Dissolution.

[1] The exposure of English commerce to pirates was always a reproach to which Wentworth was extremely sensitive.
[2] The words "but one" are wanting in the report. *Camden Debates,* 127.

were summoned to the Upper House, and in a few minutes the first Parliament of Charles I. had ceased to exist.

Such was the end of this memorable Parliament—a Parliament which opened the floodgates of that long contention with the Crown, never, except for one brief moment, to be closed again till the Revolution of 1688 came to change the conditions of government in England. And, as far as the history of such an assembly can be summed up in the name of any single man, the history of the Parliament of 1625 is summed up in the name of Phelips. At the opening of the session his hasty advocacy of an immediate adjournment met with little response. But under the pressure of events the House came gradually round to his side, and at Oxford he virtually assumed that unacknowledged leadership which was all that the traditions of Parliament at that time permitted. It was Phelips who placed the true issue of want of confidence before the House, and who, by the enquiry which he directed to Mansell, pointed out the means of testing the value of Buckingham's assertions.

It is not necessary to defend all that was said, still less all that was thought, in the House about Buckingham. No one who has studied the facts of the history in a candid spirit can deny that the speeches of the popular members were full of unfounded suspicions and unreasonable demands. But, for all that, it is impossible to assert that Buckingham could show any sufficient ground for reposing confidence in him. The account which he gave of his proceedings was singularly confused. By his own confession he had entered into engagements which he was unable to meet, and which he did not venture to ask the Commons to assist him in meeting. And, besides this, the terrible failure of Mansfeld's expedition, costing thousands of innocent lives, could not be explained away. Nor is Buckingham's a case in which further publicity than he was able to appeal to would present his ability in a better light. For some time he had been occupied in undoing the results of his own mistakes. The engagement about the Catholics and the loan of the ships to the King of France had been mainly his doing. The manner in which he had extricated himself from those entanglements was not known to the House of Commons. But it is known to us; and we may be sure that if the Commons had known what we know they would have been even more indignant than they were. As it was, the general opinion of moderate Englishmen was probably well expressed by a foreign diplomatist who took but little interest in the Parliamentary conflict. Since he had come to England, he said, he had learned the truth of two paradoxes. Under James, he found that it was better to take a bad resolution than none at all; under Charles, that it was better to give effect to a bad resolution with prudence and ability, than to give effect to a good resolution without forethought and consideration.[1]

CHAP. VIII.
1625.
Aug. 12.

Rusdorf's opinion.

The attitude which Charles would take towards this declared want of confidence in his minister would evidently depend upon the amount of confidence which he himself continued to feel in him. And unfortunately there was no chance that his reliance on Buckingham would be shaken. His own mind had nothing originative about it. When once the brilliant schemes of Buckingham had dazzled his understanding, he adopted them as his own, and from that moment all chance of inducing him to abandon

Attitude of the King.

---

[1] Rusdorf to Camerarius, Sept. $\frac{2}{12}$; *Consilia et Negotia*, 69.

them was at an end. He had no power of stepping out of himself to see how his actions looked to other people, especially when, as was certain to be the case, the real objections to his policy were mixed up with offensive imputations which he knew to be unfounded in fact.

Conflict between Crown and Parliament.

The difference of opinion between the King and the Parliament was thus reduced to a contest for power. The two great elements of the constitution which had worked harmoniously together were brought at last into open conflict. The right of enquiry before subsidies were voted would, if once it were admitted, place the destinies of England in the hands of the House from which subsidies proceeded. But it would be a mistake to suppose that either party in the quarrel were grasping at power for its own sake. Charles believed that he was defending a wise and energetic minister against factious opposition. The Commons believed that they were hindering a rash and self-seeking favourite from doing more injury than he had done already. If neither were completely in the right, the view taken by the Commons was far nearer to the truth than the view taken by Charles.

Conservatism of the House.

So far as the difference between the King and the House went beyond the mere question of confidence, the Commons stood upon a purely conservative ground. We look in vain amongst their leaders for any sign of openness to the reception of new ideas, or for any notion that the generation in which they lived was not to be as the generation which had preceded it. Their conception of the war was more suited to 1588 than to 1625, and the mazes of European politics formed for them a labyrinth without a thread. In all they had to say about the affairs of the Continent it is hard to find a single word which betrays any real know-

ledge of the wants and difficulties of the Protestants of
Germany. In home politics, too, their eyes were
equally directed to the past. The form of religion
which had grown up under the influence of the
Elizabethan struggle with Spain was to be stereotyped.
Differences of opinion were to be prohibited, and the
Calvinistic creed was to be imposed for ever upon
the English nation.

CHAP.
VIII.
1625.
Aug. 12.

But if the temper of the Commons was thus purely
conservative, its conservatism was to some extent
justified by the nature of the alternative offered to it.
Charles's foreign policy was as ignorant as that of the
Commons, and far more hazardous. Charles's ecclesiastical policy had hardly yet had time to develope
itself. But signs were not wanting that it would be
even more dangerous than that which was secure of
the popular favour. If the Commons were ready to
proscribe the religious opinions of the few, the men
whom the King honoured with his preference were
ready to proscribe the religious practices of the many.

CHAPTER IX.

THE EXPEDITION TO CADIZ.

CHAP. IX.

1625.
Aug. 12.
The leaders of the Commons untouched.

THE gloomy anticipations of some of the Commons with respect to their personal safety were not realised. Phelips and Seymour, Coke and Glanville, returned in peace to their homes. Mansell indeed was summoned before the Council. But he answered boldly that he could not be touched without a violation of the liberties of Parliament, and he was dismissed with nothing worse than a reprimand.[1]

Buckingham's intentions.

In fact it was no part of Buckingham's policy to drive the nation to extremity. Full of confidence in himself, he fancied that he had but to use the few months' breathing space allowed him to convince the electors that their late representatives had been in the wrong. The time had come which he had apparently foreseen when he conversed with Eliot at Westminster. He had asked for necessary support, and had been denied. A few days would show the King of France at peace at home, turning his sword against Spain and the allies of Spain abroad. A few months would show the great English fleet returning with the spoils of Spanish cities and the captured treasures of the New World. Then a fresh Parliament would assemble round the throne to acknowledge the fortitude of the King and the prescience of his minister.

A few days after the dissolution news came from

[1] Johnston, *Hist. Rerum Britannicarum*, 666. Tillières to Lewis XIII., Aug. 21/31; *King's MSS.*, 137, p. 121.

France which dashed to the ground the hopes which had been formed of the cessation of the civil war. There were many persons about the Court of Lewis who had no liking for Richelieu's policy of toleration. The Prince of Condé, if report spoke truly, sent a hint to Toiras, who commanded the French troops outside Rochelle, that the peace must in one way or another be made impossible. To carry such counsels into execution presented no difficulties to Toiras. The Rochellese, pleased with the news that peace had been made at Fontainebleau, pressed out without suspicion into the fields to gather in their harvest. Upon the innocent reapers Toiras directed his cannon. Many of them were slain, and Toiras then proceeded to set fire to the standing corn. Loud was the outcry of the indignant citizens within the walls. It was impossible, they said, to trust the King's word. The ratification of the treaty was refused, and it seemed as though the war must blaze up once more with all its horrors.[1] It was not long before the burden of war fell upon those who were most innocent. The English ships were now in the hands of the French admiral, and in a naval engagement which took place off Rochelle on September 5, Soubise was entirely defeated, and driven to take an ignominious refuge in an English port.

Such a calamity could hardly have been foreseen by any one. But it was none the less disastrous to Buckingham's designs of conciliating the English nation. All the long intrigue carried on with the assistance of Nicholas was rendered useless. The English ships were in French hands, and they would doubtless be used against Rochelle. What a handle this would give to Buckingham's accusers it was easy to foresee.

It is probable that this misfortune was already

CHAP. IX.

1625. Aug.

The peace with the Huguenots comes to nothing.

Aug. 10.

Sept. 5. Defeat of Soubise.

How it affected Buckingham.

[1] Resolution of the Town of Rochelle, Aug. $\frac{10}{20}$; Lorkin to Conway, Aug. $\frac{11}{21}$; *S. P. France.*

known to Charles when the Privy Council met at Woodstock on the 14th, the Sunday after the dissolution. It was evidently the King's intention to show that, so far as the assent of the Privy Council as it was then composed was worth anything, he would take no serious step without its advice. Its members unanimously approved of a proclamation for the banishment of the Roman Catholic priests, of the continuance of the preparations for sending out the fleet, and of the issue of Privy seals, to raise what was practically a forced loan, in order to meet its expenses.[1]

Yet if money had been needed for the fleet alone, there would have been no such pressing need. In addition to the 10,000*l*. borrowed in August, no less than 98,000*l*. were brought into the exchequer in the months of August and September on account of the Queen's portion,[2] and Charles, before August was over, was quietly talking to the French ambassador of diverting part of the new loan to some other purpose.[3] In point of fact the order for preparing the Privy seals was not issued till September 17,[4] and the fleet was at sea before a single penny of the loan came into the King's hands. But Charles had many needs, and he may perhaps have thought that there would be less opposition to the loan if he asked for it for the purpose of fitting out the fleet.

Charles had thus been able to dismiss his Parliament and to convince or cajole his Privy Council. But he could neither convince nor cajole his wife. The promises lightly made when hope was young he had now repudiated and flung aside. He was unable to understand why the Queen, who had upon the faith

---

[1] Meautys's Note, Aug. 14, *S. P. Dom.*, v. 41; Tillières to Lewis XIII., Aug. 24/14; *King's MSS.*, 137, p. 121.
[2] *Receipt Books of the Exchequer.*
[3] Tillières to Lewis XIII., Aug. 24/14; *King's MSS.*, 137, p. 131.
[4] The King to the Council, Sept. 17; *S. P. Dom.*, vi. 70.

of those promises, consented to leave her mother's care for a home in a strange land, should feel aggrieved when the Catholics, whom she had come to protect, were again placed under the pressure of the penal laws. A few days after the dissolution he was at Beaulieu, hunting in the New Forest, whilst Henrietta Maria was established at Titchfield, on the other side of Southampton Water. There he visited her from time to time; but in the temper in which they both were there was little chance of a reconciliation. Charles never thought of taking the slightest blame to himself for the estrangement which had arisen between them. It was a wife's business, he held, to love and obey her husband, just as it was the business of the House of Commons to vote him money. Sometimes he sent Buckingham to threaten or to flatter the Queen by turns. Sometimes he came in person to teach her what her duties were. If he was blind to his own errors he was sharpsighted enough to perceive that his wife's French attendants were doing their best to keep her displeasure alive, and were teaching her to regard herself as a martyr, and to give as much time as possible to spiritual exercises and to the reading of books of devotion.[1] To counteract these tendencies in the Queen, Charles wished to place about her the Duchess of Buckingham, the Countess of Denbigh, and the Marchioness of Hamilton, the wife, the sister, and the niece of his own favourite minister, and he desired her at once to admit them as Ladies of the Bedchamber.

The demand was not in contradiction with the

---

[1] See a curious letter, said to be from a gentleman in the Queen's household (Oct. 15, *S. P. Dom.*, vii. 85), which looks genuine. But even if it is not, the statements in it are in general accordance with what is known from other sources.

CHAP. IX.
1625.
Aug.

letter of the marriage treaty.[1] But it was in complete opposition to its spirit, and the young Queen fired up in anger at the proposal. She told Charles that what he asked was contrary to the contract of marriage. Nothing, she told her own followers, would induce her to admit spies into her privacy.

The English sermon at Titchfield.

The strife grew fierce. The guard-room at Titchfield was used on Sundays for the service of the English Church, according to the custom which prevailed in houses occupied by the King. Against this the Queen protested as an insult to herself, and argued that whilst Charles was at Beaulieu, she was herself the mistress of the house. But Lady Denbigh took part against her, and the service was not discontinued. At last the Queen lost all patience, made an incursion into the room at sermon time, and walked up and down laughing and chattering with her French ladies as loudly as possible. The preacher soon found himself a butt for the practical jokes of the Frenchmen of the household. One day, as he was sitting on a bench in the garden, a gun was fired off behind a hedge close by. The frightened man fancied an attempt had been made upon his life, and pointed to some marks upon the bench as having been made by the shot aimed at himself. Tillières, who had come back to England as chamberlain to the Queen, was called in to adjudicate, and, having sat down on several parts of the bench, gravely argued that as he could not sit anywhere without covering some of the marks, and, moreover, the clergyman was very corpulent, whilst he was himself very thin, the shot which had made the marks must certainly

Practical jokes upon the preacher.

---

[1] By Article 11 all the attendants taken from France were to be Catholics and French, and all vacancies were to be filled up with Catholics. Lewis had forgotten to provide for the case of Charles wishing to add Protestants when there were no vacancies.

TREATY WITH THE DUTCH. 307

have passed through the person of the complainant, if his story had been true.[1]

If Charles was hardly a match for his wife, he had no doubt at all that he was a match for half the Continent. Those vast enterprises which he had been unable to bring himself to disavow in the face of the House of Commons had still a charm for his mind. In vain Rusdorf, speaking on behalf of his master, the exiled Frederick, urged upon him the necessity of concentrating his forces in one quarter, and argued that the ten thousand landsmen on board the fleet would be useless at Lisbon or Cadiz, but would be invaluable on the banks of the Elbe or the Weser, where Christian of Denmark was with difficulty making head against Tilly.[2]

The attack upon Spain was the first object with Charles, and he therefore listened readily to the Dutch commissioners, who had come to England in order to draw up a treaty of alliance. Naturally the Dutchmen cared more about the war with Spain than about the war in Germany, and when the treaty which they came to negotiate was completed it fixed accurately the part to be taken by the two countries in common maritime enterprise, whilst everything relating to hostilities on land was expressed in vague generalities. The States General had already agreed to lend Charles 2,000 English soldiers in exchange for the same number of recruits, and to send twenty vessels to join the fleet at Plymouth.[3] By the treaty signed at Southampton on September 8 an alliance offensive and defensive was established between England and the

CHAP.
IX.

1625.
Sept.

Rusdorf urges Charles to assist the King of Denmark.

The Dutch commissioners in England.

Sept. 8.
The Treaty of Southampton.

---

[1] Tillières, *Mémoires*, 99–104; Rusdorf to Oxenstjerna, $\frac{\text{Sept. 30}}{\text{Oct. 10}}$; *Mem.*, ii. 73.

[2] Rusdorf's advice, $\frac{\text{Aug. 31}}{\text{Sept. 10}}$; *Mem.*, i. 611.

[3] Agreement, $\frac{\text{July 23}}{\text{Aug. 2}}$; *Aitzema*, i. 468.

x 2

CHAP. IX.
1625.
Sept. 8.

States General. The Flemish harbours were to be kept constantly blockaded by a Dutch fleet, whilst the English were to perform the same task off the coast of Spain. Whenever a joint expedition was concerted between the two nations the States General were to contribute one ship for every four sent out by England. The details of a somewhat similar arrangement for joint operations by land were left, perhaps intentionally, in some obscurity.[1]

To Rusdorf the preference shown for maritime over military enterprise was the death-knell of his master's chances of recovering the Palatinate. Charles was far too sanguine to take so gloomy a view of his situation. He had now openly broken with Spain. He had recalled Trumball, his agent at Brussels, and he had no longer any minister residing in the Spanish dominions. He had followed up this step by the issue of letters of marque to those who wished to prey on Spanish commerce. But he had no idea of limiting hostilities to a combat between England and Spain. "By the grace of God," he said to a Swedish ambassador who visited him at Titchfield, "I will carry on the war if I risk my crown. I will have reason of the Spaniards, and will set matters straight again. My brother-in-law shall be restored, and I only wish that all other potentates would do as I am doing."[2]

Open breach with Spain.

In fact it was because Charles had not been content to pursue a mere war of vengeance against Spain, that he had entered upon those extended engagements which more than anything else had brought him into collision with the House of Commons. Those engagements he had no intention of abandoning, and he

[1] Treaty of Southampton; *ibid.* i. 469.
[2] Rusdorf to Frederick, Sept. $\frac{19}{20}$; *Mem.*, i. 623.

hoped that if some temporary way of fulfilling them could be found, the success of the fleet would place him in a position to claim the gratitude of his subjects, and that he would thus be able to place himself at the head of an alliance more distinctly Protestant than when he had been hampered by the necessity of looking to France for co-operation. In the treaty of Southampton the foundation for such an alliance had been laid, and it now only remained to extend it, with the needful modifications, to the King of Denmark and the North German Princes. It was therefore arranged that Buckingham should go in person to the Hague, where the long-deferred conference was expected at last to take place. But it was useless for him to go with empty hands. If Charles could not procure the money which he had already bound himself to supply to Christian, it was hardly likely that Christian would care to enter into fresh negotiations with so bad a paymaster. Yet, how was the money to be found? One desperate resource there was of which Charles had spoken already in a rhetorical flourish, and of which he was now resolved to make use in sober earnest. The plate and jewels of the Crown, the hereditary possession of so many kings, might well be pledged in so just and so holy a cause. In England no one would touch property to which his right might possibly be challenged on the ground that the inalienable possessions of the Crown could not pass, even for a time, into the hands of a subject. On the Continent there would be no fear of the peculiar doctrines of English law. But if once the precious gems were sent to the Continent, there might be some difficulty in recovering them. At last it was decided that the plate and jewels should be carried by Buckingham to Holland. It was probably argued that in that rich and friendly country men might be found who would both accept the security and be faithful to their trust.¹

Want of money is a sad trial to any Government, and in one part of England it had already brought Charles into difficulties with his subjects. Towards the end of August serious apprehensions were entertained for the safety of Harwich. It was known that Dunkirk was alive with preparations for war, and no part of England was so liable to attack as the flat and indented coast of Essex. Orders were therefore issued by the Privy Council to put Landguard Fort in repair, and to occupy Harwich with a garrison of 3,000 men, chosen from the Essex trained bands. So far everything had been done according to rule. Each county was bound to provide men for its own defence. But the Crown was also bound to repay the expenses which it might incur, and this time there was an ominous silence about repayment. Under these circumstances a proposition was made by the Earl of Warwick, Holland's elder brother, who was now in high favour with Buckingham, which looks like the germ of the extension of ship money to the inland counties. The adjacent shires, he said, were interested in the safety of Harwich. Let them, therefore, be called on to contribute to its defence in men and money. The adjacent shires, however, refused to do anything of the kind; and the vague promises of payment at some future time, which was all that the Government had in its power to offer, were met by the firm resolution of the Essex men that they, at any rate, would not serve

---

¹ The earliest mention of Buckingham's intended journey is, I believe, in Rusdorf's letter to Oxenstjerna, Sept. $\frac{9}{19}$ (*Mem.* ii. 63.) The first hint about the jewels is in an order from Conway to Mildmay, the Master of the Jewel House, to give an account of the plate in his hands. Conway to Mildmay, Sept. 4; *Conway's Letter Book*, 227; *S. P. Dom.*

at their own charges. Making a virtue of necessity, the Council ordered the men to be sent back to their homes, and directed Pennington, who, since his return from Dieppe, had been watching, with a small squadron, the movements of the Dunkirk privateers, to betake himself to the protection of Harwich. Thus ended Charles's first attempt so to construe the obligations of the local authorities as to compel them to take upon themselves the duties of the central Government.[1]

CHAP. IX.
1625. Aug.

With all Charles's efforts to conciliate public opinion by a bold and, as he hoped, a successful foreign policy, there was no thought of throwing open the offices of state to men who were likely to be regarded with confidence by the nation. And yet it was not long before an opportunity occurred of which a wise man would have taken advantage. On September 6 Morton died of a fever which seized him a few days after his return from the Netherlands. The vacant secretaryship was at once conferred upon Sir John Coke, the only man amongst the Government officials who had incurred the positive dislike of the opposition leaders of the Commons, and whose subserviency and want of tact was to do even more damage to his patrons than they had done already.

Sept. 6. Death of Morton.

Sir John Coke, secretary.

These things were not unnoticed. Lord Cromwell, who had left his service under Mansfeld for a more hopeful appointment in the new expedition, had brought back with him from the Netherlands his old habit of speaking plainly. "They say," he wrote to Buckingham, "the best lords of the Council knew nothing of Count Mansfeld's journey or this fleet, which discon-

Sept. 8 Cromwell's letter.

[1] Coke to Buckingham, Aug. 25; Coke to Conway, Aug. 26; Order of Council, Aug. 30; Sussex to the Council, Sept. 9; Warwick to Conway, Sept. 10; Warwick to the Council, Sept. 18, 23; The Council to Warwick, Oct. 2; *S. P. Dom.*, v. 85, 99; vi. 38, 44, 76, 98; vii. 4.

312   THE EXPEDITION TO CADIZ.

CHAP.   tents even the best sort, if not all. They say it is a
IX.   very great burden your Grace takes upon you, since
1625.   none knows anything but you. It is conceived that
Sept. 8. not letting others bear part of this burden now you
         bear, it may ruin you, which Heaven forbid."[1]

  The expedition upon which so many hopes were
embarked was by no means in a prosperous condition.
For a long time the soldiers had been left unpaid.
Aug.   Before the end of August there was a new press of
Bad con- 2,000 men to fill up the vacancies caused by sickness
dition of
the troops and desertion.[2] The farmers of South Devon upon
at Ply-
mouth.   whom the soldiers were billeted refused to supply food
any longer to their unwelcome guests, as soon as they
discovered that their pockets were empty. Like Mansfeld's men eight months before, the destitute recruits
made up their minds that they would not die of starvation. Roaming about the country in bands, they
killed sheep before the eyes of their owners, and told
the farmers to their faces that rather than famish they
would kill their oxen too.[3]

  At one time there had been a talk of Buckingham's
going himself in command, and a commission had been
made out in his name. But he could not be at the
Hague and on the coast of Spain at the same time, and
he perhaps fancied that he could do better service as a
diplomatist than as an admiral. At all events, whilst
much to the amusement of the sailors he retained the
Cecil to pompous title of generalissimo of the fleet, he ap-
command
the expedi- pointed Sir Edward Cecil, the grandson of Burghley
tion.   and the nephew of Salisbury, to assume the active command with the more modest appellation of general.[4]

---

[1] Cromwell to Buckingham, Sept. 8 ; *S. P. Dom.*, vi. 30.
[2] The King to Nottingham and Holderness, Aug. 23 ; *ibid.* v. 62.
[3] Commissioners at Plymouth to the Council, Aug. 12, Sept. 1 ; *S. P. Dom.*, vi. 3.
[4] Eliot, *Negotium Posterorum*.

Cecil had served for many years in the Dutch army, with the reputation of being a good officer. But he was now for the first time to be trusted with an independent command, and the selection was the more hazardous as he was entirely unacquainted with naval warfare. But he had from the first attached himself closely to Buckingham, who had in vain supported his claims to the command in the Palatinate in 1620, and who had now sufficient influence to reverse the decision then come to in favour of Sir Horace Vere. The Earl of Essex, who was to go as Vice-Admiral, knew as little of the sea as Cecil himself; and the same might be said of the Rear-Admiral, the Earl of Denbigh, whose only known qualification for the post lay in the accident that he was married to Buckingham's sister.

Chap. IX. 1625. Aug.

Essex and Denbigh.

Whatever Cecil's powers as a general may have been, he had at least a soldier's eye to discern the deficiencies of the troops under his orders, and he professed himself as puzzled as the Commons had been to discover why, if no attempts had been made to convert the recruits into trained soldiers, they had been levied in May for service in September. Buckingham too, he complained, had been recommending officers to him who were not soldiers at all, and whom 'he neither could nor durst return.' The arms which the men should have been taught to handle were still on board ship in the harbour. On September 8, only three out of the twenty Dutch ships promised had arrived at Plymouth.¹

Sept. 8. Cecil's report on the troops.

There was, however, one direction in which Cecil's energy could hardly be thrown away. In answer to the complaints made in Parliament it had been announced that Sir Francis Steward would be sent out with a squadron to clear the English seas of

Measures taken against pirates.

¹ Cecil to Conway, Sept. 8; *S. P. Dom.,* vi. 36.

the Sallee rovers. But Steward's attempt had ended in total failure. According to the Mayor of Plymouth his ships had been outsailed by the pirates. According to his own account the weather had been against him. Parliament, instead of grumbling against the King's officers, ought to have passed an act ensuring them a fair wind.[1]

The outcry from the western ports waxed louder than ever. It was reported that danger had arisen from another quarter. No less than ten privateers had slipped through the Dutch blockading squadron in front of Dunkirk,[2] and were roaming the seas to prey upon English commerce. Cecil, when he heard the news, sent out Sir Samuel Argall in search of the enemy. Argall, after a seven days' cruise, returned without having captured a single pirate or privateer. But he was followed by a long string of French and Dutch prizes, which he suspected of carrying on traffic with the Spanish Netherlands. Amongst these was one, the name of which was, a few months later, to flash into sudden notoriety—the 'St. Peter of Havre de Grace.'[3]

By this time the King himself had paid a short visit to Plymouth to see the fleet and to encourage the crews by his presence. Buckingham, who came with him, remained behind to settle questions of precedence amongst the officers, and to infuse, if it were possible, some of his own energetic spirit into the commanders. As usual he anticipated certain success, and he was unwise enough to obtain from the King an immediate peerage for Cecil, who was from henceforth to be

[1] The Mayor &c. to the Council, Aug. 12; Steward to Buckingham, Aug. 16; *S. P.*, v. 36, 49.
[2] Hippisley to Buckingham, Sept. 9; *ibid.* vi. 67, 120.
[3] Narrative of the expedition, Sept. 16; Examination of the masters of the prizes; *ibid.* vi. 67, 120.

known as Viscount Wimbledon, on the ground that the additional rank would give him greater authority over his subordinates. Buckingham seems to have forgotten that honours assumed before success has crowned an undertaking are apt to become ridiculous in case of failure.

This was not the only foolish thing done by Buckingham at Plymouth. The sight of Glanville, the author of the last address of the Commons at Oxford, quietly fulfilling his duties as Recorder of the Devonshire port, inspired him with the idea of maliciously sending a Parliamentary lawyer to sea as secretary to the fleet. Glanville pleaded in vain that the interruption to his professional duties would cause him a heavy loss, and that, as no one but his clerk could, even under ordinary circumstances, decypher his handwriting, it was certain that when he came to set down the jargon of sailors, even that confidential servant would be unequal to the task.[1]

At last, on the 5th of October the great fleet put to sea. As it passed out of the harbour and rounded the point where the soft woods of Mount Edgcumbe slope down to the waters of the Sound, the long-expected Dutch ships were descried showing their topsails above the eastern waves, as if, as men said, they had come to escort the English fleet upon its voyage. These fair prospects were soon interrupted. The wind chopped round to the south-west, and began to blow hard. Essex, with the foremost vessels, took refuge in Falmouth, but the bulk of the fleet put back to its old anchorage. But Plymouth harbour was no safe refuge in such a gale, in the days when as yet the

[1] Glanville's reasons, Sept. ? Woodford to Nethersole, Oct. 8; *S. P. Dom.*, vi. 132; vii. 44. Was Glanville's objection the origin of the old joke, or did he use it for want of an argument?

CHAP. IX.
1625.
Oct. 6.

long low line of the breakwater had not arisen to curb the force of the rolling waves. By the next morning all bonds of discipline had given way before the anxious desire for safety, and the waters of the Sound were covered with a jostling throng of vessels, hurrying, regardless of the safety of others, to the secure retreat of the Catwater. Orders, if given at all, met with but little attention, and Wimbledon himself was forced to get into a boat, and to pass from vessel to vessel, in order to exact the least semblance of obedience.

Wimbledon's despondency.

Wimbledon had long ceased to look upon the expedition with his patron's confidence of success. Little good, he thought, would come of a voyage commenced so late in the season. And now the spectacle of disorder which he witnessed left a deep impression on his mind. The discipline which comes from an energetic and well-arranged organisation was entirely wanting, and it was not replaced by the discipline which springs from old habits of comradeship, or from the devotion which makes each man ready to sacrifice himself to the common cause. Buckingham, who in 1624 had fancied that military power was to be measured by the number of enterprises simultaneously undertaken, fancied in 1625 that the warlike momentum of a fleet or army was to be measured by its numerical size. He had yet to learn, if indeed he ever learnt it, that thousands of raw recruits do not make an army, and that thousands of sailors, dragged unwillingly into a service which they disliked, do not make a navy. But Cecil knew it, and the expedition carried with it the worst of omens in a hesitating and despondent commander.[1]

Oct. 8. The fleet again puts to sea.

On the 8th the fleet, laden with the fortunes of Buckingham and Charles, put to sea once more. It

[1] Cecil to Coke, Oct. 8, undated in *Cabala*, 370; Wimbledon to Buckingham, April 28, Sept. 26, 1626; *S. P. Dom., Addenda*.

sailed, as it had been gathered together, without any definite plan. There were general instructions that a blow should be struck somewhere on the Spanish coast before the treasure ships arrived, but no special enterprise had been finally selected. At a council held in the King's presence at Plymouth, San Lucar had been mentioned as a point of attack. But objections had been raised, and the whole question was reserved for further discussion on the spot. As soon, therefore, as the fleet rounded Cape St. Vincent, Wimbledon called a council, and was assured by seamen of experience that it would be dangerous to enter the harbour so late in the year. Upon this Argall observed that an easy landing could be effected at St. Mary Port in Cadiz Bay. From thence a march of twelve miles would bring the troops to San Lucar, and their object would thus be obtained without difficulty.[1]

Argall's advice was adopted, and orders were given to anchor off St. Mary Port. But as the fleet swept up to the station a sight presented itself much too tempting to be resisted. Far away on the opposite side of the Bay lay twelve tall ships with fifteen galleys by their side,[2] covering a crowd of smaller vessels huddled under the walls of Cadiz. Essex, who led the way in

CHAP. IX.

1625. Oct. 8.

Oct. 20. The council of war at sea.

Oct. 22. The fleet in Cadiz Bay.

[1] Wimbledon's Journal, printed in 1626, has been usually accepted as the authority for the voyage. But it should be compared with his own despatches, and with the letters of other officers, such as Sir W. St. Leger, Sir G. Blundell, and Sir T. Love, which will be found amongst the State Papers. The Journal of the 'Swiftsure' (S. P. Dom., xi. 22) gives a full narrative of the proceedings of the squadron under Essex, whilst the proceedings of Denbigh and Argall are specially treated of in an anonymous journal (S. P. Dom., x. 67). In Geronimo de la Concepcion's Cadiz Ilustrada, we have the Spanish story. In the Tanner MSS. (lxxii. 16) there is a MS. copy of Wimbledon's Journal, annotated by some one hostile to the author, thus bearing witness to the correctness of his assertions where they are not questioned.

[2] There is a discrepancy about the numbers. I take them from Wimbledon's Journal.

CHAP. IX.

1625.
Oct. 22.

Argall's ship, the 'Swiftsure,' dashed at once upon the prey.

It was not Wimbledon's fault that Essex narrowly escaped a grave disaster. Sailing through Essex's division, he shouted orders to right and left to crowd all sail after the Vice-Admiral. But he shouted now as vainly in Cadiz Bay as he shouted a few weeks before in Plymouth harbour. The merchant captains and the merchant crews, pressed unwillingly into the service, had no stomach for the fight. Essex was left alone to his glory and his danger, and Wimbledon, who did not even know the names of the vessels under his command, was unable to call the laggards to account.

Flight of the Spaniards.

Of all this the Spanish commanders were necessarily ignorant. Instead of turning upon the unsupported 'Swiftsure,' they cut their cables and fled up the harbour. It was a moment for prompt decision. Had a Drake or a Raleigh been in command, an attempt would doubtless have been made to follow up the blow. But Wimbledon was no sailor, and he allowed his original orders for anchoring to be quietly carried out.

Puntal to be attacked.

At nightfall a council of war was summoned on board the flagship. The project of marching upon San Lucar was tacitly abandoned. Had it been known that a mere handful of three hundred men formed the whole garrison of Cadiz,[1] some voices would perhaps have been raised for an immediate attack upon the town. As it was, the pursuit of the ships was regarded as the preferable alternative. But it was resolved first to attack the fort of Puntal which guarded the entrance, barely half a mile in width, leading to the inner harbour where the vessels were. The obstacle did not seem a serious one. "Now," said one of the old sailors,

[1] *Geronimo de la Concepcion*, 458.

ATTACK ON FORT PUNTAL.

"You are sure of these ships. They are your own. They are in a net. If you can but clear the forts to secure the fleet to pass in safely, you may do what you will." Nothing could be easier, it was thought, than to take the fort. Sir William St. Leger alone protested against the delay. Part of the fleet, he argued, would be sufficient to batter the fort. The remainder might sail in at once against the ships whilst the enemy's attention was distracted. But St. Leger, like his commander, was not a sailor, and in a council of war composed mainly of sailors, his advice met with no acceptance.

CHAP. IX.
1625.
Oct. 22.

Five Dutch ships and twenty small Newcastle colliers were accordingly ordered to attack the fort at once. As Wimbledon watched the flashes of the guns lighting up the night, he flattered himself that his orders had been obeyed. But when morning dawned he learned that the English colliers had taken advantage of the darkness to remain quietly at anchor, whilst the Dutchmen, overmatched in the unequal combat, had been compelled to draw off at midnight with the loss of two of their ships.

Failure of the first attack.

Oct. 23.

A rope at the yard-arm would doubtless have been Drake's recipe for the disease. Wimbledon was of a milder nature. Rowing from ship to ship, he adjured the cowards to advance for very shame. Finding that he might as well have spoken to the winds, he went on board the 'Swiftsure' and directed Essex to attack. The 'Swiftsure' was at once placed opposite the enemy's batteries, and was well seconded by her comrades of the Royal Navy. But nothing would induce the merchant captains to venture into danger. Clustering timidly behind the King's ships, they contented themselves with firing shots over them at the fort. At last one of them clumsily sent a shot

Second attack.

right through the stern of the 'Swiftsure,' and Essex, losing patience, angrily ordered them to cease firing.

Such an attack as this was not likely to compel the garrison to surrender, and it was only upon the landing of a portion of the troops that the fort capitulated. The Spanish commander was struck by the gallant bearing of the 'Swiftsure,' and asked who was in command. "Do you know," was the reply, "who took Cadiz before?" "Yes," he said, "it was the Earl of Essex." "The son of that Earl," he was told, "is in the ship." "Then," replied the Spaniard, "I think the devil is there as well." A request that he might be allowed to pay his respects to Essex was promptly accorded, and his reception was doubtless such as one brave man is in the habit of giving to another.

It was late in the evening before Puntal was in the hands of the English. By that time all hope of taking Cadiz by surprise was at an end. Whilst Essex was battering Puntal, Spanish troops were flocking into Cadiz, and that night the town was garrisoned by four thousand soldiers. It was true that the place was only provisioned for three days, but the Spanish galleys soon learned that they could bring in succours in spite of the English, and Cadiz was soon provisioned as well as guarded.

For the present, however, the ships at the head of the harbour were the mark at which Wimbledon aimed. But he contented himself with directing Denbigh to see that the work was accomplished. He himself saw to the landing of the greater part of the troops still on board on the following morning, and called a council of war at noon to decide what was next to be done.

Scarcely, however, had the council met, when a

scout hurried in with intelligence that a large force of
the enemy was approaching from the north, where the
island, at the southern end of which Cadiz was situated,
swelled out in breadth till it was cut off from the
mainland by a narrow channel over which a bridge was
thrown. Fearing lest he should be taken between this
force and the town, Wimbledon gave hasty orders to
advance to meet it. But the Spaniards were in no
hurry to bring on an action against superior numbers,
and prudently drew back before him.

CHAP. IX.
1625.
Oct. 24.

After a six miles' march the English discovered
that no enemy was in sight. But Wimbledon did not
appear to be in the least disconcerted. "It seemeth,"
he said to those who were near him, "that this alarm
is false. But since we are thus forwards on our way, if
you will, we will march on. It may be we may light
on some enemy. If we do not, we may see what kind
of bridge it is that hath been so much spoken of."[1]

Wimbledon, in fact, lighted on an enemy upon
whose presence he had failed to calculate. In the
hurry of the sudden march no one had thought of
seeing that the men carried provisions with them.
Many of the soldiers had not tasted food since they had
been landed to attack Puntal the day before. Ever
since noon they had been marching with the hot
Spanish sun beating fiercely on their heads. Wimbledon, in mercy, ordered a cask of wine to be
brought out of a neighbouring house to solace the
fasting men. Even a little drop would have been too
much for their empty stomachs, but the houses around
were stored with wine for the use of the West India

The soldiers among the wine casks.

[1] This would be almost incredible, if it did not stand on Wimbledon's
own authority. The marginal note in the copy amongst the *Tanner MSS.*
remarks: "The first time an army marched so far to answer a false alarm,
and it were fit his Lordship would name those some of the council he
spake to, that were not against his going to the bridge."

VOL. I.   Y

fleets. In a few minutes casks were broached in every direction, and well-nigh the whole army was reduced to a state of raving drunkenness. Interference was useless, and the officers were well content that the enemy was ignorant of the chance offered him.

Disgraceful as the scene was, it had no appreciable effect upon the success or failure of the expedition. When morning dawned it was evident that the men could not be kept another day without food, even if there had been any object to be gained by remaining where they were.[1] Leaving therefore a hundred poor wretches lying drunk in the ditches to be butchered by the Spaniards, Wimbledon returned to Puntal, to learn that the attack which he had ordered upon the Spanish ships had not been carried out. Their commanders had made use of their time whilst the English were battering Puntal, and, warping their largest vessels up a narrow creek at the head of the harbour, had guarded them by sinking a merchantman at the entrance. Argall, to whom the attack had been entrusted by Denbigh, had only to report that the thing was impracticable. However great may be the risk in forming an opinion on imperfect data and with imperfect knowledge, it is diffi-

[1] Let Wimbledon be judged by his own Journal. "Now this disorder happening," he writes, "made us of the council of war to corsider that since the going to the bridge was no great design, but to meet with the enemy and to spoil the country, neither could we victual any men that should be left there, and that the galleys might land as many men as they would there to cut them off: and that when my Lord of Essex took Cadiz, Conyers Clifford was taxed by Sir Francis Vere . . . with mistaking the directions that were given him to go no further from the town than the throat of the land, which is not above two miles, where he might be seconded and relieved, and be ready to relieve others; but he went to the bridge, which was twelve miles off; so in regard there was no necessity, this disorder happening and want of victuals, we resolved to turn back again, which we did." The marginal note to this is, "Why did his Lordship then go to the bridge without victuals and to lose time, having such a precedent against it ?"

cult to resist the impression that a combined attack by sea and land would not have been made in vain, and that if Wimbledon, instead of wasting his time in pursuing a flying enemy, had contented himself with acting in conjunction with Argall, a very different result would have been obtained.

CHAP. IX.

1625.
Oct. 25.

But however this may have been, it was now too late to repair the fault committed. A reconnaissance of the fortifications of Cadiz convinced the English commanders that the town was as unassailable as the ships. The Plate fleet, the main object of the voyage, was now daily expected, and there was no time to linger any longer. On the 27th the men were re-embarked. The next day Puntal was abandoned, and the great armament stood out to sea as majestic and as harmless as when it had arrived six days before.

Oct. 27.
The men re-embarked.
Oct. 28.

On the 4th of November the English fleet arrived at its appointed station, stretching out far to seaward from the southern coast of Portugal. Though no man on board knew it, the quest was hopeless from the beginning. The Spanish treasure ships, alarmed by rumours of war which had been wafted across the Atlantic, had this year taken a long sweep to the south. Creeping up the coast of Africa, they had sailed into Cadiz Bay two days after Wimbledon's departure.[1]

Nov. 4.
The lookout for the Plate fleet.

It may be that fortune was not wholly on the side of Spain. Judging by the exploits of the merchant captains before Puntal, it is at least possible that instead of the English fleet taking the galleons, the galleons might have taken the English fleet. At all events, if the Spaniards had trusted to flight rather than to valour, the English vessels would hardly have succeeded in overtaking them. With their bottoms foul

---

[1] Atye to Acton, $\frac{\text{Dec. 28}}{\text{Jan. 7}}$; *S. P. Spain.*

CHAP. IX.

1625.
Nov. 16.
Return to England.

Bad condition of the ships and men.

Buckingham's part in the matter.

with weeds, and leaking at every pore from long exposure to the weather, they found it hard to keep the sea at all. It had been at first resolved to keep watch till the 20th, but on the 16th orders were given to make sail for home with all possible speed.

It was indeed time. The officials who had been charged with supplying the fleet had been fraudulent or careless. Hulls and tackle were alike rotten. One ship had been sent out with a set of old sails which had done service in the fight with the Armada. The food was bad, smelling 'so as no dog in Paris Garden would eat it.'[1] The cyder[2] was foul and unwholesome. Disease raged among the crews, and in some cases it was hard to bring together a sufficient number of men to work the ships. One by one, all through the winter months, the shattered remains of the once powerful fleet came staggering home, to seek refuge in whatever port the winds and waves would suffer.

It was certain that so portentous a failure would add heavily to the counts of the indictment which had long been gathering against Buckingham. After his defiant challenge to public opinion at Oxford, it would be in vain for him to argue before a new House of Commons that he was not answerable for Wimbledon's neglect of his opportunities at Cadiz, and still less for the accident by which the Plate fleet had escaped. Nor, after all allowances have been made for exaggeration, is it easy to deny that the popular condemnation was in the main just. The commanders of the expedition, and the officials at home by whom the preparations were made, were Buckingham's nominees, and the system of personal favouritism, the worst

---

[1] Sir M. Geere to W. Geere, Dec. 11; *S. P. Dom.*, xi. 49.
[2] Beverage, in these letters, means cyder. It is the usual word in Devonshire now for common cyder.

canker of organisation, had never been more flourishing than under his auspices. Nor was it only indirectly that the misfortunes of the expedition were traceable to Buckingham. If, upon his arrival at Cadiz, Wimbledon had been too much distracted by the multiplicity of objects within his reach to strike a collected blow at any one of them, so had it been with the Lord High Admiral at home. Undecided for months whether the fleet was to be the mere auxiliary of the army in the siege of Dunkirk, or whether the army was to be the mere auxiliary of a fleet whose main object was the capture of the Plate fleet, he had no room in his mind for that careful special preparation for a special object which is the main condition of success in war as in everything else.

If Wimbledon's errors as a commander were thus the reflection, if not the actual result, of Buckingham's own errors, the other great cause of failure, the misconduct of the merchant captains, brings clearly before us that incapacity for recognising the real conditions of action which was the fertile source of almost all the errors alike of Buckingham and of Charles. The great Cadiz expedition of which Raleigh had been the guiding spirit, had been animated, like all other successful efforts, by the joint force of discipline and enthusiasm. A high-spirited people, stung to anger by a lifelong interference with its religion, its commerce, and its national independence, had sent forth its sons burning to requite their injuries upon the Spanish nation and the Spanish king, and ready to follow the slightest command from the tried and trusted leaders who had learned their work through a long and varied experience by sea and land. How different was everything now! It is hardly possible to doubt that the war of 1625 never was and never could have been as popular as the war of 1588

CHAP. IX.
1625.
Dec.

and 1597. It was a political and religious rather than a national war, awakening strong popular sympathies, indeed, so long as the home danger of a Spanish marriage lasted, but liable to be deserted by those sympathies when that danger was at an end. And if the enthusiasm were lacking, its place was certainly not supplied by discipline. The commanders were personally brave men, and most of them were skilled in some special branch of the art of war, but utterly without opportunities for acquiring the skill which would have enabled them to direct the motions of that most delicate of all instruments of warfare, a joint military and naval expedition. It was possible that after eight or ten years of war so great an effort might have been successful. It would have been next to a miracle if it had been successful in 1625.

No serious investigation.

The worst side of the matter was that Charles did not see in the misfortunes which had befallen him any reason for attempting to probe the causes of his failure to the bottom. Some slight investigation there was into the mistakes which had been committed in Spain. But nothing was done to trace out the root of the mischief at home. Sir James Bagg and Sir Allen Apsley, who had victualled the fleet before it sailed, were not asked to account for the state in which the provisions had been found, and they continued to enjoy Buckingham's favour as before. No officer of the dockyard was put upon his defence on account of the condition of the spars and sails. There was nothing to warrant that another fleet would not be sent forth the next spring equally unprovided and ill equipped. In the meanwhile the King and his minister had fresh objects in view, and it was always easy for them to speak of past failures as the result of accident or misfortune.

CHAPTER X.

GROWING ESTRANGEMENT BETWEEN THE COURTS OF
ENGLAND AND FRANCE.

EVEN if the Cadiz expedition had not ended in so complete a failure, the difficulties resulting from the French alliance would have been likely to cause Charles serious embarrassment. Every step which he had taken since the meeting of his first Parliament had been in the direction of a closer understanding with the Protestant powers. He had begun again to execute the penal laws. He had signed a treaty with the Dutch, and he was about to send Buckingham to the Hague to sign another treaty with the King of Denmark and the Princes of North Germany. When Parliament met again, he hoped to be able to stand forth in the character of a leader of the Protestantism of Europe.

At Salisbury, on his way back from his visit to the fleet at Plymouth, he was reminded of the old engagements which he had contracted with France. Blainville, the new French ambassador, presented himself before him, and Buckingham, who had already started for the Hague, was summoned back to take counsel on the French proposals.

Those proposals, as far as the war was concerned, ought not to have been unacceptable. Lewis was ready to furnish 100,000*l.*, payable in two years, to the King of Denmark. He would also join Charles in

CHAP.
X.

1625.
Sept.
The French alliance.

Oct. 6.
Blainville at Salisbury.

The French overtures.

CHAP. X.
1625.
Oct.

giving support to Mansfeld's army, and he consented to an arrangement, already in progress, for transferring that force to Germany, and placing Mansfeld under the command of Christian.[1] If Lewis, however, was prepared to do as much as this, he was prepared to ask for something in return. He could hardly avoid asking for the fulfilment of Charles's promise to free the English Catholics from the penal laws; and now that Soubise had been defeated he would be likely to press for the entire submission of Rochelle, though he was ready to promise that the Huguenots should enjoy religious liberty, a privilege, as he wrote to Blainville, which was not allowed to the Catholics in England.[2]

Such questions, however, difficult as they were to settle, were far from forming the whole of the barrier which stood in the way of the maintenance of the French alliance. Lewis's idea of that alliance was evidently that of a man who wishes to play the first part. But Buckingham wished to play the first part too. He would refuse to negotiate on the war with Blainville. He would cross over at once to Holland, and then, when the foundations of a great Protestant alliance had been surely laid, he would pass on to Paris. Once more he would summon the King of France to join England in open and avowed war against Spain and her allies. And he would summon him, not as he had done in May, as the representative of England alone, but as the leader of a mighty Protestant confederacy, offering to France the choice between the acceptance of English leadership or the isolation of neutrality.

Buckingham's plans.

His proposed visit to France.

Buckingham, indeed, had no difficulty in persuading

[1] Lewis XIII. to Blainville, $\frac{\text{Sept. 25}}{\text{Oct. 5}}$; Blainville to Lewis XIII., Oct. $\frac{6}{16}$; *King's MSS.*, 137, p. 274, 350; Villermont, *E. de Mansfeldt*, ii. 321.
[2] Lewis XIII. to Blainville, Oct. $\frac{11}{21}$; *King's MSS.*, 137, p. 385.

himself that the offer which he made was worthy of Lewis's acceptance. The Spanish treasure of which Wimbledon had gone in search was already his by anticipation. When the fleet returned there would be enough to keep up the war in Germany for many a year, and the Flemish ports, the objects of his desire for so many months, could at last be snatched from Spinola's tenacious hold.[1]

CHAP.
X.
1625.
Oct. 7.

There were reasons enough why the husband of Anne of Austria should be unwilling to receive a visit from the audacious upstart who had ventured to pay public court to the Queen of France, and Lewis, as soon as he heard of the proposal, peremptorily instructed Blainville to refuse permission to Buckingham to enter his kingdom.[2] But politics had undoubtedly as much part as passion in the matter. The

Lewis objects.

[1] The views of the English Government may be gathered from a passage in the instructions drawn up as a guide to some one whom it was intended to send to Gustavus. "And because we are seated most properly and best furnished for maritime actions, we have undertaken that part, though it be of greatest cost, and which will, in a short time, by the grace of God, render all the land service easy and profitable to those that shall attempt it. And therefore we shall expect that both our dear uncle the King of Denmark and the King of Sweden will, upon your reasons heard, go on cheerfully for the stopping of the progress of the enemy's conquests by land, without calling to us for contribution in that, wherein principally must be regarded the present conservation of all the sea towns which might any way give Spain a port of receipt for their ships that may come from thence that may be bought or built in these parts, or may correspond with the ports of Flanders. And it will not be amiss when you shall fall into deliberation with that king, to consult and consider with him the great importance of taking away the harbours of Flanders from the King of Spain, and to prove how far he might be moved to join with us, our uncle of Denmark, and the States, to make one year's trial to thrust the King of Spain from the seacoasts of Flanders." Instructions for Sweden, Oct. 17; *Rymer*, xviii, 212.

[2] "Je me passionne de sorte pour votre contentement que je ne crains point de vous mander si franchement mon avis, et vous êtes assez du monde pour pénétrer ce qui ne me seroit pas bienséant d'écrire," is Ville-aux-Clercs' explanation on giving the orders to Blainville, $\frac{\text{Sept. 24}}{\text{Oct. 4}}$; *King's MSS.*, 137, p. 313.

question between Lewis and Buckingham was the question of the leadership of half Europe. And Lewis had to guard against the interference of England nearer home. Buckingham was instructed, as soon as he reached Paris, to demand the immediate restoration of the English ships which had been used at Rochelle, and to ask that an end should at once be put to the unnatural war between the King and the Huguenots.

The demand, that Charles should be empowered to interfere between Lewis and his subjects, was to be made in the most offensive way. Buckingham's instructions ran in the following terms:—"To the end they," that is to say, the French Protestants, "may not refuse the conditions offered them for the only doubt of not having them kept, you shall give them our Royal promise that we will interpose our mediation so far as that those conditions shall be kept with them; and if this will not satisfy them, you shall give them our kingly promise that if by mediation you cannot prevail for them, we will assist them and defend them." In other words, when Lewis had once given his promise to the Huguenots, it was to be considered as given to the King of England, and if any disputes again arose between him and his subjects, the King of England would be justified in intervening in their favour if he thought fit so to do.

Buckingham, in fact, not content with taking the lead in Germany, was to dictate to Lewis the relations which were to exist between himself and his subjects; and that too at a moment when the English Government was fiercely repudiating a solemn contract on the ground that it did not become a king of England to allow a foreign sovereign to intervene between himself and his people.[1]

[1] Conway to Carleton, Oct. 7; *S. P. Holland.* Instructions to Buckingham; *Rymer,* xviii.

On October 11 Blainville was admitted to an audience. To the Frenchman's remonstrances about the English Catholics, Charles at first replied that he had only promised to protect the Catholics as long as they behaved with moderation. It was for himself to interpret this promise, and he took upon himself to say that they had not behaved with moderation. He then added the now familiar argument that the secret article had never been taken seriously, even by the French Government.

The tone of the conversation mutually grew warmer, and a fresh demand of the ambassador did not serve to moderate the excited feelings on either side. Soubise had brought with him to Falmouth the 'St. John,' a fine ship of the French navy, which he had seized at Blavet.[1] This ship Lewis naturally claimed as his own property which Charles was bound to restore. Charles, on the other hand, being afraid lest it should be used, as his own ships had been used, against Rochelle, hesitated and made excuses.

The state of the Queen's household, too, ministered occasion of difference. Charles wished to add English officials to those which had been brought over from France, and he peremptorily refused to discuss the question with Blainville. He intended, he said, to be master in his own house. If he gave way, it would be from the love he bore to his wife, and for no other reason.

The next day the ambassador waited on Buckingham. The conversation was carried on in a more friendly tone than that of his conversation with Charles. But in other respects it was not more satisfactory. Buckingham treated all the subjects in dispute very lightly. If anything had gone wrong the fault was in the necessities of the time. Instead of troubling himself with such trifles, the King of France ought to treat at

[1] P. 151.

once for an offensive league against Spain. As for himself, he was said to have ruined himself for the sake of France. He was now going to the Hague to save himself by great and glorious actions. If France pleased, she might take her place in the league which would be there concluded. If she refused, England would have all the glory.

Buckingham, as Blainville pointed out, had two irreconcilable objects in view. On the one hand he wished to ingratiate himself with English public opinion by placing himself at the head of a Protestant League. On the other hand he wished to show by driving France to follow his lead on the Continent, that his original overtures to that power had not been thrown away.[1]

Neither Lewis nor Richelieu were likely to stoop as low as was expected of them. Blainville was instructed to announce that the 'Vanguard,' as being Charles's own property, should be given up, but that he had no claim upon the merchant vessels, which had been expressly hired for eighteen months. The Huguenots could not be allowed to carry on a rebellion against their lawful sovereign, and if Charles was so solicitous for religious liberty, he had better begin the experiment with his own Catholic subjects.[2]

Buckingham was too anxious to reach the Hague as soon as possible, to await the issue of these negotiations at Salisbury. But before he left the King, arrangements had been made for dealing in various ways with those Peers who had taken part in the opposition in the last Parliament. Of these Abbot might safely be

[1] Tillières, *Mémoires*, 105; Blainville to Lewis XIII., Oct. $\frac{12}{22}, \frac{14}{26}$; *King's MSS.*, 137, p. 409, 438.

[2] Memoir sent by De Vic, Oct. $\frac{16}{26}$; Lewis XIII. to Blainville, $\frac{\text{Oct. 29}}{\text{Nov. 8}}$; *King's MSS.*, 137, p. 470, 482.

disregarded. He had nothing popular about him except his firm attachment to the Calvinistic doctrine, and he had long been left in the shadow by James, who displayed a strong preference for the cleverness and common sense of Williams, as Charles displayed a strong preference for the sharp decision of Laud.[1] But it was a different matter to deal with Pembroke, the richest nobleman in England,[2] who commanded numerous seats in the House of Commons,[3] and whose influence was not to be measured by the votes thus acquired. At first, indeed, Charles's temper had got the better of him, and on his journey to Plymouth he had treated Pembroke with marked disfavour. The Earl was not accustomed to be slighted, and he replied with a counter-demonstration. As he passed through Sherborne he paid a formal visit to Bristol, who was still in disgrace, at Sherborne Castle. The significance of the step could not be misinterpreted, and Charles lost no time in renewing the old familiarity to which Pembroke was never insensible. When Buckingham was with the King at Salisbury on his return journey, he made an early call at Wilton, and though Pembroke was still in bed and could not see him, it was after-

CHAP.
X.

1625.
Sept.

[1] The idea, almost universal amongst historians, that Abbot was thrown into the shade by his accidental homicide in 1621, is not borne out by contemporary writers, and his want of influence may be easily accounted for from the causes mentioned above. Fuller is doubtless the original authority for the usual opinion, but Fuller's story has long ago been shown by Hacket to have been based upon a misapprehension of the facts.

[2] To the first subsidy of the reign Pembroke paid 700l., standing alone; then came Northumberland, Rutland, and Devonshire, with 600l.; Buckingham, Derby, Cumberland, Hertford, Northampton, Petre, and Robartes, with 400l. *Book of the Subsidy of the Nobility,* Oct. 2; *S. P. Dom.,* vii. 6.

[3] Rudyerd to Nethersole, Feb. 3, 1626; *S. P. Dom.,* xx. 23. 'All my Lord's letters were sent out,' means Pembroke's letters, not 'the Duke's,' as given in the *Calendar.* See also a letter from Sir James Bagg, in *S. P., Addenda.*

334 ESTRANGEMENT BETWEEN ENGLAND AND FRANCE.

CHAP. X.

1625. Sept.

Arundel and Williams.

wards understood that the temporary estrangement was at an end.[1]

Abbot and Pembroke belonged to that section of the opposition which it was Buckingham's object to conciliate. Arundel and Williams were in different case. As a great nobleman, not mixing much in the business of government, Arundel could hardly be touched. But Williams had incurred Buckingham's bitterest displeasure, and was easily assailable in his official position. His strong sense had led him to condemn alike the extravagances of the new reign and the shifts to which Charles had been driven in order to cover those extravagances from popular condemnation. He had shown a sad want of confidence in the success of those vast armaments in which Buckingham trusted, and he had been sufficiently uncourtierlike to dissuade the King from summoning the Commons to Oxford, and to suggest that if Charles had really given his word to the King of France that he would relax the penal laws, it was dangerous as well as impolitic to break it.

Oct. 25. Dismissal of Williams.

It was easier to resolve to get rid of the Lord Keeper than to find an excuse for dismissing him. At first he had been charged with entering upon conferences at Oxford with the leading members of the opposition in the Commons. But this charge he was able to meet with a denial, and it was hardly possible to disgrace him on the mere ground that he had given unpalatable advice, or even on the ground that he had agreed with the Commons in thinking that a reinforcement of the Privy Council was advisable. At last some courtier reminded the King that his father had entrusted the Great Seal to Williams for three years on probation, and that the time fixed had now expired.

[1] North to Leicester, Sept. 28, Oct. 17; Pembroke to Leicester, Sept. 29; *Sydney Papers*, ii. 360, 363.

Charles caught at the suggestion, and Williams, unable to defend himself against a form of attack in which no direct imputation on himself was necessarily implied, surrendered his office. Charles, glad to be rid of him, spoke to him fairly at the last. But the tone amongst Buckingham's followers was different. "May the like misfortune," wrote one of them to his patron, " befall such as shall tread in his hateful path, and presume to lift their head against their maker!"[1]

With Lord Keeper Williams, worldly wisdom departed from the councils of Charles. If he could never have ripened into a great or a high-souled statesman, he had always at command a fund of strong common sense which saved him from the enormous blunders into which men more earnest and energetic than himself were ready to fall. Government was to him a balance to be kept between extreme parties. War was distasteful to him, and he cared little or nothing for Continental politics. Dogmatism of all kinds he regarded with the utmost suspicion. He had no sympathy with the persecution of the High Church clergy by the House of Commons, no sympathy with the coming persecution of the Puritans by the High Church clergy. If he had been maintained in power Charles's reign would hardly have been eventful or heroic. But it would not have ended in disaster. England would have gained a great step on its way to liberty, by the

[1] Not 'their heel,' as calendared. Suckling to Buckingham, Oct, 24 ; *S. P. Dom.*, viii. 37. I have no belief in the theory that Williams had intrigued against Buckingham. It is itself in the highest degree unlikely, and the only scrap of evidence in its favour is a story told in Rushworth that Williams said that he meant to stand on his own legs. But Rushworth is no authority for this period, and even if the story is true, its meaning depends on the question which preceded the answer. Williams may have meant, "I am not engaged in any intrigue with the opposition, I am standing on my own legs, giving the advice which I think best ; " and this would probably be a true account of the matter.

Margin: CHAP. X. 1625. Oct. — Greatness of the loss to Charles.

permission which would within certain broad limits have been granted to the free development of thought and action. The last clerical Lord Keeper in English history was in reality less clerical than any of his predecessors.

The Great Seal was given to Coventry, whose legal knowledge and general ability were beyond dispute, and whose leanings were against all concessions to the Catholics. His accession to office therefore was one more announcement of the Protestant tendencies of Buckingham. " The Duke's power with the King," said a contemporary letter writer, " for certain is exceeding great, and whom he will advance shall be advanced, and whom he doth but frown upon must be thrown down."[1] Heath succeeded as Attorney-General; and with far less excuse, Shelton, whose only distinction was that he had been employed by Buckingham in his private affairs, followed as Solicitor-General.

The meaning of the change was soon manifest, at least to the Catholics. The order for banishing the priests, given immediately after the dissolution, had not been followed at once by any attempt to interfere with the laity. On the 5th of October directions were given for a general disarmament of the Recusants, but it was not till Coventry had succeeded Williams that any further step was taken. On the 3rd of November the blow fell. A commission was issued to provide for the execution of the penal laws, with instructions to pay over the fines levied to a special fund to be employed in the defence of the realm. On the 7th orders were given to prohibit all minors from leaving England without license from the King, and to silence all schoolmasters whose teaching was open to suspicion.[2]

---

[1] Ingram to Wentworth, Nov. 7; *Strafford Letters*, i. 28.
[2] Commission, Nov. 3. *S. P. Dom. Sign Manuals.* i. 87; the King to Buckingham, Nov. 7, *S. P. Dom.* Addenda.

Charles had probably an instinctive apprehension that the persecution of the Catholics would not alone be sufficient to secure for him the approbation of the next House of Commons. But he was never keen-sighted in discerning the real causes of popular dissatisfaction, and he ascribed the attack upon Buckingham at Oxford to a mere ebullition of factious spite. The inference was obvious. If by any means the assailants of his minister could be excluded from seats in the coming Parliament, the really loyal nature of Englishmen would find unimpeded expression. It was like Charles, too, to fancy that if only legal right were on his side no one could be justly dissatisfied. With this idea in his head, nothing could seem simpler than the course he adopted. A sheriff was bound to attend to his duties in his own county, and if the opposition leaders were named as sheriffs it was plain that they could not take their seats at Westminster. Coke, Seymour, and Phelips were of course marked out for the unwelcome honour. With them were Alford, who had explained that the subsidies voted in 1624 had not been voted for the recovery of the Palatinate, and Sir Guy Palmes, who had referred unpleasantly to the fate of Empson and Dudley. And to these five was added a sixth, Sir Thomas Wentworth. Charles knew well that Wentworth had little in common with Seymour and Phelips. He was anxious, if possible, to obtain service under the Crown and to exercise his undoubted powers of government. But the war, whether it was to be in Spain or Germany, was in his eyes sheer madness, and it was plain that he would be as cool about the King's Protestant crusade in 1626 as he had been cool about his attack upon Spain in 1625. "Wentworth," said Charles, as the names were read over to him, "is an honest gentleman." But the

CHAP. X.
1625. Nov.

The opposition leaders made sheriffs.

Wentworth's peculiar position.

reasons for his exclusion were equally valid whether he was honest or not.[1]

Such a manœuvre stands self-condemned by the very fact that it was a manœuvre. It had, however, at least one supporter amongst those who favoured the vigorous prosecution of the war. "The rank weeds of Parliament," wrote Rudyerd, "are rooted up, so that we may expect a plentiful harvest the next. I pray God so temper the humours of our next assembly that out of it may result that inestimable harmony of agreement between the King and his people."[2]

It was not by such tricks as these that Charles would regain the confidence of the nation. By this time he had hoped to receive news of great results from Buckingham's diplomacy in the Netherlands. But though the Lord Admiral, taking the courtly Holland with him, had left Charles at Salisbury in the second week in October, his voyage had been sadly delayed. On the 13th a terrific storm swept over the Channel and the North Sea. The Dutch fleet before Dunkirk was driven from its port, and great was the alarm in England when it was told that twenty-two vessels, it was said with 4,000 soldiers on board, had escaped to sea. But the blow fell upon the Dutch fishing vessels, and the English coast was spared.[8]

With the Dunkirk privateers loose upon the world, the Lord Admiral could not cross without a convoy.

---

[1] Ingram to Wentworth, Nov.; *Strafford Letters*, i. 29. The name of Sir W. Fleetwood is here given as a seventh. He had not sat in the last Parliament, but in the Parliament of 1624. He was found ineligible for the shrievalty, and was neither a sheriff nor a member of the Commons in 1626. The first suggestion of making sheriffs in this way which I have met with, is in a letter from Sir G. Paul to Buckingham, Oct. 24; *S. P. Dom.*, viii. 34.

[2] Rudyerd to Nethersole, Nov. 23; *S. P. Dom.*, x. 16.

[3] Downing to the Navy Commissioners, Oct. 19; Pennington to Buckingham, Oct. 23; *S. P. Dom.*, viii. 5, 28.

And a convoy could not be easily found. The great fleet was still away at Cadiz, and three English ships had been cast away with all hands upon the cliffs between Calais and Boulogne. What vessels were to be had must be hurried together for the defence of the country before the Duke's convoy could be thought of.

At last, however, ships were found for the purpose. On November 9 Buckingham was at the Hague, and was astonishing the sober citizens of the Dutch capital by the lavish splendour of his dress and the gorgeous display of pearls and diamonds with which it was adorned. He soon allowed it to be known that he had brought with him no friendly feeling towards France. "I acknowledge," he said, "the power of the King of France. But I doubt his good will."[1]

Buckingham had brought with him, too, his old plan for a joint attack with the Dutch upon Dunkirk. The effort, he told the Prince of Orange, should be made at once, as the Spaniards were in no condition to defend the place. The wary Prince knew too much about war to relish the idea of a siege to be begun in November, and refused to entertain the proposition till the spring. Then Buckingham asked that Sluys should be put in his master's hands as a basis of operations for the English army which was to hem in the Flemish ports on the land side. But the Prince met him with the same dilatory response. He was probably of opinion that the English army of which Buckingham spoke would never have any real existence;[2] and, even if it had been otherwise, he would certainly have been unwilling to confide to it the guardianship of so important a fortress.

[1] Vreede, *Inleiding tot eene Geschiedenis der Nederlandsche Diplomatie*, ii. 2, 83.
[2] *Ibid.* ii. 2, 85, Note 2; Carleton to Conway, Nov. 14; *S. P. Holland.*

The Congress of the Hague, when it met at last, was but a poor representation of that great anti-Spanish Confederacy for which Gustavus had hoped when he first sketched out the plan. Though he was himself engaged in the Polish war, he had ordered his ambassador to take part in the assembly. But the ambassador was taken ill, and died a few days before Buckingham's arrival, and Sweden was therefore entirely unrepresented. The French minister stood aloof, and the North German Princes took no share in the discussions. The representatives of the King of Denmark were there alone, to beg for money and men.

Christian IV. was indeed in sore need. Trusting to the promises made to him by Charles, he had gone to war. But after the first month's contribution Charles had no money to send, and he was in no better plight in November than he had been in June. In fact, if Buckingham had carried out his original intentions, the war in Germany would in all probability have come to a sudden end. For his instructions, undoubtedly drawn up with his concurrence, authorised him to acquaint the Danish ambassadors that the original offer of 30,000*l*. a month, or its equivalent in men, paid by the English exchequer, had only been made to give encouragement to the German Princes. When those Princes had once taken the field it was only to be expected that they would submit to provide a fair share of the expense. Buckingham was therefore to insist upon a large reduction of the monthly charge, though he was first to make sure that Christian was thoroughly embarked in the cause, lest by threatening to stop the supplies he might drive him to make his peace with the Emperor.[1]

It is probable that a little conversation with the

---

[1] Instructions to Buckingham and Holland, Oct. 17; *Rymer,* xviii. 211.

Danish ambassadors convinced Buckingham that if the King of England thus withdrew from his engagements Christian would without doubt submit to the Emperor. At all events, nothing, as far as we know, was heard of the proposed reduction. On November 29 the Treaty of the Hague was signed between England, Denmark, and the States General.

CHAP. X.
1625.
Nov. 29. Treaty of the Hague.

The Dutch agreed to supply the Danes with 5,000*l.* a month, whilst Buckingham engaged more solemnly than ever that the 30,000*l.* a month originally promised from England should be really sent.

Large as the sum was, there is every reason to suppose that the promise was made in good faith. Parliament would soon meet, and, as Buckingham hoped, all difficulties would then be smoothed away. For the immediate future he could trust to the Crown jewels, which would soon be pawned to the merchants of Amsterdam. The disaster at Cadiz was as yet unknown, and every day might bring the happy news of victory. A new fleet was to be speedily prepared to relieve Wimbledon's force, and to take up the task of blockading the Spanish ports. The flood of mischief would thus be arrested at the fountain head, and when gold no longer flowed from Spain, the armies by which Christian was assailed would break out into open mutiny.[1]

Dec. 5. Buckingham's expectations.

Proud of victories yet to be won, Buckingham had meditated a continuance of his journey to Paris in order that he might add the name of the King of France to the signatures appended to the Treaty of the Hague. But his hopes had been cut short by the French ambassador, who plainly told him that till better satisfaction were given to his master's just demands in England, he would not be allowed to enter France.[2]

He is refused permission to enter France.

Buckingham therefore returned to England by the

[1] Buckingham to Christian IV., Dec. $\frac{5}{15}$; *S. P. Holland.*
[2] Lewis XIII. to Blainville, Dec. $\frac{4}{14}$; *King's MSS.*, 137, p. 819.

way that he had come. He was at once met by news of the failure at Cadiz and the return of the fleet. Alone, probably, of all Englishmen alive, Charles and Buckingham failed to realise the magnitude of the disaster, or the influence which it would exercise upon the deliberations of the coming session.[1] On December 16 the Lord Keeper was directed to issue writs for a new Parliament.[2]

It was possible that Parliament might have work on hand even more serious than voting supplies for the King of Denmark. It was by no means unlikely that by the time the members were collected at Westminster, England would be at open war with France. Charles had been seriously vexed at the failure of his effort to frustrate the employment of English vessels at Rochelle, and the first resolution taken in council after Buckingham's return was that a new fleet should be sent out to succour Rochelle, and to bring home the ships by force.[3]

Orders were accordingly issued that the soldiers who had come back from Cadiz should be kept under their colours for future service.[4]

Nor were the differences relating to the fulfilment of the marriage treaty in a fairer way to an accommodation. Lewis, indeed, had sent messages to Buckingham after his return, that if the English Catholics were relieved from ill-treatment, and if his sister's household were permitted to remain as it had been arranged by the contract, he would make no further objection to receiving him in France.[5] But on the first point

---

[1] 'Quod vero Regem et Buckinghamium attinet, illi non multum moventur aut indignantur.' Rusdorf to Oxenstjerna. Dec. *Mémoires*, ii. 138.

[2] *Rymer*, xviii. 245.

[3] Blainville to Lewis XIII., Dec. 12/22; *King's MSS.*, 137, p. 948.

[4] *Coll. Proclamations*, Car. I., Dec. 16, No. 31 ; *S. P. Dom.*

[5] Lewis XIII. to Blainville, Dec. 4/14; The Bishop of Mende to Ville-aux-Clercs, received Dec. 27/Jan. 6; *King's MSS.*, 138, p. 819, 1043.

Buckingham could not yield without alienating Parliament. On the second he could not yield without alienating the King.

CHAP. X.
1625.

Whilst Buckingham was still at the Hague, Charles's exasperation at his wife's French attendants had risen to fever heat. To their interference, and not at all to his own failure to keep his promises, he attributed his domestic troubles, and he threatened to send them all back to France. More prudent counsels prevailed for a time, and he now contented himself with announcing to the Bishop of Mende, the Queen's almoner, his intention of introducing English ladies into her household. A man, he repeated once more, ought to be master in his own house. The utmost to which he would agree was to wait a few days till his resolve had been communicated to the Court of France.[1]

The Queen's household.

Dec. 25.

To Richelieu the threatened breach between France and England, bringing with it a death struggle with the Huguenots of Rochelle, must have been infinitely displeasing. In spite of his master's strong feeling that he had been ill-treated, he contrived to obtain permission to address overtures to Buckingham, assuring him of a good reception in France if certain conditions, of which we have no particular information, were fulfilled. If he could not come on these terms, let him at least send confidential ambassadors to smooth away the differences between the two Crowns.[2]

French offers to Buckingham.

[1] The King to Buckingham, Nov. 20; *Hardwicke S. P.*, ii. 23. The Bishop of Mende to Lewis XIII., $\frac{\text{Dec. 25}}{\text{Jan. 4}}$; *King's MSS.*, 138, p. 1056.

[2] "M. Bautru is on his way for England with letters from the Duke de Chevreuse and Marquis d'Effiat, but concerted with the Queen Mother and the Cardinal, to invite my Lord Duke of Buckingham to come over, which many wish, but few hold it counselable." De Vic to Conway, Dec. $\frac{19}{26}$. "We may not conceal what we understand, that what the Cardinal told us of Blainville's revocation was conditional, in case the Lord Duke of Buckingham came over upon such invitements as were sent

CHAP. X.
1625.
Dec. 27.
Embassy of Holland and Carleton.

The latter alternative was accepted. Holland was once more to go to Paris to make himself agreeable to the Queen Mother and the ladies of her court. But the real business was entrusted to Carleton, who had at last been recalled from the Hague, and was now Vice-Chamberlain and a Privy Councillor. A diligent, well-informed man, too dependent upon office to be likely to take a course of his own, and sympathising entirely with the movement against Spain without rising into any large view of contemporary politics, Carleton was exactly suited for the service for which Buckingham required him, and was likely, as time went on, to establish himself firmly in his favour.

Objects of the mission.

Carleton's present work was to mediate a peace between the French Government and the Huguenots, and to persuade Lewis to surrender the English ships and to join in the alliance of the Hague.[1]

Sept.
The neutrality of France.

The differences between the two Courts were serious enough in themselves. Unhappily there was a political difference which was more serious still. In September, whilst the Cadiz fleet was still at Plymouth, a string of French prizes had been brought in, charged with carrying goods for the use of the Spanish Netherlands. Under ordinary circumstances it is hard to persuade neutrals and belligerents to take the same view of the law of prize, and there was in this case a special difficulty arising from the fact that at Whitehall French neutrality was regarded as an underhand contrivance for reaping the benefits of war without sharing its burdens.

The French prizes.

There was clearly need of enquiry into the nature of the cargoes on board the vessels. Besides the French

him.' Holland and Carleton to Conway, Feb. 26, 1626; *S. P. France*. It can hardly be said, therefore, that Buckingham could not go to France without first declaring war.

[1] Instructions to Holland and Carleton, Dec. 30; *S. P. France*.

prizes, there were many of Dutch nationality, and a few from other parts of Europe. If they had on board goods which were the property of Spaniards, those goods, according to the ideas of the day, would be subject to immediate confiscation. Contraband of war again, being carried to Spain or the Spanish Netherlands, would be liable to seizure, whether it was Spanish property or not. But it was by no means a matter of universal agreement what contraband of war was. In the treaty of Southampton indeed, England and the States General had recently agreed upon a sweeping definition, including in that category provisions and the precious metals as well as munitions of war and materials used in shipbuilding,[1] and had declared not only such articles, but even the ships and men engaged in the traffic, to be lawful prize. Such an interpretation of the customary maritime law was not likely to commend itself to a neutral seafaring nation.

Even if this knotty point had been settled, there was another behind it. What evidence was to be accepted that the contraband goods were or were not destined for Spanish use. Every one of the eleven French vessels seized had sailed from a Spanish port, and all of them, with one exception, were owned by Calais merchants.[2] It was, however, notorious that there were men at Calais whose business it was to pass goods as soon as landed over the frontier into Flanders, in much the same way as goods were passed over into Russia from Memel in the time of the Crimean war.[3]

It happened that Buckingham was at Plymouth when the prizes were brought in. Gold and silver

[1] Art. 20 of the Treaty; *Dumont*, v. 2, 480.
[2] Examinations of the masters of the prize ships, Sept. 29; *S. P. Dom.*, vi. 120.
[3] Marten to Conway, Nov. 8; Joachimi to ——; *S. P. Holland.* —— to Quester; *S. P. France.*

being contraband of war, according to the view taken in England, he ordered 9,000*l*. or 10,000*l*. which were on board to be sequestered,[1] and the remainder of the goods to be placed in safe keeping. A few weeks later the cargoes were stowed again on board, and the prizes brought up to London to pass through a legal investigation before the Court of Admiralty. By the beginning of November the number of captured French vessels had increased to twenty-two.[2]

So far there was no reasonable ground of complaint. But in the needy circumstances of the King's treasury the sequestered property was too tempting a bait to be long resisted. In October Buckingham had attempted to borrow 70,000*l*., in order that he might carry with him something to the Hague for the immediate supply of the armies of Christian IV. and Mansfeld. But the security which Charles could offer fell short of the required sum by 20,000*l*., and Ley and Weston proposed to fill the gap by giving security upon the first sale of condemned prize goods. The suggestion in itself was innocent enough. But either it was not thought sufficient, or Charles fancied that he could do better. On October 27 the money from the French ships was taken to be spent on warlike preparations, and on November 5 orders were given to sell goods at once to the required value of 20,000*l*., without waiting for a sentence from the Court.[3]

To Charles the difference may have seemed slight. If the decision of the Court was against him he would

---

[1] Minutes by Nicholas, Feb. (?) 1626; *S. P. Dom.*, xxi. 99.

[2] Minute of the replacing of the goods on board, calendared in September, but it was almost certainly in October. Receipt by Marsh, Oct. 11; *S. P. Dom.*, vi. 126; xxii. 12, 1. Blainville to Lewis XIII., Nov. $\frac{8}{18}$; *King's MSS.*, 138, p. 659.

[3] Coke to Conway, Oct. 27; *S. P. Dom.*, viii. 26. Warrant, Nov. 5; *Sign Manuals*, i. 90.

refund the money. But there was another side of the question which he had forgotten to consider. Blainville reminded him that as the cargoes had not been made up for the English market, they would not fetch anything like their full value on a compulsory sale in London.[1]

The impression produced by Charles's hasty act was likely to be worse than the act itself would justify. It gave to the Admiralty Court the appearance of being merely an official instrument for enforcing confiscation for the benefit of the Crown. Sir Henry Marten, the Judge of the Court, felt the indignity keenly. "For my part," he wrote, in answer to an appeal from Conway for arguments in support of the course which had been taken, "I can profess to know no other disposition yet intended, but that all the goods should be landed, inventoried, and appraised; and, on Saturday next, all who pretend to any of those ships or goods to appear and propound their claims."[2]

Before this remonstrance Charles gave way for a time. Buckingham was absent at the Hague, and there was a period of indecision till the guiding spirit of the Government was once more in England. The Council took up the question, and on December 4 fresh orders were given to proceed with the sale, orders which were retracted shortly afterwards.[3] Sir John Coke, who, as a prominent personage on the Navy Commission, was eager for money that he might be enabled to meet the expenses of the fleet, and whose small official mind could not catch sight of the

CHAP. X.

1625. Nov. 5. Blainville protests.

Nov. 8. Marten declines to support the seizure.

Charles's indecision.

Dec. 4.

---

[1] Blainville to Lewis XIII., Nov. $\frac{6}{16}$; *King's MSS.*, 138, p. 659.
[2] Conway to Marten, Nov. 7; *Conway's Letter Book*; Marten to Conway, Nov. 8; *S. P. Dom.*, ix. 32.
[3] Joachimi to ——; *S. P. Holland.*

larger aspects of the case, was eager for instant and sweeping action. "If you shall limit the sales," he wrote to Conway, on hearing that some half-measure was in contemplation, " as I hear you intend, to goods which are out of question, I know not what goods can be sold; since there is neither ship nor particular goods therein to which no man doth pretend."[1]

Before Charles had made up his mind, the mere announcement of his intention had called forth reprisals in France. Villars, the governor of Havre, was himself interested in the 'St. Peter' of that port, and on December 7 he arrested two English vessels lying at Rouen. A fortnight later it was known in London that the French authorities were contemplating a general embargo upon all English property in France, which was only delayed till there was some certain intelligence of the course finally adopted in England.

By this time Buckingham was again at Court, and the acceptance of Richelieu's overtures had opened a prospect of averting the impending quarrel. "It is necessary for me," said Charles, "to preserve my friends and allies." Just as Holland and Carleton were starting, an Order in Council was drawn up to form the basis of a settlement of the dispute.[2]

According to this order the 'St. Peter of Havre de Grace,' against which the presumptions were less than against vessels belonging to the merchants of Calais, was to be delivered to its owners. Of the remaining ships and their cargoes, whatever was clearly French property should be given up at once. Against whatever was questionable proceedings should be taken,

---

[1] Coke to Conway, Dec. 17; *S. P. Dom.*, xii. 1.
[2] *Commons' Journals*, i. 823; Palloysenu to Hippisley, $\frac{Dec. 23}{Jan. 2}$; *Harl. MSS.*, 1583, fol. 171; Joachimi to the States General, $\frac{Dec. 27}{Jan. 6}$, Jan. $\frac{7}{17}$; *Add. MSS.*, 17677, L. fol. 130, 119.

'without any further restraint of sale, or other proceeding warrantable by law or the course of the Admiralty.'[1]

On January 11 the ambassadors had their first interview with Richelieu. He received them in the most friendly way; but he gave it to be understood that till the Huguenot rebellion was at an end there could be no open war with Spain, and that his master could not tolerate the interference of a foreign king between himself and his subjects. But they might rest assured that there was no intention of persecuting the Protestant religion in France. The 'Vanguard' would be restored as soon as Soubise's prize was given up. The other vessels had been hired from the merchants, and as long as Rochelle was in arms it was impossible to dispense with their services.

The irritation at the French Court at the tone assumed by Charles was such that no minister could afford to disregard it, and least of all was Richelieu likely to think lightly of the honour of his sovereign. Lewis himself was particularly displeased at the proposal to include him in the treaty signed at the Hague without his concurrence. "The league," he wrote to his ambassador in the Netherlands, "is not aimed at the liberty of the Empire or the abasement of Spain, but at the abasement of the Catholic religion and of all the princes who profess it, and particularly of myself." One of his ministers expressed himself in much the same tone. "There is a great difference," he wrote, "between proposing to the King things done or things to be done. To communicate a design and to wish to do nothing without his advice would oblige his Majesty, but to propose to him to take part in a

---

[1] Order in Council, Dec. 8; *S. P. Dom.*, xii. 72.

matter already arranged would have the contrary effect."[1]

In Lewis's place Charles would have felt precisely in the same manner. But he had not the tact to perceive that concession must be made to the feelings of others, and, with the consciousness that he had himself contributed, or appeared to have contributed, to the misfortunes of Rochelle, he determined to support the town against its sovereign, at whatever cost to the interests of the rest of Europe. Pennington had for some time been getting ready a fleet at Plymouth, which was destined in case of necessity to escort Soubise with provisions for the blockaded Huguenots, and at a council held on January 20 it was resolved that the fleet should be at once despatched. In order to impart greater energy to the crews it was arranged that Buckingham should command in person. The deputies from the insurgent city, who were in England seeking for aid, were informed that the fleet would proceed to drive the troops of the King of France out of Rhé and Oleron, if they would consent to the deposit of the islands in Charles's hands till the expenses of the undertaking had been repaid to him.[2]

No secret was made of the resolution taken. Buckingham informed Blainville that his master could no longer remain neutral. He had contributed to the ruin of the Protestants by the loan of his ships, and now, with one voice, his Council and his people called upon him to undertake the defence of those whom he had so deeply injured. If war were once

[1] Extracts given by Vreede, *Inleiding tot eene Geschiedenis der Nederlandsche Diplomatie*, ii. 2, 85, 87.

[2] Blainville to Lewis XIII., Jan. 21; *King's MSS.*, 138, p. 1206. Conway to Holland and Carleton, Jan. 21; *S. P. France.* Buckingham to Pennington, Jan. 7; Pennington to Buckingham, Jan. 17; *S. P. Dom.*, xviii. 18, 75.

declared he would show the world that he was not so destitute of men and money as was commonly supposed.[1]

The resolution thus taken at Court could not fail to have its effects on the prospects of the owners of the French prizes. As far as the 'St. Peter' was concerned everything had proceeded regularly. Suspicion only attached itself to some hides and a few other articles on board. Bonds were accepted in the Admiralty Court for the payment of their value, in case of their proving to be Spanish property, and on January 26 Marten gave orders for the delivery of ship and cargo to the owners.

The proprietors of the other vessels had before this fancied that their difficulties were at an end. Soon after the Order in Council of December 28, goods to the value of 30,000l. were given up to them, as being beyond question legitimately French property. But when the news of the difficulties made in France about the surrender of the English vessels reached England, the Government took another tone. On January 24 the goods were again seized for the King, and out of that part of the cargo which was considered contraband by the Crown lawyers, though it had not yet been condemned by any court of law, property to the value of 7,000l. was sold by auction. Having made up his mind to war, it would seem that Charles no longer thought it necessary to keep terms with the subjects of the King of France.[2]

With the King and Buckingham in this temper, it was not likely that even the 'St. Peter' would be

[1] Order for taking bonds, Jan. 21; *Book of Acts, Admiralty Court,* 159, fol. 30, b. Order for release, Jan. 26; *S. P. Dom.,* xix. 52.

[2] Joachimi to ———; *S. P. Holland.* Joachimi to the States General, Feb. $\frac{8}{18}$; *Add. MSS.,* 17677 L., fol. 143. Blainville to Lewis XIII., $\frac{\text{Jan. 25}}{\text{Feb. 4}}$; *King's MSS.,* 138, p. 1270, 1273.

allowed to escape. As soon as the order had been issued for its release, Apsley, the Lieutenant of the Tower, remonstrated with the Lord Admiral, assuring him that he could bring as good evidence against that vessel as against the others. To Apsley's statements Buckingham gave too easy credence, and on February 4, having previously obtained the King's consent, he ordered the detention of the ship. It is perhaps not an unreasonable conjecture that the real motive in these proceedings was the desire to detain as many pledges as possible for the English ships at Rochelle, the recovery of which had been the subject of repeated messages to the ambassadors at Paris. Buckingham might well doubt his chances of obtaining from the approaching Parliament a favourable consideration of his policy, if Lewis were still engaged in war with the Huguenots with the help of English vessels.

All this time the despatches sent to Paris had been growing more peremptory. On January 23 the ambassadors were ordered to hasten home if the ships were not surrendered. On the 26th Charles was still unyielding. He had just received a letter from Holland and Carleton, telling him that Richelieu, in his master's name, insisted on the maintenance of the King's garrison in Fort Louis and in the islands of Rhé and Oleron, as well as on the right to send a Royal Intendant of Justice into Rochelle. The Huguenot deputies objected to all three points, and asked for the full execution of the treaty of Montpellier. After a time, however, they expressed their readiness to withdraw their demands. They would reluctantly agree to admit the Intendant, and to allow the garrison to remain in the islands. Even at Fort Louis they would not insist upon an immediate disarmament, if they could hope for its demolition in course of time.

The ambassadors were satisfied that peace was virtually made. But Charles was not satisfied. He thought that the conditions were insufficient for the safety of Rochelle. Nothing less than the terms of the treaty of Montpellier should receive his assent. The ambassadors were also to ask for the immediate release of the ships, and if that were refused, they were to come home at once.[1]

The error of Lewis was coming home to him. If he had been faulty in appending to his sister's marriage contract a condition which involved an interference with the administration of English law, Charles was now interfering far more incisively in French domestic politics. And when once it was understood that the Huguenots were to owe their recovered independence to English help, a situation would be created which would be intolerable even to a king of France far less sensitive than Lewis on all matters connected with his personal authority. In the preceding August Richelieu might wisely have argued that it would be better for him to grant all the demands of his Protestant subjects, in order that he might turn his attention to external war. But it was one thing to grant such demands upon conviction; it was another thing to grant them to the menaces of the King of England. Rochelle, freed from the control of its own sovereign by Charles's interposition, would practically be an independent republic, resting for security upon the support of England. The work of uniting France, handed down as the task of centuries from one generation of monarchs to another, would receive a blow from which it would be hard to

CHAP. X.

1626. Jan. 26.

The English ships to be positively demanded.

Interference of Charles in French politics.

---

[1] Buckingham to Holland and Carleton, Jan. 23; Holland and Carleton to Conway, Jan. 23; Conway to Holland and Carleton, Jan. 19; *S. P. France.*

VOL. I.　　　　　　A A

1626.
Jan. 26.

The Queen refuses to be crowned.

Jan. 21.

Charles angry with Blainville.

recover. An English Rochelle would be a far more potent instrument of mischief than even an English Calais had ever been.

Such a view of the case was not likely to present itself to Charles. All that he saw was that as his ships had been used for the defeat of Soubise, it was his business to take care that the Huguenots suffered no loss. And by this time he had a fresh grievance in his own domestic circle, which kept his mind in a state of irritation. He had arranged that his own coronation should take place before the opening of Parliament, and he fondly hoped that the Queen would be at his side on that solemn occasion. To his surprise he found that his young wife had religious scruples about taking part in a Protestant ceremony, and he at once appealed to her brother to convince her that she was in the wrong. The coronation, Conway wrote to the ambassadors, was but a form. "Yet," he added, "it is a wonder, it is a disorder, it is a misfortune, so apparent a declaration of a difference in judgment, obedience, and conformity." But he got no help from Lewis. The view taken at the French Court was that there would be no harm done if the Queen submitted to coronation, provided that none of the Protestant clergy took any part in the ceremony.[1]

As this was clearly inadmissible, Charles had to resign himself to be crowned alone. Such a consequence he ought to have foreseen when he decided upon marrying a Roman Catholic princess. But he was bitterly disappointed, and he threw the whole blame upon the French ambassador. Blainville, according to him, had given himself, since his coming into England, to stirring up ill-will between himself

[1] Lewis XIII. to Blainville, Jan. $\frac{15}{25}$; *King's MSS.*, 138, p. 1121. Conway to Holland and Carleton, Jan. 21; *S. P. France.*

and the Queen. Blainville was certainly not conciliatory in his dealings with a Government against which he had many and bitter grievances, and he had listened more sympathizingly than became an ambassador to the Queen's complaints; but it is undeniable that the Queen's troubles had their root in causes which existed before Blainville set foot in England.

The day fixed for the coronation was the 2nd of February. The curtained seat which had been prepared for Henrietta Maria, at a time when it was still hoped that she might be present as a spectator, if she would not take her part in the ceremony, was empty. Its emptiness must have reminded Charles bitterly of the misery of his home life and of the most conspicuous failure of his political life. Yet there was no want of loyalty in the hearty shout—the echo of that old cry which had once given to English kings their right to sit upon the throne—which greeted him as he stood in the pride of youthful·dignity in the face of the assembled multitude. As yet, though the first enthusiasm which greeted his accession had passed away, no personal unpopularity had gathered round him. Whatever was ill-done was attributed to the influence of Buckingham.[1]

---

[1] Mead to Stuteville, Feb. 3; D'Ewes to Stuteville, Feb. 3; *Ellis*, ser. 1, iii. 220, 213. Mr. Forster is mistaken in supposing that the incident of Charles's stumbling, and of his answering 'when Buckingham offered to assist him, "I have as much need to help you as you to assist me,"' took place 'when all was over, and the King and the Duke came wearily away.' It really happened before the coronation, and D'Ewes adds that the words were spoken 'with a smiling countenance.' Charles doubtless merely meant that he was able to recover his footing without help. It would not have been worth while mentioning this, but for the doubt which I entertain whether Mr. Forster is right in attributing any sort of foreboding of coming evil to Charles. There is no evidence either way; but my impression, from what I know of Charles's character and actions, is that he never foreboded evil, and that he was so convinced

CHAP. X.

1626.
Feb. 2.

The new king was thus, to use words spoken by his direction a few days later, married to his people. He chose that day to be clothed in white,[1] as the sign of the virgin purity with which he came to play a bridegroom's part, instead of in the purple robe of sovereignty. *Amor civium, Regis præsidium* was the motto which in trustful confidence he placed upon the coins which still bore the Royal arms impressed upon the sails of a ship careering through the waves, the emblem doubtless of that great naval victory with which he hoped to illustrate the annals of his reign. If Wimbledon had failed at Cadiz, Buckingham, he might think, would hardly fail at Rochelle. Charles, so far as it is possible to judge by the indications which have reached us, was preparing to meet the new Parliament with all the buoyancy of hopefulness. Neither Coke, nor Phelips, nor Seymour would be there to distract the hearts of his faithful Commons with factious opposition. So little did the King suspect that he would meet with any difficulty in the Upper House that he neglected the

New earldoms.

that he was always in the right, that the idea of Parliamentary opposition would not occur to him till he was called to face it.

As for the people not shouting at the coronation when Arundel first asked them to do so, I am content with D'Ewes's explanation: "Whether some expected he should have spoken more, or others hearing not so well what he said, hindered those by questioning which might have heard, or that the newness and greatness of the action busied men's thoughts, or the presence of so dear a thing drew admiring silence, or that those which were nearest doubted what to do, but not one word followed till my Lord of Arundel told them they should cry out, 'God save King Charles!' upon which, as ashamed of their first oversight, a little shouting followed. At the other sides where he presented himself there was not the like failing." Joachimi, as Ranke has observed, has no hesitation to tell of. He says the answer was given 'with great cry and shouting.' Joachimi to the States General, Feb. $\frac{3}{13}$; *Add. MSS.*, 17,677 L. fol. 148.

[1] Heylin, *Life of Laud*, 144. After Charles's death, this was pointed to as a presage of the innocence of martyrdom, as was also the text taken by the preacher, "I will give thee a crown of life."

opportunity which the coronation afforded of raising to the Peerage persons in whom he could confide. No additional votes were gained by the earldoms which he distributed amongst members of the existing peerage, and it was only a matter of personal importance to themselves that Lord Ley, for instance, would for the future be known as Earl of Marlborough, Lord Mandeville as Earl of Manchester, and Lord Carew as Earl of Totness.

There were yet a few days before the meeting of Parliament, and if Charles had been capable of rising into a statesmanlike view of his relations with France, he would have seized the opportunity of reconsidering his position which was offered him during those days. Holland and Carleton had left no stone unturned to bring about a pacification. The stumbling-block was Fort Louis. The French minister frankly averred that unless the King kept up a garrison in it, he could have no security that when he was engaged in war abroad the Rochellese would not rise in insurrection as they had done the year before. With equal energy the Huguenot deputies argued that unless the fort were demolished, they could have no security for the freedom of their commerce. On the evening of the 25th of January it was believed on both sides that the negotiation was at an end.

The next morning a chosen number of the French clergy were to be admitted to the King to declare their readiness to open their purses to support him in the holy war which they had done their best to render imminent. But they had reckoned without the Cardinal. Seizing a pretext for deferring the audience for a time, he had proposed a compromise through the English ambassadors. When at last the deputation

CHAP. X.
1626.

Jan. 25.
Negotiations between Lewis XIII. and the Huguenots.

Jan. 26.
An agreement come to.

CHAP. X.
1625.
Jan. 26.

swept into the Royal presence they found that they were too late. The Huguenot deputies were already on their knees before the King, and the baffled priests had come only to see the King reconciled at last with his Protestant subjects.

Terms of the agreement.

Unhappily the terms of reconciliation announced on the following day by the Chancellor, were such as by no means to preclude the probability of a renewal of the strife at no distant future. Under pressure from Holland and Carleton, the deputies agreed to give up all the points at issue, including the demolition of Fort Louis. In return they were to have from the King an assurance that 'by long services and continued obedience they might expect that which they most desired,' and that 'in fitting time he would listen to their supplications made with due respect and humility.'[1] Before the words were spoken a private exposition of their meaning was given by the French ministers to the effect that they pointed to the eventual demolition of Fort Louis.

Jan. 29.
Accepted by the Huguenots through expectations of English support.

Holland and Carleton had certainly taxed their authority as mediators to the uttermost. The deputies plainly told them that they had agreed to the treaty 'because they might now lawfully accept assistance from his Majesty.' When the ambassadors attended the Protestant church at Charenton on the following Sunday, they found themselves the objects of universal enthusiasm. The preacher took for his text, "How beautiful are the feet of them that preach the gospel of peace."

It was all very natural, but it was very dangerous.

[1] Answer of the Chancellor in the name of the King of France, $\frac{\text{Jan. 6}}{\text{Feb. 27}}$; *S. P. France.* This date, however, must be merely that on which a written copy of the speech was delivered. It was spoke on $\frac{\text{Jan. 26}}{\text{Feb. 5}}$.

[2] Declaration by Holland and Carleton $\frac{\text{Jan. 31}}{\text{Feb. 10}}$; *S. P. France.*

PEACE ACCORDED TO THE HUGUENOTS. 359

To thrust the foreign mediation in the face of Lewis was the very way to disgust him with the arrangement which had been made, and if Charles had been wise he would have kept his part in the treaty in the background. If the French Government were once engaged in earnest in the conflict with Spain, any renewal of persecution would be virtually impossible.

In such a course Charles would have had every assistance from Richelieu. The treaty was signed on the 28th, and the Cardinal at once assured the ambassadors that the English ships would be speedily restored, and that his master would practically, if not in name, join England in the war in Germany. On the 29th Holland and Carleton reported that the French ministers dealt with them more freely than they expected, 'for they have not denied those of the Religion any of their demands, so as all parties are satisfied.'[1]

On the 5th of February the ambassadors were able to write of offers still more definite. Richelieu had assured them that his master, besides carrying on the war in Italy, was ready to create a diversion for the King of Denmark by sending into Germany an army nominally commanded by some German prince, but in reality supported jointly by France and England. In addition to this he would give the aid already promised to the King of Denmark. The army thus proposed would not cost Charles a third of the expense of the force which he had proposed to send against Dunkirk, whilst it would be of far greater advantage to the common cause.[2]

Whether Charles, after his numerous failures, would

CHAP. X.

1625.
Jan. 11.

Richelieu ready to take up the conflict against Spain.

Definite offers made by him.

Feb. 10. Satisfactory prospect.

[1] Holland and Carleton to Conway, Jan. 27, 29; Declaration by Holland and Carleton, $\frac{\text{Jan. 31}}{\text{Feb. 10}}$; The state of Holland and Carleton's negotiation, Aug. (?); *S. P. France.*
[2] Holland and Carleton to Conway, Feb. 5; *S. P. France.*

CHAP. X.
1626.
Feb. 10.

have now been able to persuade his Parliament to grant the supply necessary for this or for any other enterprise, may well be doubted. But it was at least in his power to meet Parliament with the proposal of a definite joint action with France, which was the very object at which he had been so long driving. In a few days the English ships would have returned and the establishment of peace in France would have justified the policy upon which their loan had originally depended, whilst it might be taken for granted that when once England and France were actively co-operating in Germany, there would be no disposition on the part of the French Government to return to the system of annoyance of which the Huguenots had previously complained, nor even to scrutinise very closely Charles's failure to observe the provisions of his marriage contract.

Feb. 6.
Dissatisfaction of Charles.

Such however was not the view which Charles took of the situation. On the 6th of February, when the first news of the agreement had reached England, Conway was directed to write ironically to the ambassadors that his Majesty was confident that there must be in the treaty 'some excellent good warrants and reservations provided that are not expressed.'[1] The

Feb. 7.

next day Charles had an opportunity of reading the treaty itself. "It seems," wrote Conway again, "something strange that your Lordships had concluded the peace with so little surety for those of the Religion, for ought appeared here. But his Majesty is persuaded if your Lordships have, as it seems, placed the confidence of all those of the Religion and those of Rochelle upon him for the maintaining of their surety, that you have some very good grounds that such underhand promises as may have been made, which

[1] Conway to Holland and Carleton, Feb. 6; *S. P. France*.

DISSATISFACTION OF CHARLES. 361

appear not, shall be kept ; or that, now that the King is satisfied in point of honour, of his goodness he will presently withdraw all his forces from Rochelle, and will appoint a certain time when he will demolish the fort.

CHAP. X.
1626. Feb. 7.

"His Majesty's pleasure is that you protest to that king and his ministers that, under the hope and confidence of the real and present performance of those things, you had employed your mediation, and had engaged the authority of his Majesty to move and almost constrain the deputies to accept the peace upon these conditions.

The ambassadors to protest against the treaty.

"And further, you are, by the advice of the deputies, to move for such conditions as may be for their surety, and so to carry that business betwixt that king and those of the Religion that, if his Majesty's honour must be pledged for the due observation of the treaty, his Majesty may be called and admitted to that office by that king and those of the Religion ; and that there may be some ground and possibility for such a surety to be in the power and possession of those of the Religion and those of Rochelle, in the strength of which they may subsist until such time as they may make their grievances known to his Majesty, and for him to apply his mediation and set his endeavours on work. But in these things his Majesty can give you no exact limits, but must leave you to that restraint or latitude your Lordships' own wisdom will take in your own negotiation. But it is his Majesty's precise commandment that you demand the present restitution of his Majesty's ship, and of the merchants' ships ; and that in that point you admit no delay, but take a delay as a denial."

Charles, in short, blind to the fact that the force of circumstances under Richelieu's guidance was working

Charles's mistake.

CHAP.
X.
1626.

Feb. 11.
Charles persists in treating the offer of French co-operation with coolness.

for him, would be content with nothing less than an open acknowledgment of his position as mediator between Lewis and his subjects. A few more despatches such as this would make even Richelieu powerless to preserve peace between France and England.

On the 11th the news of the French offer of co-operation in Germany had reached England. Sir John Coke was directed to answer as follows :—

"Concerning the raising of a new English-French army,—which strange overture you have kept afoot by undertaking to procure an answer from hence,— that this may not serve them for any pretence to colour their withdrawing of contribution from the King of Denmark and Mansfeld, you are to lay before them his Majesty's great charges both by sea and land, and the impossibility of levying more armies of that kind ; and further directly to profess that if that king perform not what he hath promised for the support of those forces, his Majesty in like manner will presently hold his hand and employ all his means for the strengthening of his fleet, which he well knoweth to be the best support of his own honour and state, all the rest having a principal relation to his allies. And, since the diversion in Germany concerneth chiefly the security of France against which the Imperial forces were evidently designed, if the King of Denmark had sat still ; you are to make them sensible of this interest and of his Majesty's resolution to bear that burthen no longer, if that king shall cast it off, or not contribute at least in an equal proportion."[1]

An alliance impossible on these conditions.

On such terms a working alliance was impossible. A foreign government would find now, as domestic parties were to find afterwards, that it was not

[1] Coke to Holland and Carleton, Feb. 11 ; *S. P. France.*

enough to give way to Charles in some things, unless it was prepared to give way to him in all. What he asked was merely that a high-spirited and sensitive nation should first submit its domestic affairs to his arbitration, and should then enter upon a war precisely in such a manner and on such conditions as it pleased him to prescribe.

CHAP. X.
1626.
Feb. 11.

If knowledge of character be worth anything, it is to Charles rather than to Buckingham that these unsatisfactory despatches are to be ascribed. Charles too had annoyances at home which may well have served to put him in a bad temper during the days in which they were dictated. His dissatisfaction with his wife had reached a crisis. Parliament was opened on the 6th, and arrangements had been made for the Queen to witness the procession from one of the windows of the Banqueting Hall at Whitehall. Charles, however, always anxious to separate her from the French attendants, and to bring her as much as possible in communication with the ladies of the Villiers family, expressed a wish that she should take a seat in a balcony occupied by the old Countess of Buckingham. The Queen assented, but when the time came she either saw or fancied she saw that it was raining, and asked to be excused from going out into the street in the wet. Charles, on the other hand, insisted that it did not rain, but finding that his words produced no impression, withdrew from the altercation. Dissatisfied at his rebuff,—so at least the French accounts of the affair assert,—he betook himself to Buckingham. "How can you expect," said the favourite, "to be obeyed by your Parliament if you cannot secure the obedience of your wife?" Charles, conscious perhaps of his own inability to impress the Queen with sufficient awe of his commands, sent Buckingham to try his powers upon

Feb. 6.
The Queen at the procession of the opening of Parliament.

Altercation with her husband.

her. Buckingham rated her soundly for her disobedience, and as Blainville, who had perhaps objected originally to her showing herself in Lady Buckingham's company, now advised submission, she took Buckingham's hand, and was led across the street to the house in which his mother was.

Even this act of submission caused fresh umbrage to Charles. The Queen, it would seem, would not obey him, but would obey the French ambassador. With some reminiscence, perhaps, of the 'Taming of the Shrew,' he sent orders to her to come down from the window at which she was, and with these orders Henrietta Maria meekly complied.

For three days Charles kept entirely aloof from his wife, waiting sulkily till she should come to beg his pardon. At last, weary of his silence, she sought him out and asked in what she had offended him. He expected her, he answered, to acknowledge her error. She was unable, she said, to accuse herself of anything wrong. Would he not tell her what her fault had been? The question seemed to take him by surprise. After some hesitation he answered: "You told me that it rained when I said that it did not rain." "I should never have thought that to be an offence," she replied; "but if you think so, I will think so too." Pleased with such evidence of humility, Charles took his wife in his arms, and kissed her.[1]

[1] *Mémoires de Tillières*. It seems so unlikely that Charles should have quarrelled with Blainville on this point, that it is as well to give the words of the English narrative: "In the meantime a difference that fell out about the place for the Queen to see the King ride to Parliament (she affecting to stand in the Banqueting House, or in the Privy Gallery, when the King had given reasons for her better sight in the house of the Countess, mother to the Duke of Buckingham, next the gate in King Street), was a subject for some discontent, and so far as the Ambassador Blainville seeming to his Majesty to have been the causer of it, had the

The quarrel was over for the time. The Queen had perhaps begun to open her eyes to the truth that with such a character as Charles's the outward appearance of complete and unreasoning obedience is the surest way to mastery in the end.

CHAP. X.
1626.
Feb. 10.

Unhappily this misunderstanding between man and wife became another element in the misunderstanding between two kingdoms. On the day after the offence was given, the courier who carried the despatch expressive of Charles's dissatisfaction with the Huguenot treaty, took with him a letter from Charles to Lewis himself, asking for Blainville's recall, on the ground that he had done everything in his power to bring about a misunderstanding between himself and the Queen. At the same time he directed Conway to inform the ambassador that he would no longer be permitted to appear at Court.[1]

Feb. 7.
Charles refuses to allow Blainville to appear at Court.

Such were the conditions under which Charles met his second Parliament. A great French minister, amidst unexampled difficulties, had steered the vessel of state on to the track in which it was hereafter to be borne to victory on behalf of a noble cause. In spite of the hesitations of Lewis and of the opposition of the clergy and of a large portion of the aristocracy, Richelieu had firmly planted the banner of monarchical France on the basis of toleration. He had gained his point by unwearied patience, by yielding in details whilst never losing sight of his main object, by the appearance of being but the servant of his king, whilst in reality he was bending the king and France itself to

Circumstances under which Charles meets Parliament.

next day a message brought him by the Lord Conway." Affair of Blainville. Undated. *S. P. France.*

[1] Message sent to Blainville, Feb. 7. The King to Lewis XIII., Feb. 7. *S. P. France.*

his own ends. One thing he yet wanted, that the ruler whom fortune had placed upon the English throne should be capable of understanding his meaning. As long as Charles was King of England no such good fortune was likely to be his.

END OF THE FIRST VOLUME.

LONDON: PRINTED BY
SPOTTISWOODE AND CO., NEW-STREET SQUARE
AND PARLIAMENT STREET

www.ingramcontent.com/pod-product-compliance
Lightning Source LLC
Chambersburg PA
CBHW032030220426
43664CB00006B/421